# THE WORLD BANK ANNUAL REPORT 1996

THE WORLD BANK, WASHINGTON, D.C.

Photo credits    Cover photo montage: The Magazine Group (oil drilling photo by Comstock, copyright 1995)
                 Frontispiece: Kay Chernush; Page 13: World Bank; Page 24: Kay Chernush
                 Page 43: World Bank; Page 46: Kay Chernush; Page 54: Curt Carnemark/World Bank
                 Page 65: Kay Chernush; Page 70: Sally Wiener Grotta; Page 73: Kay Chernush; Page 84: Franck Charton
                 Page 92: Kay Chernush; Page 104: Tim Cullen; Page 112: Curt Carnemark/World Bank
                 Page 123: Kay Chernush; Page 165: Neeraj Jain; End page: Kay Chernush

Design           Book design: Joyce Petruzzelli, Graphic Design Unit, The World Bank Group
                 Chart design: May Eidi, Graphic Design Unit, The World Bank Group
                 Typography: Graphic Design Unit, The World Bank Group
                 Cover design: Glenn Pierce, The Magazine Group

Editorial        Peter C. Muncie, Office of the Publisher, The World Bank Group


ISSN: 0252-2942
ISBN: 0-8213-3254-6

This *Annual Report*, which covers the period July 1, 1995, to June 30, 1996, has been prepared by the executive directors of both the International Bank for Reconstruction and Development (IBRD) and the International Development Association (IDA) in accordance with the respective by-laws of the two institutions. James D. Wolfensohn, president of the IBRD and IDA and chairman of the boards of executive directors, has submitted this *Report*, together with accompanying administrative budgets and audited financial statements, to the board of governors.

The executive directors would like to take this opportunity to thank the staff of the World Bank for its support for the new agenda for change, which aims through quality improvements to more effectively help borrowing countries to reduce poverty, the Bank's *raison d'être*.

Annual Reports for the International Finance Corporation (IFC), the Multilateral Investment Guarantee Agency (MIGA), and the International Centre for Settlement of Investment Disputes (ICSID) are published separately.

| **Executive Directors** | **Alternates** |
| --- | --- |
| Khalid M. Al-Saad | Mohamed W. Hosny |
| Khalid H. Alyahya | Ibrahim M. Al-Mofleh |
| Marc-Antoine Autheman | Arnaud Chneiweiss |
| Ali Bourhane | Luc-Abdi Aden |
| Andrei Bugrov | Eugene Miagkov |
| Marcos Caramuru de Paiva | Jorge Cock-Londoño |
| Huw Evans | David Stanton |
| Jean-Daniel Gerber | Jan Sulmicki |
| Leonard Good | Winston Cox |
| Eveline Herfkens | Sergiy Kulyk |
| Ruth Jacoby | Jorgen Varder |
| Li Yong | Zhu Guangyao |
| Abdul Karim Lodhi | Kaçim Brachemi |
| Leonard Mseka | Joaquim R. Carvalho |
| Peter W.E. Nicholl | Christopher Y. Legg |
| Atsuo Nishihara | Rintaro Tamaki |
| Julio Nogués | Carlos Steneri |
| Franco Passacantando | Helena Cordeiro |
| Jan Piercy | Michael Marek |
| Walter Rill | Luc Hubloue |
| Helmut Schaffer | Erika Wagenhöfer |
| Surendra Singh | Mushfiqur Rahman |
| Suwan Pasugswad | Khin Ohn Thant |
| Jorge Terrazas | Roberto Jimenez-Ortiz |

August 1, 1996

The World Bank, which consists of the International Bank for Reconstruction and Development (IBRD) and the International Development Association (IDA), has one central purpose: to promote economic and social progress in developing nations by helping raise productivity so that their people may live a better and fuller life. This is also the aim of the International Finance Corporation—which works closely with private investors from around the world and invests in commercial enterprises in developing countries—and the Multilateral Investment Guarantee Agency (MIGA)—which was established to encourage direct foreign investment in developing countries by protecting investors from noncommercial risk. Collectively, the World Bank, the IFC, and MIGA are known as the World Bank Group.

Of the four institutions, the IBRD, established in 1945, is the oldest and largest. The IBRD is owned by the governments of 180 countries that have subscribed to its capital. Under its Articles of Agreement, only countries that are members of the International Monetary Fund (IMF) can be considered for membership in the IBRD. Subscriptions by member countries to the capital stock of the IBRD are related to each member's quota in the IMF, which is designed to reflect the country's relative economic strength.

The IBRD makes loans only to creditworthy borrowers. Assistance is provided only to those projects that promise high real rates of economic return to the country. As a matter of policy, the IBRD does not reschedule payments, and it has suffered no losses on the loans it has made. It has earned a net income every year since 1948.

The IBRD obtains most of its funds through medium- and long-term borrowings in the capital markets of Europe, Japan, and the United States. It also borrows funds at market-based rates from central banks and other government institutions. The IBRD's solid standing in the markets is based upon the combination of conservative lending policies, strong financial backing by its members, and prudent financial management.

Apart from borrowings, significant amounts also come from the IBRD's paid-in capital, from its retained earnings, and from the flow of repayments on its loans.

The International Development Association was established in 1960 to provide assistance to the poorer developing countries on terms that would bear less heavily on their balance of payments than IBRD loans. IDA's assistance is concentrated on the very poor countries—mainly those with an annual per capita gross national product of less than $865 (in 1994 U.S. dollars). By this criterion, about seventy countries are eligible.

Membership in IDA is open to all members of the IBRD, and 159 have joined. The funds lent by IDA come mostly in the form of contributions from its richer members, although some developing countries contribute to IDA, as well. IDA's resources have also been augmented by frequent transfers from the net earnings of the IBRD.

IDA credits are made only to governments. They have to be repaid over a period of thirty-five to forty years. They carry no interest, but there is an annual service charge of 0.5 percent on the undisbursed amount of each credit. Although IDA is legally and financially distinct from the IBRD, it shares the same staff, and the projects it assists have to meet the same criteria as do projects supported by the IBRD.

The success of the Bank's operations depends upon the trust it has established with borrowers, and this trust is based on the experience and technical skills the Bank has demonstrated over the years in working with its member developing countries.

Under its Articles of Agreement, the Bank cannot allow itself to be influenced by the political character of a member country: Only economic considerations are relevant. It also seeks to ensure that the developing country gets full value for the money it borrows. Bank assistance, therefore, is untied in that it may be used to purchase goods and services from any member country.

The IFC was established in 1956. Its function is to assist the economic development of developing countries by promoting growth in the private sector of their economies and helping to mobilize domestic and foreign capital for this purpose. One hundred seventy countries are members of the IFC. Legally and financially, the IFC and the World Bank are separate entities. The IFC has its own operating and legal staff, but draws upon the Bank for administrative and other services.

In its project-financing role, the IFC provides loans and makes equity investments. Unlike most multilateral institutions, the IFC does not accept government guarantees for its financing. Like a private financial institution, the IFC prices its finance and services, to the extent possible, in line with the market, while taking into account the cost of its funds, and seeks profitable returns. The IFC shares full projects risks with its partners.

MIGA, the newest member of the World Bank Group, was established in 1988. It has as its principal responsibility the promotion of investment for economic development in member countries through guarantees to foreign investors against losses caused by noncommercial risks and through advisory and consultative services to member countries to assist them in creating a responsive investment climate and information base to guide and encourage the flow of capital.

MIGA is also an entity separate from the World Bank. Like the IFC, it has its own operating and legal staff but draws upon the Bank for administrative and other services. MIGA currently has 134 members.

BOXES

This *Annual Report*, covering July 1, 1995 to June 30, 1996, details a critical period in the history of the World Bank Group, one of transition designed to create an institution that is stronger, more agile, and more effective in response to the needs of its developing country clients.

This transition has been made necessary by the extraordinary change taking place in the global economy, with explosive growth in worldwide trade and private investment centering on the emerging market economies. In the 1990s, developing countries have contributed 70 percent of the growth in global GDP and half the growth in world trade. Private investment flows to the developing world have more than tripled, from around $44 billion in 1990 to nearly $170 billion by the end of 1995.

Economic change is about far more than numbers. It is about change in people's lives. For many people, this change has been for the better. Many countries have cut their poverty rates by more than half and have expanded access to health, education, and social services to their entire population. Far more people now have access to economic opportunity than in the recent past. Further, just a decade ago, only about 1 billion people lived in economies that could be called market-oriented; today, the figure is around 5 billion people. Meanwhile, communications technology is drawing people from around the world closer together. Today, doctors in Africa, Latin America, or Asia can teleconference with top medical researchers around the world; entrepreneurs can get the latest global market information instantly; and students in the most remote parts of the globe have the possibility of access to the world's best libraries and teaching resources. The potential of what the information revolution is unleashing is extraordinary.

But growth and prosperity cannot be taken for granted. In many of the world's poorest countries, global change has not brought significant improvements to people's lives. We still live in a world where 1.2 billion people live below the line of what the World Bank considers absolute poverty—$1 per day—and in Africa, the number of poor people is expected to continue growing into the next century. A quarter of the developing world's population lacks access to safe drinking water, and almost half of it has no electricity. One hundred thirty million children, most of them girls, are not getting the chance to go to school. In too many places the poor—and most particularly women—are shut out of the opportunities that would allow them to improve the conditions of their lives.

Despite the explosive growth in the world economy, many countries are being left behind. Seventy-five percent of private capital flows to the developing world are concentrated in just twelve countries (and East Asia receives 60 percent of the total). At the same time, official development assistance—which might have filled the gap—has fallen to its lowest point in real terms ($59 billion) in twenty-three years. And many of the world's poorest countries are so deeply in debt as to make it practically impossible for them to sustain vital economic reforms.

Armed violence continues to plague the world. Just last year, there were some fifty armed conflicts worldwide. We are all aware of the horror in Bosnia, where a quarter of a million people have been killed, and unspeakable horrors committed. But Bosnia is far from the only site of such abominations. In the past decade, 70 million people have been displaced from their homes or become refugees.

And the world remains under the growing threat of environmental deterioration, uncontrolled population growth, epidemic disease, and an emerging shortage of water resources.

The current change under way around the world carries great opportunities—and risks. The role of the World Bank under these conditions is to help its clients seize the opportunities, avoid the pitfalls, and—for those countries just beginning to make the transition to soundly managed market economies—build the capacity to stay on course.

This means we must stay close to our clients and develop our own ability to adapt to their changing needs. It means we must be able to respond quickly to conditions on the ground, and particularly to the challenge of post-conflict situations; create innovative new mechanisms for assisting the poorest; help build sound market systems; and ensure that development is environmentally sustainable. If we are to be truly effective, we must expand and deepen our partnerships with the UN system, regional development banks, bilateral assistance agencies, nongovernmental organizations, foundations, the private sector, and others; and we must develop the professional capabilities of our own staff to the highest possible level. We must also work with the International Monetary Fund, other multilateral development banks, and the governments of creditor nations to reduce the burden of debt in the poorest reforming countries. And we must lead the way in ensuring that concessional resources—particularly in the form of IDA funds—continue to be adequate to finance our clients' development priorities.

This *Annual Report* reviews what we have already done and where we are headed in these areas, in addition to covering the Bank's ongoing development activities around the world. It provides the essential facts about Bank operations in all regions of the world, and in all sectors of development.

In the end, however, the *Report* is not only about financial statistics or percentages; it is about people—the people who live in the countries we serve. It is about the immeasurable improvements that the World Bank is bringing to people's lives. In the end, this will be the gauge by which we judge our success.

JAMES D. WOLFENSOHN

Poverty reduction and sustainable development remain the central objectives of the World Bank. In fiscal 1996, several initiatives were launched to strengthen the Bank's development effectiveness and to focus Bank efforts more on the needs of its clients and results on the ground *(see accompanying box on the Bank's change process)*.

The change agenda of the institution is focusing on two main areas: (a) immediate steps to raise the standards of all client services and (b) measures to improve the Bank's longer-term ability to meet client needs more effectively.

In particular, the Bank's ability to respond quickly to the needs of its clients has been strengthened. For example:

• Three months after the signing of the Dayton Peace Accords in December 1995, a $150 million Trust Fund for Bosnia and Herzegovina was created to support vital reconstruction work in advance of Bosnia becoming a World Bank member and clearing its arrears with the institution. The Bank, together with the European Union, convened two donor conferences during the year, at which the international community pledged a total of $1.83 billion in reconstruction aid. A field office for the World Bank opened in early January 1996 in Sarajevo to coordinate the Bank's reconstruction effort. And, by the end of fiscal 1996, seven projects financed through the Trust Fund—emergency recovery; water, sanitation, and solid waste urgent works; emergency farm, transport, power, and education reconstruction; and war-victims rehabilitation—had been approved; two IDA-assisted projects—education reconstruction and war-victims rehabilitation—had also been approved. Commitments in fiscal 1996 totaled $160 million, $150 million from the Trust Fund and $10 million from IDA. It is expected that, subject to approval of individual operations by the Bank's executive board, a positive net transfer of funds to Bosnia of about $450 million over the next four years will take place. *(For further details, see Box 4-3 on page 100.)*

• In the Middle East, the border closure that followed the tragic events of late February and early March delivered a massive shock to the economy of the West Bank and Gaza. As the dimensions of the closure emerged, it became imperative that Bank strategy must adjust to tackle immediate goals; without some provision of relief, there might be little need to plan for the medium term. A two-stage Bank response strategy was quickly agreed to with the Palestinian Authority and put into motion. Stage one comprised the immediate provision of emergency assistance: In April, the Bank, through the Holst Trust Fund, approved a program to finance 21,000 short-term jobs. Stage two involved the creation of more productive short-term employment: The $90 million replenishment of the Trust Fund for Gaza and the West Bank has been directed to four projects that respond in various ways to the employment crisis. Two of the projects had been approved by the end of fiscal 1996.

• Responding quickly to a request made by the Bank's African governors at the October 1995 annual meetings to expand the institution's capacity-building efforts in the region, a joint Africa–World Bank "partnership for capacity building" was announced in February 1996. In March and early April, leading experts in capacity building met in subregional meetings with representatives from various African countries to define the partnership's purview, goals, tasks, and methods. In addition, a dozen countries have begun to conduct internal assessments of their individual capacity needs, and a working party of experts is reviewing the way Bank policies and procedures have affected capacity in Africa in the past. The group will offer suggestions for improving the capacity-building impact of Bank-supported operations in the future.

Changes in operational approaches are also taking place

# CHANGING THE BANK

*Under new leadership, an integrated effort is under way for the Bank to better meet client needs, provide high-quality results on the ground, further improve efficiency and cost effectiveness, strengthen external partnerships, and increase Bankwide professional excellence. Examples of initiatives in each of these areas appear throughout the pages of this Annual Report.*

*An institutional framework for facilitating the change process has been established. It has four main goals:*

*• developing an institutional strategy that provides a clear sense of direction about how the Bank will serve borrowers, donors, other shareholders, beneficiaries, and partners;*

*• enhancing institutional capacity by strengthening management capabilities and improving incentive mechanisms;*

*• redesigning and putting into place improved and more efficient business processes with a view to improving the quality of the Bank's services; and*

*• pursuing a communications strategy that builds institutional and external support for implementing the program of change.*

*Although it is still in its early stages, the momentum for change is steadily building, and several initiatives are under way.*

*Examples of the simplification of business processes and project documentation, steps to accelerate the project cycle and reduce elapsed time for processing, as well as efforts to improve the quality of the Bank portfolio of projects are documented in Section Two and the various regional sections of this Annual Report.*

*Measures to strengthen the management of the Bank's human resources are reported on in the "Administrative Budget, Corporate Planning, and Resource Management" section of the* Report.

*With a view to increasing the country focus of the Bank's work, country directors are being appointed in Africa and Latin America to lead country teams. Some—the country director for the new Mexico department and the country director for Kenya and Djibouti—are already located in the field. The intention is to increase, over time, the number of country directors in the field. In the Africa Region, fifteen country directors, reporting directly to the regional vice presidents, lead country teams. The teams, which include the resident representative as "co-pilot," contract technical staff to work on specific projects and programs. Country directors are responsible for allocating the operational budget across the work program and are accountable for delivering the services agreed on the country-assistance strategy (CAS), including portfolio management, disbursement performance, and the quality of services. Details of many change initiatives under way in the Latin America and the Caribbean Regional office may be found on page 115.*

*Measures aimed at strengthening technical units in the Bank and the capacity to share knowledge across the institution are being pursued to facilitate professional excellence in the Bank's work.*

*To sharpen focus on client needs, a new generation of CASs was designed in fiscal 1996 in closer consultation with borrowers and in collaboration with a much broader array of partners. Special efforts were made to solicit the views of government officials and donors throughout the CAS process for the Philippines, for example, with government officials participating in a series of workshops to clarify development strategies and the most productive areas for Bank focus.*

*These and other efforts will be pursued further in fiscal 1997, targeted primarily at the four main goals of the change agenda.*

throughout the Bank. During fiscal 1996, for example, there has been considerable progress in upgrading country-assistance strategies (CASs) so that they (a) articulate the Bank's approach to country-specific development challenges by defining the appropriate mix of lending and advisory services and (b) set out monitorable indicators (both qualitative and quantitative) to assess the Bank's performance in addressing these challenges.

Many examples of change at the regional level have also taken place.

• In Africa, approaches to different countries are increasingly being modulated according to clients' commitment to poverty reduction, economic reform, and debt management.

- In East Asia and Pacific, work priorities and the allocation of resources are being redirected from middle-income to low-income countries.

- In South Asia, new initiatives are being financed from redeployed economic and sector work (ESW), and cost reductions are coming from securing increased borrower responsibility for project preparation and supervision.

- In Europe and Central Asia, a major effort is under way to improve disbursements and portfolio implementation.

- In Latin America and the Caribbean, increased resources are being allocated to portfolio management, and the redeployment of resources, responsibilities, and activities to the field is expected to enhance the Bank's responsiveness to client needs.

- In the Middle East and North Africa, more focused and flexible CASs are being developed in concert with clients and other stakeholders. Decentralized decisionmaking and redesigned business processes are aimed at increasing cost effectiveness and results.

These initiatives that are taking place at the regional level are being supported by the recently established Quality Assurance Group. The group aims to strengthen accountability for quality and results by providing line managers with independent assessments of their work and by helping to address critical problem areas in the portfolio.

A number of other institutional initiatives have been put into place, or are being proposed, to accelerate and sustain the Bank's change agenda *(see accompanying box)*. They aim to improve substantially the Bank's level of performance and its ability to meet changing client needs. These initiatives include:

- The strengthening of top management—including the assignment of direct line responsibilities to five managing directors—to provide more strategic direction to the institution.

- The training and renewal of the professional skills of Bank staff, to be coordinated and managed by the Learning and Leadership Center. In-house training programs are being strengthened; professional skills for staff at all levels in major sectors are being expanded; selected managers and staff are being sent to leading international management and business schools; and staff exchange and secondment programs, involving private sector organizations and autonomous agencies in selected countries, are being developed.

- A significant expansion of the activities of the Economic Development Institute (EDI) has been proposed, including (a) expansion of high-impact core programs in an increasing number of countries, (b) development of more partnerships to enable countries to deliver their programs, and (c) integration of the work of the EDI into CASs and tying it more closely to the rest of the Bank.

- Creation of a coordination mechanism to develop the Bank Group's overall strategy for private sector development (PSD). The mechanism, which comprises senior management from the Bank, the IFC, and MIGA, will (a) foster synergy among PSD activities through CAS coordination, (b) facilitate PSD operations that involve two or more Bank Group institutions, (c) develop partnerships with the private sector, and (d) promote the sharing of expertise within the Bank Group.

The purpose of the Bank's agenda for change is to increase the development effectiveness of its services by improving the quality of work across the board—lending, advice, and state-of-the-art financial products. Change that improves the quality of the Bank's staff and multiplies the effectiveness of the Bank's programs can have a significant effect on the Bank's performance as a development institution.

Improvements are being delivered in an increasingly cost-effective, responsive, and flexible manner. The need to enhance efficiency has been recognized explicitly through a reduction in the Bank's real net administrative budget by some 6 percent a year during fiscal years 1996 and 1997. In the process, the Bank has made hard choices that have led to well-balanced efficiency gains and selective programmatic reduction, while permitting significant new initiatives and expanding programs.

Other immediate priorities were addressed throughout the past fiscal year, as well:

• Representatives of more than thirty donor countries agreed on new funding for the International Development Association. Donors meeting in Tokyo on March 19, 1996, endorsed a package that will allow concessional lending of $22 billion to poor countries over the period fiscal 1997–99 *(see accompanying table)*. Although the level of donor funding is half that of IDA-10, it is expected that the total available resources will be adequate to meet foreseen needs because of factors such as a large carryover of funds from IDA-10.

The three-year package begins with a one-year interim fund of about $3 billion running from July 1, 1996, with decisionmaking and procurement limited to contributing donors and developing countries *(see accompanying table)*. In each of the two subsequent years, starting July 1, 1997, all IDA donors will contribute about $4 billion to the Eleventh Replenishment of IDA.

These donor contributions, when complemented by other sources of IDA funds, will be adequate to meet foreseen needs of some SDR 14.5 billion. They do not, however, leave room for contingencies—future operations that are not now foreseen—in countries currently inactive or borrowing below expected levels due to absorptive capacity constraints, for example. Bosnia is the most recent example of an unexpected demand for IDA funding. While the current program for Bosnia can now be funded, IDA would have great difficulty in financing new, unexpected demands within the available window.

Donor representatives (IDA Deputies) reaffirmed IDA's special commitment to Africa within its overarching objective of poverty reduction, emphasized that private sector-led growth and social and environmental sustainability are the foundations of effective poverty reduction, and called upon recipient countries to improve governance and to broaden participation by the poor in development. The Deputies emphasized that access to primary education, clean water, health services, and basic infrastructure were vital to the emergence of families from poverty. They called on

IDA management not only to continue strong support for such investments but also to help governments restructure public spending, wherever possible, toward these sectors and away from nonproductive purposes.

• In April 1996, the Bank's shareholders welcomed the joint proposal of the Bank and the International Monetary Fund of the "Framework for Action" aimed at addressing the debt burden of heavily indebted poor countries (HIPCs). The proposal followed the request, made in October 1995 by the Development and Interim Committees, that the two institutions undertaken further analysis of the debt problems of these countries.

On the basis of staff analysis, the executive boards of the institutions agreed that there was a number of HIPCs, most of which are in sub-Saharan Africa, for whom the burden of debt was likely to remain above sustainable levels over the medium term, even with strong policy performance and the full use of existing debt-relief mechanisms.

Directors agreed that the following broad principles should guide further action:

(a) The objective should be to target overall debt sustainability on a case-by-case basis, focusing on the totality of a country's debt.

(b) Action should be envisaged only when the debtor has shown, through a track record of reform and sound policies, the ability to put to good use whatever exceptional support is provided to achieve a sustainable outcome.

(c) New measures should build, as much as possible, on existing mechanisms.

(d) Additional action for the problem cases should be coordinated among all creditors involved, with broad and equitable participation.

(e) Any action to relieve the burden of debt owed to multilateral creditors should preserve the financial integrity of the institutions and their preferred creditor status, and be consistent with the constraints of their charters in order that the institutions can continue to provide financing to all member countries on appropriate terms.

(f) New external finance for the countries concerned should be on appropriate concessional terms so as to support their efforts

## TABLE 1. CONTRIBUTIONS TO THE ELEVENTH REPLENISHMENT OF IDA RESOURCES

*(amounts in millions)*

| Contributing member | Basic contributions | | Supplementary contributions | Total contributions |
|---|---|---|---|---|
| | Share (percent) | SDR amount | SDR amount | SDR amount |
| Argentina [a] | 0.10 | 5.05 | | 5.05 |
| Australia [b] | | | | |
| Austria | 0.90 | 45.46 | | 45.46 |
| Belgium | 1.55 | 78.29 | | 78.29 |
| Botswana [a/f] | 0.01 | 0.67 | | 0.67 |
| Brazil [c/f] | 0.16 | 8.08 | | 8.08 |
| Canada | 3.75 | 189.40 | | 189.40 |
| Czech Republic | 0.05 | 2.53 | | 2.53 |
| Denmark [f] | 1.30 | 65.66 | | 65.66 |
| Finland | 0.50 | 25.25 | | 25.25 |
| France [d] | 7.02 | 354.56 | 14.14 | 368.71 |
| Germany | 11.00 | 555.58 | | 555.58 |
| Greece | 0.05 | 2.53 | | 2.53 |
| Hungary [f] | 0.06 | 3.00 | | 3.00 |
| Iceland | 0.03 | 1.52 | | 1.52 |
| Ireland [c/f] | 0.13 | 6.57 | 2.68 | 9.25 |
| Italy | 4.35 | 219.71 | | 219.71 |
| Japan | 18.70 | 944.49 | 65.66 | 1,010.15 |
| Korea, Republic of [f] | 0.23 | 11.62 | 3.54 | 15.15 |
| Kuwait [e] | 0.14 | 7.07 | | 7.07 |
| Luxembourg [c] | 0.10 | 5.05 | 0.95 | 6.00 |
| Mexico | 0.10 | 5.05 | | 5.05 |
| Netherlands | 3.30 | 166.68 | | 166.68 |
| New Zealand | 0.12 | 6.06 | 3.19 | 9.25 |
| Norway [f] | 1.42 | 71.72 | | 71.72 |
| Poland [f] | 0.03 | 1.52 | | 1.52 |
| Portugal [c] | 0.20 | 10.10 | | 10.10 |
| Russia [a] | 0.20 | 10.10 | 6.90 | 17.00 |
| Saudi Arabia | 0.65 | 32.92 | | 32.92 |
| Slovak Republic | 0.04 | 2.00 | | 2.00 |
| South Africa | 0.08 | 4.04 | | 4.04 |
| Spain | 1.00 | 50.51 | | 50.51 |
| Sweden | 2.62 | 132.33 | | 132.33 |
| Switzerland [c] | 2.43 | 122.73 | | 122.73 |
| Turkey | 0.10 | 5.00 | | 5.00 |
| United Kingdom | 6.15 | 310.62 | | 310.62 |
| United States | 20.86 | 1,053.59 | | 1,053.59 |
| Subtotal | 90.89 | 4,590.79 | 97.06 | 4,687.85 |
| Supplementary contributions | 1.92 | 97.06 | | |
| Change in encashment | 0.14 | 7.04 | | 7.04 |
| Unallocated | 7.05 | 355.88 | | 355.88 |
| Total | 100 | 5,050.77 | | 5,050.77 |

a. Argentina, Botswana, and Russia are donors to IDA-11 who did not participate in IDA-10.

b. In Australia, a new government has recently been sworn in and is expected to announce its pledge to the Interim Trust Fund and to IDA-11 in the near future.

c. Brazil, Ireland, Luxembourg, Portugal, and Switzerland increased their basic share from that in IDA-10.

d. France's contribution amounts to 7.3 percent. France's objective is to maintain a global national currency contribution to IDA of at least 7.3 percent.

e. Kuwait is not in a position to commit to a final contribution to IDA-11. The level shown is therefore indicative.

f. Botswana, Brazil, Denmark, Hungary, Ireland, Korea (Republic of), Norway, and Poland made additional efforts by agreeing to accelerate the encashment of their contributions.

# TABLE 2. CONTRIBUTIONS TO IDA'S INTERIM TRUST FUND

*(amounts in millions)*

| Contributing member | Basic contributions | | Supplementary contributions | Total contributions |
|---|---|---|---|---|
| | Share (percent) | SDR amount | SDR amount | SDR amount |
| Argentina [a] | 0.10 | 3.00 | | 3.00 |
| Australia [b] | | | | |
| Austria | 0.90 | 27.00 | 3.00 | 30.00 |
| Belgium | 1.55 | 46.50 | | 46.50 |
| Botswana [a/f] | 0.01 | 0.33 | | 0.33 |
| Brazil [c/f] | 0.16 | 4.80 | | 4.80 |
| Canada | 3.50 | 105.00 | | 105.00 |
| Czech Republic | 0.05 | 1.50 | | 1.50 |
| Denmark [f] | 1.30 | 39.00 | | 39.00 |
| Finland | 0.50 | 15.00 | | 15.00 |
| France [d/f] | 7.02 | 210.60 | 8.40 | 219.00 |
| Germany | 11.00 | 330.00 | | 330.00 |
| Greece | 0.05 | 1.50 | | 1.50 |
| Hungary [f] | 0.07 | 2.00 | | 2.00 |
| Iceland | 0.03 | 0.90 | | 0.90 |
| Ireland [c/f] | 0.13 | 3.90 | 0.67 | 4.57 |
| Italy | 4.02 | 120.60 | | 120.60 |
| Japan [f] | 18.70 | 561.00 | 39.00 | 600.00 |
| Korea, Republic of [f] | 0.23 | 6.90 | 2.10 | 9.00 |
| Kuwait [e] | 0.14 | 4.20 | | 4.20 |
| Luxembourg [c] | 0.10 | 3.00 | | 3.00 |
| Mexico | 0.10 | 3.00 | | 3.00 |
| Netherlands [f] | 3.30 | 99.00 | 60.00 | 159.00 |
| New Zealand | 0.12 | 3.60 | 0.97 | 4.57 |
| Norway [f] | 1.42 | 42.60 | 10.00 | 52.60 |
| Poland [f] | 0.03 | 0.90 | | 0.90 |
| Portugal [c] | 0.20 | 6.00 | | 6.00 |
| Russia [a] | 0.20 | 6.00 | 2.00 | 8.00 |
| Saudi Arabia | 0.55 | 16.46 | | 16.46 |
| Slovak Republic | 0.03 | 1.00 | | 1.00 |
| South Africa | 0.08 | 2.40 | | 2.40 |
| Spain | 1.00 | 30.00 | | 30.00 |
| Sweden | 2.62 | 78.60 | | 78.60 |
| Switzerland | 1.74 | 52.20 | | 52.20 |
| Turkey | 0.07 | 2.00 | 0.23 | 2.23 |
| United Kingdom | 6.15 | 184.50 | | 184.50 |
| | | | | |
| Subtotal | 68.63 | 2,058.80 | 126.38 | 2,185.17 |
| Supplementary contributions | 4.21 | 126.38 | | |
| Change in encashment | 1.09 | 32.64 | | 32.64 |
| Unallocated [g] | 26.07 | 782.19 | | 782.19 |
| | | | | |
| Total | 100 | 3,000.00 | | 3,000.00 |

a. Argentina, Botswana, and Russia are donors to the Interim Trust Fund who did not participate in IDA-10.

b. In Australia, a new government has recently been sworn in and is expected to announce its pledge to the Interim Trust Fund and to IDA-11 in the near future.

c. Brazil, Ireland, Luxembourg, and Portugal increased their basic share from that in IDA-10.

d. France's objective is to maintain a global national currency contribution to IDA of at least 7.3 percent.

e. Kuwait is not in a position to commit to a final contribution to the Interim Trust Fund. The level shown is therefore indicative.

f. Botswana, Brazil, Denmark, France, Hungary, Ireland, Japan, Korea (Republic of), Netherlands, Norway and Poland made additional efforts by agreeing to accelerate the encashment of their contributions.

g. The unallocated amount exists because the United States (which pledged 20.86 percent in IDA-10) is not participating in the Interim Trust Fund and the IDA-10 basic shares did not add up to 100 percent, but included a "structural" gap of 8.72 percent.

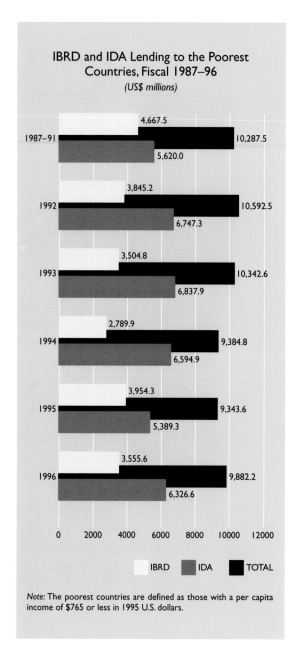

**IBRD and IDA Lending to the Poorest Countries, Fiscal 1987–96**
*(US$ millions)*

1987–91
4,667.5
10,287.5
5,620.0

1992
3,845.2
10,592.5
6,747.3

1993
3,504.8
10,342.6
6,837.9

1994
2,789.9
9,384.8
6,594.9

1995
3,954.3
9,343.6
5,389.3

1996
3,555.6
9,882.2
6,326.6

0   2000   4000   6000   8000   10000   12000

☐ IBRD   ▨ IDA   ■ TOTAL

*Note:* The poorest countries are defined as those with a per capita income of $765 or less in 1995 U.S. dollars.

to pursue reform and establish a track record of good policy.

At their April 1996 meetings, the Development and Interim Committees, after their study of the joint proposal, asked the Bank and the Fund, in close collaboration with all involved, to move swiftly to produce a program of action to implement this framework. Ministers urged that a decision be reached on this program and its financing as soon as possible, aiming to do so by the annual meetings of the two institutions in early October 1996. The Group of 7 (G-7)

asked the president of the Bank to participate in its discussions on debt at its annual summit, held in June 1996 in Lyons. In their *communiqué* following the Lyons meeting, the seven heads of governments stated that the solution for some heavily indebted poor countries (HIPCs) should "provide an exit for unsustainable debt and be based on a case-by-case approach adapted to the specific needs of each country concerned, once it had shown its commitment to pursuing economic adjustment." The G-7 also endorsed an overall World Bank contribution of the order of $2 billion for a trust fund initiative aimed at assisting the HIPCs in dealing with their debt situation. The president of the Bank subsequently stated that the exact amounts allocated by the Bank would be determined by its shareholders and would depend on coordination of required action by all creditors involved and those countries that would make voluntary contributions to the trust fund.

• Collaboration with existing and new partners was accelerated and deepened. Nongovernmental organization (NGO) liaison officers have been assigned in the Bank's offices worldwide, including seventeen in Africa, ten in Latin America, four in Europe and Central Asia, three in South Asia, and one in East Asia and Pacific. The goal is to have an NGO liaison officer in every Bank resident mission to facilitate participatory approaches in Bank-supported projects. Participatory approaches to development have been mainstreamed. The *World Bank Participation Sourcebook*, published early in 1996, is a tool intended to encourage Bank task managers to use participatory approaches in their work.[1] The Private Sector Development Group, comprising senior managers from the Bank, the IFC, and MIGA, has become the focal point for private investors seeking assistance from, or cooperation with, the Bank Group. Coordination with other multilateral development banks (MDBs) is also being strengthened. The heads of the five principal MDBs have agreed to meet every six

1. World Bank. 1996. *World Bank Participation Sourcebook.* Washington, D.C.

# INFORMATION FOR DEVELOPMENT (INFODEV) PROGRAM IS LAUNCHED

*InfoDev, a cooperative program managed in the World Bank's Industry and Energy Department, brings together finance and expertise from governments, mutilateral institutions, such as the World Bank and the European Union, and the private sector to promote reform and investment in the developing world through improved access to information technology. InfoDev receives project proposals from governments, private firms, and international and nongovernmental organizations wishing to foster such development in four main categories: creating a market-friendly environment to accelerate access to information; reducing poverty and exclusion; promoting education, improving health, and protecting the environment; and improving the efficiency and transparency of governments. InfoDev focuses on fostering partnerships among the World Bank, governments, the private sector, and civil society.*

*InfoDev was launched in September 1995. Since then, it has received more than 144 project proposals from all over the world, ranging from distance education and sophisticated agricultural mapping to medical data bases. Of these, four have already been approved as part of infoDev's Initiating Work Program: the African Virtual University; Telematics for African Development; Jamaica: Partnership for Technology in Basic Education; and the Sixth International Telecommunications Union Regulatory Colloquium. The standard funding amount per project is around $250,000. Dozens more projects are in the process of being evaluated, of which infoDev hopes to fund ten to fifteen annually. Available funds for calendar year 1996 are expected to reach about $4.5 million from sources in the private sector, member governments, and multilateral institutions.*

months to develop their collaborative approach, including the sharing of best practice, while respecting the value of diversity, competition, and the individual characteristics of each institution. In addition, the Bank's independent operations evaluation unit and its partners in the regional banks have established a voluntary coordination group to help develop more consistent approaches and methodologies to evaluation across the MDBs.

• Work with clients to attract private and public investment in high-quality projects— including capacity building in governments, strengthening legal and accounting systems and property rights, the marketing of opportunities and providing assurance to investors that the rules of the game will be followed—is being enhanced.

The Bank has stepped up its lending and advisory work in such areas, providing support for finance-sector reform and the private sector in Moldova; reform of the banking system in Vietnam; export development in Jordan; private infrastructure finance in India; and land titling in the Lao People's Democratic Republic. The Bank is also working with business organizations in many countries to provide business opportunities in developing countries (the annual meetings

now feature investment seminars for private sector participants, for example). It has also launched infoDev, an initiative to bring new resources—from corporations, foundations, and governments—to promote reform and investment in the developing world through improved access to information technology *(see accompanying box).* More efforts are being undertaken on mainstreaming the guarantee facility to encourage investment and on other services that will catalyze private investment in developing countries.

Against this background, commitments by the Bank were $21,520 million—$14,656 million from the IBRD and $6,864 million from IDA *(see accompanying table).* A total of 256 projects were approved (129 by the IBRD and 127 from IDA). Two loans on IDA-like terms, totaling $60 million, from resources provided by the Trust Fund for Gaza, were approved for the West Bank and Gaza. Seven projects in Bosnia and Herzegovina, totaling $150 million from the Trust Fund for Bosnia and Herzegovina, were also approved. Partial guarantees, totaling $275 million, were approved for three countries—China, Jordan, and Pakistan. Gross disbursements amounted to $19,256 million—

## TABLE 3. WORLD BANK OPERATIONAL AND FINANCIAL OVERVIEW, 1992–96

*(millions of us dollars unless otherwise noted; fiscal years)*

| Item | 1992 | 1993 | 1994 | 1995 | 1996 |
|---|---|---|---|---|---|
| **IBRD** | | | | | |
| Commitments[a] | 15,156 | 16,945 | 14,244 | 16,853 | 14,656[b] |
| Disbursements[a] | 11,666 | 12,942 | 10,447 | 12,672 | 13,372[b] |
| Net disbursements to current borrowers, excluding prepayments[a] | 2,502 | 2,865 | 19 | 1,651 | 2,100 |
| | 2,767 | 3,319 | 983 | 2,238 | 2,882 |
| Net disbursements to all borrowers[a] | 1,828 | 2,331 | -731 | 897 | 1,213 |
| Net income | 1,645 | 1,130 | 1,051 | 1,354 | 1,187 |
| Financial return on average investments | 8.07% | 6.07% | 3.53% | 5.69% | 4.43% |
| New medium- and long-term (MLT) borrowings after swaps[b] | 11,789 | 12,676 | 8,908 | 9,026 | 10,883 |
| Average cost of new MLT borrowings after swaps | 6.69% | 5.97% | 4.99% | 6.31% | 5.28% |
| Subscribed capital | 152,248 | 165,589 | 170,003 | 176,438 | 180,630 |
| Statutory lending limit | 168,368 | 183,312 | 189,189 | 198,988 | 201,125 |
| Loans and callable guarantees outstanding | 100,968 | 104,606 | 109,468 | 123,676 | 110,369 |
| As a % of statutory lending limit | 60 | 57 | 58 | 62 | 55 |
| Headroom | 67,400 | 78,706 | 79,721 | 75,312 | 90,756 |
| Liquidity ratio | 48% | 48% | 51% | 46% | 43% |
| Interest-coverage ratio | 1.24 | 1.16 | 1.16% | 1.19% | 1.18% |
| Reserves-to-loans ratio | 11.7% | 11.7% | 13.9% | 14.3% | 14.1% |
| **IBRD/IDA Joint Activities** | | | | | |
| Administrative expenses | 1,074 | 1,254 | 1,389 | 1,540 | 1,376 |
| **IDA** | | | | | |
| Commitments | 6,550 | 6,752 | 6,592 | 5,669 | 6,864 |
| Disbursements | 4,765 | 4,947 | 5,532 | 5,703 | 5,884 |
| Net disbursements | 4,441 | 4,581 | 5,110 | 5,205 | 5,322 |
| Development credits outstanding | 52,304 | 56,158 | 62,810 | 72,032 | 72,821 |
| Accumulated surplus | 1,363 | 1,194 | 1,365 | 1,995 | 1,790 |

a. *Excludes guarantees and loans to the IFC.*
b. *Includes the refinanced/rescheduled overdue charges of $168 million for Bosnia and Herzegovina.*

$13,372 million from the IBRD and $5,884 million from IDA.

Assistance to the poorest countries—those with a per capita gross national product of $765 or less (in terms of constant 1995 United States dollars) totaled $9,883 million—$3,556 million from the IBRD and $6,327 million from IDA *(see figure on page 20)*.

Some 32 percent of total Bank investment lending during the year was directly targeted to the poor, the same as in fiscal 1995 . These projects supported activities to increase the productivity of and economic opportunities for the poor, to develop their human resources, and to

provide social safety nets (for a description of each such targeted project, turn to the project summaries, which begin on page 127).

Grants during the year from the Debt-reduction Facility for IDA-only Countries totaled $77 million. They were advanced to four countries: Albania, Ethiopia, Mauritania, and Nicaragua. The Debt-reduction Facility provides low-income countries with grant funds to reduce their commercial debt that is public, external, noncollateralized, and unguaranteed. The facility is financed through contributions from the IBRD's net income and donors.

On the financial side, the IBRD borrowed the equivalent of $10,883 million in the world's financial markets. Its net income was $1,187 million.

And, at the end of the fiscal year, the executive board approved two initiatives that provide borrowers flexibility in determining the currency composition of their IBRD loans. One permits borrowers to select loans in a single currency for new loan commitments without volume restriction. The other allows borrowers to convert the terms of their existing currency-pool loans to the offered currency of their choice.

During the fiscal year, Bosnia and Herzegovina fulfilled the required formalities to succeed to the membership of the former Socialist Federal Republic of Yugoslavia as a member of the IBRD. Brunei Darussalam became a member of the IBRD on October 10, 1995, increasing the IBRD's membership to 180.

At the end of the fiscal year, action was pending on membership in the IBRD for the Federal Republic of Yugoslavia (Serbia/Montenegro).

Bosnia and Herzegovina also fulfilled the required formalities to succeeed to the membership of the former Socialist Federal Republic of Yugoslavia as a member of IDA, bringing the total membership of IDA to 159.

At the end of the fiscal year, action was pending on membership in IDA for Brunei Darussalam, Ukraine, and the Federal Republic of Yugoslavia (Serbia/Montenegro).

The board of executive directors is responsible for the conduct of the general operations of the Bank and performs its duties under powers delegated to it by the board of governors. As provided in the Articles of Agreement, five of the twenty-four executive directors are appointed by the five member governments having the largest number of shares; the rest of the board is elected by the other member governments, who form constituencies in the election process every two years.

The executive directors consider and decide on the IBRD loan and IDA credit proposals made by the president, and they decide policy issues that guide the general operations of the Bank and its direction. The executive directors are also responsible for presenting to the board of governors at the annual meetings an audit of accounts, an administrative budget, and the *Annual Report* on the operations and policies of the Bank, as well as any other matters that, in their judgment, require submission to the board of governors. During fiscal 1996, the executive directors met 114 times in formal board meetings and another forty-one times in seminars, informal sessions, and as the Committee of the Whole. In addition, most of the executive directors serve on one or more of five standing board committees: Audit Committee, Committee on Development Effectiveness,

Budget Committee, Personnel Committee, and Committee on Executive Directors' Administrative Matters. The executive directors' Steering Committee, an informal advisory body, also meets regularly.

In addition to the meetings and committee work, the executive directors accompany the president of the Bank when he travels to their constituencies. Groups of executive directors and alternate executive directors at times make special trips to borrowing countries to observe Bank-supported operations and its assistance strategy first hand. They meet with a wide range of people, including staff of the Bank's resident mission or field office, government officials and project managers, NGOs and project beneficiaries, and the business community. In fiscal 1996, groups of executive directors visited Eastern and Southern Africa (Ethiopia, Kenya, Mozambique, Zambia), Latin America and the Caribbean (Brazil, El Salvador, Guyana), and Central Asia (Kazakstan, Kyrgyz Republic, Uzbekistan).

## Shaping Policy

The board of executive directors' oversight role covers virtually all Bank policy, so its role cannot be clearly separated from most of the Bank activities and initiatives covered in this *Report*. This oversight role is exercised in part through the process of board approval of each Bank or IDA lending operation and the annual budget process. Although

a board committee cannot make a decision for the entire executive board, the committees increasingly look in depth at specific issues or Bank practices and report their findings and recommendations to the board. Also, the executive directors review major policy areas in order to keep them current. In a sense, the board of executive directors in its oversight role seeks to ensure that Bank policies are being interpreted and implemented correctly. The Operations Evaluation Department, an independent body within the Bank that reports directly to the executive board, assists in this function. It was through this oversight role that it became clear that the Bank should take a serious look at the type of results it was achieving, which resulted in the Task Force on Portfolio Management and its follow-up in recent years.

The executive directors are agents of change and also exercise a strong and important role in shaping more rapid shifts or innovations in Bank policy. It is in this role that the directors represent the changing perspectives of their shareholder governments regarding the Bank's role, particularly in response to international economic shocks. In this context, the need for a new role or emphasis for the Bank may become widely recognized by shareholders within a relatively short time. Examples are the visible refocusing of the Bank on poverty reduction about ten years ago and the emergence of such new areas of concern as governance, financial sector reform, and private sector development.

These policy initiatives normally reflect needs perceived by shareholders and involve a process of consensus building, both among executive directors and with Bank management. That process is presently ongoing on the issue of how to find a solution to the official debt problem of the heavily indebted poor countries. The Bank and shareholder governments are working to define their various roles in a coordinated approach.

The Development Committee's Task Force on Multilateral Development Banks was a different type of shareholder initiative that resulted in recommendations for change in the Bank and the other major MDBS.

The Task Force on Multilateral Development Banks was established in October 1995 by the Development Committee with a mandate to assess the implications that economic change in the world has had for the priorities, instruments, operations, and management of the world's five principal multilateral development banks (MDBS). In its April 1996 report to the Development Committee, the task force set forth five priorities that multilateral development banks must support in order to achieve sustainable development. Poverty reduction, the task force said, is the main challenge of development. The remaining four priorities were promotion of effective government and a strong civil society, assurance that development be environmentally sustainable, investment in infrastructure and utilities, and encouragement of private sector development.

The priorities should be carried out, the task force continued, by enhancing the strategic role of the MDBS' executive boards; strengthening national ownership of reforms, programs, and projects; learning from experience, developing better ground rules for sharing country economic information more widely; and demonstrating heightened cost-consciousness, especially in the light of the fact that their costs are borne by the world's developing countries through fees and charges.

The directors agreed that the Bank will make a progress report to the Development Committee in two years.

## Poverty Reduction

The executive board in fiscal 1996 continued its efforts to see poverty reduction, the Bank's overriding objective, more comprehensively integrated into the country-assistance strategies and all Bank work and analysis in borrowing countries. Directors made it clear that the poverty-reduction objective must not get downplayed in the course of the changes that are being made to increase Bank efficiency. Although recognizing considerable progress in the past few years, directors stressed the importance of keeping current with poverty assessments for borrowing countries, since it was difficult to begin serious work to help a country reduce poverty on a sustainable basis without the basic information. They also asked for more efforts to identify the real causes of poverty in any country so that efforts to lessen it could be appropriately targeted.

## Institutional Initiatives

The Budget Committee reviewed institutional initiatives proposed by the president with an eye to their effect on the budget and the board's desire to stay very close to previously agreed budget reductions. They asked management to explain its justifications for the initiatives, as well as detailed cost estimates, possible tradeoffs with other Bank programs, and redeployment options. The new initiatives will be paid for largely out of efficiency gains or budget reductions elsewhere.

The Personnel Committee reviewed business-process innovation in the Bank to date, particularly what had been done under pilot programs. It has expressed the need for management to take a more comprehensive approach to personnel issues and monitor the effects of change management on personnel issues.

The Audit Committee considered a report on the effectiveness of controls and supported the use of the framework defined by the Committee of Sponsoring Organization (COSO) of the

Treadway Commission to carry out a Bankwide review of internal controls. This review began in fiscal year 1996.

### Development Effectiveness

The board Committee on Development Effectiveness continued urging management to develop indicators of development effectiveness, or development impact, that could be applied to operations *ex ante*. This would constitute one major follow-up to the Task Force on Portfolio Management, and it would help in efforts to design higher-quality projects.

The committee is also interested in having the IFC develop indicators to measure the developmental effectiveness of its investments.

Supervision and portfolio evaluation and management are other areas of major follow-up to that task force report, and the board now reviews it via an "Annual Report on Portfolio Performance." It has expressed satisfaction that active portfolio restructuring and management have become increasingly employed by Bank staff and country officials.

### New Auditors

On the recommendation of the Audit Committee, the board in fiscal 1995 decided to periodically rotate external auditors. In fiscal 1996, procedures for getting bids from five international firms were decided. The actual bidding process and the selection of the new auditor are expected to take place in fiscal 1997.

## Increasing Development Effectiveness

Increasing development effectiveness is the absolute priority of today's World Bank. For only by increasing the effectiveness of what the Bank does can its goals—reducing poverty and fostering sustainable development—be met.

To enhance the quality and impact of its operations, the Bank gave heightened priority in fiscal 1996 to meeting client needs more effectively, improving the quality of new operations entering the portfolio, improving portfolio management, measuring the performance and development effectiveness of its activities, and feeding back the lessons of experience into new initiatives.

Actions taken by the Bank during the year and, in fact, since the publication in fiscal 1993 of the report of the Task Force on Portfolio Management, are in line with the recommendations of the Development Committee's Task Force on Multilateral Development Banks, which, in April 1996, strongly endorsed the need to instill an organizational culture based not on approvals but results, and not on the quantity of lending but on the developmental impact of loans and other services.

In pursuit of efforts to improve development effectiveness, the interface between the executive board and Bank management improved through the work of the board's Committee on Development Effectiveness (CODE).

This committee addresses issues—including operational policy and portfolio-management issues—that have an important bearing on the relevance, efficiency, and effectiveness of the Bank Group's operations, and it monitors the implementation of board decisions on these issues. The committee oversees the work of the independent Operations Evaluation Department (OED) and the responses of Bank management to evaluation findings and recommendations, so as to identify policy issues for consideration by the board. Within the forum offered by CODE, fiscal 1996 saw an intense process of debate and decisionmaking; while maintaining their distinctive institutional roles and perspectives, the CODE, Bank management, and OED initiated a collaborative process aimed at creating a learning culture in the Bank and shaping organizational change to make the Bank more responsive to the needs of clients and more accountable for results on the ground.

*Meeting client needs.* During fiscal 1996 the Bank made considerable progress in focusing its country-assistance strategies (CASS) more clearly on clients' specific needs, both for lending and for advice, and in linking its budget decisions more closely to the goals of these strategies. More systematic efforts were made to ensure that the CASS reflected the views of interest groups likely to be affected; Bank resident missions played a larger role in organizing opportunities for discussion with, and feedback from, key stakeholders.

Fundamental to the Bank's ability to meet client needs more effectively were the steps taken in fiscal 1996 to improve management. The president strengthened the functions of senior management, assigning direct line responsibilities to five managing directors. The two managing directors for operations have given priority to lightening the process burden and reducing reviews, giving operational staff more time and scope to focus on results "on the ground." Efforts to lighten processes, reduce reviews, and delegate responsibility are not without risks to quality. But Bank management is convinced that quality resides in its staff, that reliance on lengthy documentation and multiple reviews provides false comfort, and that the key to improved quality lies in reformed personnel incentives, enhanced skills, and tightened management.

In discussions with the executive board and CODE, Bank management sought to signal a break with the past by more thorough reporting on the status of the lending program, the quality of portfolio management, disbursement performance, and nonlending services, as well as on the implementation of management responses to recommendations from the Operations Evaluation Department. In the same vein, the CODE agreed to review with top management specific examples of significant project restructuring and country-portfolio performance reviews, so that all parties can better understand the management issues.

Business-innovation programs are now under way in all the Bank's regional offices. In the Africa region, changes in organization are designed to make operational approaches more responsive to clients' differing needs and differing levels of commitment to poverty reduction, economic reform, and better debt management. Measures are being implemented to simplify work processes and make lending and economic and sector studies more timely and responsive to needs. In East Asia and Pacific, work priorities and resources are being redirected from middle- to low-income countries, and operational processes have been accelerated. The South Asia region is increasing its focus on social and environmental risks. Borrowers' increased responsibility for project preparation and implementation has helped to increase development effectiveness and reduce costs.

In the Europe and Central Asia region, a major effort is in progress to strengthen portfolio implementation and improve rates of loan disbursement. The region is reducing its unit costs of lending and is making its economic and sector studies more succinct and better focused. Resources freed by these efforts, and by increased selectivity, are helping make possible a swift Bank response to urgent needs in Bosnia and Herzegovina. The Latin America and the Caribbean region is allocating increased resources to portfolio management. A high-level Brazil-Bank commission has been set up to reform portfolio-management processes. And, seeking closer relations with its clients, it is decentralizing resources, responsibilities, and activities to the field. The Middle East and North Africa region is developing more focused and flexible CASs, in concert with clients and other stakeholders. Decentralized decisionmaking and redesigned business processes aim at increasing cost-effectiveness and improving results on the ground.

To strengthen accountability for quality and results, the president of the Bank established the Quality Assurance Group in fiscal 1996. The new group provides line managers with independent assessments of their work and identifies and helps to address critical problem areas in the portfolio. The group is reviewing operational products on a sample basis, initially focusing on project-cycle activities—including reviews of supervision, checks on the quality of proposed new projects, and troubleshooting for problem projects—and on CASs and country-portfolio performance reviews.

*Staff training and education.* The Bank began a new education and training effort to raise the professional standards and diversify the skills of its staff. In-house professional training programs were upgraded, and expanded training for technical staff promoted the sharing of best practices and lessons from evaluation experience. The Bank expanded staff opportunities for executive education and for exchange and secondment, including exchanges with, and secondment to, private sector organizations and autonomous agencies, and it established a Presidential Fellows Program to bring eminent scholars and leaders to the Bank. The education and training programs will help strengthen management capacity across the Bank, restore the Bank's skills base, and ensure professional excellence at all levels, enhancing the Bank's awareness and competitiveness. Ultimately the result should be more effective services to clients.

*Improving the quality of new operations.* The Bank continued with initiatives to improve the quality of new operations. At the president's request, the Operations Policy Department and the OED jointly reviewed the economic analysis of new operations proposed for financing and made recommendations for action. They found that today's operations are based on somewhat better analysis than those approved three years ago; nevertheless, a continuing need for much more analytical rigor in project appraisal, particularly in analyzing poverty-reduction impacts, was identified. Another review confirmed the value of the Bank's economic and sector work in client countries. It noted that in-depth economic and sector studies facilitate the dialogue with clients, encouraging project designs that are tailored to specific circumstances. Projects that were able to build on the results of economic and sector studies were found to give more thorough attention to institutional support, budgetary provisions, project alternatives, and risks. The CODE endorsed the recommendations of both these studies, and throughout fiscal 1996, the OED reviewed the early documentation for selected new lending operations and drew the attention of operational staff to relevant lessons of experience.

*Improving portfolio management.* The Bank's regional offices have been giving increased attention to portfolio management since the

"Next Steps" Program began in fiscal 1993 *(see Box 2-1)*. Actions in progress include identifying concentrations of problem projects and making concerted efforts to deal with them. They also include more intense portfolio supervision, greater reliance on reviews of country portfolio performance, and making portfolio performance a more important consideration in the design and adaptation of CASS.

Monitoring and evaluation of ongoing projects are fundamental to getting results on the ground. In fiscal 1996, the Bank began introducing more objective indicators for measuring projects' progress toward development goals. Responding to OED findings that the

---

## BOX 2-1. "NEXT STEPS": A SECOND PROGRESS REPORT

*In the wake of the November 1992 report of the Task Force on Portfolio Management, which examined the quality of the Bank's project portfolio and made recommendations on ways to reverse its decline, a commitment was made in July 1993 to undertake eighty-seven specific actions ("next steps") to enhance portfolio management.*

*These actions were grouped into the seven major themes of the task-force report to facilitate progress assessment and track specific deadlines. They were: linking country portfolio performance to the Bank's core business practices; providing for more active project and portfolio restructuring; improving the quality of projects entering the portfolio; defining the Bank's role in, and improving the management of, project performance; enhancing the role of the Operations Evaluation Department; creating a supportive internal environment for better portfolio management; and finally, generic issues affecting portfolio performance were included.*

*According to a first progress report (June 1994), almost all of those actions had either been completed or were at an advanced stage of completion by June 30, 1994.*

*The board reviewed a second report early in fiscal 1996. While it warned that "next steps" activities should not be viewed in isolation because they are interrelated and together they form a whole, it examined the program under four general categories of activities to illustrate progress in implementing the program. Thus:*

• *Studies, policy papers, and related policy changes had, for the most part, been completed; for example, a new information-disclosure policy had been adopted, and the operational policies and procedures for the economic analysis of investment projects had been improved.*

• *New approaches to improve projects were either in active use, or, in the case of performance-monitoring indicators, were at an early stage of implementation. Their impact will only become evident over time.*

• *Strengthened approaches to country- and project-level implementation had also progressed, with evidence of many instances of good practices.*

• *Changing the environment and organizational incentives to support conscientious portfolio management also showed progress, with relevant changes made to staff incentives, more targeted recruitment, and redesigned training, as well as simplification and more transparent and flexible mnagement processes.*

*The report did not attempt to assess the effect of these actions or claim that the goals espoused in the task-force report had been achieved.*

*This second report was the final report on the implementation of "next steps." Because the* Annual Report on Portfolio Performance *is the primary tool for assessing the development effectiveness of the Bank's portfolio, it will be used in the future to measure the overall effect of the "next steps" actions.*

monitoring and evaluation of ongoing operations still need major improvement, management undertook to ensure that appropriate monitoring and evaluation provisions are built into new operations and the portfolio, and to provide better technical leadership and support services to operational staff for monitoring and evaluation.

Menus of sector-specific project-performance monitoring indicators have been developed. As of the end of fiscal 1996, seventeen sector "first edition" notes have been issued, as well as a handbook for task managers. The sector notes cover each sector in which the Bank works and areas of emphasis that cross economic and social sectors, such as environmental concerns, poverty reduction, public sector management, and technical assistance. The only note that remains to be issued is on public sector management; it is expected later in calendar 1996. All the notes will be revised as the Bank and its clients gain experience with the use of indicators.

The indicators are currently being incorporated into the Bank's work in several ways. To enhance the quality of projects at entry, the Bank's six operational regions are responsible for ensuring that project designs and implementation plans include appropriate monitoring indicators. Borrower and staff training, including regional workshops, on the appropriate uses of performance-monitoring indicators have taken place and will continue. The process of selecting indicators should help the borrower, implementing agency, other stakeholders, and Bank staff clarify project objectives.

The Bank expects that better-defined project objectives will lead to more objective project monitoring, which, in turn, will improve the realism of project ratings.

*Assessing performance.* The *Annual Report on Portfolio Performance (ARPP)* is the Bank's principal means of informing management and the executive board of the overall status of the portfolio, as well as of identifying additional measures to improve portfolio performance and management. The *ARPP* for fiscal 1995, reviewed by the executive board in December 1995, examined 1,742 ongoing operations in 138

countries with a total commitment value of $143.1 billion.[1]

The *ARPP* provides an overview of portfolio performance, using the Bank's project-rating system that assesses projects' likelihood of achieving their development objectives (DO) and their implementation progress (IP). Under the first criterion, achievement of development objectives, the share of problem projects—those that get an "unsatisfactory" rating because they are not likely to achieve their developmental objectives—in the portfolio fell from 13.4 percent in fiscal 1994 to 11.5 percent in fiscal 1995. The modest improvement reflects two factors. First, reflecting efforts to clean up problematic country portfolios, fiscal 1995 saw the closure of many projects with higher-than-average unsatisfactory ratings. Second, projects that entered the portfolio during the year were rated positively at this early stage of their implementation.

In terms of implementation progress, the status of the portfolio seems to have stabilized since about fiscal 1992, with 17 percent-to-18 percent of the ongoing projects rated unsatisfactory each year. The gap between the IP and DO ratings—about 6 percent—reflects overoptimistic assessments during project preparation and offers a measure of the risks that projects will not achieve their objectives. Greater attention to the quality of supervision ratings is being encouraged, in part, through the development of specific sets of performance indicators for each sector.

*Independent review of the ARPP.* In its "Process Review of the FY95 Annual Report on Portfolio Performance," also reviewed by the board, the OED noted that operational units are becoming steadily more realistic about the performance of ongoing operations. But it emphasized that a reduction in the failure rate of Bank operations is still elusive. Concerned that about a third of Bank operations are still rated unsatisfactory on their completion, and that the failure rate has

1. World Bank. 1996. *Annual Report on Portfolio Performance— Fiscal 1995*. Washington, D.C.

been stuck at about this level for five years, the OED pointed to the continuing need to deal aggressively with weaknesses in the portfolio. It recommended the regions continue to push for more careful treatment of portfolio matters in the development and review of CASS, linking assistance more closely to the performance of ongoing operations. It urged that country portfolio performance reviews take on a greater strategic thrust, leading to agreements with borrowers on broad qualitative goals, and that progress toward these goals be systematically reviewed.

*Performance of completed operations.* The OED's independent analysis of completed operations evaluated in calendar 1994, *Evaluation Results 1994*, which was reviewed by the board in fiscal 1996, pointed to some encouraging signs, but confirmed the need to improve performance and accountability further for results.[2] Sixty-six percent of the completed operations that were evaluated in 1994 had satisfactory outcomes—a figure somewhat better than the average for 1990–94, but still low. Only 44 percent of the evaluated operations were expected to sustain their benefits throughout the operational phase that follows the completion of Bank loan disbursements. This proportion differed little from the average for 1989–94, though there was a noticeable drop in the share of operations judged clearly *un*likely to sustain their benefits. Institutional development goals were substantially achieved in 39 percent of the operations, better than the 30 percent in the 1993 cohort and the average of 31 percent for the last five years, but again a low figure. Adjustment operations performed better, on average, than investment projects.

*Evaluation and feedback.* As well as providing "report cards" on the Bank's record, evaluation supported the Bank's effort to improve development effectiveness in two ways: by providing lessons of experience for policies and projects, and by helping to enhance quality management through links to training programs, the work of the Quality Assurance Group, and monitoring and evaluating of ongoing operations.

*Self-evaluation by regional offices.* Under arrangements introduced in fiscal 1995, the Bank's regional staff and borrowers prepare implementation completion reports (ICRS) for the executive board on all completed lending operations. Unlike project completion reports (PCRS), which were prepared prior to fiscal 1995, ICRS are sent directly to the executive board rather than through the OED. In fiscal 1996, the OED reported on the experience with the first cohort of implementation completion reports. In general, it found that the reports were providing candid reviews with thoughtful insights on lessons learned. Borrower involvement in completion reporting had, however, remained somewhat superficial, confirming a need that the Bank has already recognized—for strengthening evaluation capacity in its client countries.

*New emphases in independent evaluation.* Responding to the Bank's new operational emphases, the OED increased the country focus of its work (by undertaking country-assistance reviews (CARS), for example); undertook follow-up studies to report on the Bank's progress in implementing earlier OED recommendations; and produced process evaluations of the Bank's implementation-completion reports, environmental impact assessments, and the ARPP. It issued impact evaluations that assessed the long-run development effectiveness of a wide range of operations, drawing out the implications for today's policies and programs.

*Dissemination of evaluation findings.* A Bankwide task force on dissemination of evaluation findings examined how the Bank learns from evaluation work and other Bank experience; it made recommendations for greater efforts by the OED and the central vice presidencies to disseminate these lessons and by operational staff to apply them.

## Operations Evaluation

Operations evaluation at the World Bank has a threefold mandate: to measure how far, how effectively, and how efficiently the Bank's activities are achieving their desired results; to draw and disseminate lessons for application in

2. World Bank. 1996. *Evaluation Results 1994*. Washington, D.C.

policies, operations, and processes; and to help the Bank and its member countries improve their evaluation capabilities.

Evaluators responded in fiscal 1996 to the new president's emphasis on meeting clients' needs, introducing better business processes, and achieving development impact on the ground. Assessing the extent to which these goals are translated into practice, and making recommendations for further progress, are integral to the Bank's evaluation function. Some of the evaluation activities in support of greater development effectiveness were outlined earlier in this section.

Evaluation work in the Bank is overseen by the director general, operations evaluation, who reports to the board of executive directors through the Committee on Development Effectiveness (CODE) and keeps a watching brief over the large volume of self-evaluation work done by the regional offices and other vice presidencies. Independent evaluation is done by the Operations Evaluation Department (OED). Results and recommendations from evaluation are reported to the executive directors and fed back into the design and implementation of policies and lending operations.

*Lending.* All lending operations are evaluated on completion by the regional offices responsible for them; borrower agencies contribute to these completion reports. The OED reviews the performance ratings presented and, for each completed operation, provides the board with an independent assessment of overall outcome, sustainability, impact on the borrower's institutional development, borrower performance, and Bank performance, as well as the lessons to be drawn.

For a representative sample of completed operations, the OED produces performance audits.

In fiscal 1996 the OED reviewed 250 completion reports and reported on their quality to the Bank's board and management, and audited 100 completed operations. The cumulative total of Bank operations subjected to *ex post* evaluation reached 4,126 at the end of the fiscal year.

The OED's *Evaluation Results 1994* provided an overview of performance in recently completed operations, as noted earlier in this section. It also broke new ground with a quantita-

tive analysis of the determinants of performance in more than 1,000 completed operations. The Bank's board and management discussed the implications of this analysis. In particular, the findings suggested that in countries without a cohesive strategy to address economic fundamentals, the odds of successful investment operations are poor, and that, in consequence, the Bank should revisit its practice of maintaining substantial lending levels in countries with unhelpful economic environments.

In its impact evaluations, the OED, assisted by agencies in borrower countries, analyzes the development effectiveness of projects five to eight years after the close of loan disbursements. These evaluations assess the economic worth of projects and their long-term effects on people and the environment. They provide unique insights into what makes development efforts sustainable. Among the twenty-two impact evaluations produced in fiscal 1996, subjects included urban improvement projects in Kenya and India; a steel project in Egypt; assistance to refugees in Pakistan; road projects in Morocco; and irrigation projects in South and Southeast Asia. Several of these impact evaluations put into effect a new set of guidelines for more systematically involving stakeholders—including communities directly affected by Bank operations—in evaluations, so as to assess more accurately the social impact of Bank lending.

*Nonlending services.* Following recommendations made by a Bankwide working group, Bank management enhanced the arrangements for evaluating the development impact of nonlending services—including economic and sector work, trust funds, development training, research, and technical assistance—which now account for more than a third of the Bank's administrative budget.

The OED began a review of the self-evaluation processes of the Bank's economic and sector work and of the Economic Development Institute and, jointly with the Controller's Department, designed a process for evaluating the Bank's administration of trust funds, which currently finance more than 3,000 schemes and collaborative programs.

*Country and sector assistance, business processes*. The OED's evaluation studies examine Bank processes and broader development issues, including policies and experience in countries, regions, and sectors. Recommendations arising from the studies are discussed by the CODE, along with responses from Bank management, and agreements on follow-up actions are recorded in a policy ledger to have their implementation monitored by the OED. In fiscal 1996, the OED sent twelve studies to the board. These included evaluations of country-assistance programs in Argentina and Zambia, and reviews of lending for agricultural research and for electric power development in Africa.

OED's country-assistance review for Ghana raised generic issues for the Bank's planning and management of CASs. The CODE pursued these issues with management. They included the Bank's propensity to underestimate the time required to implement policy-reform programs and achieve a sustained response from producers; the need for CASs to reflect the political economy; the need to design trade-liberalization programs flexibly, with an eye to costs as well as benefits; the need for consistent, thoroughgoing efforts to promote partnership and borrower participation in Bank operations; the need for high-quality, judiciously timed economic and sector work and thorough analysis of proposed operations; and skill mix, staffing, and work-location issues.

Through follow-up studies, the OED assessed the progress the Bank had made in implementing earlier OED recommendations on agricultural credit policy and on monitoring and evaluation of ongoing operations. The latter study highlighted examples of best practices and noted an improving trend in the use of key performance indicators. But it also found that institutional capacity among borrowers and in the Bank, and data collection at the project level, had not kept pace, and that the record of tracking the developmental impact of projects under implementation was uneven.

*Dissemination and outreach*. In line with the Bank's disclosure policy on evaluation results, all impact evaluations and country- and sector-evaluation studies were released to the public

through the Public Information Center. The OED expanded its publications program, and its offerings on the Internet led to a large volume of requests for evaluation information.

The OED gave seminars within and outside the Bank, including in borrower countries, to discuss evaluation design and results, and issues raised by evaluation results for the management of ongoing programs.

Several activities expanded and strengthened the professional links between the OED and evaluators in other agencies. First, the OED participated as an observer in meetings of the DAC Expert Group. Second, the multilateral development banks (MDBs) established an Evaluation Cooperation Group, through which they will systematically learn from each other's experiences in evaluation approaches and practices. In this context, OED commissioned an independent review of project-evaluation methods and standards among the MDBs. Third, OED pursued professional contacts with Australian government evaluators, resulting in workshops for the Indonesian government and for Bank staff on Australia's well-established integration of evaluation into strategic planning and budgeting. Fourth, evaluation staff contributed to several professional evaluation meetings, including the first international conference on evaluation sponsored by the North American Evaluation Association.

*Support for evaluation in borrower countries*. Bank country departments and the OED responded to requests for advice on evaluation capacity development from Colombia, Indonesia, Turkey, and Zimbabwe.

*Executive board review*. In fiscal 1996 the executive directors reviewed the OED's *Evaluation Results 1994*, the director general's "Annual Report on Operations Evaluation in the Bank," and the "Annual Report of the CODE." They found that, overall, the Bank's evaluation system was performing well. But they called for efforts to (a) strengthen borrower participation in completion reporting and borrowers' evaluation capacity; (b) ensure more timely preparation of reports on completed lending operations; (c) improve the economic analysis of proposed projects and the monitoring and evaluation of ongoing operations; and (d) make further progress in the evaluation of nonlending services. And they asked for more concrete evidence that lessons learned from experience are being implemented in lending, portfolio management, nonlending services, and CASS.

## Commitments and Guarantees

World Bank commitments (IBRD and IDA combined) amounted to $21,520 million in fiscal 1996, a decrease of $1,002 million (5 percent) over fiscal 1995's total (see Table 2-1). Commitments by the IBRD (including the refinanced/rescheduled overdue charges of $168 million for Bosnia and Herzegovina) amounted to $14,656 million, while IDA credits totaled SDR4,616 million, or $6,864 million equivalent. A total of 129 IBRD loans to forty-five countries were approved; the 127 IDA credits went to forty-nine countries.

The biggest increase in commitments was in the Middle East and North Africa region, where twenty-one projects were approved for a total of $1,595 million. Comparable figures for the previous year were fourteen projects for $979 million. Lending volume also increased in the Africa region. The sharpest drop occurred in Latin America and the Caribbean.

Adjustment lending amounted to 21 percent of Bank commitments, down from the previous year's 24 percent (see Table 2-2). The fiscal 1996 adjustment total includes $65 million in rehabilitation-import loans and $30 million in debt-reduction loans.

The three largest borrowers from the IBRD were China ($2,490 million), Russia ($1,816 million), and Argentina ($1,509 million). The three largest borrowers of IDA credits were India ($1,301 million), Vietnam ($502 million), and China ($480 million).

Two projects in the West Bank and Gaza, totaling $60 million and funded from the Trust Fund for Gaza, were approved. Seven projects, totaling $150 million and funded by the Trust Fund for Bosnia and Herzegovina, were approved for Bosnia and Herzegovina.

Lending for electric power—at $3,247 million—led all sectors by volume, followed by

## TABLE 2-1. TRENDS IN IBRD AND IDA LENDING, FISCAL YEARS 1994–96

(amounts in millions of US dollars)

| Sector | 1994 | | | 1995 | | | 1996 | | |
|---|---|---|---|---|---|---|---|---|---|
| | IBRD | IDA | Total | IBRD | IDA | Total | IBRD | IDA | Total |
| Agriculture | 2,194.3 | 1,674.0 | 3,868.3 | 1,171.4 | 1,540.4 | 2,751.8 | 1,160.3 | 1,416.4 | 2,576.7 |
| Education | 1,499.9 | 658.1 | 2,158.0 | 1,280.6 | 816.2 | 2,096.8 | 920.8 | 784.9 | 1,705.7 |
| Electric power and other energy | 1,613.3 | — | 1,613.3 | 1,802.5 | 439.0 | 2,241.5 | 2,899.2 | 347.9 | 3,247.1 |
| Environment | 679.5 | 17.3 | 696.8 | 557.1 | 40.5 | 597.6 | 348.1 | 36.8 | 384.9 |
| Finance | 1,093.5 | 411.1 | 1,504.6 | 2,935.4 | 129.3 | 3,064.7 | 1,199.2 | 161.4 | 1,372.7 |
| Industry | 375.0 | 267.1 | 642.1 | 175.0 | 23.2 | 198.2 | 217.0 | 14.8 | 239.8 |
| Mining/Other extractive | 14.0 | — | 14.0 | — | 24.8 | 24.8 | 570.8 | 109.0 | 679.8 |
| Multisector | 606.3 | 896.5 | 1,495.3 | 2,295.0 | 867.8 | 3,116.5 | 906.3 | 758.6 | 1,685.5 |
| Oil and gas | 957.3 | 186.2 | 1,143.5 | 461.5 | 141.6 | 603.1 | 30.0 | 25.6 | 55.6 |
| Population, health, and nutrition | 366.0 | 519.7 | 885.7 | 451.3 | 711.0 | 1,162.3 | 1,495.2 | 858.2 | 2,353.4 |
| Public sector management | 378.3 | 260.1 | 646.0 | 636.2 | 230.1 | 872.6 | 1,036.0 | 943.1 | 1,938.4 |
| Social sector | 130.0 | 20.6 | 150.6 | 596.5 | 51.0 | 627.5 | 240.0 | 554.5 | 794.5 |
| Telecommunications/ Informatics | 405.0 | 18.0 | 423.0 | 325.0 | — | 325.0 | 35.0 | — | 35.0 |
| Transportation | 2,202.5 | 1,117.7 | 3,320.2 | 2,026.8 | 104.1 | 2,130.9 | 2,236.9 | 535.7 | 2,772.6 |
| Urban development | 857.0 | 442.4 | 1,299.4 | 1,466.0 | 241.0 | 1,727.0 | 632.0 | 236.5 | 868.5 |
| Water supply and sanitation | 872.0 | 103.2 | 975.2 | 672.3 | 309.2 | 981.5 | 729.1 | 80.7 | 809.8 |
| Total | 14,243.9 | 6,592.1 | 20,836.0 | 16,852.6 | 5,669.2 | 22,521.8 | 14,655.9 | 6,864.1 | 21,520.0 |

# TABLE 2-2. WORLD BANK ADJUSTMENT OPERATIONS, FISCAL 1996

*(amounts in millions of US dollars)*

| Country | Project | World Bank financing | | |
|---|---|---|---|---|
| | | IBRD | IDA | Total |
| *Sector-adjustment loans* | | | | |
| Argentina | Bank Reform Loan | 500.0 | — | 500.0 |
| Argentina | Health Insurance Reform Loan | 350.0 | — | 350.0 |
| Bangladesh | Jute Sector Adjustment Credit (IDA reflows) | — | 3.4 | 3.4 |
| Bolivia | Capitalization Program Adjustment Credit | — | 50.0 | 50.0 |
| Bolivia | Capitalization Program Adjustment Credit (IDA reflows) | — | 8.0 | 8.0 |
| Cameroon | Structural Adjustment Credit II | — | 150.0 | 150.0 |
| Cameroon | Structural Adjustment Credit II (IDA reflows) | — | 30.3 | 30.3 |
| Côte d'Ivoire | Agriculture Sector Adjustment Credit | — | 150.0 | 150.0 |
| Côte d'Ivoire | Agriculture Sector Adjustment Credit (IDA reflows) | — | 73.6 | 73.6 |
| Côte d'Ivoire | Private Sector Development Adjustment Credit | — | 180.0 | 180.0 |
| Guyana | Private Sector Development Adjustment Credit (IDA reflows) | — | 2.9 | 2.9 |
| Jordan | Economic Reform and Development Loan | 80.0 | — | 80.0 |
| Kazakstan | Financial Sector Adjustment Loan | 180.0 | — | 180.0 |
| Kyrgyz Republic | Financial Sector Adjustment Credit | — | 45.0 | 45.0 |
| Mauritania | Private Sector Development Credit (IDA reflows) | — | 0.8 | 0.8 |
| Mauritania | Public Resource Management | — | 20.0 | 20.0 |
| Morocco | Financial Markets Development Loan | 250.0 | — | 250.0 |
| Nicaragua | Emergency Recovery Credit (IDA reflows) | — | 5.8 | 5.8 |
| Romania | Financial and Enterprise Sector Adjustment Loan | 280.0 | — | 280.0 |
| Russia | Coal Sector Adjustment Loan | 500.0 | — | 500.0 |
| Senegal | Agricultural Sector Adjustment Credit (IDA reflows) | — | 2.8 | 2.8 |
| Ukraine | Enterprise Development Adjustment Loan | 310.0 | — | 310.0 |
| Zambia | Economic Recovery and Investment Promotion Credit | — | 140.0 | 140.0 |
| Zambia | Economic Recovery and Investment Promotion Credit (IDA reflows) | — | 12.1 | 12.1 |
| Total | | 2,450.0 | 874.7 | 3,324.7 |
| *Structural adjustment loans* | | | | |
| Algeria | Structural Adjustment Loan I | 300.0 | — | 300.0 |
| Armenia | Structural Adjustment Credit | — | 60.0 | 60.0 |
| Cambodia | Economic Rehabilitation Credit | — | 40.0 | 40.0 |
| Chad | Structural Adjustment Credit | — | 30.0 | 30.0 |
| Georgia | Structural Adjustment Credit | — | 60.0 | 60.0 |
| Ghana | Private Sector Adjustment Credit (IDA reflows) | — | 4.8 | 4.8 |
| Honduras | Public Sector Modernization Structural Adjustment | — | 55.0 | 55.0 |
| Honduras | Public Sector Modernization Structural Adjustment (IDA reflows) | — | 26.4 | 26.4 |
| Kenya | Structural Adjustment Credit | — | 126.8 | 126.8 |
| Lao People's Democratic Rep. | Structural Adjustment Credit III | — | 40.0 | 40.0 |
| Malawi | Fiscal Restructuring and Deregulation Program | — | 102.0 | 102.0 |
| Malawi | Fiscal Restructuring and Deregulation Program (IDA reflows) | — | 4.4 | 4.4 |
| Mali | Economic Management Credit | — | 60.0 | 60.0 |
| Papua New Guinea | Economic Recovery Program | 50.0 | — | 50.0 |
| Sierra Leone | Structural Adjustment Credit II (IDA reflows) | — | 0.3 | 0.3 |
| Togo | Economic Recovery and Adjustment Credit | — | 50.0 | 50.0 |
| Yemen | Economic Recovery Credit | — | 80.0 | 80.0 |
| Total | | 350.0 | 739.7 | 1,089.7 |
| *Debt-reduction loan* | | | | |
| Panama | Debt and Debt-service Reduction Loan | 30.0 | — | 30.0 |
| Total | | 30.0 | — | 30.0 |
| *Rehabilitation-import loan* | | | | |
| Azerbaijan | Rehabilitation Credit | — | 65.0 | 65.0 |
| Grand total | | 2,830.0 | 1,679.4 | 4,509.4 |

— Zero.

transportation ($2,773 million) and agriculture ($2,577 million).

Fiscal 1996 saw the expansion of its partial risk and credit-risk gurantee program that was revitalized and amended during the previous year to catalyze the flow of private capital to infrastructure projects. Three such projects, totaling $275 million, were approved.

## Disbursements

Gross disbursements by the IBRD to countries totaled $13,372 million, an increase of 5.5 percent over fiscal 1995's $12,672 million. IDA disbursements amounted to $5,884 million, up $181 million from the previous year.

*Disbursements, by source of supply.* Projects financed by the World Bank require procurement from foreign and local sources to achieve project goals. Disbursements are made primarily to cover specific costs for foreign procurement and some local expenditures.

Three procurement considerations generally guide the Bank's requirements: the need for economy and efficiency in the execution of a project; the Bank's interest, as a cooperative

institution, in giving all eligible bidders from developing countries and developed countries an opportunity to compete in providing goods and works financed by the Bank; and the Bank's interest, as a development institution, in encouraging the development of local contractors and manufacturers in borrowing countries. The Bank prescribes conditions under which preferences may be given to domestic or regional manufacturers and, where appropriate, to domestic contractors.

Table 2-3 shows consolidated foreign and local disbursements for the IBRD and IDA through the end of fiscal 1991 and for the period fiscal 1992 through fiscal 1996. Advance disbursements consist of payments made into special accounts of borrowers, from which funds are paid to specific suppliers as expenditures are incurred. Because balances in these accounts cannot be attributed to any specific supplying country until expenditures have been reported to the Bank, these are shown as a separate category.

Table 2-4 provides details for foreign disbursements by OECD and non-OECD countries for the IBRD and IDA separately.

### TABLE 2-3. FOREIGN AND LOCAL DISBURSEMENTS, BY SOURCE OF SUPPLY

*(amounts in millions of US dollars)*

| Period | IBRD and IDA | | | | | | |
|---|---|---|---|---|---|---|---|
| | Foreign[a] | | Local | | Net advance disbursements[b] | | Total amount |
| | Amount | % | Amount | % | Amount | % | |
| Cumulative to June 30, 1991 | 103,433 | 58 | 70,923 | 40 | 4,592 | 3 | 178,948 |
| Fiscal 1992 | 9,038 | 55 | 6,807 | 42 | 537 | 3 | 16,381 |
| Fiscal 1993 | 9,813 | 56 | 7,887 | 45 | -325 | -2 | 17,375 |
| Fiscal 1994 | 9,010 | 56 | 7,442 | 47 | -473 | -3 | 15,979 |
| Fiscal 1995 | 9,094 | 51 | 8,724 | 49 | -97 | -1 | 17,720 |
| Fiscal 1996 | 10,013[c] | 52 | 8,787 | 46 | 456 | 2 | 19,256 |
| Cumulative to June 30, 1996 | 150,401 | 57 | 110,570 | 42 | 4,690 | 2 | 265,660 |

NOTE: Details may not add to totals because of rounding.
a. Amounts exclude debt-reduction disbursements of $313 million in FY91, $50 million in FY92, $515 million in FY93, and $655 million in FY95. Amounts include $556 million in disbursements under simplified procedures for structural and sectoral adjustment loans in FY 96.
b. Net advance disbursements are advances made to special accounts net of amounts recovered (amounts for which the Bank has applied evidence of expenditures to recovery of the outstanding advance).
c. Disbursements for FY96 include the refinanced/rescheduled overdue charges of $168 million for Bosnia and Herzegovina.

## TABLE 2-4. FOREIGN DISBURSEMENTS, BY SOURCE OF SUPPLY

*(amounts in millions of US dollars)*

| Period | IBRD OECD Amount | % | Non-OECD Amount | % | Total amount | IDA OECD Amount | % | Non-OECD Amount | % | Total amount |
|---|---|---|---|---|---|---|---|---|---|---|
| Cumulative to June 30, 1991 | 66,071 | 86 | 11,104 | 14 | 77,176 | 20,783 | 79 | 5,475 | 21 | 26,258 |
| Fiscal 1992 | 5,116 | 76 | 1,585 | 24 | 6,701 | 1,541 | 66 | 796 | 34 | 2,337 |
| Fiscal 1993 | 5,104 | 73 | 1,873 | 27 | 6,976 | 1,786 | 63 | 1,050 | 37 | 2,837 |
| Fiscal 1994 | 3,995 | 73 | 1,462 | 27 | 5,457 | 2,209 | 62 | 1,344 | 38 | 3,553 |
| Fiscal 1995 | 4,584 | 78 | 1,312 | 22 | 5,896 | 1,987 | 62 | 1,210 | 38 | 3,197 |
| Fiscal 1996 | 4,982 | 73 | 1,824 | 27 | 6,806 | 1,712 | 65 | 940 | 35 | 2,652 |
| Cumulative to June 30, 1996 | 89,852 | 82 | 19,160 | 18 | 109,012 | 30,018 | 74 | 10,815 | 26 | 40,832 |

NOTE: *Amounts exclude disbursements for debt reduction, net advance disbursements, and disbursements under simplified procedures for structural and sectoral adjustment loans. Details may not add to totals because of rounding. OECD amounts are based on current OECD membership, excluding Czech Republic and Hungary, which became OECD members in December 1995 and May 1996 respectively.*

Appendix 7 shows disbursements made in fiscal 1996 by the IBRD and IDA for local procurement by current borrowing countries and disbursements made for goods, works, and services procured from them by other Bank borrowers (foreign procurement) for projects funded by the Bank.

Appendix 8 shows the amounts disbursed from the IBRD and IDA separately for foreign procurement of goods, works, and services from selected member countries in fiscal 1996 and cumulatively through fiscal 1996.

Appendix 9 shows the proportion of foreign disbursements from the IBRD and IDA for specific categories of goods and services provided by selected member countries in fiscal 1996.

Appendix 10 provides a summary listing of the amounts paid to OECD and non-OECD country suppliers in each fiscal year from 1994 to 1996 under investment projects. Amounts disbursed are compared with respect to significant categories of goods procured from foreign suppliers. The extent to which OECD and non-OECD countries participated in supplying these major categories of goods in each of the past three fiscal years is also compared.

In all these tables and appendixes, IBRD figures exclude disbursements for loans to the IFC and "B" loans. IDA figures include Special Fund and Special Facility for sub-Saharan Africa credits. Disbursements for Project Preparation Facility advances are excluded for both the IBRD and IDA.

### Cofinancing and Trust-fund Programs

Cofinancing is an essential tool in mobilizing resources for development and in harmonizing Bank assistance with other institutions, both official and private. The volume of cofinancing anticipated in support of World Bank projects approved in fiscal year 1996 was $8.35 billion,[3] remaining within the range of $8 billion-$9 billion achieved during the past two years *(see Table 2-5)*. These funds helped finance 131

3. Cofinancing figures, which represent planned cofinancing, are compiled at the time of presentation of each IBRD and IDA operation to the Bank's executive board. The amounts of official cofinancing, in most cases, are firm commitments by that stage; export credits and private cofinancing, however, are generally only estimates, since such cofinancing is actually arranged as required for project implementation, and the amounts get firmed up within a year or two after board approval. The amounts of private cofinancing in Table 2-5 for any fiscal year do not necessarily reflect market placements.

# TABLE 2-5. WORLD BANK COFINANCING OPERATIONS, BY REGION, FISCAL YEARS 1995–96

*(amounts in millions of US dollars)*

| | Projects cofinanced | | Official[a] | | Export credit | | Total Private | | (of which IBRD guarantees) | | World Bank contribution | | Total project costs |
|---|---|---|---|---|---|---|---|---|---|---|---|---|---|
| Region and year | No. | Amount | No. | Amount | No. | Amount | No. | Amount | No. | Amount | IBRD | IDA | |
| **Africa** | | | | | | | | | | | | | |
| 1995 | 36 | 1,296 | 34 | 1,285 | — | — | 3 | 11 | — | — | 65 | 1,349 | 3,683 |
| 1996 | 34 | 1,155 | 33 | 1,146 | — | — | 2 | 9 | — | — | — | 1,618 | 4,828 |
| **East Asia and Pacific** | | | | | | | | | | | | | |
| 1995 | 16 | 1,765 | 14 | 987 | 2 | 348 | 5 | 340 | (1) | (64) | 1,336 | 334 | 6,186 |
| 1996 | 9 | 869 | 7 | 664 | — | — | 2 | 205 | (1) | (50) | 1,109 | 207 | 3,805 |
| **South Asia** | | | | | | | | | | | | | |
| 1995 | 9 | 1,108 | 9 | 527 | 1 | 50 | 1 | 531 | (1) | (240) | 609 | 374 | 3,344 |
| 1996 | 12 | 2,032 | 11 | 1,271 | 3 | 433 | 3 | 328 | (1) | (75) | 900 | 710 | 6,669 |
| **Europe and Central Asia** | | | | | | | | | | | | | |
| 1995 | 41 | 870 | 39 | 588 | 1 | 50 | 4 | 232 | — | — | 2,542 | 424 | 4,961 |
| 1996 | 41 | 1,342 | 41 | 1,340 | — | — | 1 | 2 | — | — | 1,544 | 153 | 4,020 |
| **Latin America and the Caribbean** | | | | | | | | | | | | | |
| 1995 | 27 | 3,053 | 26 | 3,032 | — | — | 2 | 21 | — | — | 2,773 | 242 | 7,542 |
| 1996 | 26 | 2,081 | 25 | 1,901 | — | — | 2 | 180 | — | — | 1,266 | 262 | 4,944 |
| **Middle East and North Africa** | | | | | | | | | | | | | |
| 1995 | 11 | 639 | 11 | 639 | — | — | — | — | — | — | 559 | 53 | 1,807 |
| 1996 | 9 | 871 | 9 | 871 | — | — | — | — | — | — | 364 | 196 | 1,912 |
| **Total** | | | | | | | | | | | | | |
| 1995 | 140 | 8,731 | 133 | 7,058 | 4 | 448 | 15 | 1,225 | (2) | (304) | 7,883 | 2,777 | 27,523 |
| 1996 | 131 | 8,350 | 126 | 7,194 | 3 | 433 | 10 | 724 | (2) | (125) | 5,183 | 3,146 | 26,179 |

— Zero.

NOTE: *The number of operations shown under different sources add up to a figure exceeding the total number of cofinanced projects because a number of projects were cofinanced from more than one source. Cofinancing data are reported by the fiscal year in which the project is presented to the Bank's executive board. Details may not add to totals because of rounding.*

a. *These figures include cofinancing with untied loans from the Export-Import Bank of Japan.*

Bank-assisted projects, or about half of the total number of projects approved during the year.

About 86 percent of cofinancing came from official sources, both bilateral (37 percent) and multilateral (49 percent). Japan remained the most important bilateral source in fiscal year 1996. Japan's Overseas Economic Cooperation Fund (OECF) and the Export-Import Bank of Japan (JEXIM) together cofinanced ten projects for a total of $1.1 billion. Other important bi-

lateral sources of cofinancing during the year were Germany ($394 million), France ($217 million), the United Kingdom ($159 million), and the United States ($96 million).

The Inter-American Development Bank (IDB), which provided $1.6 billion in cofinancing during the year, remained the Bank's largest multilateral cofinancier. The second largest multilateral source of cofinancing came from European Union (EU) institutions, including the European Investment Bank (EIB). Together these institutions accounted for $829 million in cofinancing. The Asian Development Bank ($703 million) and the European Bank for Reconstruction and Development ($181 million) also cofinanced a significant number of operations with the Bank during the year.

Fourteen percent of cofinancing was provided by export-credit agencies (ECAS) and the private sector. Private sector cofinancing amounted to $724 million in fiscal 1996, compared with $1.2 billion in 1995. Export credit cofinancing was $433 million during the year, about the same as last year.

Investment loans attracted the largest share of cofinancing, at 75 percent. The trend towards lower levels of cofinancing for adjustment lending and other fast-disbursing loans resumed during fiscal 1996, after temporarily rising in fiscal 1995 due to two large, fast-disbursing operations in Mexico and Argentina. On a sectoral basis, cofinancing in infrastructure (power, energy, telecommunications, transportation, water supply) once again attracted the most cofinancing, amounting to $3.8 billion, or 45 percent of the total. Cofinancing in the social sectors rose significantly, mainly due to large loans to Argentina, Brazil, and Egypt.

Regionally, the largest amount of cofinancing ($2.1 billion) continued to go to Latin American countries, reflecting the Bank's close collaboration with the Inter-American Development Bank. Cofinancing fell in East Asia, in part because of the stronger reliance of many East Asian countries on private sector financing, particularly for infrastructure. This was offset by a significant rise in cofinancing for South Asia, due to a few big infrastructure projects in India and Pakistan. In Eastern Europe and Central Asia, cofinancing grew in line with donor readiness to support the needs of the transition economies and reconstruction efforts in Bosnia. Cofinancing in Africa and the Middle East and North Africa remained at about the previous year's level.

The Special Program of Assistance for Sub-Saharan Africa (SPA) continued to constitute the largest single on-going donor coordination effort. The third phase of the SPA (SPA-3) was launched in October, 1993, to cover the 1994–1996 period. To date, seventeen donors have pledged $6.7 billion under SPA-3, and the number of eligible countries grew to thirty-one. Other large cofinancing efforts during the year included those with the Global Environmental Facility (GEF) and with special efforts for reconstruction in Bosnia and Herzegovina, as well as in the West Bank and Gaza.

*Cofinancing management.* In order to strengthen its capacity to generate resources and to better leverage funds for development from other sources, the Bank consolidated its resource mobilization and cofinancing functions into a single vice presidency for Resource Mobilization and Cofinancing (RMC). This change, effective March 15, 1996, was made to better enable the Bank to forge more effective partnerships with the donor community and the private sector.

RMC (and its predecessor Cofinancing and Financial Advisory Services) carried out a number of specific activities during fiscal year 1996 to further enhance the Bank's cofinancing partnerships. A new Cofinancing Framework Agreement was finalized with Australia, and an agreement on processing Fifth Dimension cofinancing was signed with Norway. A total of twenty cofinancing consultations were held with sixteen major partners. Bank/donor consultations help firm up cofinancing arrangements for specific projects in the Bank's lending program, deepen the Bank's policy dialogue with its partners, and focus on coordinating official flows with private sector investment in developing countries.

RMC took steps, as well, to improve the Bank's ongoing relations with ECAs and with the Berne Union, which comprises insurers of export credit and private foreign investment. Activities during fiscal year 1996 included: (a) a two-day meeting with ECAs in Washington, in which prospects for increasing cofinancing were discussed, (b) a meeting between the Berne Union's Cofinancing Committee and the Bank where participants gained a better understanding of cofinancing issues, and (c) consultations with major ECAs in order to build on the improving dialogue with the Berne Union.

During the year, RMC sought to improve the services and information it provides its clients.

As part of this effort, it kept donors informed of cofinancing prospects through its biannual Cofinancing Opportunities Publication. It also kept Bank task managers informed of donor programs and procedures through an updated version of the "Cofinancing Handbook." As part of its overall review of cofinancing activities, it issued a report, "Cofinancing With the World Bank—Twenty-Five Years of Cooperation."

*Trust funds.* Despite constraints on national aid budgets, donors continued to increase their funding in support of technical assistance trust-fund programs. During the year, the two main programs, the Policy and Human Resources Development (PHRD) Fund—financed by Japan—and the Consultant Trust Fund (CTF) program—financed by twenty-six donors—both increased their activities.

The PHRD Fund extends untied grants to meet the technical assistance needs of developing countries. During the past fiscal year, the PHRD Fund provided 270 grants for $162 million to support project-preparation activities of Bank-financed operations (270 grants for $177 million were extended in fiscal 1995). Fifty-nine percent of projects approved during the year were prepared with grant assistance from the PHRD Fund. The balance of the PHRD Fund is allocated to financing the training and development activities of the Economic Development Institute; the funding of Japanese experts through the Japan Consultant Trust Fund; and other special programs.

During the year, the Japanese government also provided, through the PHRD, financial support to assist regions emerging from civil strife. This program began with $9 million in cofinancing funds allocated for the Emergency Recovery Project to assist Bosnia and Herzegovina.

The Consultant Trust Fund (CTF) Program provides consultancy services to support the Bank's operational and technical assistance work. The CTF program financed a total of $78 million in new allocations in fiscal year 1996, a 23 percent increase over the previous year. During the year, two new CTFs were established (by Austria and Canada) to support activities in the environmental sector, bringing the total number of CTFs to forty-nine, funded by twenty-six donors. The growth in the program reflects the continuing need for consultancy services, particularly in the environmental sector and in the transitional economies of Europe and Central Asia. It also reflects the continuing support for the program by donors who, despite constraints on aid budgets, made special efforts to increase their contributions to support the Bank's programs of assistance.

During the year, the Bank sought to improve its management and monitoring of trust funds. Towards this end, a first "Annual Report" on CTF activities was issued, internal controls on the use of funds were strengthened, and CTF resource information was placed "on-line" for easy access by Bank staff.

In order to improve flexibility and effectiveness in the use of trust funds, the Bank reviewed with donors ways to reduce the degree to which CTF funds are restricted in terms of procurement. As a result, a number of donors (ten to date) have agreed to untie CTFs by at least 25 percent on the basis of reciprocity.

*Trust-fund management.* In response to the rapid growth in the use of trust funds, the Bank has introduced a series of initiatives to strengthen the institutional procedures for administering externally funded trust funds. The Bank's principal policy objectives are to ensure that trust funds are: (a) used in accordance with institutional priorities; (b) consistent with country-assistance strategies; and (c) fully effective from a development perspective, particularly in the case of country-specific technical assistance in which recipient ownership of the product can be a critical factor. A report on the status of trust-fund programs was submitted to the executive board in April 1996.

In order to strengthen the coherence of these efforts, the newly created vice presidency for Resource Mobilization and Cofinancing was designated as the focal point in the Bank to establish trust-fund policies and strategies, to be the institutional link with donors and the main channel for trust-fund resource mobilization, and to improve trust-fund processing, monitoring, and accountability.

The Debt-reduction Facility for IDA-only Countries provides grant funds to heavily indebted IDA-eligible countries, which use these funds to buy back their commercial debt at a deep discount. Four operations (Albania, Ethiopia, Nicaragua, and Mauritania) were completed in fiscal year 1996 under facility auspices. They utilized $77 million in IBRD resources from the facility and $135 million in cofinancing to extinguish a total of $1.7 billion in eligible principal debt.

### Technical Assistance

Technical assistance (TA) is an important ingredient in the Bank's menu of operational activities. It provides the resources and expertise countries need to build up institutions critical for development success—institutions that facilitate a flourishing private sector, invest in people, and protect natural resources and the environment.

In calendar 1995 World Bank funding for technical assistance totaled $1.9 billion. Of this amount, $1.3 billion was for the technical assistance components of investment or economic reform projects and $610 million was for twenty-four freestanding technical assistance loans.

While funding for technical assistance fluctuates from year to year, the overall share of Bank lending geared to TA has remained stable at about 10 percent.

Argentina was the largest single user of the Bank's technical assistance funding ($250 million), followed by China ($227 million), India ($218 million), and Indonesia ($159 million).

The Bank's Project Preparation Facility (PPF), as its name suggests, provides funds for countries that lack the resources to prepare projects for external funding. Use of the PPF does not signal a funding commitment to the project by the IBRD or IDA. In calendar 1995, the Bank made 122 PPF advances totaling $96.2 million. Sixty-six of these (54 percent) were to countries in the Africa region, which traditionally has been the largest user of the facility.

The Bank approved 105 Institutional Development Fund grants to sixty-one countries totaling $24.2 million. These covered a wide range of activities, including a grant of $446,800 to Eritrea to help build the government's capacity for budgeting, monitoring, and coordinating projects; a grant of $489,000 to Tanzania to help establish a Revenue Authority; and a grant of $198,000 to Vietnam to support water management.

*Measuring technical assistance effectiveness.* For many years, the Bank has used performance indicators to measure the performance of investment operations—mostly the physical aspects of a project rather than its TA components. Recognizing that an effective means of measuring capacity building is also essential in allocating scarce resources and identifying best practice, the Bank expanded its system of performance indicators this past year so that the performance of technical assistance operations can also be measured. These indicators measure performance by results and outputs (rather than by inputs) and distinguish between quantitative and qualitative yardsticks.

*The Bank and the United Nations Development Programme (UNDP).* The Bank maintained a frequent policy dialogue with the UNDP at the highest levels of management throughout the year. A letter to field staff, jointly signed by the Bank's president and the UNDP's administrator, reinforced the institutions' commitments to enhance their collaboration, and agreement was reached on coordination mechanisms for consultative group and roundtable activities.

### Inspection Panel

An independent inspection panel was established by the executive directors in September 1993 to help ensure that the Bank's operations adhere to the institution's operational policies and procedures regarding the design, preparation, or implementation of a project. Any group of individuals who may be directly and adversely affected by a Bank-supported project or projects can ask the panel to investigate complaints that the Bank has failed to abide by its policies and procedures. The executive directors decide, on the recommendation of the panel, whether an inspection will take place.

The panel has received numerous queries concerning potential requests for inspection. To date, however, it has received only five formal requests for inspection, three of which were found to be admissible. Two of those requests were acted upon in fiscal 1996.

One relates to the execution of the Rondonia Natural Resources Management Project (Brazil), where the requesters claimed that the Bank's lack of enforcement of several covenants of the project's legal documents caused material adverse effects on, among other things, their

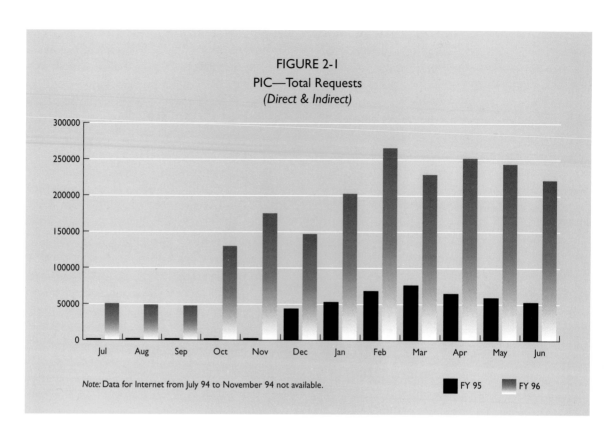

FIGURE 2-1
PIC—Total Requests
(Direct & Indirect)

Note: Data for Internet from July 94 to November 94 not available.

■ FY 95   ■ FY 96

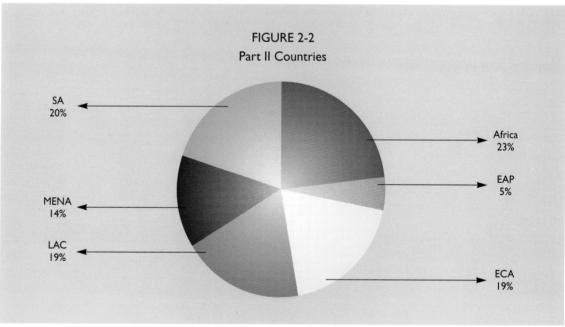

FIGURE 2-2
Part II Countries

SA
20%

Africa
23%

EAP
5%

MENA
14%

LAC
19%

ECA
19%

incomes and health. The panel recommended an investigation, but the executive board requested more information on which to base the decision of whether an investigation should be carried out.

The panel conducted an "Additional Review" of the request for inspection and of the information provided by Bank management, and in December 1995, it submitted to the executive board a report on the Additional Review. Later in the month, Bank management submitted a status report on project implementation to the board, which included a plan of action dealing with the principal issues raised by the panel. The executive directors considered the request for inspection, and, in light of the action plan presented by management and the follow-up now under way, concluded that it would not be advisable to proceed with the investigation as recommended by the panel. However, in view of the complexity of the project and the Bank's desire to help ensure its success, the executive directors agreed to review a progress report by management and to invite the panel to assist in the review.

The second involved a request related to the provision of IDA financing for an emergency power project in Tanzania. The requesters claimed that there was private sector financing (to be provided by the firm they owned or worked for) available for the project on reasonable terms. The board accepted the panel's recommendation that no inspection take place, as the panel had found that IDA management had followed its policies in this regard. The panel also declared a related complaint on alleged possible adverse environmental effects of the proposed emergency project not eligible.

The resolution that established the panel requires a review of its functions by the Bank's executive board after two years of operations. It is expected that the review process will have been completed early in fiscal 1997.

## Public Information Center

Since the Bank's disclosure-of-information policy was endorsed by the executive directors in August 1993, the Public Information Center (PIC) has worked to make available a wider range of operational information—formerly available only to official users—to a wider audience, in user-friendly ways. The PIC provides information related to Bank-assisted projets, including project-preparation documents, environmental studies, and evaluations. The PIC's aim is to support accountability and transparency of the Bank's operations.

The PIC continued to expand its activites in fiscal 1996. Several new initiatives were taken

to inform the public about the center's services. A brochure on PIC services was distributed at the annual meetings. Printed copies, as well as an electronic version on the Internet, are available in English, French, and Spanish. The PIC also made its Internet program more user-friendly and added abstracts of many documents that fall under the Bank's disclosure policy.

The PIC's usage continues to grow *(see Figure 2-1)*. Requests for information received at the PIC totaled more than 2 million, a fivefold increase over fiscal 1995; users of the Internet program numbered almost 2 million. In fiscal 1996, the highest demand for information from the PIC came from the business community, followed by public agencies and the academic community. *Figure 2-2* depicts the breakdown of requests by developing country region.

The PIC manager visited Bank field offices in Côte d'Ivoire, Kenya, Madagascar, and Senegal to review progress in implementing the Bank's disclosure policy, orient field staff on the policy, and help establish a PIC section in their libraries. New PICs were opened in Colombia, Ecuador, and Tunisia, and several others are in the advanced planning stage. Many Bank field offices that do not have PICs are making great efforts to make information available to the public.

## Human Capital Development (HCD)

When children in a kindergarten in India, Kazakstan, or Kenya enjoy a nutritious meal, play with educational toys, or get a health checkup through one of the World Bank-funded programs for early child development, they do not know that this is the last link in a long chain of planning, coordinating, and implementing one of the strategies for investing in human capital. Countries around the world are investing in people and building human capital with the help of the World Bank and other international aid agencies.

Children enrolled in early child development programs are just some of the beneficiaries of these efforts. They will get a better chance to grow up healthy, well educated, and prepared to become productive and successful members of their society. Thus they help the World Bank accomplish its basic mission—reducing poverty and creating better lives for people in the developing countries.

One of the important lessons from decades of experience in development is that there is no more direct road to improving living standards in developing countries than investing in the well-being of people. Healthy, well-educated people will not only ensure better lives for themselves and their families but also contribute to the wealth and progress of their societies.

That is what investing in people is about, and why "human capital" are the key words in today's development economics.

Investing in people is at the center of the Bank's work in the 1990s. It is one of the fastest growth areas of Bank activities. Lending for human capital development has increased by more than fivefold since the early 1980s. Loans totaling $35 billion have been extended to more than 100 countries for education, health, population, and nutrition programs since the first loan in support of human capital investments was approved in 1962. From 5 percent annually in the early 1980s, lending for human capital development increased to 18 percent of total Bank lending in the five-year period fiscal 1992–96. Average yearly lending amounts during this period totaled more than $4 billion.

The World Bank is now the world's single largest provider of external financing for social services or human capital development. In recent years social sector spending has included new activities such as pensions, unemployment compensation, safety nets, and gender equity. The Human Capital Development (HCD) vice presidency is the focal point for the Bank's activities in this field.

People in developing countries today are, on average, better off than they were fifteen years ago: Household

incomes in developing countries have more than doubled, and, in some countries, they have grown by a factor of five or even ten. Average life expectancy in developing countries has risen from about forty years to sixty-three years in the past four decades. Infant mortality rates have been cut by two thirds. Child immunization, almost nonexistent in the 1950s, now covers 80 percent of all children. Smallpox has been eradicated. A generation ago only 40 percent of children entered primary school in the poorer countries—today, that many enter high schools, and many developing countries have achieved close to universal primary education. But there is no room for complacency. Disease, malnourishment, and hunger are still a constant curse for many millions of poor people faced with suffering and tragedy each day. Despite progress, the lot of the most deprived and vulnerable remains a serious development challenge.

The World Bank, therefore, continues to increase its support for investments in human capital. Special attention has been paid to the provision of primary health and education services, which have the greatest impact on economic growth and poverty reduction. In fiscal 1996, lending in support of primary health and education services amounted to $1,595 million and $686 million, respectively. The essence of the Bank's approach combines two complementary tracks: investing in people and sound economic policies.

Investments in people will not be effective unless governments establish an economic framework that ensures macroeconomic stability, markets that are open for trade and investments, the right structure of incentives, proper social sector policies, and efficiently functioning capital and labor markets. It is not a question of choosing between investing in people and sound economic policies—it must be both. They go hand in hand and reinforce each other to replace the vicious circle of poverty with the virtuous circle of growth and progress. This approach is at the core of the work and research performed by HCD's two departments, Poverty and Social Policy (PSP) and Human Development (HDD).

The expertise and advice that the Bank provides to donors and developing countries is as important as the dollar amounts that it lends for HCD projects. Important decisions must be made on education strategies, labor-market policies, policies to advance gender equity or to reduce poverty, health-care programs, HIV/AIDS prevention, or how to target food subsidies for the poor. HCD focuses much of its effort on providing such advice and helping developing countries design and implement proper social sector policies. To disseminate the Bank's experiences and the knowledge of best practices, HCD has released a number of reports and studies dealing with different aspects of human capital development and poverty reduction.

## Poverty-reduction Activities

A thorough analysis of the Bank's work in reducing poverty is presented in *Poverty Reduction and the World Bank: Progress and Challenges in the 1990s*—a comprehensive report on global poverty trends and the Bank's efforts and strategy to alleviate the suffering of the poor.[1] The report takes a more wide-ranging approach than previous reports in its analysis of methods, results, and future strategies based on the lessons learned.

The poverty-reduction strategy that the Bank is implementing today, while still based on broad-based growth, human capital development, and safety nets, is much more targeted to the needs of each region and, within regions, to specific country needs.

The report shows that, although inroads have been made in reducing poverty between the late 1980s and the early 1990s, the gains have been small. While the incidence of poverty is estimated to have fallen from 30.1 percent in 1987 to 29.4 percent in 1993, the *number* of poor has increased from 1.23 billion to 1.31 billion. Efforts to reduce poverty have been more successful in some regions than in others, and success rates are unevenly distributed.

The incidence of poverty has declined in East Asia, the Middle East, Northern Africa, and in South Asia. It has remained more or less stable in Latin America and sub-Saharan Africa, and it has increased in East Europe and Central Asia. About 90 percent of the poor live in South Asia, sub-Saharan Africa, Indochina, Mongolia, Central America, Brazil, and China.

The Bank recognizes the importance of understanding, on a country-by-country basis, the many dimensions of poverty: its causes, whether it is increasing or decreasing, what works best to reduce it. The Bank has made tremendous gains in measuring and monitoring poverty through poverty assessments, so that poverty analysis can be built into planning, policy dialogue, and decisions about lending operations.[2] Country-assistance strategies (CASs) are the primary tool for incorporating poverty analysis into countries' overall development strategies. Developed in consultation with borrowing governments and discussed by the executive board, CASs describe the unique circumstances each country faces. Because the problem of poverty is so overwhelming in many countries, its reduction is almost invariably the key element of the Bank's CASs, and the CAS enables the most

---

1. World Bank. 1996. *Poverty Reduction and the World Bank: Progress and Challenges in the 1990s.* Washington, D.C.
2. Through June 30, 1996, a total of eighty-four poverty assessments—they provide the basis for a collaborative approach to poverty reduction by country officials and the Bank—had been completed.

## TABLE 3-1. PROGRAM OF TARGETED INTERVENTIONS, 1994–96

*(millions of us dollars; fiscal years)*

|  | 1994 | 1995 | 1996 |
|---|---|---|---|
| Total World Bank PTI lending | 4,440.5 | 5,436.7 | 5,408.1 |
| As share of investment lending (%) | 25 | 32 | 32 |
| As share of all Bank lending (%) | 21 | 24 | 25 |
| Total number of projects in the PTI | 63 | 75 | 79 |
| Total number of investment projects | 197 | 208 | 224 |
|  |  |  |  |
| IDA PTI lending | 1,853 | 2,423.2 | 3,246 |
| As share of IDA investment lending (%) | 43 | 54 | 63 |
| As share of all IDA lending (%) | 28 | 43 | 47 |
| Number of IDA PTI projects | 35 | 48 | 51 |

NOTE: *Investment lending is defined as all lending except for adjustment, debt and debt-service reduction operations, and emergency-reconstruction operations.*

appropriate package of instruments for supporting the government's poverty-reduction efforts to be defined.

The Bank has supported projects in a number of sectors that, among other objectives, aim to reduce poverty. During fiscal 1992–96, the Bank provided $16 billion to support agricultural productivity, about $14 billion to improve transportation, slightly under $10 billion for education, more than $7 billion for population, health, and nutrition programs, over $6 billion for urban development, and about $5 billion to improve water supply and sewerage systems.

During fiscal 1996, $5.4 billion, or about 32 percent of World Bank investment lending, was channeled directly for poverty-targeted projects, the same percentage as in fiscal 1995 *(see Table 3-1)*. For IDA countries, lending for projects in the Program of Targeted Interventions (PTI) amounted to 63 percent, up from 54 percent of investment lending in the previous year. During fiscal 1996, seventeen of the twenty-nine adjustment operations that were approved contained specific poverty-reduction measures.[3]

Economic growth remains the cornerstone of the Bank's strategy for reducing poverty, but the study shows that growth by itself does not automatically translate into the fastest possible rate of poverty reduction. Many constraints prevent the poor from benefiting from the opportunities presented by growth. The Bank aims to take steps to remove these constraints with programs that (a) improve the access of the poor to essential factors of production through affordable credits; (b) increase the productivity of and returns to the poor's factors of production in agriculture or the informal sector; (c) help markets work to the benefit of the poor by urging governments to lift unnecessary or burdensome regulations; and (d) support efforts to overcome discrimination of the poor and increase their access to the opportunities that arise from economic growth.

Due to the importance the Bank attaches to reducing poverty in its operations, it will prepare annual poverty updates, with a more detailed and wide-ranging report monitoring poverty trends every five years. The *World Development Report* will focus on poverty issues every ten years.

3. A description of each project in the PTI that was approved in fiscal 1996 can be found in the "project summaries" section of this *Annual Report*. The PTI projects are marked by an (§). A description of each poverty-focused adjustment operation is also included; they are marked by a (†).

## Gender Issues Mainstreamed

The World Bank took active part in the preparation of the United Nations Conference on Women held in Beijing in September 1995. Two publications, *Toward Gender Equality: The Role of Public Policy* and *Advancing Gender Equality: From Concept to Action*, highlighted the Bank's strategy[4]—first introduced in the executive board–approved policy paper, *Enhancing Women's Participation in Economic Development*[5]—for empowering women and described how gender issues are incorporated in Bank projects. Focusing on the economic arguments for gender equality, the reports presented solid evidence that investing in women is good economics, gender inequality hampers growth, and investing in women enhances the quality of growth.

The Bank's commitment to promoting gender equality was underlined by the participation at the conference of James Wolfensohn, who had assumed his position as World Bank president only a few months earlier. In his speech and meetings with nongovernmental organizations (NGOs) and other participants, he left no doubt about the Bank's commitment.

Mr. Wolfensohn's speech focused on the role education plays in eliminating gender inequalities, particularly when special attention is given to girls' education. He defined a new goal—achievement of universal primary education by 2010 and attendance by 60 percent of children in secondary school. For girls, attainment of the first goal would mean an additional 90 million completing primary school; realizing the second objective would imply that an additional 90 million would go on to secondary school. The estimated extra cost would amount to $30 billion. Realizing that more resources are needed to make girls' enrollment equal to that of boys, Mr. Wolfensohn committed the Bank to allocate $900 million yearly for girls' education.

Responding to a petition from thousands of women at the Beijing conference, the Bank issued a progress report on its gender activities, "Implementing the World Bank's Gender Policies." It reviews the evolution and the current status of Bank operations and describes the initiatives that have been undertaken in support of the Beijing agenda.

The Bank focuses on three strategic areas in its operations in mainstreaming gender issues:
- building up women's economic capacity by investing in their human capital;
- helping improve economic conditions and opportunities for women; and
- improving institutional capacity to advance women's welfare and status.

Each region in the Bank is formulating a Gender Action Plan, which, when finalized, will make up the basis for a coherent, Bankwide gender strategic framework.

An internal gender committee has been formed, which will report to the Bank's president on a regular basis on progress in integrating gender issues into operations, and an external Gender Consultative Group was established to strengthen the Bank's partnership with NGOs and women's organizations. It provides a forum for discussion of gender issues, and, at the same time, is a mechanism for promoting NGO-Bank cooperation and following the Bank's progress in implementing the Beijing agenda. The formation of the consultative group is consistent with the Bank's efforts to enhance participation and partnership as an essential part of its development strategy.

## Participation in World Bank Activities

Fiscal 1996 saw the publication of the *World Bank Participation Sourcebook*, a how-to guide written by more than 200 Bank task managers to highlight the importance of the participatory approach in economic and social development. The importance of the issue is also being recog-

4. World Bank. 1995. *Advancing Gender Equality: From Concept to Action.* Washington, D.C.; World Bank. 1995. *Toward Gender Equality: The Role of Public Policy.* Development in Practice Series. Washington, D.C.

5. World Bank. 1994. *Enhancing Women's Participation in Economic Development.* A World Bank Policy Paper. Washington, D.C.

nized in the Bank's Change Management Agenda, which encourages greater awareness of client-oriented and participatory approaches to create a greater sense of ownership, achieve better results on the ground, and enhance sustainability of Bank-supported operations.

The Bank chairs the Inter-Agency Group on Participation. At the group's second meeting in March 1996, strategies for mainstreaming participation, monitoring and evaluation, and strengthening in-country capacity to support participatory approaches to development were discussed. The Bank is working on several projects to help design appropriate monitoring and evaluation instruments to better assess the efforts and impacts of the participatory processes. To highlight and help focus on these issues, the Bank has set up a discussion network, called "Participation Exchange," on the World Wide Web.

The Bank is also taking steps to broaden public consultation in the shaping of CASs by increasing the use of participatory poverty assessments in which the poor and their organizations are involved in the analytical process. The use of qualitative information on the needs and perceptions of the poor has increased greatly in Bank operations. Of the twenty-two poverty assessments (PAs) completed in fiscal 1996, twelve were participatory PAs.

## NGO Involvement Increases

As in recent years, a considerable proportion of projects approved in fiscal 1996 involved NGOs.[6] It is clear that the depth of NGO involvement is increasing, with NGOs being a central feature in both the design and implementation of a growing number of projects. For example, NGOs were actively engaged in the planning of the Ghazi-Barotha dam in Pakistan; implementation of the planned Pilot Participation Project (to tackle hunger) in Mali is to be the sole responsibility of NGOs; and a trust fund to finance NGO activities has been designed and launched for the West Bank and Gaza. NGO involvement in economic and sector work also continues to expand.

The principal factor promoting enhanced Bank-NGO interactions during the past year was the direct interest of the Bank's president. He meets NGOs in most countries he visits and has had structured meetings with civil society leadership on poverty, the environment, adjustment, gender, and sustainable agriculture. Some of these have led to important follow-up, such as the creation of the previously mentioned Gender Consultative Group and the planning of a joint Bank-NGO initiative to study the impact of adjustment in a number of countries. At the time of the annual meetings, he joined leaders of major NGO networks in a media event to highlight threats to the funding of development assistance, including that to IDA. Strong emphasis has been placed on field-level interactions (see Box 3-1) and the notion of partnership with civil society.

In addition to these issues, policy dialogue with NGOs has centered on multilateral debt, private sector development, and the disclosure and dissemination of Bank information. A Bank-NGO working group on the last-named has helped improve the implementation of the Bank's disclosure policy and has encouraged innovations at the field level. The NGO–World Bank Committee continues to be the principal forum for policy dialogue; annual meetings are now supplemented by regional meetings, held during the past year in Accra, Managua, and Manila. Major international gatherings, such as the Women's Conference in Beijing and the Habitat II Conference in Istanbul (the City Summit), are also important fora for policy interactions.

The Bank seeks opportunities to draw governments' attention to the importance of NGOs and civil society. It has launched studies of state-NGO relations in Bangladesh and Indonesia, it has organized government/civil society/donor "trialogues" in Guinea-Bissau, Lesotho, and Vietnam, and is preparing a handbook, "Global Standards and Best Practices for Laws Governing NGOs."

6. Projects involving NGOs that were approved in fiscal 1996 are marked by a ◊ in the "project summaries" section that begins on page 127.

## Labor-market Issues

Labor-market issues are increasingly attracting the Bank's attention, both in its lending operations and its analytical work. The Bank is expanding its links with international partners, such as the International Labor Organization and the International Confederation of Free Trade Unions, to undertake joint studies and organize conferences. And a series of seminars in the Bank on labor markets focused on issues covered in *World Development Report 1995: Workers in an Integrating World.*[7]

HCD's Social Insurance group is undertaking analysis of the need for pension-system reform, especially in middle-income countries that face an increasingly aging population. Some countries (in Eastern and Central Europe, the former Soviet Union, and Uruguay, for example) are facing short-term imbalances with long-term unfunded liabilities often in excess of their gross domestic product (GDP). The challenge for the Social Insurance group is to identify the options for reducing unfunded liabilities and assist countries to move ahead toward a system that distorts labor markets less. The 1994 Policy Research Report, *Averting the Old Age Crisis:*

*Policies to Protect the Old and Promote Growth*, made the case that countries need a "multipillar" pension system, where part of the pension is publicly and part privately funded, to minimize poverty in old age, boost future growth through greater savings and work, and to discourage evasion.[8] There has been a wave of pension-system reforms since then, particularly in Latin America but also in transition economies with relatively old populations, where pension expenditures absorb a large share of the budget. The Bank is assisting these countries to undertake reforms that are fiscally sustainable, protect the poorest and most vulnerable, create incentives for savings and work, and promote growth.

## Education Strategies and Child Interventions

Education is a particularly important investment because it affects the health and life expectancy of people and equips them with the

7. World Bank. 1995. *World Development Report 1995: Workers in an Integrating World.* New York: Oxford University Press.

8. World Bank. 1994. *Averting the Old Age Crisis: Policies to Protect the Old and Promote Growth.* World Bank Policy Research Report. New York: Oxford University Press.

knowledge and the means to live healthier lives. Education is a critical factor for a country's sustained economic growth, and no country in the Information Age can compete in world markets if it neglects education.

The World Bank's education strategy supports enhancing the productive use of labor, which is the poor's main asset. The book, *Priorities and Strategies for Education: A Review*, emphasizes the need for quality education systems as one of the keys to progress and economic growth.[9] Public spending on education remains inefficient and inequitable in many cases. In Africa, for example, spending per student in higher education is about forty-four times that of expenditures per student in primary education. Yet, one half of Africa's primary school–age children are not enrolled in school.

Primary education deserves high priority for four reasons. It is the foundation on which higher education must build; the returns, as measured by individual wage gains, tend to be largest for primary education; the poor, in particular, benefit from public spending on primary education; and primary education brings broad additional benefits such as lower mortality and fertility, and better health, nutrition, and literacy.

But waiting until children go to school may often be too late because the earliest stages of a child's life can be decisive for success later. A child's earliest years are of critical importance for the individual, the family, and society. Millions of children suffer from malnourishment, lack of appropriate health care, and stimulation through interaction with adults.

Children deprived in this way are more likely to fail in school, drop out, be functionally illiterate, and be only marginally employable. Consequently, they affect labor productivity and the economic prosperity of their country. The earlier intervention programs are implemented the better, and experience shows that children under two years of age should be priority targets.

Building on this knowledge, HCD has taken the lead with its children's initiative to create more understanding and support for early child development programs as a key to breaking the intergenerational cycle of poverty. The publica-tion, *Early Child Development: Investing in the Future*, presents the theory in an overview of the many programs that target children from birth to age eight.[10] It also examines Bank-supported "early child" projects around the world and recommends nutrition, health, and education interventions that have proved to be successful and cost-effective.

To highlight the importance of early child interventions HCD organized a conference in cooperation with the Carter Center in Atlanta and the Task Force for Child Survival and Development, an affiliate of the Carter Center. Some of the themes and issues that were analyzed at the conference, such as the integration of nutrition, health, and psychosocial programs, active learning and play, and the importance of parents' involvement, will help HCD devise new projects and map new directions for the Bank's work in supporting early child development programs.

**Challenges of Population Growth**

Population growth is a major concern confronting the developing world. In 2020, world population will total 7.9 billion (2.2 billion more than today). Although some regions have demonstrated that they can still register impressive per capita GDP growth despite rapid population growth, others face a bleak future. This implies that with expected population growth the number of poor will continue to grow. Without a substantial increase in economic growth or a marked drop in fertility rates, more than three times as many people will live in poverty by the year 2020.

In publications such as *Population in Asia* and *Key Indicators for Family Planning Projects*, HCD has analyzed the challenges posed by population growth and presented its recommendations for mitigating them.[11] Improved economic

9. World Bank. 1995. *Priorities and Strategies for Education: A Review*. Development in Practice Series. Washington, D.C.

10. Young, Mary Eming. 1995. *Early Child Development: Investing in the Future*. Directions in Development Series. Washington, D.C.: World Bank.

11. Sanderson, Warren C., and Jee-Peng Tan. 1995. *Population in Asia*. A World Bank Regional and Sectoral Study. Washington, D.C.; Bulatao, Rodolfo A. 1995. Key *Indicators for Family Planning Projects*. World Bank Technical Paper No. 297. Washington, D.C.

growth through human capital investments is one key tool to curb population growth. Strong policies are needed to put in place programs that can provide the necessary social services and, at the same time, ensure that people have the capability to use those services appropriately. Social capacity is a central parameter. The challenge for governments is not just to ensure, for example, that contraceptive services are delivered but also to understand that expanding social capacity (for example, by educating girls) can be even more important.

**Meeting the Challenges of the Future**

In an effort to increase the professional excellence of its staff, HCD launched a new training program during fiscal 1996. Professional Development Week brought together staff and counterparts from around the world for a week of intensive and stimulating training.

Through seminars and workshops, the training week gave participants exposure to the most recent research, best practices, and cutting-edge programs in various disciplines. Apart from knowledge sharing, the training week also provided participants with the opportunity to explore partnership possibilities with other development agencies and discuss and define new leadership challenges. Over the next three years, the training program aims to give all HCD staff the opportunity to acquire the knowledge and skills to help them do their work more effectively.

**Environmentally Sustainable Development (ESD)**

As the Bank has helped countries understand the economic, environmental, and social consequences of ignoring depletion and degradation of natural resources, demand for its help to mitigate these effects has grown.

A polluted river or stream is not only an eyesore, it poisons drinking and irrigation water, promotes waterborne diseases, kills off fish that are a valuable source of protein for local people, and adversely affects tourism. Loss of forests, likewise, has many repercussions—biological diversity is lost forever, indigenous people lose their homes, and the atmosphere loses a valuable source of oxygen. But these are the most obvious environmental problems developing countries face. New environmental challenges, including those arising from urban growth, increasing motorization, and from a recent lack of attention to rural development, are emerging as priority concerns for the Bank and its borrowers. In addition, the continuing need to extend basic services in water, sanitation, and transport to both urban and rural populations must be addressed in environmentally sustainable ways.

The Environmentally Sustainable Development (ESD) vice presidency, created in 1993, is the focal point of the Bank's environmental expertise where a critical mass of environmental professionals works to link environmental objectives to the agricultural and infrastructure sectors. These specialists undertake an active program of policy work, provide technical support to regional staff, and help establish partnerships with external institutions so that the Bank's technical understanding of environmental issues is strengthened and its ability to develop operational solutions to on-the-ground problems is enhanced.

The primary challenge facing the Bank today is to improve the quality of the development impact of its assistance. This effort includes ensuring that new operations are responsive to beneficiaries and are designed to be sustainable and that measures are identified and undertaken to strengthen the effectiveness of ongoing operations. Work is under way to ensure that the Bank's environmental assistance is in-line with borrower priorities. Environmental concerns are included in country-strategy formulation, and state-of-the-art expertise is applied to sectoral and project problems which the Bank is being asked to address. The ESD portfolio, which ac-counts for about half of total lending, is being evaluated so that lessons learned can be built into projects in the pipeline.

## Strategic Approaches to Meet the Challenge

*Environmental management.* An important part of the ESD portfolio is the Bank's targeted lending for the environment. The primary focus of the Bank's environmental work is to reduce the potential harm from Bank-assisted projects and to ensure successful implementation of the young and rapidly growing portfolio of environmental projects. A key challenge is finding ways to effectively and appropriately integrate global and local environmental dimensions in the Bank's traditional lending sectors.

As the Bank's lending portfolio has grown and matured, the Bank has added new dimensions of environmentally and socially sustainable development to its activities. It has strengthened its capacity to reduce adverse environmental and social impacts of projects. Operational policies covering environmental and social issues have been updated and refined, and there has been a significant increase in the numbers of Bank staff working on these issues. The Bank now has 288 higher-level environment staff, of whom two thirds have been recruited since 1992. Similarly, of the ninety-nine staff specializing in the social sciences, more than 60 percent have been recruited within the past three years.

*Social policy.* Social concerns are becoming more prominent in the Bank's operations, and to reduce the piecemeal approach to them social assessments are being prepared, incorporating participatory processes. A preliminary review of forty-two social assessments found that they are being used as a tool for social analysis and as a mechanism to identify stakeholders and put participatory processes in place in Bank operations. In addition, they are helping the Bank and its partners reach the poor and build local capacity.

*Rural development and sustainable agriculture.* Doubling food supplies over the next thirty years will require greatly accelerated efforts to develop and support the adoption of more intensive agricultural production systems.

Involving poor farmers and rural communities in rapid and sustainable technological change is an important challenge to which the Bank must respond. But this challenge can be met only if policies, institutional frameworks, and public expenditures adjust to reflect better the value of natural resources, more thoroughly involve local people in development planning and implementation, more effectively target research and extension investments, and more equitably share access to land and natural resources.

During the past year, the Bank's activities have entailed analysis and synthesis of best practices on (a) decentralization of the financing and implementation of Bank-supported rural development activities; (b) tailoring public and private investments that will both increase output in a sustainable manner and contribute to widely shared growth in rural incomes; and (c) more effective targeting of poverty-reduction efforts.

The agricultural action plan, "From Vision to Action in the Rural Sector," produced during fiscal 1996, will guide the Bank's future activities in support of rural, agricultural, and natural resource operations. It proposed that the Bank (a) incorporate key elements of the rural strategy into CASS, (b) improve portfolio implementation and performance so as to increase the ratio of projects receiving a "satisfactory" rating, (c) increase the international community's commitment to improve rural development and reduce rural poverty, and (d) rebuild and enhance the Bank's capacity to support agriculture and rural development. Bank staff and managers identified reasons for reduced support for the rural sector in recent years and identified the policy, staffing, and budgetary changes needed to revitalize that support. The action plan was presented to the Bank's president in March 1996, and modalities to implement its recommendations are being devised. Promoting development programs to benefit small farmers will be the central focus of Bank efforts to reduce rural poverty. These programs will include, in particular, measures to improve the access of poor people to financial services and to decentralize decisionmaking in planning rural investments.

*Delivery of transport, water, sanitation, and urban sector services.* Rapid urban growth has accompanied economic development in all regions of the world. However, the pace of the change in low-income countries from societies that have been predominantly rural to those that are mostly urban presents enormous challenges in urban management and finance, environmental regulation, and the provision of basic services, especially to the poor.

Similarly, it has become evident in recent years that more effective management of water is critical to all aspects of the Bank's development work—the reduction of poverty, economic growth, and environmentally sustainable development.

To this end, effective delivery of transport, water, sanitation, and urban sector services to the poor and institutional and policy reform were important elements of the ESD work program in fiscal 1996. This included work on sustainable fiscal policies and targeting mechanisms, as well as effective institutional arrangements for the delivery of basic infrastructure services to low-income communities in rural and peri-urban areas. The Bank has been closely involved in conceptual work and operational support to help client countries improve infrastructure services, management, and finance through sector reform (including commercialization and restructuring) and by redefining the role of public and private participants in each subsector.

## Mainstreaming the Global Environment

As parties to global environment conventions, the Bank's country clients have committed themselves to internalize global environmental concerns into their ongoing economic development activities. The Bank assists them to meet the obligation in three ways: first, by identifying and helping mitigate any negative global impacts of its own development assistance; second, by factoring global environment implications into its sector work; and third, by mobilizing grants from the Global Environment Facility (GEF) and the Multilateral Fund of the Montreal Protocol (MFMP) to meet the incremental costs of actions to further global environmental objectives.

The Bank shares responsibility for implementing GEF activities with the United Nations Environment Programme (UNEP) and the United Nations Development Programme (UNDP). The Bank's executive board approved $118 million of grant financing for thirteen GEF projects during the past year, bringing the total GEF portfolio to nearly $500 million for fifty-six projects covering four focal areas: biodiversity, climate change, ozone-depleting substances phaseout, and international waters. The MP Multilateral Fund portfolio also grew and now totals $188.1 million for 241 projects. The MP is charged with reducing consumption of two groups of ozone-depleting substances; the Bank is one of the Fund's implementing agencies.

The Bank is also mobilizing NGO experience and capacity, as well as private sector know-how and capital, for global environmental benefit. Examples of partnerships with NGOs, foundations, and the private sector include the Forest Market Transformation Initiative for sustainable forestry and the Photovoltaic Market Initiative for solar energy dissemination. The Bank has also helped leverage scarce grant funds through establishing Venture Capital Funds (biodiversity, renewable energy/efficiency) and by pioneering market-based instruments for the phase-out of ozone-depleting substances in developing countries.

During the year, the Bank, with support from the Energy Sector Management Assistance Program (ESMAP), a program funded by a consortium of donors and the Bank, advanced a solar energy initiative that aims to introduce the use of highly efficient, up-to-date, solar technologies in developing countries. Identification and preparation of solar and renewable energy projects are under way in at least fourteen countries, including Bolivia, Cameroon, Indonesia, Kenya, and Mali.

## The Bank's Portfolio and Environmentally Sustainable Development

In fiscal 1996, the Bank committed $1.63 billion and leveraged another $1.64 billion from other sources for twenty new environmental projects. These new commitments brought the Bank's active environmental portfolio to 153 projects totaling $11.4 billion. The portfolio supports catalytic and innovative work on natural resources management ("green projects"), as well as actions focused on the urban environment (the "brown" agenda), specifically control of water and air pollution, energy-related issues, and environmental institution building.

The *Second Environmental Assessment Review: The Impact of Environmental Assessment*, completed in fiscal 1996, takes stock of the Bank's progress in implementing its environmental assessment (EA) policy, focusing on the quality of EAS, the effects of EA on project design and implementation, and the application of EA in contexts such as privatization and financial intermediary lending. The review concluded that, although significant progress had been made in recent years, weaknesses still exist (for example, in the areas of public consultation and project supervision). There is evidence that high-quality EAS, now demanded by the Bank, are becoming, in a growing number of countries, the norm in investments financed by others.

## Identifying Best Practice: Learning by Doing

In fiscal 1996 the Bank focused on environmental activities with high potential for demonstrating best practice or for testing innovative approaches to rural poverty reduction. One example is the workshop convened in Africa to examine soil-degradation issues with the international community and to set in motion a consensus-building process on how best to reverse it. And in Indonesia and Nigeria, support was provided to small farmers and herdsmen to help them find ways to identify and introduce more relevant approaches of sustainable smallholder livestock development.

The Bank has assisted a wide range of countries in commercializing or involving the private sector in water and sanitation utilities and in all modes of transportation so as to mitigate the pervasive problems of poor performance (for example, in Albania, Brazil, Guinea, India, the Philippines, Romania, and South Africa). Work is under way on the development of a "toolkit" for preparing projects with public/private partnerships. The Bank is also helping to develop and implement innovative projects to provide sustainable water and sanitation services to the poor (in Bolivia, Brazil, India, Indonesia, Uganda, and Uzbekistan, for example).

In related efforts, the Bank is distilling lessons of experience in the performance of large-scale rural systems and facilitating partnerships between nonformal institutions—community groups and small-scale private sector providers, for example—and utilities in peri-urban areas. The Bank is assessing its operational experience in implementing the water-resources policy paper,[12] drawing on recent operations in managing water quality and mechanisms for water allocation (in Brazil, China, South Africa, sub-Saharan Africa, and Venezuela, for example). Similarly, work to distill and disseminate lessons of experience with programs for targeting basic services and environmental improvements in poor urban settlements is under way.

Important conceptual and methodological work in support of the Bank's work on environmentally and socially sustainable development was undertaken during the past year. The publication, *Monitoring Environmental Progress: A Report on Work in Progress*, reported on a new system for measuring the wealth of nations by integrating economic, social, and environmental factors.[13] The system is a major addition to international perspectives that have looked only at income and represents the first effort to calculate wealth for nearly all countries of the world. The system measures the real wealth of nations based on a combination of natural capital, produced assets, human resources, and social capital. The concept fits in well with the traditional measures of economic performance commonly employed by the Bank.

The vision for the Bank Group's transport-sector activities was set out in "Sustainable Transport," considered by the executive board in September 1995. The paper recommends the Bank pay greater attention than in the past to the transport needs of the rural and urban poor, environmental issues, competition and markets,

and appropriate roles for the private and public sectors. A work program was developed from the recommendations focusing on three themes: (a) reforming transport sector institutions and financial policies (economic sustainability); (b) transport and poverty reduction (social sustainability); and (c) motorization and the environment (environmental sustainability).

Several "best practice" papers produced during the year will help improve the Bank's operations, including those on rural finance, livestock management and environmental degradation, improving biodiversity in agriculture, and successful examples of water users' associations. A best practice discussion paper, "Rural Finance: Issues, Design, and Best Practices," examines the case for intervention in rural financial markets, promoting policies for creating a conducive environment for rural finance, and principles for building viable rural financial intermediaries. The paper, intended for a broad, worldwide audience of policymakers and practitioners of rural finance issues, proposes measures to create a conducive environment and build self-sustaining institutions that mobilize primarily local funds.

"Livestock and the Environment" (June 1996) examines sources of environmental degradation caused by improper livestock management, ranging from extensive grazing to intensive animal-management practices. A follow-up to a 1992 global assessment of livestock development by ten donor agencies, the study is the outcome of joint Bank/United States Agency for International Development/Food and Agriculture Organization of the U.N. (FAO) research that concentrated not only on interactions between livestock and the environment but also identified practices that should be encouraged and discouraged.

Together with the Bank's Economic Development Institute (EDI), ESD has fostered a south-south exchange of success stories in promoting decentralized water management. The Participatory Irrigation Management network, estab-

12. World Bank. 1993. *Water Resources Management. A World Bank Policy Study.* Washington, D.C.

13. World Bank. 1995. *Monitoring Environmental Progress: A Report on Work in Progress.* Washington, D.C.

lished by the EDI, has widely disseminated the story of Mexico's successful devolution of responsibility for irrigation operations and maintenance throughout the world. The Mexican experience of water-users' associations setting their own charges and managing their own resources is being applied in Turkey and is being used to guide similar undertakings in several other countries.

**Training Activities Are Intensified**

The Bank's environmental training activities were intensified in fiscal 1996. Building on the previous year's initiatives, a core training program was developed for nonenvironmental specialists Bankwide. It focuses on improving the understanding of environmental issues and the mastery of cross-sectoral linkages among policy, institutions, sociocultural factors, and technology. The program was launched in January 1996. Similarly, a Bankwide core training program was initiated for agricultural staff. Four one-day modules have been piloted and are now being mainstreamed, with the objective of having all 360 agricultural staff participate in the four modules over the next three years. ESD staff organized a large menu of specialized training activities, supplemented by workshops and study tours tailored to the needs of the Bank's, and its clients', technical staffs. Seminars and familiarization tours for water-policy, irrigation-management, transport, and urban development specialists were emphasized. Other activities focused on soils, crop, pest-management, and rural finance issues.

**Strengthening Existing Partnerships; Searching for New Ones**

While the Bank continues to learn from its experience, it recognizes that other institutions and organizations have rich experiences that can be tapped and are better placed than the Bank to experiment with innovative environmental and social work, as well as to secure input from in-country stakeholders. Strategic partnerships with these groups promise high payoffs. Links with such external partners were

therefore deepened during the past year, and the Bank began integrating its work with partners as a matter of course. An agreement to work jointly with the World Conservation Union has been established, and joint activities are being conducted, among others, with the Earth Council, the World Wildlife Federation, the U.S. National Wildlife Federation, Conservation International, the U.S. National Academy of Sciences, and the Federation of American Scientists.

More than 1,400 leaders of governments, NGOs, businesses, and international institutions, as well as noted scholars and financiers, participated in the Third Annual ESD Conference, "Effective Financing," held in October 1995 in Washington, D.C. Thematic roundtables included the role of the private and public sectors, effective financing at the global and regional levels, water issues, community participation, and resource conservation and policy. Ten associated events, cosponsored by the World Bank and various NGOs and other institutions, were held concurrently with the conference.

Agreement to create the Global Water Partnership (GWP) was reached at a meeting of the Bank, the UNDP, and the Swedish International Development Authority in Stockholm in December 1995. The GWP is to serve as a coherent, integrated, and collaborative framework to help local, national, and regional authorities implement internationally endorsed water-management principles. The GWP would consolidate the existing UNDP–World Bank Water Program and bring together key partners on a wide range of water issues.

Partnerships were also forged with urban development practitioners in developing countries—through Bank-sponsored retreats and seminars—to help the Bank develop new responses to client needs. These efforts aim *first*, to support the overall improvement of urban management and the financial sustainability of urban services, and *second*, to assist in developing programmatic solutions that directly address the needs of the poor.

With significant contribution from UNEP and the United Nations Industrial Development Organization, as well as technical advice from the United States Environmental Protection Agency and the World Health Organisation, the new "Pollution Prevention and Abatement Handbook" was prepared. The handbook summarizes the lessons learned from Bank experience in addressing industrial and municipal pollution and provides advice on how to set priorities in pollution management.

The preparations for the City Summit, held in Istanbul in June 1996, provided a unique opportunity to generate interest and visibility for the challenges of growing urban poverty, urban environmental degradation, and urban financing needs. As part of the preparatory effort, inter-agency support (involving the United States government, the United Nations Centre for Human Settlements, and the Bank) was mobilized for the Urban Finance Colloquium in September 1995, which helped develop a consensus on financing issues to be reflected in the Summit's Global Plan of Action. The Bank expects to define further the agenda for action during fiscal 1997 to develop cities in a sustainable way.

**A Renewed CGIAR Becomes Operational**

Fiscal 1996 saw the completion of the changes begun by the Consultative Group on International Agricultural Research (CGIAR) in New Delhi in 1994. International Centers Week, held from October 30 to November 3, 1995 in Washington, D.C., formally brought the Bank-led renewal program to closure and charted new directions for the future of the CGIAR system. The renewal program, implemented in eighteen months, was the outcome of a collective effort involving CGIAR cosponsors (the Bank, the FAO, UNEP, and the UNDP), other CGIAR members, the centers themselves, CGIAR's Technical Advisory Committee (TAC), national agricultural research systems (NARs), and outside experts. The effort was based on a comprehensive and critical self-examination of the CGIAR; it built on past strengths and aimed at eliminating weaknesses.

On January 1, 1996, the renewed CGIAR became operational. The renewal program developed a more open and participatory system. Four areas were specifically targeted:

• expanding developing country membership to strengthen the CGIAR as a "south-north" coalition and to enhance the basis of support for agricultural research;

• encouraging full participation of developing country NARs in setting priorities for the CGIAR;

• expanding the dialogue between the CGIAR and institutions with compatible interests; and

• increasing interaction with the private sector.

Nine developing countries have joined the CGIAR since its renewal program was launched in New Delhi, bringing the total membership to sixteen—as compared with twenty-one industrial member countries—marking considerable progress on broadening the base of developing country membership.

To further the aim of broadened partnerships, an NGO committee was formed and met in Washington, D.C. in October 1995. Similarly, a private sector committee, established to provide the CGIAR with a private sector perspective on global agricultural research and to serve as a link to agroindustrial companies, was convened in December.

The twin pillars of CGIAR research—productivity increases and natural resources management—were reaffirmed. In addition, three additional objectives were endorsed: saving biodiversity, improving agricultural policy, and strengthening national research. CGIAR programs will now be more firmly anchored in the context of global agricultural R&D efforts and will be carried out in collaboration with other actors.

Financial support for the CGIAR has rebounded since the onset of the renewal program. Support for the 1996 research agenda is estimated at $300 million, including a Bank contribution of $45 million.

Many challenges still face the CGIAR. The relevance of its research agenda must be maintained and the scientific excellence of its work nurtured. The CGIAR's TAC is working on recommendations for a new set of priorities and strategies to help guide the research system into the next century.

## Private Sector Development

Countries throughout the world are working to enhance the role of the private sector in their national development because it is central to reducing poverty. Private sector development stimulates economic growth and creates jobs, and privatizations create the fiscal space that allows governments to allocate greater resources to the social sector. Many country initiatives—economic policy reform, regulatory innovation, ownership changes, and capacity building—have all been used to buttress this powerful trend. The Bank Group encourages and supports the expanded role of the private sector through its various financial instruments, advisory services, training, and the nurturing of business partnerships.

In fiscal 1996, the Bank Group—the Bank, the IFC, and MIGA—mounted a diverse program of assistance to continue and enhance its support of member countries' private sector development. World Bank assistance to sectors in which private sector development is making the most rapid inroads totaled more than $5.6 billion through fifty-one projects—in the financial, power, telecommunications/information technology, oil and gas, and industry and mining sectors. These operations supported the structural changes needed to attract private funding to productive enterprises. Operations were designed in many cases to leverage substantial private capital flows. The Bank also provided nonlending services, including technical assistance, research, and knowledge brokering—often in cooperation with bilateral donors, private companies, and NGOs.

In fiscal 1996, the IFC reached a record level in financing approvals of $3.2 billion for 264 projects, compared with $2.9 billion for 231 projects in fiscal 1995. It was a banner year, as well, for the IFC's resource-mobilization activities: $4.9 billion in financing was approved through loan syndications and the underwriting

of securities issues and investment funds. Syndications with banks and institutional investors exceeded the IFC's combined loan and equity investments for the sixth year in a row, underscoring the growing catalytic role of this program. Projects approved by the IFC had total investment costs of $19.6 billion; other investors and lenders provided a total of $5.13 for every dollar approved by the IFC. Projects were approved in sixty-eight countries in fiscal 1996. In addition, eight projects were regional or international in scope.

Fiscal 1996 was another successful year for MIGA's guarantee program. Business increased by all measures compared with the results of fiscal 1995. Sixty-eight guarantee contracts were issued for $862 million in coverage, and income earned from premiums and commitment fees amounted to $21.9 million. The contracts issued in fiscal 1996 facilitated an estimated $6.6 billion in foreign direct investment in twenty-seven developing countries, the highest amount facilitated by MIGA in a single year so far. These projects will generate an estimated 9,200 jobs and will involve substantial training programs for their employees. Overall, forty developing countries have benefited from investments guaranteed by MIGA, and more than $15 billion of foreign direct investment has been facilitated.

Reflecting the importance the Bank Group attaches to private sector development and in an effort to be more responsive to clients, a managing director was given the specific mandate to coordinate the Bank Group's private sector activities and strengthen its outreach to business audiences. This office has been facilitating policy coordination across the Bank Group institutions on a range of environmental, social, and other issues, fostering closer working relations among the institutions in developing joint country-assistance strategies, and coordinating financial sector strategies, multi-institutional projects, and a more effective IBRD guarantee instrument. The office has also been promoting Bank Group representation at conferences and trade fairs and helping strengthen partnerships with business associations, NGOs, and other groups. It will soon launch a Business Partnership Center, which will provide a focal point for communications with the private sector.

World Bank assistance for private sector development is grounded in the institution's long experience with its clients, familiarity with the global financial community, and the strong technical skills of its staff. In fiscal 1996, work was under way in every region of the Bank to improve the business environment through encouraging countries to identify and overcome constraints to competitiveness, supporting privatization and enterprise reform, facilitating greater investment in infrastructure, and promoting microfinance.

**Improving the Business Environment**

The Bank assists countries in privatization and enterprise reform by providing direct advice and analysis, making loans for technical assistance to facilitate transactions, designing adjustment projects to help governments face the one-time costs that may be associated with privatization, making investment loans to help privatized companies restructure, and providing guarantees to cover risks to private investors. During the past year, the Bank stepped up the pace of technical assistance to help governments implement step-by-step, practical measures leading to greater privatization of ownership; to prepare sales strategies for large enterprises, to design worker-participation and related schemes, and to recruit and supervise investment advisers for large transactions. An example of results-oriented technical assistance in Pakistan is detailed in Box 3-2.

The Bank continued to be active in preparing private sector assessments (PSAs), which describe the structure of a country's private sector, identify the key constraints to its development, and lay out economically efficient ways to remove those constraints. They represent the beginning of a process of dialogue with a government and form a baseline for joint work on policy and institutional reform.

Originally mandated by the executive board in 1992 to strengthen the Bank's private sector perspective in economic and sector work, PSAs were further emphasized when the board mandated that the Bank and the IFC collaborate on an initial set of twenty PSAs.[14] As of June 30, 1996, thirty-one PSAs had been completed, covering countries in every region in which the Bank works—including, for example, Côte d'Ivoire and Ghana in Africa, Indonesia and the Philippines in East Asia, India and Pakistan in South Asia, Hungary and Poland in Eastern and Central Europe, Brazil and Mexico in Latin America, and Egypt and Morocco in the Middle East and North Africa. At least a half dozen additional PSAs are targeted for completion in fiscal 1997. Moreover, the Bank and its client countries have embarked on a variety of follow-up studies to explore issues identified in the PSAs in more depth.

The "competitiveness framework"—the legal and policy framework affecting business decisions—is critical to the success of private sector development Without such frameworks many privatization, infrastructure investment, and financial sector initiatives cannot realize their full potential. The Bank is helping focus the attention of key policymakers in client countries on how to increase the competitiveness of the local business environment through joint competitiveness assessments, conferences to develop a common vision of actions needed, and technical assistance to develop competition law, competition strategy, and firm-led capacity building. The goal is to create a sustained dialogue for change among the Bank's borrowing countries. Earlier, successful application of these approaches in Morocco was replicated in El Salvador during the past fiscal year, and preliminary work has begun in Egypt and Jordan.[15]

---

14. The Bank and the IFC have also begun a pilot program of a limited number of joint country-assistance strategies (CASs), which provide a vehicle for executive board discussion of the Bank's views of a particular country's developmental constraints and priorities and the proposed Bank-assistance strategy. These CASs would be considered jointly by the executive directors of the Bank and the executive directors of the IFC. Eight countries in the pilot program have been agreed upon: Brazil, Côte d'Ivoire, Egypt, India, Indonesia, Kazakstan, Mexico, and Poland. The objective of the joint CAS is to ensure that there is a coordinated Bank Group private sector country view and strategy.

15. In Morocco, four public-private "clusters" are working—with support from the Bank—on policy changes and action programs, for example, the Northwest Regional Tourism Development Program.

## BOX 3-2. ACCELERATING PRIVATIZATION IN PAKISTAN

*When the Pakistani government requested technical assistance to accelerate its privatization program, a team of experts was mobilized by the Bank—supported in part with Japanese trust funds—to work with Pakistan's Privatization Commission. Team members provided technical assistance on the design and implementation of the government's privatization program, recruited and supervised consultants, strengthened the Commission's staffing through training, drafted an operational strategy and action plan, and prepared valuations and bidding rules.*

*As a result, twenty manufacturing units were sold in fiscal 1996, raising Rs.9.4 billion ($268 million).*

*These included Wah Cement and Pak Saudi Fertilizer. In addition, the Kot Addu Power Plant was sold for Rs.7.5 billion ($215 million), and the sale of Banker's Equity Limited (BEL)—a development finance institution—raised Rs.314 million ($9 million). The Commission expects the telecom utility (PTC), gas company (SNGPL), two banks, three firms in the power sector, and other medium- and large-scale units to be privatized later in the calendar year. In addition, the government has begun initial work on privatizing the national airline, PIA.*

## Private Provision of Infrastructure

The Bank's focus on private sector development comes together most vividly in private provision of infrastructure (PPI). While divestiture of assets through privatization is an essential step in facilitating private sector-led economic growth, the provision of new infrastructure with private financing cannot get under way without a credible business climate. Creating a conducive climate is a complex process that requires appropriate market structures and economic regulations for infrastructure development. The Bank is helping countries develop strategies for "unbundling" infrastructure industries where competitive supply is possible, and, where natural monopoly elements remain, to develop economic regulations that protect consumers and provide incentives for efficient supply. The Bank is providing advisory services to deal with this critical set of issues such as the technical assistance loan, approved during the past year, to Mexico in support of PPI.

The Bank has also begun to develop a structured network of developing-country regulatory leaders and institutions to promote capacity building in PPI. It includes expert meetings, hands-on seminars for regulators and stakeholders, and dissemination of best-practice information on planning and sequencing regulatory change. The Bank has also developed a world-wide data base of 3,500 private infrastructure projects (including those situated in industrialized countries) to support its best-practice work.

The Bank facilitates PPI through loans and credits and guarantee operations. Over the past nine years, some 138 such operations were approved. These include adjustment loans for policy reform, technical assistance, wide-ranging and diverse investment operations, and guarantees *(see Box 3-3)*. Among the twenty-three PPI projects approved in fiscal 1996 was an adjustment credit in Yemen, which is paving the way for multisector regulatory changes to allow private participation in infrastructure. A technical assistance loan in Congo is facilitating private participation in the telecommunications, energy, power, and transport sectors, and a railways-rehabilitation loan in Côte d'Ivoire is supporting the transition from state to private management.

## Selected Instruments for Addressing Private Sector Development

*The guarantee program.* In fiscal 1996, the Bank expanded its partial risk and partial credit guarantee programs and integrated them into its comprehensive package of development-assistance instruments. Guarantees can lower project risks and induce private capital investments and can be applied flexibly based on the

## BOX 3-3. WORLD BANK CONTRIBUTION TO PRIVATE PARTICIPATION IN INFRASTRUCTURE

*A wave of private sector participation in infrastructure (PPI) is sweeping the globe: More than 2,200 PPI projects are under preparation in developing countries as disparate as Albania and Colombia. The World Bank's lending and guarantee programs have supported this worldwide movement. During the period fiscal 1988–96, the Bank provided funds for some 138 loans and credits, as well as partial risk and credit-risk guarantees. Each operation embodied significant PPI components, including the privatization of public utilities, onlending to private sector operators, and franchising operations involving leases, concessions, and management contracts. The Bank's primary focus has been to support policy-related reforms and work on less developed regions—particularly Africa. The range of this activity is shown in the table below.*

***Adjustment and technical assistance loans.*** *Since 1988, the Bank has developed single-sector and multisector adjustment loans to support major policy improvements in, among other countries, Argentina, Bolivia, Mexico, Peru, and Venezuela. In fiscal 1996, the Bank supported multisectoral PPI components as part of adjustment loans in Yemen and Ukraine. These loans depend on and require long-term government commitment to an infrastructure-privatization agenda. Support to multisectoral PPI agendas has also been provided through stand-alone technical assistance loans, such as those provided in fiscal 1996 to Congo and Mexico. These loans support the design of stable, comprehensive, and consistent legal and regulatory frameworks for PPI, striving to ensure the sustainability of reforms undertaken.*

***Investment loans.*** *World Bank investment loans for physical infrastructure play a catalytic role in privatizing infrastructure services. Transport-sector projects in Armenia and Georgia, for example, funded road maintenance and investment in new equipment, thereby facilitating the privatization of trucking and road-repair operations. Since 1988, similar loans with PPI-related policy components have been undertaken in some ninety-nine other countries.*

***Franchises.*** *The Bank is helping to design management contracts, leases, or concessions for infrastructure services in a number of investment loans that involve franchise arrangements. Franchise arrangements are most common in Africa, where sixteen were supported by Bank infrastructure loans from fiscal 1988 to 1996. In some PPI operations, Bank funds are onlent to private sector operators of infrastructure services, including power projects in India and Turkey, water and telecommunications projects in Argentina and the Philippines, and transport-sector operations in Ethiopia and Mexico.*

***Guarantees.*** *The Bank has provided eight guarantees since the inception of the program in 1994. Catalyzing private funding for mostly public sector projects, these operations have also involved guarantees to the private sector in two power projects in Pakistan, formed an important component in facilitating the eventual privatization of Jordan's publicly held telecom entity, and assisted with the financing of a loan involving an independent power project in the Philippines.*

### World Bank PPI Operations, Fiscal 1988–96

| Instrument | Africa | East Asia and the Pacific | South Asia | Europe and Central Asia | Latin America | Middle East and North Africa | Total |
|---|---|---|---|---|---|---|---|
| Adjustment: single sector | 4 | 0 | 0 | 1 | 1 | 0 | 6 |
| Adjustment: multisector | 0 | 0 | 0 | 1 | 7 | 1 | 9 |
| Technical assistance | 4 | 1 | 1 | 1 | 9 | 0 | 16 |
| Investment lending | 33 | 17 | 15 | 13 | 17 | 4 | 99 |
| Guarantees | 0 | 4 | 2 | 0 | 1 | 1 | 8 |
| Total | 41 | 22 | 18 | 16 | 35 | 6 | 138 |

characteristic of each project and on country conditions. In fiscal 1996, the executive board approved three such operations totaling $275 million.

These included a partial risk guarantee for the privately sponsored Uch Power Project in Pakistan ($75 million guarantee), a complex package involving an IFC loan of $115 million, United States Exim Bank guarantees, and direct loans from the Bank of China. This project exemplifies growing cooperation among the Bank, the IFC, and other cofinanciers in financing major infrastructure investments. Other operations included a guarantee to mobilize $150 million of private debt financing on favorable terms for China's Ertan II Hydro Project and the guarantee of a bond issue of $50 million to support the Telecommunications Company of Jordan. This last operation led to unprecedented access—for a Jordanian company—into the Eurobond market.

The Bank also accelerated guarantee processing by streamlining documentation requirements and developing model agreements for legal documents. Action frameworks were created and specific projects were identified in consultation with several borrower governments to build a pipeline of guarantee operations over the medium term. A broader program to market the Bank's guarantees included convening a seminar on guarantees at the Bank's 1995 annual meetings. A solid pipeline of prospective guarantees now includes more than three dozen operations, across all the Bank's regions, covering virtually all major infrastructure sectors.

*CGAP.* Over the past decade, microcredit and savings services have proved to be an effective means of job creation and income generation among the very poor. Participation of the poor in credit and savings systems improves family welfare, nutritional and educational status among children, and lowers birth rates. To broaden and deepen this success, the Consultative Group for Assistance to the Poorest (CGAP), established late in fiscal 1995, is now implementing microfinance operations that provide assistance to the poorest.

CGAP channels funds through sound microfinance institutions that meet CGAP-approved eligibility criteria; improves donor coordination for systematic financing of such programs; and provides governments, donors, and practitioners with a vehicle for learning and disseminating best practices for delivering these services. By the end of fiscal 1996, the consultative group had twenty-three members. The Bank manages the CGAP secretariat, which administers a pool of pilot project-oriented external funding amounting to $32 million, of which $18.8 million was received in fiscal 1996, including a Bank contribution of $14 million. Some fifty-seven initial project requests from NGO and microenterprise-funding facilities from about thirty countries and several regional programs were reviewed during the past year, and fourteen were approved for implementation.

CGAP also provides training and information services on best practices in microfinance to policymakers and practitioners in the field. A seminar on methodologies for microfinance was held in Ghana, for example, and a study tour for Tunisian policymakers to Guatemala and Honduras was undertaken.

*The Foreign Investment Advisory Service (FIAS).* FIAS is a joint Bank-IFC program that provides advisory services to governments to help them improve the policy environment for foreign private investment. The program—funded by the IFC, the Bank, other donors, and paying customers among the developing countries receiving advice—carries out projects in twenty-five to thirty countries each year. During the year FIAS launched more-intensive work in Africa, with operations under way or expected soon in seven countries to help increase levels of foreign investment to the region. FIAS also carries out a large advisory program in East Asia and the Pacific—supported by its new regional office in Sydney—as well as in others regions of the developing world.

## Financial Sector Development

A well-functioning financial sector is essential for private enterprise to grow and flourish. In turn, a healthy financial sector depends on a favorable policy environment and on strong institutions, banks, capital markets, and specialized institutions in areas such as housing finance, pension systems, and banking-sector supervision. In fiscal 1996, the Bank approved seventeen projects designed to help its clients develop their financial sectors.

The Bank's role in the financial sector is rapidly changing; in the past, Bank operations focused primarily on improving the policy framework and mandating basic prudential supervision. While still important in many countries, the Bank is increasingly becoming involved in assisting countries facing internal and external shocks (such as Argentina and Mexico) that result in pressure on their banking systems from high real interest rates and economic slowdown. Deterioration in asset quality increases the potential for runs on banks' liabilities, and responses must deal with underlying problems in banking systems, accounting standards, and bank management. Operations must be designed quickly since situations can soon become systemic within a country rather than affecting one or a few banks.

Lending in support of the financial sector in fiscal 1996 included support to banking reform in Argentina, Ghana, India, Moldova, Morocco, Tanzania, and Vietnam. In addition, supervision of earlier financial sector loans was intensive in both Argentina and Mexico to deal with the systemic aspects of their banking systems. Loans to Ghana and India are assisting nonbanking financial institutions—primarily leasing and other financial services organizations—to expand their financing of development-related infrastructure activities. These new-style financial sector operations rely heavily on staff with a high degree of expertise in resolving systemic liquidity and solvency problems. They include specialists in bank restructuring and privatization, banking supervision, central banking, liquidity management, and the collection and sale of bad assets. The Bank is building up its technical capability in these areas.

Training client-country staff is an important element of the Bank's assistance to the financial sector. During fiscal 1996, seven courses, attended by about 400 participants, were held, covering issues such as payment systems, banking supervision, and social security and pension reform. A total of 1,100 Bank staff also underwent short-course training in financial sector issues throughout the fiscal year.

Assistance in capital markets development—in close cooperation with the IFC—is a growing area of Bank support. In fiscal 1996, the Bank provided technical assistance in market building, including the regulation and supervision of capital markets, and in developing new financial instruments to address investor concerns about risk. Examples include upgrading regulatory and supervisory capacity and providing a backstop facility in Argentina, creating market infrastructure in Russia, promoting debt-market development in India, and developing regional capital markets in West Africa.

## Operations in the Power Sector

The Bank's assistance to the power sector emphasizes restructuring, private sector involvement in financing and management, innovative energy sources, energy for the rural and urban poor, energy efficiency, and environmentally sound energy technologies. The lending program was robust in fiscal 1996, with twenty projects totaling $3.2 billion in all regions of the Bank. The Bank also carried out an expanding program of nonlending services including conferences and roundtables, direct technical assistance, and knowledge dissemination aimed at energy-sector decisionmakers in the Bank's borrowing countries.

The Bank aims to buttress borrower efforts to increase private sector participation in the power sector. The past year's lending program included power-generation loans with reform and institutional strengthening components in Bolivia, Cambodia, China, Colombia, El Salvador, India, Madagascar, Pakistan, and Romania—among others. The loan for Colombia supports power-sector reform by facilitating the operation of a competitive bulk supply market for electricity. In India, the Bank supported a pathbreaking operation in Orissa to unbundle the state's power generation, transmission, and distribution businesses and to achieve full privatization of power transmission by the year 2000.

## Supporting Reform in Telecommunications and Information Technology

The Bank is shifting from investment in telephone-company infrastructure to support for sector reform that sets the stage for competition and mobilization of private capital and management. Traditional telecom lending is declining accordingly while technical assistance to prepare regulatory regimes and restructure programs is increasing. In Ghana, for example, the Bank's technical assistance has resulted in a competitive telecommunications-sector strategy. With Bank assistance, increased private participation in financing and management is now a reality in many borrowing countries, including Bolivia, Hungary, India, and Indonesia. IFC's private sector activities in the sector have increased.

The Bank and the IFC have worked together closely on telecommunications financing and reform. During the past year that collaboration became even closer, as the Bank and IFC telecom divisions "co-located" their operations to facilitate joint work—for example in evaluating industry proposals for fiber cable systems in Africa.

In the new information age, economic development is intimately connected to the growth of telecommunications services. In recent years, up to 10 percent of project lending has funded information technology-related procurement.

However, before fiscal 1996 the Bank did not have a visible, freestanding program for applying information-technology solutions to the full range of developing country problems and priorities.

In July 1995, some 150 donors, industry representatives, and information-technology experts participated in the Bank Group's first conference on information infrastructure. The conference explored the role of information in economic development, and participants discussed how the Bank, together with the private sector, can most effectively help developing countries build, access, and utilize modern information infrastructure. The conference led to the creation of infoDev (the Information for Development Program), designed to bring together industry experts, other donors, the Bank, and its borrowers, to focus on meeting development needs through technology applications *(see box on page 21)*.

TechNet, an information-dissemination and networking program, has also been launched to assess the technology status and requirements in developing countries and link practitioners around the world through seminars, best-practice papers, and electronic communications. TechNet is working with partners, such as foundations, the United States National Research Council, and the European Union, to improve understanding of the role of science and technology in economic development.

### Oil and Gas Sector Activities

Privatization of the oil and gas sector is well advanced in many of the Bank's borrowing countries. The Bank's role is catalytic; it provides financing for the infrastructure that must be put into place along with private investments, and develops worldwide methodologies and standards for procurement to facilitate bid preparation. In fiscal 1996, the Bank joined with private sector partners in the oil and gas sector to find ways to overcome bottlenecks to private investment arising from traditional contracting procedures. Bank staff, country experts, and industry representatives held a productive

seminar to suggest faster, more innovative contracting procedures to facilitate investment flows, for example through structured, direct negotiations.

The Bank also provides technical assistance loans to speed up the privatization process. In fiscal 1996, for example, a technical assistance credit helped the Bolivian government design and execute a hydrocarbon-sector adjustment program and capitalize YPFB, the state-owned oil company.

### Mining Sector: Active Bank Involvement

The mining sector is an important engine of growth for many of the Bank's borrowing countries. During fiscal 1996, the Bank actively facilitated private sector involvement in a number of ways. Bank lending is supporting a series of reforms, including rewriting mining laws, reforming public mining institutions, strengthening environmental protection capabilities, privatizing state companies, and addressing social safety net issues. The Bank also works closely with the IFC, MIGA, other multilateral banks, and private investors to help governments carry out broad, complex programs of mining-sector privatization, restructuring, and new investment—for example the mining industry in Zambia.

### Forging Links with External Partnerships

The Bank is forging wider and stronger linkages with private industry, NGOs, trade groups, and investors. For example, the Bank hosts an annual review of progress and problems for private power-sector companies that invest in developing countries. Information-technology companies are involved in infoDev as both donors and colleagues and are helping to carrying out pilot projects. Two private energy groups, Marubeni of Japan and EnergyNet of the Netherlands, have joined the ESMAP consultative group and participate in its deliberations and funding. Links with trade associations and industrial organizations are increasing—with the Japanese Keidanren, the International Business

Roundtable, the Milan and Turin Chambers of Commerce, the Global Information Infrastructure Commission, and the International Institute of Finance—to name a few. Contacts with the petroleum industry are close, both in project development and in dialogue on strategic issues. Groups such as the Prince of Wales Business Leaders Forum provide the opportunity to advance the concept of corporate responsibility.

In fiscal 1996, a network that provides technical assistance in developing countries, the Senior Volunteer Advisory Service, was invited to participate in the Bank's work; it is supporting Bank development activities in a number of countries. Linkages with bilateral donors are long-standing (through ESMAP), as well as new (through infoDev and CGAP). Increasingly, the Bank is collaborating with bilateral donors in planning and implementing technical assistance projects.

Best-practice knowledge in private sector development, financial sector development, and industry and energy is disseminated through publications and access to Bank data bases (for example, in the private provision of infrastructure). The Bank is stepping up its secondment of private sector staff into the Bank—and the assignment of its regular staff to enrichment programs in private companies.

# AFRICA

Sub-Saharan Africa's gross domestic product (GDP) is estimated to have grown by 4.0 percent in 1995—a significant improvement over the period 1991–94 (1.4 percent on average)—and economists are forecasting an even higher rate of growth in 1996. Aggregate numbers such as these mask wide variations by country, as in the past. Thus, while at least fifteen countries grew by 5 percent or more in 1995 (four—Angola, Lesotho, Malawi, and Uganda—experienced growth rates in excess of 10 percent), others (Burundi, Congo, Seychelles, Sierra Leone, Somalia, Zaire, Zambia, and Zimbabwe) registered declines. Africa's exports also expanded in 1995—by 5.7 percent, or roughly twice as fast as the year before. In this case, too, performance varied widely—from a negative 38 percent (Sierra Leone) to a positive 23 percent (Mauritania)—thereby confirming that "there is no single African reality," the conclusion of "A Continent in Transition—Sub-Saharan African in the Mid-1990s" (World Bank 1995).

Several trends are clear, nevertheless:

• Africa's economic performance *is* improving; thirty countries, accounting for 61 percent of the region's population, recorded positive per capita income growth in 1995. In some cases (such as Cameroon and Gabon), GDP growth fell short of the rate of population growth; nonetheless, this represented a reversal from the negative growth rates of the previous year.

• Performance *is* responding to policy reforms, which are spreading. (In 1995, for example, the sharpest increases in exports were registered by the group of countries in the CFA zone that had adjusted their exchange rates in early 1994.)

• In most of the continent, growth is not nearly sufficient to make a dent in poverty reduction, and despite recent improvements, Africa's GDP and export growth rates, savings and investment levels, and social indicators remain below those of other regions.

Africa's recent development experience and current situation are consistent with both the Bank's strategic agenda in the region and its operational approach to it. The strategic agenda aims to accelerate and spread growth dramatically—to achieve a quantum jump—to reduce poverty and to improve the quality of people's lives; the operational approach aims to maximize "results on the ground" by working in *partnership* with all parties with a stake in the outcomes and who can make a difference. The following sections highlight how the Bank has pursued its strategic agenda over the past twelve months.

## A Compact for Poverty Reduction

Countries must realize income growth of between 6 percent and 7 percent annually if significant progress in reducing poverty is to be achievable. Even then, such progress is not possible, let alone probable, unless poverty reduction is at the center of the development efforts of all stakeholders: multilateral and bilateral donors, international and local nongovernmental organizations (NGOs), and African countries themselves. In addition, all parties must work in true and strong partnership. The Bank's strategy aims to put in place a "compact for poverty reduction in Africa," the main components of which are:

• a more vigorous commitment by African governments to increase economic growth rates and reduce poverty, and, to this end, to improve governance;

• more systematic attention by African policymakers to economic reform, including reform of public finances and reform aimed at macroeconomic stability, to ensure a strong broad-based and sustained supply response;

• an improved pattern of public expenditure that enhances both the efficiency of investment and focuses expenditure on priority needs in the key social and economic sectors; and

• an improved environment for the private sector, which will lead to increased private sector investment.

Clearly, achieving these results requires strong national commitment and efforts. It is encouraging that a number of countries have strengthened the focus on poverty reduction in the formulation of their policies and investment programs.

## Working with External Partners

The Special Program of Assistance for Africa (SPA), established in December 1987, has been the most important forum for the coordination of aid to the subcontinent. Its objectives have been twofold: to mobilize adequate and timely financing in support of African countries that are undertaking economic reforms and to improve the effectiveness of donor assistance. The program is currently in the final year of its third phase. Bilateral and multilateral donors disbursed $16 billion in balance-of-payments finance during the years of the program's first two phases (1988–93). Planned financing for the current phase, 1994–96, totals $13 billion, although current budget pressures in many capitals are expected to affect donors' ability to fulfill these plans. Overall, the SPA has succeeded in providing much needed external financing to recipient countries. Annual net official development assistance (ODA) in real terms to them has been more than two thirds higher, on average, since the onset of the SPA (during 1988–94) than during the preceding seven-year period (1981–87). Just as real net ODA has increased sharply during the SPA period itself, so, too, have real net transfers. These resources, plus debt relief, are aimed at ensuring that the programs of economic reform are adequately funded.

Over time, the agenda of the SPA has evolved to include the developmental context of economic reform. Various working groups have focused on key subjects such as civil service reform; economic reform in an era of political liberalization; gender, poverty, and social policy; and public expenditure management. The SPA has begun to explore ways to improve the design, sequencing, and implementation of economic reform programs in order to promote greater country "ownership" of them and achieve sharper impact. Concurrently, the Bank initiated a comprehensive review of its policy-based lending instrument, which complemented the discussions in the SPA fora. This review took into consideration the views expressed by a broad range of African partners and donors during consultations on "A Continent in Transition," as well as discussion of policy-based lending in government, academic, and nongovernmental fora in the early 1990s. The aim of the review, and of the subsequent modifications, was to get economic reform programs to achieve quicker, stronger, and longer positive effects on the ground. Progress was also made under the SPA in refining the concept, and addressing the operational aspects, of Sector Investment Programs (SIPs), which are intended to enhance the impact of development lending in Africa by coming to grips with the problems created by the fragmentation of donor-driven projects and overburdened African capacity.

There are indications that the deep continentwide economic crisis that led to the birth of the SPA has been largely overcome. Many challenges still remain, however. Even the strongest performers among the countries of the region must still aspire to raise income beyond current levels. Debt problems and weak capacity continue to act as significant constraints on development. These and other issues will be discussed as SPA-3 completes its final year and donors agree on an agenda for a fourth phase beginning in 1997.

Steps were also taken by the Bank to strengthen its collaboration with UN agencies. It participated actively in the preparation of the Secretary-General's Special Initiative for Africa, which was launched on March 15, 1996. The initiative defines a program of concrete actions to accelerate African development and a partnership to reduce the fragmentation of development assistance. It seeks to greatly expand basic education and health care, to promote peace and better governance, and to improve water and food security. Up to $25 billion may be required to finance the Special Initiative over a ten-year period (this is an estimate of the cost of all the investments necessary in the sectors covered by the initiative). Funding will come, to a significant extent, from a continuation of the current programs of support for the sectors involved and a reallocation of resources to initiative activities. The World Bank will participate in all areas covered by the initiative and take on particular responsibility for mobilizing resources for basic education and health care on the basis of well-prepared sector programs supported by local stakeholders and donors.

The Bank also worked closely with the United Nations Economic Commission for Africa (UNECA) in a number of areas such as private sector development. The collaboration with UNECA and other UN agencies has evolved into one among "genuine partners." In addition, the Bank has strengthened its collaboration with multilateral lending institutions such as the Islamic Development Bank and the African Development Bank (AfDB). It responded, for example, to a request from the AfDB to provide extensive technical advice in selected areas (such as portfolio management, treasury operations, and procurement) as part of its major restructuring.

## Partnership for Private Sector Development

Close consultation with the private sector and other stakeholder groups has become an integral part of project design and policy reforms for private sector development. Workshops that bring all stakeholders together to discuss problems and develop an action program are becoming a popular and increasingly effective tool to this end. A private sector workshop in Mali, for example, led to the restructuring of the $12 million Private Sector Assistance Project approved in November 1993. Workshops are sometimes focused on specific issues, such as those held on export strategies in Madagascar and small and micro enterprises in Benin. The Africa Region of the Bank is working with the Bank's Economic Development Institute to develop consultation and training programs in these and other countries to facilitate increased dialogue between the public and private sectors.

In countries such as Chad, Malawi, Senegal, Uganda, Zambia, and Zimbabwe, partnership among the Bank, governments, and the private sector, established through project-preparation task forces during the past year, has evolved to the creation of joint steering committees or

units to oversee project implementation. Positive initiatives taken by countries themselves include the establishment of private sector foundations in Madagascar, Senegal, and Uganda to provide support to private businesses and to improve the dialogue between the government and the private sector. Mozambique and the Central African Republic have established annual private sector conferences.

In addition to supporting these national efforts, the Bank is encouraging dialogue with the private sector *across* countries. It joined with UNECA, the United Nations Development Programme, the Global Coalition for

Africa (GCA), and other bilateral and international agencies in sponsoring a regionwide Conference on Reviving Private Investment in Africa, held in Ghana in June 1996. More narrowly focused subregional forums were held on "Agribusiness in Southern Africa" (March 1996) and on the "Informal Sector and Micro Finance in Western Africa" (June 1996). A symposium in Johannesburg on Power Sector Reform and Efficiency in December 1995 brought together ministers of finance and CEOs of utilities from forty-three African countries to discuss reforms, investment requirements, and greater private sector involvement. These activities also involved cooperation with other international and national agencies and NGOs.

In a growing number of countries, the Bank is acting as a low-key catalyst to help facilitate and foster improved dialogue between African governments and private sector representatives. Government-private sector competitiveness-review groups and fora have been set up (notably in Ghana, Madagascar, and Senegal) to assess major bottlenecks to private sector competitiveness and to propose solutions for adoption by the authorities. These can be instrumental in building ownership for policy reform.

Meanwhile, in the area of private investment promotion, strengthened coordination between the Bank, the IFC, and MIGA is enhancing Bank Group efforts to assist client countries to design business-environment reforms—notably through the Bank/IFC-run Foreign Investment Advisory Service—and to execute promotion programs with MIGA assistance. Increasingly, in project finance for private investment, the Bank is finding opportunities to catalyze IFC and MIGA involvement, both for major new projects (in the energy sector, for example) and for postprivatization and postliberalization private investments (in telecommunications, for example).

## Partnership with Local Communities and NGOs

The Bank is strongly committed to going beyond traditional cooperation with member governments to include participation in decisionmaking by NGOs, community groups, cooperatives, women's organizations, the poor and the disadvantaged, as well as the private sector. Using participatory approaches, the Bank is doing more listening than imposing. The Bank has identified nineteen "flagship" participatory operations—including five in Africa—that it is monitoring, and systematic participatory approaches are becoming the normal way of doing business for all major activities. In agriculture, the utility of systematic farmer participation is illustrated by the beneficiary assessment undertaken in Senegal. In addition, in three "gender" pilot projects—in Burkina Faso, Mali, and Mozambique—gender-related concerns are being introduced in policy-based operations in close collaboration with beneficiaries.

One of the "flagship" operations, the Tanzania Human Resources Development Pilot Project, currently under preparation, is an example of the close partnership being developed among the Bank, governments, and local communities. After three years of participatory consultation with parent associations, community leaders, school teachers, and health workers, the Tanzanian government designed three pilot programs to be financed by the project that aim at making schools and health facilities more accountable to their clients and at promoting a feeling of ownership among beneficiaries, who provide financial support.

The Mali Pilot Participation Project—a "flagship" operation under advanced preparation—was conceived at the June 1995 Mali Hunger Workshop as a vehicle to experiment with partnership approaches in the fight against hunger and poverty. The steering committee designing the project is composed of representatives of the central government and district authorities, community-based organizations, and NGOs. Two confederations of NGOs are involved, one containing local NGOs only and the other both local and international NGOs. These actions and others are expected to help build a basis for partnership between the government

## TABLE 4-1. LENDING TO BORROWERS IN AFRICA, BY SECTOR, 1987–96

*(millions of US dollars; fiscal years)*

| Sector | Annual average, 1987–91 | 1992 | 1993 | 1994 | 1995 | 1996 |
|---|---|---|---|---|---|---|
| Agriculture | 671.1 | 707.4 | 318.3 | 152.6 | 415.1 | 328.0 |
| Education | 197.6 | 402.9 | 417.4 | 325.5 | 201.2 | 131.6 |
| Electric power and other energy | 145.1 | 130.0 | 356.0 | 90.0 | 255.3 | 73.3 |
| Environment | 4.4 | — | — | 2.6 | — | 11.8 |
| Finance | 283.3 | 619.9 | 279.6 | 400.1 | 7.2 | 59.2 |
| Industry | 122.0 | 200.0 | 20.9 | 16.8 | — | 11.4 |
| Mining/Other extractive | 16.2 | 6.0 | — | — | 24.8 | — |
| Multisector | 604.2 | 895.0 | 451.2 | 724.1 | 470.9 | 407.8 |
| Oil and gas | 66.5 | — | 2.4 | 186.2 | — | — |
| Population, health, and nutrition | 179.8 | 110.3 | 131.2 | 161.6 | 311.5 | 158.7 |
| Public sector management | 103.3 | 128.1 | 139.8 | 61.0 | 117.3 | 654.4 |
| Social sector | 5.8 | 59.0 | 12.0 | — | — | 257.5 |
| Telecommunications/Informatics | 73.8 | — | 89.1 | — | — | — |
| Transportation | 389.4 | 233.0 | 483.0 | 501.9 | 74.8 | 420.7 |
| Urban development | 225.9 | 184.6 | 49.2 | 111.4 | 158.0 | 190.0 |
| Water supply and sanitation | 167.3 | 297.4 | 67.2 | 74.1 | 248.2 | 35.7 |
| Total | 3,255.7 | 3,973.6 | 2,817.3 | 2,807.9 | 2,284.3 | 2,740.1 |
| Of which: IBRD | 992.3 | 738.4 | 47.0 | 127.7 | 80.7 | — |
| IDA | 2,263.4 | 3,235.2 | 2,770.3 | 2,680.2 | 2,203.6 | 2,740.1 |
| Number of operations | 80 | 77 | 75 | 60 | 58 | 53 |

NOTE: *Details may not add to totals because of rounding.*
— *Zero.*

and NGOs in the delivery of social services to the poor.

Bank-NGO dialogue on Africa was strengthened in fiscal 1996 through systematic consultation and the appointment of twenty-three NGO liaison officers, who are attached to Bank resident missions to facilitate participatory approaches in Bank-financed projects. The Third African World Bank-NGO Consultation meeting was held in Accra at the Bank's offices in February 1996. This meeting was attended by Bank staff, forty African NGOs, four international NGOs, several African academics, and a representative from the host government.

### Partnership for Project Success

A significant characteristic of the 1990s has been the increasing divergence among African countries in terms of economic performance, completed political and structural reforms, global integration, and domestic capacity for economic management. At the same time, it has become increasingly apparent that the policy-based lending instrument needed modification if it were to continue to be a potent instrument for structural change and meet the emerging needs of such a diverse group of countries. Several innovations were introduced during the year, including the use of standard as well as of floating tranches on loans to minimize resource disruptions and accommodate uncertainties associated with difficult institutional reforms; greater reliance on in-country knowledge at the farm and firm level; a more intensive study of the potential effects of economic reforms on various groups, especially the poor and women; and closer linkages between support for structural reforms and the total package of lending and nonlending assistance given to a country. Clearly, mainstreaming such innovations involves much closer and continuous interaction between African countries and donors, and among the different stakeholders in civil society within the African countries themselves.

Performance of projects in the Bank's Africa portfolio continues to improve. The proportion of problem projects, based on the development-objectives rating, eased from 17 percent in fiscal 1993 to 16 percent in fiscal 1995. On the basis of the implementation-progress rating, the proportion of problem projects fell from 24 percent to 18 percent over the same period. These improvements reflect the Bank's proactive

management of its portfolio in the region, close collaboration with borrowing countries in project implementation, and efforts by the various implementing agencies concerned. Many of the problems of poorly performing projects stem from a lack of government ownership or their low priority in the current policy framework. Projects in the portfolio are being restructured to make them more consistent with the current country and sector priorities, and those elements no longer considered to be of priority are being eliminated. Project restructuring is especially common in the social sectors and in Nigeria, in particular. In addition, a review of completed operations in the agriculture sector has helped identify lessons from experience that are expected to lead to improved project outcomes. The review concluded, among other things, that while sound macroeconomic framework, political stability, and governmental commitment are important, complex project design that does not take into account weaknesses in local capacity can severely affect the results; beneficiary participation during project preparation and implementation is crucial for project success; and pilot projects can be helpful by offering opportunities to minimize implementation problems and to test innovative approaches.

### TABLE 4-2. WORLD BANK COMMITMENTS, DISBURSEMENTS, AND NET TRANSFERS IN AFRICA, 1991–96

*(millions of US dollars; fiscal years)*

| Item | Côte d'Ivoire start 1996 | 1996 | 1991–96 | Ghana start 1996 | 1996 | 1991–96 | Kenya start 1996 | 1996 | 1991–96 | Total region start 1996 | 1996 | 1991–96 |
|---|---|---|---|---|---|---|---|---|---|---|---|---|
| Undisbursed commitments | 284 | | | 1,158 | | | 459 | | | 11,659 | | |
| Commitments | | 464 | 1,634 | | 276 | 1,621 | | 314 | 1,184 | | 2,740 | 18,017 |
| Gross disbursements | | 251 | 1,368 | | 261 | 1,244 | | 169 | 1,027 | | 2,914 | 16,923 |
| Repayments | | 180 | 1,051 | | 23 | 106 | | 105 | 637 | | 1,120 | 6,247 |
| Net disbursements | | 71 | 316 | | 238 | 1,138 | | 64 | 390 | | 1,794 | 10,676 |
| Interest and charges | | 114 | 900 | | 22 | 119 | | 54 | 401 | | 756 | 5,073 |
| Net transfer | | -43 | -584 | | 216 | 1,019 | | 10 | -11 | | 1038 | 5,603 |

NOTE: *Disbursements from the IDA Special Fund are included. The countries shown in the table are those with the largest borrowings of Bank funds during fiscal 1995–96. Details may not add to totals because of rounding.*
— *Zero.*

New approaches adopted in recent years are expected to contribute to the quality-at-entry of new projects and to project success. Leading the way is the greater emphasis that is being placed on operations patterned on the SIP approach, whose main characteristics are coherent sector policy; sectorwide or subsectorwide scope; preparation by local stakeholders; efficient coordination of all major donors in the sector, including common implementation arrangements; and minimal resort to long-term technical assistance. Fifteen SIP operations were approved in fiscal 1996, compared with five in the previous year.

**Partnership for Capacity Building**

Capacity—of human resources as well as of institutions—permits countries to achieve (as well as define) their development goals. For that reason, capacity has long received deserved attention; however, efforts in Africa, where the challenge is the greatest, have been generally ineffective. The need to correct this situation urgently, comprehensively, and effectively was put on the agenda as never before during the past year—this time on the initiative of the African countries themselves. Through their governors in attendance at the annual meetings of the two Bretton Woods institutions, African countries asked the president of the World Bank to work with them to take concrete steps toward improving capacity in Africa.

Toward that objective, the executive directors for African countries and Bank staff organized a series of consultations, including workshops in Abidjan, Addis Ababa, Johannesburg, Libreville, and Nairobi, to gain a better understanding of the problems and concerns (including the reasons for past successes and failures), and to explore innovative approaches and pragmatic solutions in the realm of capacity building. Participants were drawn from a wide range of experience and expertise: government, private sector, academia, "think tanks," professional associations, and NGOs. Participants were asked to comment, for example, on ways to form better partnerships with the World Bank and donors to build African capacity. In parallel, a nine-member high-level group, of whom six are from

Africa, was brought together to review the impact of World Bank policies and operations on capacity building and utilization. Also, in May 1996, a workshop was held in Mauritius, bringing together Africans and East Asians to explore the role of capacity building in the East Asian "miracle" and its implications for Africa.

The work at all three levels (consultations, evaluation by the high-level group of the Bank's role, national assessments) is well advanced. While the conclusions are not apparent yet, they are likely to reflect the ideas that have emerged to date:

• capacity building is central to sustainable development in Africa;

• African countries must grasp the initiative in building capacity and take steps to ensure its optimal utilization;

• a new partnership for capacity building, leading to changes in the way both donors and borrowers do business, is essential. If donors change but countries do not or if African countries change but donors do not, both will fail in their capacity-building task; and

• The World Bank can be a leader in supporting African efforts to build capacity by making capacity building a central objective of all its development activities.

**Partnership for Consensus Building and Regional Cooperation**

The Global Coalition for Africa, which was launched following the Maastricht Conference on Africa in 1990, has been a key forum for building consensus on development issues among African countries and their external partners and in generating political validation at the highest levels in Africa on economic reform and governance measures. A key element of the consensus is that regional cooperation/integration should be accelerated while integrating the African countries into the global economy. The Second Maastricht Conference, held in November 1995, agreed that the GCA should continue its catalytic role in focusing attention on critical issues and development priorities in

# TABLE 4-3. PROJECTS APPROVED DURING FISCAL YEAR 1996, AFRICA

| Country/project name | Date of Approval | Maturities | Principal amount (millions) SDR | US$ |
|---|---|---|---|---|
| **Angola** | | | | |
| Social Action Project | December 21, 1995 | 2006/2035 | 16.1 | 24.00 |
| **Cameroon** | | | | |
| Privatization and Private Sector Technical Assistance Project | June 13, 1996 | 2006/2036 | 8.9 | 12.60 |
| Transport Sector Project | May 30, 1996 | 2006/2036 | 41.7 | 60.70 |
| Second Structural Adjustment Credit (IDA reflows) | April 2, 1996 | 2006/2035 | 20.4 | 30.30 |
| Second Structural Adjustment Credit | February 8, 1996 | 2006/2035 | 100.7 | 150.00 |
| **Cape Verde** | | | | |
| Capacity Building Project for Private Sector Promotion | May 21, 1996 | 2006/2036 | 7.9 | 11.40 |
| **Chad** | | | | |
| Structural Adjustment Credit | February 15, 1996 | 2006/2036 | 20.2 | 30.00 |
| Capacity Building for Economic Management Project | February 15, 1996 | 2006/2036 | 6.4 | 9.50 |
| **Congo** | | | | |
| Privatization and Capacity Building Project | September 5, 1995 | 2005/2035 | 5.8 | 9.00 |
| **Côte d'Ivoire** | | | | |
| Integrated Health Services Development Project | June 27, 1996 | 2006/2036 | 27.7 | 40.00 |
| Private Sector Development Adjustment Credit | April 11, 1996 | 2006/2036 | 123.9 | 180.00 |
| Railway Rehabilitation Project | November 28, 1995 | 2006/2035 | 13.5 | 20.00 |
| Agricultural Sector Adjustment Credit | September 26, 1995 | 2006/2035 | 95.8 | 150.00 |
| Agricultural Sector Adjustment Credit (IDA reflows) | December 12, 1995 | 2006/2035 | 49.1 | 73.60 |
| **Eritrea** | | | | |
| Community Development Fund Project | February 29, 1996 | 2006/2036 | 11.8 | 17.50 |
| **Ethiopia** | | | | |
| Social Rehabilitation and Development Fund Project | April 9, 1996 | 2006/2036 | 80.8 | 120.00 |
| Water Supply Development and Rehabilitation Project | April 9, 1996 | 2006/2036 | 24.0 | 35.73 |
| **Ghana** | | | | |
| Basic Education Sector Project | June 18, 1996 | 2006/2036 | 34.7 | 50.00 |
| Public Enterprise and Privatization Technical Assistance Project | June 11, 1996 | 2006/2036 | 18.2 | 26.45 |
| Highway Sector Investment Program | May 14, 1996 | 2006/2036 | 67.8 | 100.00 |
| Urban Environmental Sanitation Project | March 26, 1996 | 2006/2036 | 47.8 | 71.00 |
| Private Sector Adjustment Credit (IDA reflows) | December 12, 1995 | 2005/2035 | 3.2 | 4.80 |
| Non-Bank Financial Institutions Assistance Project | December 5, 1995 | 2005/2035 | 16.0 | 23.90 |
| **Guinea** | | | | |
| Mining Sector Investment Promotion Project | June 4, 1996 | 2006/2036 | 8.3 | 12.20 |
| National Agricultural Services Project | April 2, 1996 | 2006/2035 | 23.6 | 35.00 |
| Higher Education Management Support Project | November 28, 1995 | 2006/2035 | 4.5 | 6.60 |
| **Kenya** | | | | |
| Structural Adjustment Credit | June 18, 1996 | 2006/2036 | 61.8 | 90.00 |
| Structural Adjustment Credit (IDA reflows) | June 18, 1996 | 2006/2036 | 24.5 | 36.80 |
| Nairobi-Mombasa Road Rehabilitation Loan | January 30, 1996 | 2006/2035 | 34.0 | 50.00 |
| Urban Transport Infrastructure | January 30, 1996 | 2006/2035 | 77.1 | 115.00 |
| Arid Lands Resource Management Project | December 14, 1995 | 2006/2035 | 14.8 | 22.00 |
| **Lesotho** | | | | |
| Road Rehabilitation and Maintenance Project | May 9, 1996 | 2006/2036 | 26.8 | 40.00 |
| **Madagascar** | | | | |
| Energy Sector Development Project | April 16, 1996 | 2006/2035 | 31.8 | 46.00 |
| Social Fund II Project | September 14, 1995 | 2006/2035 | 25.5 | 40.00 |

| Country/project name | Date of Approval | Maturities | Principal amount (millions) | |
| --- | --- | --- | --- | --- |
| | | | SDR | US$ |
| **Malawi** | | | | |
| Social Action Fund Project | May 9, 1996 | 2006/2036 | 38.0 | 56.00 |
| Fiscal Restructuring and Deregulation Program | April 30, 1996 | 2006/2036 | 70.3 | 102.00 |
| Fiscal Restructuring and Deregulation Program (IDA reflows) | April 30, 1996 | 2006/2036 | 2.9 | 4.40 |
| Primary Education Project | January 25, 1996 | 2006/2035 | 15.1 | 22.50 |
| **Mali** | | | | |
| Economic Management Credit | June 27, 1996 | 2006/2036 | 41.6 | 60.00 |
| Selingue Power Rehabilitation Project | April 25, 1996 | 2006/2036 | 18.5 | 27.30 |
| Vocational Education and Training Consolidation Project | March 14, 1996 | 2006/2036 | 9.0 | 13.40 |
| **Mauritania** | | | | |
| Public Resource Management Project | June 20, 1996 | 2006/2036 | 13.9 | 20.00 |
| Urban Infrastructure and Pilot Decentralization Project | March 26, 1996 | 2006/2035 | 9.7 | 14.00 |
| Private Sector Development Credit (IDA reflows) | December 12, 1995 | 2005/2035 | 0.5 | 0.80 |
| **Mozambique** | | | | |
| Health Sector Recovery Program | November 30, 1995 | 2006/2035 | 66.3 | 98.70 |
| **Niger** | | | | |
| Natural Resources Management Project | December 14, 1995 | 2006/2035 | 18.0 | 26.70 |
| **Senegal** | | | | |
| Higher Education Project | June 4, 1996 | 2006/2036 | 18.4 | 26.50 |
| Pilot Female Literacy Project | June 4, 1996 | 2006/2036 | 8.7 | 12.60 |
| Agricultural Sector Adjustment Credit (IDA reflows) | December 12, 1995 | 2005/2035 | 1.8 | 2.80 |
| **Sierra Leone** | | | | |
| Transport Sector Project | June 27, 1996 | 2006/2036 | 24.3 | 35.00 |
| Integrated Health Sector Investment Project | March 14, 1996 | 2006/2035 | 13.6 | 20.00 |
| Structural Adjustment Credit (IDA reflows) | December 12, 1995 | 2004/2033 | 0.2 | 0.30 |
| **Tanzania** | | | | |
| Urban Sector Rehabilitation Project | May 23, 1996 | 2006/2036 | 72.3 | 105.00 |
| Financial Institutions Development Project | August 3, 1995 | 2005/2035 | 7.5 | 10.90 |
| **Togo** | | | | |
| Economic Recovery and Adjustment Credit | April 25, 1996 | 2006/2035 | 32.2 | 50.00 |
| **Uganda** | | | | |
| Agricultural Sector Management Project | April 16, 1996 | 2006/2036 | 12.1 | 17.90 |
| Private Sector Competitiveness Project | December 14, 1995 | 2006/2035 | 8.3 | 12.30 |
| Environmental Management Capacity Building Project | September 14, 1995 | 2006/2035 | 7.5 | 11.80 |
| **Zambia** | | | | |
| Economic Recovery and Investment Promotion Technical Assistance | June 4, 1996 | 2006/2036 | 16.0 | 23.00 |
| Economic Recovery and Investment Promotion Credit (IDA reflows) | December 12, 1995 | 2005/2035 | 8.0 | 12.10 |
| Economic Recovery and Investment Promotion Credit | July 11, 1995 | 2005/2035 | 90.0 | 140.00 |
| **Zimbabwe** | | | | |
| Enterprise Development Project | April 25, 1996 | 2006/2036 | 47.5 | 70.00 |
| Total | | | 1,831.20 | 2,740.10 |

n.a. = not applicable (IBRD loan).

## BOX 4-1. NEW PARTNERSHIP FOR WATER MANAGEMENT

*Recent events in sub-Saharan Africa demonstrate the strategic importance that water plays in the region's food production, health, and economic development. In 1995, drought in Southern and Eastern Africa, as well as localized droughts in the Sahel, led to significant drops in crop production and the risk of price hikes and malnutrition. Increased water pollution and lack of accessibility to clean water and sanitation services throughout the region are having a direct impact on human health. At the same time, water management is an issue of geopolitical importance and hence requires close cooperation among riparian countries. This appreciation has led the Nile Basin states[1] to create a forum for continuous dialogue, while in 1995, the states of the Southern African Development Community (SADC)[2] signed a Protocol calling for the equitable use and management of shared river basins.*

*In an effort to shed some light on this increasingly important area, the Bank put out a report entitled "African Water Resources: Challenges and Opportunities for Sustainable Development." The strategy document provides a counterpoint to the old supply-driven approach in the sector that focused on a single stakeholder (the public sector). The strategy calls upon donors to conduct business in new ways based on (a) the principle that water-resources management needs to be country-driven, with Africans taking the lead in integrated, multisectoral approaches in the development and implementation of national water strategies that involve all stakeholders and (b) a new emphasis on partnership among donors and countries.*

*The strategy builds on these two points by identifying five development priorities: enhanced drinking water and sanitation service coverage, with priority for the poor; food security through irrigation and collection of rainfall; water quality and human health; protection of watersheds and wetlands; and intercountry river-basin cooperation. It also calls for more emphasis on rural and peri-urban areas, stake-holder participation, privatization of water utilities (including small-scale irrigation and suppliers of water), and demand-management approaches. The strategy also suggests that the international community needs to develop new instruments to promote international cooperation and river-basin management, including, among other things, multicountry lending programs and projects within countries that create an even playing field between coriparian states.*

*The concept of partnership shaped the way in which the strategy itself was prepared. A group of senior advisers from nine African countries was brought together by the Bank, in consultation with other donors, in 1994 to form the African Advisory Group (AAG). The AAG reviewed working drafts of the strategy in 1994 and 1995, gave advice, and provided a crucial Africa voice in the process. Donor agencies, including the Food and Agriculture Organization of the U.N., the United Nations Environment Programme, the United Nations Educational, Scientific, and Cultural Organisation, the International Center for Research in Agroforestry, the United Kingdom's Overseas Development Administration, and the World Bank, authored building-block papers integral to the strategy. The strategy was presented at two stakeholder workshops held in Africa in early 1996 attended by 235 participants from forty-one countries. One immediate result of the workshops was the agreement to form a Pan-African Partnership, to be led initially by the AAG, for fostering intercountry dialogue; sharing knowledge, experience, and best practices; developing consensus on key issues and actions; and reviewing progress on agreed action plans.*

*1. Burundi, Egypt, Ethiopia, Eritrea, Kenya, Rwanda, Sudan, Tanzania, Uganda, and Zaire.*
*2. The members of SADC, the former Southern African Development Coordination Conference (SADCC), are Angola, Botswana, Lesotho, Malawi, Mozambique, South Africa, Swaziland, Tanzania, Zambia, and Zimbabwe.*

Africa. The Bank has supported the GCA from its inception and remains committed to providing technical and financial support to the coalition, together with other interested partners and donor countries.

In line with the consensus on the importance of regional cooperation in the development process, the Bank supports a new vision of regional integration in Africa based on the promotion of factor mobility among countries, while, in parallel, integrating African countries into the world economy. Together with the International Monetary Fund, the European Union, and other interested institutions and donors, the Bank is supporting efforts by groups of African countries based on such a vision of integration. These include the Cross-Border Initiative to facilitate private investment, trade, and payments in Eastern and Southern Africa and in the Indian ocean countries; the East African Cooperation among Kenya, Tanzania, and Uganda; the West African Economic and Monetary Union; and the Central African Monetary Union. The countries participating in these arrangements are taking steps to remove the barriers to cross-border flows of goods, factors, and people. The Bank supports these efforts through technical and policy advice, institution building, and financing in the context of country-specific assistance programs.

### Partnership Is Necessity, Not Optional: The Case of Water Management

The view that partnership is a necessity rather than an option applies to nearly all areas in Africa, given the constraint on resources—domestic and external—and the distance that needs to be covered to achieve significant sustainable improvement in well-being. Both these factors put a premium on using available resources (human and financial, internal and external) as judiciously and effectively as possible through partnership. The management of water resources epitomizes the need to view partnership as a necessity, not an option *(see Box 4-1)*. In Africa, fifty-four rivers or lakes are shared by more than one country, and major drainage basins and aquifers are each shared by seven or more countries. Recent developments have demonstrated anew the vulnerability of Africa's food production, health, and economic development to the availability of water.

East Asia and the Pacific is a region of spectacular development success and huge development challenges. In 1995, the region outperformed other developing regions again and posted the most rapid growth rate in the world: 9.2 percent, up slightly from 8.9 percent in 1994. Growth in gross domestic product (GDP) accelerated in most countries: The Republic of Korea, Malaysia, and Vietnam were in the 9 percent range, while the economies of Indonesia and Thailand grew from between 7 percent and 8 percent. The Philippines recorded a satisfying increase in its growth rate to 4.8 percent, while Mongolia's economy advanced by 6 percent. China cooled an overheated economy without stalling growth: Inflation declined from 22 percent in 1994 to 15 percent, and growth eased from 12 percent to 10 percent. Growth in Fiji also eased, down from 4.5 percent in 1994 to 2.5 percent. Papua New Guinea was the only country in the region that experienced economic decline (4.7 percent).

The region is faced with many development challenges as it moves toward the Twenty-first Century. It has immense diversity and contains the world's largest and smallest developing countries, landlocked states and both large and small island countries, some of the most prosperous nations, and some of the poorest. Despite huge successes, it is still, on average, a low-income region with an estimated per capita gross national product of $940. Eighty percent of its people, about 1.3 billion, live in low-income countries, almost entirely accounted for by the six economies in transition (Cambodia, China, the Lao People's Democratic Republic, Mongolia, Myanmar, and Vietnam). Reducing poverty and developing the institutions for a market economy are the primary challenges facing these countries. Throughout the region, rapid growth and urbanization are placing heavy pressures on infrastructure, and environmental degradation threatens to undermine the hard-fought gains made to date. Under these circumstances, the Bank's role in East Asia has become increasingly diverse, complex, and challenging.

## The Record

Market-based East Asian economies have been exemplars of fast and relatively equitable growth that leads to rapid reduction in poverty; the mixed economies of China and Vietnam have experienced rapid poverty reduction early in their transitions. Although the number of people who live on incomes below $1 a day has declined from 413 million in 1990 to 392 million in 1993, equivalent to a quarter of the population in East Asia, that number nevertheless represents about 34 percent of the poor in all developing countries (4 percent if China's total number of poor are excluded). Social indicators have improved remarkably. The infant mortality rate (per 1,000 live births) has declined from an already low 44 in 1987 to 35 in 1993, compared with 54 in all developing countries. Life expectancy has risen from 67 to 68 years in the same period, compared with 64 years for all developing countries. Adult illiteracy has been reduced from 29 percent in 1985 to 24 percent in 1990, and given the current secondary enrollment rate of 52 percent (46 percent for girls), the region is likely to achieve the Bankwide objective—set by Bank President James Wolfensohn at the United Nations Conference on Women in Beijing—of providing access to secondary education to 60 percent of children by 2010.

East Asian countries have been successful in integrating with the world market for both capital and goods. Since 1990, the region has become the predominant destination of private capital flows. In 1995 alone, developing countries in the region received an estimated $108 billion in foreign capital flows, of which $98 billion was from private sources, including $54 billion in direct investment. The surge in foreign capital flows was induced by rapid economic growth, sound economic fundamentals, and a high level of

## TABLE 4-4. LENDING TO BORROWERS IN EAST ASIA AND PACIFIC, BY SECTOR, 1987–96

*(millions of US dollars; fiscal years)*

| Sector | Annual average, 1987–91 | 1992 | 1993 | 1994 | 1995 | 1996 |
|---|---|---|---|---|---|---|
| Agriculture | 827.8 | 826.7 | 1,089.3 | 1,735.4 | 891.1 | 865.6 |
| Education | 308.0 | 474.1 | 478.9 | 436.6 | 526.5 | 437.9 |
| Electric power and other energy | 610.1 | 1,745.9 | 760.0 | 1,048.5 | 1,383.0 | 1,683.0 |
| Environment | — | 125.0 | 300.0 | 216.5 | 110.0 | 150.0 |
| Finance | 373.7 | — | 457.0 | 100.0 | — | 49.0 |
| Industry | 287.5 | 82.7 | — | — | 195.0 | 271.0 |
| Mining/Other extractive | — | — | — | — | — | 35.0 |
| Multisector | 423.0 | 70.0 | 200.0 | 82.7 | 167.0 | 130.0 |
| Oil and gas | 29.8 | 100.0 | 225.0 | 266.0 | 245.0 | — |
| Population, health, and nutrition | 65.9 | 129.6 | 200.4 | 160.0 | 242.2 | 296.0 |
| Public sector management | 18.5 | 17.0 | 173.0 | — | 88.0 | — |
| Social sector | — | — | — | 9.7 | — | 40.0 |
| Telecommunications/Informatics | 83.8 | 375.0 | 134.0 | 250.0 | 325.0 | — |
| Transportation | 573.6 | 1,182.5 | 1,132.2 | 1,380.0 | 960.0 | 916.9 |
| Urban development | 285.1 | 168.0 | 110.0 | 349.0 | 486.0 | 542.7 |
| Water supply and sanitation | 105.4 | 150.0 | 310.0 | — | 75.0 | 57.0 |
| Total | 3,992.2 | 5,446.5 | 5,569.8 | 6,034.4 | 5,693.8 | 5,420.1 |
| Of which: IBRD | 3,263.5 | 4,386.9 | 4,404.8 | 4,623.8 | 4,592.6 | 4,252.2 |
| IDA | 728.6 | 1,059.6 | 1,165.0 | 1,410.6 | 1,101.2 | 1,167.9 |
| Number of operations | 37 | 45 | 45 | 43 | 42 | 46 |

NOTE: Details may not add to totals because of rounding.
— Zero.

integration with the world market. East Asians are large investors in both their own economies and in their neighbors: Domestic savings rates have been 35 percent or higher of GDP, and more than 70 percent of foreign direct investment is from within the region. Furthermore, these countries have been able to use the foreign capital inflows more effectively than other developing regions, thereby contributing to rapid technological upgrading. Foreign direct investment has also wrought structural changes by increasing manufacturing output as a share of GDP and exports; for example, in China, ex-ports of foreign-invested enterprises (mostly joint ventures) account for nearly 40 percent of all exports.

The past year witnessed further rapid growth in trade throughout the region. Exports and imports grew at annual rates of 21 percent and 18 percent, respectively. East Asian developing countries currently account for over one third of all developing country trade and just under 10 percent of total world trade. It is projected that these countries will account for over one third of all incremental trade between 1992 and

sector (with Vietnam phasing in its liberalization over a somewhat longer period). APEC is becoming a unique forum of both developing and industrial countries with implications encompassing cooperation in areas that go far beyond trade issues, including financial flows, human resources, and the environment.[2]

Continued strong commitment to international integration; high levels of saving and investment; emphasis on health, education, and human capital development; plus a stable macroeconomic environment have enabled East Asian countries to propel themselves successfully on a rapid poverty-reducing growth path. Its rapid growth will continue to effect the global economy and serve as an important source of stability for the rest of the world.

**Challenges Ahead**

Several global and regional economic and social processes underlie the present situation and future outlook for East Asia and Pacific. The processes include:

• rising integration of international markets with growing trade, capital flows, and international migration;

• the transition by several countries from central planning to market-based economies and its effect on two thirds of the region's population who are entering the international market via trade integration;

• the transition from predominantly rural to predominantly urban societies. In the early 1990s, only about 500 million East Asians lived in towns. By 2020 this figure will have grown to about 1.5 billion. By then, seven East Asian cities (outside Japan) are expected to have populations in excess of 10 million. As a result, infrastructure requirements for the region are expected to surge to some $200 billion a year by 2000 (from $70 billion in 1992);

• the move by 30 percent of the work force from informal to formal sectors by the year

2002, and their share in world trade is likely to continue to expand. The determination of these countries to liberalize their trade was reconfirmed by (nonbinding) commitments undertaken at the Asia Pacific Economic Cooperation (APEC) meeting in Tokyo in November 1995. China announced plans to cut tariffs from an average of 36 percent to 23 percent during 1996. The seven members of the Association of Southeast Asian Nations (ASEAN)[1] agreed to shorten the timeframe for tariff cuts under the ASEAN Free Trade Agreement (AFTA) to reduce tariffs to the 0 percent-to-5 percent range by the end of 2002 (instead of 2007) and to expand the coverage to include the agriculture

1. Brunei, Indonesia, Malaysia, the Philippines, Singapore, Thailand, and Vietnam.

2. APEC membership includes Australia, Brunei, Canada, Chile, China, Hong Kong, Indonesia, Japan, Republic of Korea, Malaysia, Mexico, New Zealand, Papua New Guinea, the Philippines, Singapore, Thailand, the United States of America, and Taiwan, China.

2020 and increased demand for skilled workers brought about by the structural changes that have occurred as countries move from agricultural to manufacturing-based economies;

• the rapid aging of the population, the result of increased life expectancy and a rapid decline in total fertility.[3] By 2020, the percentage of the old in the Chinese population, for example, will be equal of that in most industrial countries today. Korea's population is aging even faster. This regional trend will not only put pressure on national social security systems but, in addition, will have profound implications for long-term economic growth in East Asian countries; and

• environmental degradation, as deforestation has been more rapid than in any other region, and problems related to water availability and air and water pollution are severe.

All countries are facing policy and institutional challenges even though most have been successful in implementing the fundamentals of development policy. Future challenges are likely to be more complex and difficult. The character of the challenges varies greatly between the transition and market economies, and among the low-, middle-, and high-income countries. Yet because they also have many common issues, a common agenda within the region is emerging, of which the key ingredients are: reducing poverty and achieving growth with equity; meeting growing infrastructure needs; developing the institutions for market economies; providing social insurance; managing structural change and upgrading labor; and dealing with environmental problems.

The challenges faced by the Pacific island economies differ in many important respects from most of East Asia. While life is relatively safe and secure, economic growth has been slow. Unless the island economies achieve moderate sustainable economic growth, improvements in the quality of life may not be possible. The island economies face major constraints to development, such as long distances to large external markets, a narrow resource and production base, high unit costs of infrastructure, limitations in the skilled work force, and vulnerability to external shocks and natural disasters. To build a more resilient base, these countries will need to diversify their economic base and obtain higher return for their natural capital, principally forest and marine resources.

There are a number of ways in which the Bank can make a significant contribution in helping the Pacific Islands build a more resilient economic base and move toward a higher and more sustainable growth path. Although support is tailored to the specific needs of each economy, it may include: high-level policy advice; economic and sector analyses; technical assistance in specific areas in which the Bank has a comparative advantage; strengthening partnerships with key stakeholders, including NGOs; and selected lending activities in areas where the Bank can provide positive support to national development strategies.

## The Bank's Strategy and Activities

The Bank's activities in the region have been directed by this emerging development agenda. There has been a shift in its lending activities from the region's middle-income countries to the low-income Indochinese countries. Total commitments in fiscal 1996 were $5.4 billion, while gross disbursements and net disbursements were $4.1 billion and $1.3 billion, respectively. Net transfers, taking account of interest as well as of principal repayment, were a negative $925 million (see table 4-5). Lending to China, a "blend" country, accounted for 55 percent of the total. Thirteen percent of the lending volume was to low-income, IDA-only countries (Cambodia, Lao PDR, Mongolia, and Vietnam), compared with 6 percent in the period fiscal 1993–95. Net transfers to China and the three Indochinese nations—Cambodia, Lao PDR, and Vietnam—amounted to almost $1.4 billion, while the mature borrowers—Korea (which "graduated" from IBRD lending in fiscal 1995), Malaysia, and Thailand—became net repayers as their share of new lending from the Bank either stabilized or declined. These borrowers, however, continue to make use of the Bank for special studies and projects in innovative areas.

---

3. The population in developing East Asian countries is aging at a relatively faster pace than did the population in today's industrial countries. In thirty-four years, for example, China will double its share of elderly in the population (from 9 percent to 18 pecent), a process that took place over a span of 100 years in Belgium.

TABLE 4-5. WORLD BANK COMMITMENTS, DISBURSEMENTS, AND NET TRANSFERS IN EAST ASIA AND PACIFIC, 1991–96

*(millions of US dollars; fiscal years)*

| Item | China start 1996 | China 1996 | China 1991–96 | Indonesia start 1996 | Indonesia 1996 | Indonesia 1991–96 | Vietnam start 1996 | Vietnam 1996 | Vietnam 1991–96 | Total region start 1996 | Total region 1996 | Total region 1991–96 |
|---|---|---|---|---|---|---|---|---|---|---|---|---|
| Undisbursed commitments | 9,831 | | | 4,984 | | | 625 | | | 19,172 | | |
| Commitments | | 2,970 | 16,317 | | 992 | 7,991 | | 502 | 1,242 | | 5,420 | 32,728 |
| Gross disbursements | | 2,219 | 10,419 | | 959 | 6,742 | | 35 | 201 | | 4,136 | 23,932 |
| Repayments | | 364 | 1,616 | | 1,213 | 5,330 | | 1 | 4 | | 2,859 | 15,089 |
| Net disbursements | | 1,855 | 8,803 | | -254 | 1,412 | | 35 | 198 | | 1,277 | 8,843 |
| Interest and charges | | 534 | 2,178 | | 901 | 5,182 | | 2 | 5 | | 2,202 | 12,252 |
| Net transfer | | 1,321 | 6,625 | | -1,155 | -3,770 | | 33 | 193 | | -925 | -3,409 |

NOTE: *Disbursements from the IDA Special Fund are included. The countries shown in the table are those with the largest borrowings of Bank funds during fiscal 1995–96. Details may not add to totals because of rounding.*

Nonlending services are becoming broader based, since they cover not only middle- and low-income countries but also activities in high-income countries. For example, the regional study, *East Asia's Trade and Investment*, was widely used at the 1994 APEC meeting, and policy recommendations for a concerted unilateral trade liberalization were accepted.[4]

*Reducing poverty* remains a central priority of the Bank's activities in East Asia. While much lending has strong indirect effects on poverty reduction, 18 percent of total new commitments in fiscal 1996 was included in the Program of Targeted Interventions. The Bank's poverty-reduction strategy varies across countries. In low-income countries, projects aim at generating effective rural development and delivering social services to the poor. For example, a poverty-reduction project approved during the past year in China facilitated "market-friendly" income generation and labor mobility so that higher-income opportunities could be generated for the rural poor. Two health projects in Vietnam and a disease-prevention project in China are helping to provide basic health care to vulnerable groups such as poor women and their children. Rural finance and land-titling projects in Vietnam and Lao PDR, respectively, are helping to strengthen institutions that support the poor and other vulnerable groups. In several countries, the need is to focus on the special difficulties of groups at risk of being left out of the development process due to geographic isolation, ethnicity, or lack of skills. In the Population and Family Health Project in Vietnam, for example, a model outreach system will be tested to supplement commune health-center (the country's lowest-level health facility) services in remote mountainous areas where most disadvantaged ethnic minority populations live. Village-based health posts will be established in remote mountainous areas in the fifteen provinces covered by the project and then extended to cover all such areas in the provinces if evaluated as being successful. The Bank continued to monitor and provide policy advice by conducting poverty assessments in Lao PDR, Mongolia, and the Philippines, and through dissemination of the Vietnam poverty assessment in provincial participatory workshops. Other recently completed studies—on health, education, and rural development—also included a poverty-reduction component. A regional paper on poverty is currently under preparation, with publication targeted for late in calendar year 1996.

*Meeting the infrastructure needs* of the region has become the most significant component of

4. World Bank. 1994. *East Asia's Trade and Investment: Regional and Global Gains from Liberalization.* Development in Practice Series. Washington, D.C.

# TABLE 4-6. PROJECTS APPROVED DURING FISCAL YEAR 1996, EAST ASIA AND PACIFIC

| Country/project name | Date of Approval | Maturities | Principal amount (millions) SDR | US$ |
|---|---|---|---|---|
| **Cambodia** | | | | |
| Economic Rehabilitation Credit | September 28, 1995 | 2005/2035 | 25.40 | 40.00 |
| Phnom Penh Power Rehabilitation Project | September 28, 1995 | 2006/2035 | 25.80 | 40.00 |
| **China** | | | | |
| Yunnan Environment Project[a] | June 25, 1996 | 2006/2031 | 17.40 | 25.00 |
| Yunnan Environment Project[a] | June 25, 1996 | 2002/2016 | n.a. | 125.00 |
| Seed Sector Commercialization Project[a] | June 18, 1996 | 2001/2016 | n.a. | 80.00 |
| Seed Sector Commercialization Project[a] | June 18, 1996 | 2006/2031 | 13.80 | 20.00 |
| Chongqing Industrial Pollution Control Reform Project | June 18, 1996 | 2002/2016 | n.a. | 170.00 |
| Gansu Hexi Corridor Project[a] | May 30, 1996 | 2006/2031 | 61.80 | 90.00 |
| Gansu Hexi Corridor Project[a] | May 30, 1996 | 2002/2016 | n.a. | 60.00 |
| Second Henan Provincial Highway Project | May 30, 1996 | 2002/2016 | n.a. | 210.00 |
| Animal Feed Project | April 16, 1996 | 2001/2016 | n.a. | 150.00 |
| Shanxi Poverty Alleviation Project | March 26, 1996 | 2006/2031 | 67.30 | 100.00 |
| Second Shaanxi Provincial Highways Project | March 21, 1996 | 2001/2016 | | 210.00 |
| Second Shanghai Sewerage Project | March 21, 1996 | 2001/2016 | | 250.00 |
| Third Basic Education Project | March 21, 1996 | 2006/2031 | 67.30 | 100.00 |
| Henan (Qinbei) Thermal Power Project | February 27, 1996 | 2001/2016 | n.a. | 440.00 |
| Labor Market Development Project[a] | December 19, 1995 | 2006/2030 | 13.40 | 20.00 |
| Labor Market Development Project[a] | December 19, 1995 | 2001/2016 | n.a. | 10.00 |
| Hubei Urban Environmental Project[a] | December 19, 1995 | 2006/2030 | 16.80 | 25.00 |
| Hubei Urban Environmental Project[a] | December 19, 1995 | 2001/2016 | n.a. | 125.00 |
| Disease Prevention Project | December 12, 1995 | 2006/2030 | 67.00 | 100.00 |
| Ertan II Hydroelectric Project | August 22, 1995 | 2001/2015 | n.a. | 400.00 |
| Shanghai-Zhejiang Highway Project | August 1, 1995 | 2001/2015 | n.a. | 260.00 |
| **Indonesia** | | | | |
| Strategic Urban Roads Infrastructure Project | June 25, 1996 | 2000/2012 | n.a. | 86.90 |
| East Java and East Nusa Tenggara Junior Secondary Education Project | June 18, 1996 | 2002/2016 | n.a. | 99.00 |
| Higher Education Support Project-Development of Undergraduate Education | June 18, 1996 | 2002/2016 | n.a. | 65.00 |
| Social Sector Strategy and Capacity Building Project | June 4, 1996 | 2002/2016 | n.a. | 20.00 |
| Second East Java Urban Development Project | May 16, 1996 | 2002/2016 | n.a. | 142.70 |
| Sulawesi Agricultural Area Development Project | April 30, 1996 | 2002/2016 | n.a. | 26.80 |
| Kerinci-Seblat Integrated Conservation and Development Project | April 30, 1996 | 2002/2016 | n.a. | 19.10 |
| Nusa Tenggara Agricultural Area Development Project | March 5, 1996 | 2001/2016 | n.a. | 27.00 |
| HIV, AIDS and STDs Prevention and Management Project | February 27, 1996 | 2000/2011 | n.a. | 24.80 |
| Second Power Transmission and Distribution Project | February 20, 1996 | 2001/2016 | n.a. | 373.00 |
| Secondary School Teacher Development Project | February 20, 1996 | 2001/2016 | n.a. | 60.40 |
| Industrial Technology Development Project | December 21, 1995 | 2001/2016 | n.a. | 47.00 |
| **Lao People's Democratic Republic** | | | | |
| Land Titling Project | March 21, 1996 | 2006/2036 | 14.00 | 20.70 |
| Third Structural Adjustment Credit | February 22, 1996 | 2006/2035 | 26.90 | 40.00 |
| **Mongolia** | | | | |
| Coal Project | May 7, 1996 | 2006/2036 | 23.80 | 35.00 |
| Poverty Alleviation for Vulnerable Groups Project | July 6, 1995 | 2005/2035 | 6.50 | 10.00 |
| **Papua New Guinea** | | | | |
| Economic Recovery Program | August 29, 1995 | 2001/2015 | n.a. | 50.00 |
| **Philippines** | | | | |
| Manila Second Sewerage Project | May 21, 1996 | 2002/2016 | n.a. | 57.00 |
| Transmission Grid Reinforcement Project | April 4, 1996 | 2001/2016 | n.a. | 250.00 |
| Second Rural Finance Project | September 14, 1995 | 2001/2015 | n.a. | 150.00 |
| **Thailand** | | | | |
| Technical Education Project | June 25, 1996 | 2000/2011 | n.a. | 31.60 |
| Secondary Education Quality Improvement Project | June 25, 1996 | 2000/2011 | n.a. | 81.90 |
| Fifth Highway Sector Project | December 21, 1995 | 2001/2013 | n.a. | 150.00 |
| **Vietnam** | | | | |
| Rural Finance Project | May 7, 1996 | 2006/2036 | 82.70 | 122.00 |
| Power Development Project | February 20, 1996 | 2006/2035 | 121.00 | 180.00 |
| National Health Support Project | January 16, 1996 | 2006/2036 | 68.00 | 101.20 |
| Population and Family Health Project | January 16, 1996 | 2006/2036 | 33.60 | 50.00 |
| Payment System and Bank Modernization Project | November 21, 1995 | 2006/2035 | 32.90 | 49.00 |
| Total | | | 785.40 | 5,420.10 |

n.a. = not applicable (IBRD loan).

a. "Blend" loan/credit.

the Bank's lending program, accounting for about two fifths of the new commitments (by volume) in fiscal 1996. To cope with rapid modernization, rising urbanization, and international integration, it is estimated that developing East Asian countries will need to invest between $1.2 trillion and $1.5 trillion, or 7 percent of regional GDP, in transportation, power, telecommunications, and water and sanitation facilities in the next decade. Meeting this challenge will require large-scale private sector involvement for financing and efficiency. During the past year, in "Infrastructure Development in East Asia and Pacific: Towards a New Public-Private Partnership," the Bank laid out an overall agenda to enhance private sector participation. The Bank explored the possibility of establishing an Infrastructure Fund in the Philippines, developed a cofinancing strategy with the private sector, and undertook a large number of other activities at the project, sector, and country level to enhance private sector involvement. In addition, recent economic and sector work has included infrastructure studies for China, Indonesia, Mongolia, and Vietnam.

*Building market-oriented institutions* in the financial and enterprise sectors is another priority for East Asia. Well-functioning market economies require effective and increasingly sophisticated institutions. These include efficient financial systems, sound structure for corporate governance and industrial relations, and well-functioning governmental institutions. To this end, the Bank has recently conducted studies and provided policy advice on banking sector reforms, capital market development, and state-owned enterprise (SOE) reforms in China, Indonesia, the Philippines, and Vietnam. Two regional studies, *Managing Capital Flows in East Asia* and *The Emerging Asian Bond Market*, were widely disseminated in an international conference in Hong Kong in mid 1995.[5] The conference was a success on all fronts: Participation was greater than expected, both public and private sectors showed keen interest, and press coverage was comprehensive and highly favorable.

*Providing social insurance systems* is an emerging issue in the region. Urbanization, movement of labor into the formal sector, and aging populations create the need and demand for formal mechanisms of social insurance. The design of social insurance systems is critical because poorly designed systems can have large and potentially adverse fiscal and labor-market consequences. There are potentially significant benefits from sharing experience in developing sound systems of old age, health, unemployment, and disability insurance. To this end, the Bank has recently carried out formal and informal studies on pension reforms in China, Indonesia, and Thailand, and provided policy advice on the design of these systems based on its worldwide experience. A Health Care Financing study was conducted for China, and Education Cost and Financing studies were undertaken for the Philippines and Vietnam. Because development of social insurance systems is still at an early stage, lending projects were few and accounted for less than 1 percent of the past year's commitments. In the $20 million Labor Market Development Project in China, employee benefits—pensions, unemployment insurance, and medical coverage—are being transferred on a pilot basis from SOEs to the administration of five municipalities. This action is the first step in overall social insurance reform and is intended to accelerate the redeployment of surplus labor to other productive activities.

*Managing structural change and upgrading labor* are also emerging issues in the region. Rising integration and swift technological change are encouraging rapid structural changes and shifting workers from rural to urban areas and from informal to formal sectors. Labor reallocation and career changes for workers raise the issue of how to design education and training systems that provide flexible skills and mechanisms to support workers' mobility. During fiscal 1996, the Bank published a report, *Involving Workers in East Asian Growth*, a by-product of *World Development Report 1995*;[6] a labor-market study in Indonesia; and an education financing study in Vietnam.

5. World Bank. 1996. *Managing Capital Flows in East Asia*. Washington, D.C.; World Bank. 1995. *The Emerging Asian Bond Market*. Washington, D.C.

6. World Bank. 1995. *Involving Workers in East Asian Growth*. Washington, D.C.

*Dealing with environmental problems* continues to be a top priority of the Bank's activity. The Bank's strategy is to help the region's countries correct the underpricing of environmental costs and to build the institutional capacity for sound environmental management and a healthy and attractive urban environment. A study, *East Asia's Environment: Principles and Priorities for Action*, focused on underpricing, proposed market-based instruments for government regulations, and recommended priorities for action.[7] Subjects of economic and sector work (ESW) included industrial pollution control (Indonesia and Vietnam), renewable energy (China), and biodiversity and forestry (Cambodia).

*Maintaining macroeconomic stability* has been at the heart of East Asia's success. The Bank continues to analyze the macroeconomic situation in relation to structural reforms. For example, it is helping China build institutional capacities to deal with an overheated economy and is supporting government efforts at economic recovery and growth in the Philippines. In addition to country economic memoranda, which each year analyze individual macroeconomic conditions, the Bank conducted public expenditure reviews in the Lao PDR and the Philippines and provided public investment analysis to China on ways to maintain a sound fiscal and macroeconomic policy environment. It also provided advice on how to manage the macroeconomic impact of large capital flows.

The Bank's strategies for the Pacific island nations were articulated in the 1996 economic report, "Pacific Island Economies." Recommendations were made on helping these economies maintain an enabling macroeconomic environment, reducing anti-export biases in trade policy and the tax regime, and reducing barriers to domestic and foreign direct investment.

## Mainstreaming Business Innovations

The Bank's East Asia and Pacific Regional Office began to mainstream comprehensive business innovations at the beginning of fiscal 1996. These innovations, which were based on pilot work completed during the previous year, are designed to allow the Bank to provide member countries with increased operational outputs and a mix of products and services that better respond to their fast-changing needs.

The initial results of these innovations have been encouraging. Elapsed time and staff costs of preparing projects and economic and sector work under the new procedures are about one third lower. Simultaneously, greater emphasis is being placed on preparing focused policy notes in response to urgent government requests. Overhead costs have been reduced significantly, as a larger proportion of staff time is being devoted to direct client work. Results during fiscal 1997 are likely to be even more dramatic as the full benefits of the business innovations are harvested.

Greater attention is being given to portfolio management. Portfolio performance in the East Asia and Pacific region has traditionally been strong and it remains so. Studies by the Bank's Operations Evaluation Department (OED) of completed projects approved since 1980 show that 81 percent of projects in the region have met their development objectives. While this showing is a good one, there can be no sense of complacency.

Two complementary objectives have been adopted to improve the performance of the portfolio: *first*, to focus on project quality at entry by better defining project objectives and simplifying designs at the concept stage, improving economic analysis, and introducing key performance impact indicators; *second*, to improve the overall quality of the existing stock of projects, with major and visible results in the "development objectives" ratings and disbursement ratios.[8] The Regional Office has stepped up the attention it pays to the semiannual portfolio reviews and is looking hard at every problem project and the proposed action plan designed to move it out of the unsatisfactory category within six to twelve months.

7. Hammer, Jeffrey S., and Sudhir Shetty. 1995. *East Asia's Environment: Principles and Priorities for Action*. World Bank Discussion Paper No. 287. Washington, D.C.

8. Disbursement ratio is the amount of loans disbursed during the fiscal year as a percentage of the outstanding commitments at the beginning of the year.

In 1995, South Asian economies grew by 5.3 percent. India continued to reap substantial benefits from the trade and investment-liberalization reforms undertaken after 1991. Helped by favorable monsoons, growth is estimated to be around 6 percent, while manufacturing output growth has averaged 10 percent in the past two years. In Nepal growth reached a respectable 4.5 percent, and in Pakistan growth recovered after being held down by a series of poor cotton crops. By contrast, in Bangladesh and in Sri Lanka political difficulties and the continuation of civil strife, respectively, have contributed to dampen private sector dynamism and restrain growth.

Export performance remained vigorous, reflecting trade reforms, exchange adjustments and buoyant world demand. Since 1991, the annual average export growth rate for the region has exceeded 10 percent, compared with an average of 5.6 percent for the 1981–90 period. Nevertheless, exports of goods and nonfactor services represent less than 15 percent of domestic output, well below the average for developing countries. Although recent reforms have succeeded in lowering trade barriers, South Asian tariffs remain far higher than those in other regions. As a result, they remain an impediment to growth because, in conjunction with other trade restrictions, they create distortions and can lead to resource misallocation.

Regional cooperation received a boost with the ratification by members of the South Asia Association of Regional Cooperation (SAARC) of a trade agreement that included bilateral trade concessions that brought about cuts, ranging from 10 percent to 100 percent in tariff rates covering more than 220 items. Although the trade impact is likely to be small given the low share of intraregional trade, the SAARC countries[9] have indicated their intention to initiate negotiations towards establishing a free trade area in the near future.

Reform programs and the active engagement in the world economy by South Asian countries are now paying off in terms of higher foreign investment. Private capital is becoming increasingly important and now accounts for close to 50 percent of the resource flows to the region, compared with 25 percent in 1990. Although aggregate resource flows fell in 1995 due to a decline in overall portfolio flows following the devaluation of the Mexican peso in December 1994, they were still much higher than in 1993. Foreign direct investment reached a record $2.8 billion, and although India was the largest recipient (receiving about $2 billion), the other countries in the region also shared in the increase. Debt indicators showed a marked improvement as the South Asian economies saw the growth of their export earnings outpace the increase in their debt. All countries improved their debt-to-export ratios and debt-to-gross national product ratios. South Asian economies are the only group of developing countries that has not restructured its debt in the past decade and has incurred almost no arrears to external creditors. But maintaining sound economic fundamentals and pushing ahead with economic reforms are essential if the region is to take full advantage of the enormous potential for further growth in private capital flows to the region. The reduction of poverty and the improvement of living conditions continue to be the major objectives of the countries in the region. Although the incidence and depth of poverty have declined since the late 1980s, the number of poor has increased. The most recent estimates suggest that about 43 percent of the region's population lives on incomes of less than $1 a day and that South Asia, with 22 percent of the world's population, accounts for 40 percent of the world's poor. The poor in South Asia tend to be located in rural areas, to be illiterate, and to depend on subsistence agriculture and low-skill wage employment for their livelihood.

9. Bangladesh, Bhutan, India, Maldives, Nepal, Pakistan, and Sri Lanka.

Thus the importance of policies that raise rural incomes.

High and sustained growth that takes place in an environment of sound economic management is essential for the reduction of poverty. The good performance of the 1980s that lessened poverty was not sustainable because it led to large fiscal and balance-of-payments imbalances. But growth is not by itself sufficient to reduce poverty. South Asia's social indicators are very poor. Average life expectancy at birth is sixty years, half of the adult population is illiterate, and children under the age of five experience the highest mortality rate in the world. (A key factor accounting for the poor social indicators is the region's historically low investment in education and training.) These regional averages, however, mask considerable diversity, both across countries as well as within countries. Sri Lanka and some Indian states, for example, have social indicators that are comparable with those in countries with a higher income per capita.

The status of women is of particular concern since they are less well educated, have lower life expectancy, and work longer hours than men. Increasing the access of women to basic education, health and nutrition services, and water and sanitation is essential.

## TABLE 4-7. LENDING TO BORROWERS IN SOUTH ASIA, BY SECTOR, 1987–96

*(millions of US dollars; fiscal years)*

| Sector | Annual average, 1987–91 | 1992 | 1993 | 1994 | 1995 | 1996 |
|---|---|---|---|---|---|---|
| Agriculture | 732.6 | 346.1 | 451.9 | 387.8 | 551.3 | 684.5 |
| Education | 271.9 | 145.6 | 339.0 | 220.0 | 423.7 | 499.8 |
| Electric power and other energy | 897.2 | 730.0 | 960.0 | 230.0 | 250.0 | 700.0 |
| Environment | 31.1 | — | 28.8 | 14.7 | 168.0 | — |
| Finance | 274.5 | 28.4 | 65.8 | — | 916.0 | 205.0 |
| Industry | 233.8 | — | — | 250.3 | 3.2 | 3.4 |
| Mining/Other extractive | 68.0 | — | 12.0 | — | — | 63.0 |
| Multisector | 82.2 | 680.2 | 503.5 | — | — | — |
| Oil and gas | 365.6 | 330.0 | — | — | 120.8 | — |
| Population, health, and nutrition | 156.0 | 377.5 | 827.0 | 233.1 | 257.9 | 376.7 |
| Public sector management | 9.0 | — | — | 296.8 | — | 92.0 |
| Telecommunications/Informatics | 100.4 | 55.0 | — | — | — | 35.0 |
| Transportation | 330.6 | 306.0 | 20.0 | 491.3 | — | — |
| Urban development | 191.5 | — | — | 246.0 | 39.0 | 21.5 |
| Water supply and sanitation | 161.1 | — | 208.2 | — | 275.8 | 251.6 |
| Total | 3,935.5 | 2,998.8 | 3,416.2 | 2,370.0 | 3,005.7 | 2,932.5 |
| Of which:   IBRD | 2,241.5 | 1,348.0 | 1,145.0 | 474.0 | 1,584.8 | 1,161.6 |
|              IDA | 1,694.0 | 1,650.8 | 2,271.2 | 1,896.0 | 1,420.9 | 1,770.9 |
| Number of operations | 30 | 24 | 26 | 19 | 18 | 21 |

NOTE: Details may not add to totals because of rounding.
— Zero.

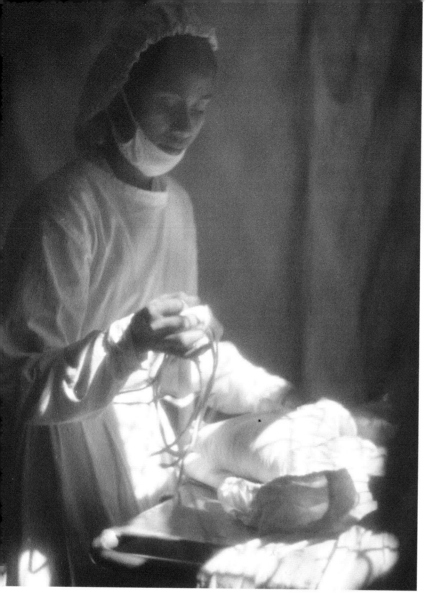

achieve these objectives through participatory approaches, decentralization, increased involvement by the private sector, and a sharper client focus.

## Consensus Building

Building consensus among project beneficiaries through various communication tools—seminars, meetings, media coverage—is an important aspect of improving ownership of, and local commitment to, projects. In many lending and nonlending activities, the Bank has followed a participatory approach, involving large numbers of stakeholders in the preparation of economic and sector work and in project design. The object is to broaden and deepen "ownership" and thus increase the developmental impact of the Bank's activities. The preparation of three studies—Sri Lanka 2000, Pakistan 2010, and Bangladesh Public Sector Management—involved close collaboration with country counterparts. Increased importance is being placed on dissemination of the Bank's analytical work. The Bank's poverty assessment for Pakistan, for example, was the sole subject of a number of seminars that brought together government officials, nongovernment organization (NGO) representatives, staff from donor agencies, private sector representatives, and academics. The assessment also received extensive press coverage.

The formulation of the Teacher Education and Teacher Deployment Project (Sri Lanka), approved in fiscal 1996, involved many in-country seminars and an informal report about solutions to the problems of teacher recruitment and assignment practices. In project preparation, participatory approaches are increasingly becoming the norm. In Bangladesh the Bank focused on building government and donor consensus around a revised scope for the Flood Action Plan that places more emphasis on change in people's behavior and less on physical works. In the Coastal Embankment Rehabilitation Project, designed to prevent the loss of life and property during cyclones and prevent salinity intrusion during normal monsoons, community participation is essential to project success. A community-participation approach is being used to deal with the issues of foreshore and

Achieving major poverty reduction is feasible. But to sustain more rapid growth and integration in the world economy in the coming years, South Asian nations will face tough policy challenges that include addressing the deficiencies in social areas, dealing with infrastructure bottlenecks, reducing still-excessive trade and investment barriers, and extending the scope of competition in domestic factor and product markets.

The Bank continues to support policies that promote sustainable growth, develop human resources, extend the benefits to currently disadvantaged groups (such as poor women), and overcome obstacles to the sustainability of growth, particularly in the environmental and human-resource areas. The current operational strategy in the region emphasizes ways to embankment afforestation, routine embankment maintenance, and the resettlement of some 2,000 families displaced by the project. NGOs are being employed to assist in community mobilization, provide training of participants, and facilitate community implementation of project activities.

The implementation of a rural water-supply and sanitation project in Nepal, currently at an advanced stage of preparation, is to be carried out with assistance of local NGOs, private firms, and community-based organizations with a track record in participatory rural development or water supply and sanitation. NGO-implemented schemes in Nepal have in the past performed better than those that have been centrally managed. NGOs have a strong presence in Nepal's water-supply sector, accounting for 10 percent of service delivery. The results of a pilot project that reviewed more than 100 water-supply schemes suggest that communities are more willing to contribute toward capital and operation and maintenance costs—up to 40 percent of the former and 100 percent of the latter—when their input is solicited.

Public participation was integral to the design of Ghazi-Barotha, a run-of-the-river energy project that will help reduce the acute energy shortages in Pakistan. Based on past experience in Pakistan and elsewhere, resettlement action plans have generally suffered from a number of weaknesses, including a lack of public consultation and participation and shortages of funds to compensate the affected population in a timely manner. As a result, an environmental resettlement and review panel was associated with project preparation from the outset. A proactive approach for public participation and consultation was ensured, including the setting up of a public information center at the project site, and sufficient funds for land acquisition were made available well in advance of eminent domain proceedings. An independent organization was also established, tasked with maintaining regular contacts with the local population on land acquisition and compensation issues.

The Nonformal Education Project in Bangladesh is expected to give "second-chance" education to some 2.5 million people between the ages of fifteen and twenty-four, of whom 1.3 million are expected to be female. The typical beneficiary is likely to be poor and malnourished, live in a rural area, own no land, have little opportunity for occupational or geographical mobility, be illiterate, and be only seasonally employed. The delivery of these programs, designed to provide young adults with literacy, numeracy, and life skills, will be made through

TABLE 4-8. WORLD BANK COMMITMENTS, DISBURSEMENTS, AND NET TRANSFERS IN SOUTH ASIA, 1991–96

*(millions of US dollars; fiscal years)*

| Item | India start 1996 | India 1996 | India 1991–96 | Pakistan start 1996 | Pakistan 1996 | Pakistan 1991–96 | Bangladesh start 1996 | Bangladesh 1996 | Bangladesh 1991–96 | Total region start 1996 | Total region 1996 | Total region 1991–96 |
|---|---|---|---|---|---|---|---|---|---|---|---|---|
| Undisbursed commitments | 9,430 | | | 2,991 | | | 1,589 | | | 14,971 | | |
| Commitments | | 2,078 | 11,989 | | 460 | 3,338 | | 239 | 1,904 | | 2,933 | 18,328 |
| Gross disbursements | | 1,309 | 10,893 | | 521 | 3,489 | | 227 | 1,780 | | 2,253 | 17,302 |
| Repayments | | 1,149 | 5,306 | | 261 | 1,100 | | 50 | 189 | | 1,482 | 6,711 |
| Net disbursements | | 161 | 5,587 | | 260 | 2,388 | | 176 | 1,590 | | 771 | 10,591 |
| Interest and charges | | 884 | 4,978 | | 241 | 1,225 | | 46 | 236 | | 1,195 | 6,566 |
| Net transfer | | -723 | 609 | | 19 | 1,163 | | 130 | 1,354 | | -424 | 4,025 |

NOTE: *Disbursements from the IDA Special Fund are included. The countries shown in the table are those with the largest borrowings of Bank funds during fiscal 1995–96. Details may not add to totals because of rounding.*

## TABLE 4-9. PROJECTS APPROVED DURING FISCAL YEAR 1996, SOUTH ASIA

| Country/project name | Date of Approval | Maturities | Principal amount (millions) SDR | Principal amount (millions) US$ |
|---|---|---|---|---|
| **Bangladesh** | | | | |
| Nonformal Education Project | February 27, 1996 | 2006/2035 | 7.10 | 10.50 |
| Agricultural Research Management Project | February 8, 1996 | 2006/2035 | 33.60 | 50.00 |
| Jute Sector Adjustment Credit (IDA reflows) | December 12, 1995 | 2004/2034 | 2.30 | 3.40 |
| River Bank Protection Project | December 5, 1995 | 2006/2035 | 78.40 | 121.90 |
| Coastal Embankment Rehabilitation Project | November 9, 1995 | 2006/2035 | 34.10 | 53.00 |
| **India** | | | | |
| Uttar Pradesh Rural Water Supply and Environmental Sanitation Project | June 25, 1996 | 2002/2016 | n.a. | 59.60 |
| Second District Primary Education Project | June 6, 1996 | 2006/2031 | 291.70 | 425.20 |
| Coal Sector Environmental and Social Mitigation Project | May 16, 1996 | 2006/2031 | 43.30 | 63.00 |
| Orissa Power Sector Restructuring Project | May 14, 1996 | 2002/2016 | n.a. | 350.00 |
| Private Infrastructure Finance Project[a] | March 28, 1996 | 2001/2016 | 3.40 | 5.00 |
| Private Infrastructure Finance Project[a] | March 28, 1996 | 2006/2030 | n.a. | 200.00 |
| Second State Health Systems Development Project | March 21, 1996 | 2006/2031 | 235.50 | 350.00 |
| Orissa Water Resources Consolidation Project | December 19, 1995 | 2006/2030 | 194.80 | 290.90 |
| Hydrology Project | August 22, 1995 | 2006/2030 | 90.10 | 142.00 |
| Bombay Sewage Disposal Project[a] | July 6, 1995 | 2001/2015 | n.a. | 167.00 |
| Bombay Sewage Disposal Project[a] | July 6, 1995 | 2005/2030 | 15.90 | 25.00 |
| **Pakistan** | | | | |
| Northern Health Program Project | June 13, 1996 | 2006/2031 | 18.40 | 26.70 |
| NWFP Community Infrastructure and NHA Strengthening Project | March 14, 1996 | 2006/2031 | 13.70 | 21.50 |
| Ghazi-Barotha Hydropower Project | December 19, 1995 | 2001/2016 | n.a. | 350.00 |
| Telecommunications Regulation and Privatization Support Project | November 9, 1995 | 2001/2015 | n.a. | 35.00 |
| Balochistan Community Irrigation and Agriculture Project | September 26, 1995 | 2005/2030 | 18.50 | 26.70 |
| **Sri Lanka** | | | | |
| Private Sector Infrastructure Development Project | June 13, 1996 | 2006/2036 | 52.90 | 77.00 |
| Teacher Education and Teacher Deployment Project | June 13, 1996 | 2006/2036 | 44.00 | 64.10 |
| Telecommunications Regulation and Public Enterprise Reform Technical Assistance Project | March 26, 1996 | 2006/2036 | 10.40 | 15.00 |
| **Total** | | | 1,188.10 | 2,932.50 |

n.a. = not applicable (IBRD loan).
a. "Blend" loan/credit.

qualified NGOs and local organizations. Nongovernmental organizations or other voluntary organizations currently provide most nonformal education instruction in Bangladesh, either in programs focusing on nonformal education only or within broader development projects. The effectiveness of the country's major NGOs (there are some 13,000 NGOs operating in Bangladesh) has been tested by both bilateral and multilateral organizations. At their best, NGO programs have had real and direct relevance to the needs and aspirations of the learners, demonstrated by classes with high attendance and low dropout rates. This has been achieved through the devel-

opment of needs-based curriculum, participatory teaching methodologies, and materials that start with the experience of the learners and the communities where they live. Beneficiary communities will participate in identifying prospective students, providing shelter for classes, and in recruiting teachers. Women will be encouraged to participate in planning and implementing project activities, and women teachers will be hired to teach female students.

## Decentralization

In many existing operations supported by the Bank there is scope for decentralizing the delivery of the programs. Pakistan and India, with their federal/provincial or state setup, provide the most scope for initiatives toward decentralization. In Pakistan, supervision of the $200 million Social Action Program Project, as well as of various health and education credits, has focused more on provincial implementation, while the Balochistan Primary Education Project, approved in fiscal 1993, has fostered a successful model of community schools *(see Box 4-2)*.

A project in India's Orissa state is representative of the Bank's new lending strategy that emphasizes a state's sector-policy framework and institutional strengthening rather than project-specific issues only. Operations focus on support for institutional and expenditure reform in states that are receptive to reform. The $290.9 million Orissa Water Resources Consolidation Project finances a program to improve the productivity and sustainability of Orissa's water resources, involves farmers in decisionmaking and planning in irrigation management, and strengthens the state institutional and technical capabilities in water development and planning. Orissa was chosen because, in formulating its

## BOX 4-2. COMMUNITY PRIMARY SCHOOLS IN BALOCHISTAN

*Involving parents in the process of delivering primary education has had positive results in Balochistan. Village education committees, made up entirely of parents, have established 295 new rural schools that enroll over 12,000 female primary students. The community schools component of the $106 million Balochistan Primary Education Project began as a pilot experiment in 1992 and is now part of a comprehensive program supported by the Bank to improve Balochistan's primary education system. The component is being implemented by the Society for Community Support for Primary Education in Balochistan, an NGO contracted by the Balochistan government.*

*The society sends teams to selected villages where they go door to door encouraging parents to form village-education committees to identify local females willing to teach and who have at least an eighth grade education. (It has been found that the involvement of parents in the selection of the teacher greatly enhances the accountability of teachers to the communities. The committees also provide assurance to fathers and husbands that it is all right for daughters or wives to work outside the family circle.) Given the short supply of qualified female teachers in rural Balochistan, finding women with enough education to be trained as teachers is the major constraint to the expansion of the program. Selected candidates must pass a competency test, undergo three months of training, and teach without compensation for three months to demonstrate their commitment to teaching and their ability to maintain enrollments. Successful teachers receive a regular teaching post, while the provincial government makes a commitment to build a permanent school in villages in*

*which "trial" schools survive for three years. The village-education committee ensures that teachers and students regularly attend classes.*

*Government support for the community schools program has grown with its obvious success, and with the growing appreciation of its cost-effectiveness.[1] The program is now poised for a major expansion. Three additional NGOs are being contracted by the government to replicate the community-school program throughout Balochistan, and a district-level support structure, which includes improved training facilities for the teachers, is under development. About 80 percent of the costs are being financed by the government; the remainder comes from a UNICEF grant. Teacher salaries are paid through the regular government recurrent budget. Because the community-school program has been so successful, the government is also experimenting with two additional measures involving further devolvement to villages. A rural fellowship program, now a year old, completely decentralizes school management and operations, including the hiring of teachers, to the community. Thirty schools, with enrollment of more than 3,000 students, are currently participating. Under the second measure, urban fellowship vouchers, which provide funds amounting to the salaries of four teachers, are transferred to urban communities, which then hire private providers. Twelve schools, with enrollment of more than 1,500 students, are participating.*

*1. Success can be measured by the high enrollment and low dropout rates at the community schools. Girls in community schools also score higher on achievement tests than those in regular government schools.*

new water-resources strategy, it had demonstrated a commitment to policy and institutional reforms; multisector water planning, development, and allocation, with attention to environmental concerns; improved service delivery; and enhanced participation by stakeholders. Farmers and other stakeholders are an integral part of the project management and implementation arrangements. Emphasis is also being placed on fostering stakeholder awareness and participation in water planning and management, in particular in areas such as farmer participation in investment decisions, operation and maintenance, monitoring of financial allocations, and achieving full cost recovery. Over time, this stakeholder involvement is expected to foster a demand-driven and client-oriented government service, as well as progressively increase involvement of nongovernment entities in project implementation.

The Second State Health Systems Development Project supports three states in putting into place a referral health-care system. The three—Karnataka, Punjab, and West Bengal—were included in the project because, in addition to their early commitment to undertake health reform, they had forged ahead of other states in setting up a framework to develop a package of policy reforms. The project will contribute to improving resource allocation, strengthening implementation capacity of the agencies in the sector, and enhancing the role of the private sector and of voluntary sectors in the delivery and management of health services.

### Bringing in the Private Sector

In South Asia, severe absorptive capacity and implementation deficiencies, coupled with financial constraints, have resulted in chronic underinvestment in infrastructure. The public sector alone does not have the resources to meet the needs of the sector. One constraint to the expansion of the private sector in this area is the lack of available finance on terms commensurate with the typical long gestation and revenue-earning capacity of infrastructure projects. In India, for example, the development of a domestic long-term debt market requires a number of significant policy reforms in the financial sector, particularly as regards regulations

applicable to contractual savings institutions. While such a reform program is being formulated, and until its key elements are implemented so that a well-functioning domestic long-term debt market can emerge, domestic financial institutions have to play a major role in supporting private investment in infrastructure. Working with a major nonbanking financial company that is majority privately owned, the Private Infrastructure Finance Project, approved during fiscal 1996, aims to develop the prototype contractual arrangements for private investment in areas such as urban bypasses and bridges, water and sewerage services, and other municipal infrastructure, thus facilitating entry of the private sector in the sector in areas heretofore dominated by the public sector.

The Private Infrastructure Finance Project, as well as the Telecommunications Regulation and Public Enterprise Reform Technical Assistance Project in Sri Lanka are setting up systems to facilitate private investment in formerly publicly provided services. The Bank has been involved in three telecommunications projects in Sri Lanka. The first, closed in 1986, was generally successful in separating the telecommunications and postal departments and supporting expansion of the telephone network. The second supported reforms that separated the service provider from the sector regulator. The most recent continues reform and efficient development of the sector through the strengthening of sector regulation and its institutions. By such strengthening, interest of potential private investors should increase.

### Client Focus and Quality of Implementation

The Bank's proactive management of its portfolio has led to major restructuring and supervision efforts to improve project performance. Portfolio management addresses generic issues of quality of entry and of implementation by keeping project designs simple; ensuring that key actions on procurement, land acquisition, and environmental and government clearances are obtained prior to project approval; improving the mechanism for channeling external funds; restructuring or canceling components with little scope for improvement; making greater use of consultants to supervise construction work;

and by adhering to the closing dates of loans and credits.

The region has undertaken a major review of internal business processes in an effort to increase efficiencies. Targets that were set for portfolio improvement, with a special focus on the Nepal and Bangladesh portfolios, were closely monitored, and cross-cutting themes in sectors where problems are concentrated (such as agriculture and urban development) were examined. As a result, several steps were taken to improve quality at entry, and ongoing projects were retrofitted with new performance indicators. Other measures included sectoral monitoring of the time taken to prepare lending operations, proactive management of droppages in the lending program, and cost-cutting measures in economic and sector work.

Local input into project supervision has been enhanced by substantial decentralization to field offices. This is the continuation of past efforts that saw the Bank shift a number of tasks—such as task management for some supervision, procurement and auditing oversight, as well as management of economic analysis work, for example—to the resident missions in Bangladesh, India, and Pakistan. The objective of the decentralization exercise, which allows the Bank to take advantage of its field offices' proximity to the client and of their familiarity with social, cultural, and political contexts, is to raise development effectiveness on the ground. During the past year, the Bank's Sri Lanka resident representative assumed responsibility for the management of the Sri Lanka and Maldives programs (including the budget), as well as for the policy dialogue with, and the preparation of the country-assistance strategies for, the two countries.

In Pakistan, responsibility for the supervision of the $200 million Social Action Program (SAP) Project, approved in fiscal 1994, was shifted to the resident mission. The SAP is a complex project that involves frequent and close interactions with federal and provincial governments, NGOs, and local donors. In India, the highly successful initiative represented by the establishment of the procurement and the social development units in the resident mission is being strengthened. In addition, the region's five field

offices, together with the Bank's headquarters, reviewed their work programs and identified specific tasks that can be devolved later in a phased manner consistent with the buildup of capacity in the field offices.

Since the beginning of fiscal 1994, the region has undertaken, with borrower participation, country portfolio-performance reviews that address generic issues affecting portfolio performance at the project or sector-specific level. These reviews have resulted, among other things, in supervision focus, at the outset, on projects deemed to be "at risk" and in increased allocation of resources to problem projects with ambitious community objectives such as the Poverty Alleviation Project (Sri Lanka) and the Rural Water Supply and Sanitation Project (Pakistan).

The work program of the Bank's South Asia Regional Office relies heavily on partnerships with other institutions. In particular, collaboration is expanding with the Asian Development Bank through the formal coordination of country-assistance strategies in both institutions. A pilot case in Pakistan has resulted in an exchange of documentation, coordination of sector strategies, and a better division of labor.

The Bank also continues to play a major role in several aid group meetings, such as those for Pakistan and Nepal. The India Development Forum which, since 1994, has included official aid agencies and private investors, last met in June 1995. The forum offers an opportunity for an open exchange of views on topics such as state-level adjustment efforts, the continuity of government policy, and the opportunities for private sector investment in sectors such as infrastructure.

Throughout Central and Eastern Europe and the Baltic countries, output continued to grow during 1995, and in several other countries of the former Soviet Union (FSU)—Armenia, Kyrgyz Republic, and Moldova—growth resumed in 1995. There is evidence that such growth is being sustained during 1996. In the other countries of the FSU, output continued to decline, although at a slower rate—about 6 percent in 1995 versus 15 percent in the year before. There is some evidence, particularly if the new emerging private sector is fully included, that 1996 will witness the bottoming out of output decline.

Private sector growth and improvements in the external sector are largely responsible for recovery of output in those countries where output grew. For the region overall, exports grew at 22 percent in 1995; Estonia, Hungary, and Kazakstan experienced export growth in excess of 40 percent in current dollar terms. Foreign direct investment nearly doubled between 1994 and 1995.

Throughout the region inflation has been reduced, notably in the countries of the FSU. In spite of progress on inflation, countries in the region continue to struggle on the fiscal front as they deal with legacies from the past while, at the same time, they work to create scaled-down, yet effective public sector structures needed in a market economy. In many countries—in particular, in Central and Eastern Europe—government spending—and revenues to finance it—continues in the range of 50 percent of gross domestic product (GDP). In some countries, however, progress has been made in reducing fiscal aggregates. For example, the share of public expenditures in GDP in Hungary was cut by some 7 percent to about 55 percent in 1995, helping to restore macroeconomic equilibria. By contrast, in some FSU countries, the decline in public expenditures reflects a failure to collect broad-based revenues.

Generally in line with growth trends, the fall in real earnings has been stemmed. Real wages increased during 1995 throughout most of Central and Eastern Europe and the Baltics. The unemployment rate declined in almost all countries of Central Europe, but it is leveling out at rates comparable with those of Western Europe, with evidence of structural unemployment and little turnover in the pool of unemployed.

By contrast, there was an upward drift in unemployment—from far lower levels—in the countries of the FSU; by the end of 1995, 3 percent of the labor force in Russia was registered as being unemployed, and 8 percent was unemployed as measured by labor-force surveys. The initial collapse of output and increase in inequality to market-economy levels reduced real incomes for large portions of the population, within both lower- and middle-income households. Many households have been able to adjust to the new opportunities, however, in particular those headed by younger and well-educated workers living in areas with a diversified resource base or employed in jobs linked to exports and the service sector. At the same time, poverty has increased, and many households remain vulnerable, even in countries where significant resources have been directed towards social protection. Those headed by the very elderly have seen their pensions eroded or, in some cases, have seen their pension eligibility vanish. Other vulnerable households include those that depend on earnings of less well-educated workers, in line with greater dispersion of wages in a market economy and their predominance in the ranks of the structurally unemployed. Growth is critical to improving household income and reducing poverty. Early evidence from Poland and Estonia, for example, indicates that growth has resulted in a decline in the number of poor in 1995. However, an important challenge of the transition is to assure that vulnerable groups are not left behind.

## TABLE 4-10. LENDING TO BORROWERS IN EUROPE AND CENTRAL ASIA, BY SECTOR, 1987–96

*(millions of us dollars; fiscal years)*

| Sector | Annual average, 1987–91 | 1992 | 1993 | 1994 | 1995 | 1996 |
|---|---|---|---|---|---|---|
| Agriculture | 210.6 | 155.0 | 525.4 | 582.9 | 202.0 | 185.8 |
| Education | 89.3 | — | — | 59.6 | 40.0 | 5.0 |
| Electric power and other energy | 285.4 | 516.0 | 93.0 | 164.8 | 191.7 | 325.4 |
| Environment | 3.6 | — | — | — | 123.0 | 30.1 |
| Finance | 351.7 | — | 55.0 | 280.0 | 232.0 | 638.9 |
| Industry | 214.9 | — | — | 375.0 | — | — |
| Mining/Other extractive | — | — | — | — | — | 540.8 |
| Multisector | 323.4 | 691.1 | 1,245.0 | 566.3 | 2,000.0 | 656.8 |
| Oil and gas | 108.0 | — | 610.0 | 691.3 | 226.3 | 10.0 |
| Population, health, and nutrition | 15.0 | 280.0 | 91.0 | — | 220.4 | 350.4 |
| Public sector management | 20.0 | 269.2 | 335.0 | 210.0 | 70.9 | 505.6 |
| Social sector | 20.0 | — | 67.0 | 10.9 | 127.5 | 12.0 |
| Telecommunications/Informatics | 68.0 | — | 30.0 | 153.0 | — | — |
| Transportation | 265.6 | — | 378.0 | 352.0 | 486.0 | 868.0 |
| Urban development | 24.0 | 200.0 | 285.0 | 171.0 | 418.0 | 44.3 |
| Water supply and sanitation | 132.0 | 32.0 | 129.5 | 109.6 | 161.0 | 221.5 |
| Total | 2,131.5 | 2,143.3 | 3,843.9 | 3,726.4 | 4,498.8 | 4,394.6[a] |
| Of which:  IBRD | 2,131.6 | 2,102.2 | 3,739.5 | 3,533.3 | 3,953.8 | 3,918.2[a] |
| IDA | — | 41.1 | 104.4 | 193.1 | 545.0 | 476.4 |
| Number of operations | 13 | 14 | 30 | 42 | 58 | 61 |

NOTE: *Details may not add to totals because of rounding.*
— *Zero.*
a. *Includes the refinanced/rescheduled overdue charges of $168 million for Bosnia and Herzegovina.*

## Activities of the Bank

During fiscal 1996, Bosnia and Herzegovina fulfilled the requirements providing for succession to membership of the Socialist Federal Republic of Yugoslavia *(see Box 4-3)*; twenty-seven countries are now active borrowers in the Europe and Central Asia (ECA) region. As shown in Figure 4-1, the volume of lending was $4.4 billion, roughly comparable to the peak of $4.5 billion in fiscal 1995. Disbursements increased sharply to more than $3.7 billion.

Over the past four years, the project portfolio for the most recent member countries has more than doubled. The entire portfolio now exceeds $20 billion, of which $12 billion represents undisbursed commitments, as illustrated in Figure 4-2. The portfolio spans a range of sectors: Support for infrastructure and energy continues to be significant; lending in support of the financial sector and onlending to the private sector is also robust, as is that for agriculture and natural resources; and the share directed to the social sectors is increasing. Adjustment lending remains an important vehicle, representing 34 percent of the portfolio.

## Enhancing Results on the Ground

As a result of the rapid increase in the portfolio and in undisbursed commitments and in response to signs of portfolio problems, the Bank is placing more emphasis on enhancing the development effectiveness of previously approved projects. Increased resources are being devoted to strengthening borrower implementation capacity so as to assist the absorptive capacity of the borrowers. During the past year, resources devoted to project supervision increased by 12 percent (to close to ninety staff years). The proportion of operations with unsatisfactory progress on implementation continued to decline in fiscal 1996, and six problem projects,

largely in the mature borrowing countries, were restructured.

Many of the projects in newer member countries are at the early stage of implementation, where, typically, projects have a slower rate of disbursement. At the same time, legal and administrative requirements within countries frequently have delayed effectiveness. The Bank has become increasingly alert to internal procedures for processing approvals in borrowing countries and in integrating them into the sequence of actions so as to avoid delays in disbursements. Clients are also becoming more familiar with Bank procedures. The translation of standard bidding documents and assistance in strengthening national procurement procedures, for example, have facilitated procurement. As a

*1996–99 period, which would be in addition to the resources provided by the Trust Fund. To respond to the country's needs for immediate significant support, to rebuild infrastructure and jump-start the economy, a significant proportion of this assistance will be front-loaded during the first two years and will support further projects in de-mining, electric power, housing, employment-creation, industry, and health. At least one Structural Adjustment Credit in support of economic reforms in the enterprise and banking sectors and in public finance, is anticipated. Bosnia is expected to borrow a comparatively large amount from IDA over the next three years. As its creditworthiness improves, IDA lending will be phased down, and loans from the IBRD are expected to increase.*

*Bosnia, which has fulfilled the conditions of succession to the membership of the former Yugoslavia in the Bank, can access the Bank's lending resources as a result of the approval late in fiscal 1996 of a loan-consolidation package of up to $620.6 million that cleared the country's outstanding obligations to the IBRD, including principal arrears, interest arrears, and principal not yet due.*

*Approval of the package follows the sanctioning by the Bank's executive board in March of an innovative arrears-clearance approach that, in addition to maintaining the financial integrity of the Bank—it does not incorporate any financial concessionality on the part of the IBRD—also ensured a substantial positive net flow of funds to Bosnia.*

*Donor contributions to pay off one of the highest-interest loans have been arranged and include contributions from the governments of Italy, the Netherlands, Norway, and Switzerland.*

*The Bank expects—subject to approval of individual operations by the board—to make a positive net transfer of funds to Bosnia of about $450 million over the next four years, most of which will be on concessional terms. The Bank's executive directors will revisit the assistance package in 1997. At that time, the shape of future assistance would be based on an assessment of Bosnia's performance and absorptive capacity and its creditworthiness.*

result, during fiscal 1996, the ratio of disbursements to opening balances for projects increased from 12 percent to 18 percent, compared with a Bankwide average of 19 percent.

To assist project implementation, several investment projects now include components that strengthen what often limits project impact: institutional capacity to effect systemic change. For example, considerable institutional strengthening in Russia's banking sector has been achieved under the Financial Institutions Development Project approved in May 1994. Among the criteria for participation in the project (and follow-up credit lines) are annual audits by international accounting firms and adherence to prudential banking norms that are much stricter than central bank regulations.

There has been keen interest among the leading Russian commercial banks to be accredited under the project: Some forty banks have been screened, and thirteen banks have been accredited. While disbursements have been limited, the project already has achieved a good part of its institution-building objectives through the introduction of international banking standards and more extensive disclosure. Again in Russia, the auctioning-off of municipal land to the private sector, a component of fiscal 1995's Housing Project, has had the effect of introducing the concept of land as an asset, establishing a transparent system of land allocation and transfer of ownership from local governments to the private sector, and introducing new market-oriented planning processes at the city and oblast levels.

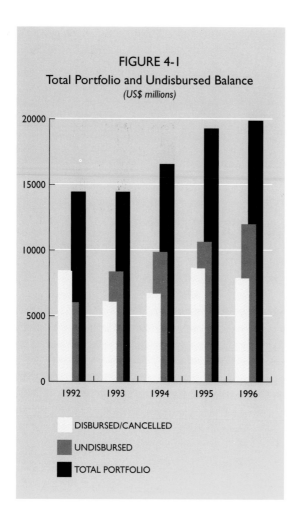

**FIGURE 4-1**

**Total Portfolio and Undisbursed Balance**
*(US$ millions)*

DISBURSED/CANCELLED
UNDISBURSED
TOTAL PORTFOLIO

The portfolio also includes an increasing number of innovative projects that are testing community approaches on ways to reduce the social cost of restructuring. In Ukraine, for example, the Bank is supporting a pilot project designed to mitigate the social and environmental impact of the government's decision to close coal mines. Ways to close mines safely will be tested, and out-of-work miners seeking employment elsewhere will be able to choose assistance from a menu of options. The lessons from the pilot project will be built into future support for coal-sector restructuring.

With implementation of the portfolio moving to center stage, high-level Country Portfolio Performance Reviews (CPPRs) with member countries are now a central vehicle for ensuring effectiveness of Bank assistance, particularly in those countries experiencing implementation difficulties. Eight CPPRs were held during the

fiscal year. During the CPPR for Russia, for example, important bottlenecks were resolved, quantitative performance indicators and key targets were established, and corrective actions were identified for both the government and the Bank so as to improve the pace of implementation of the project portfolio. By the end of the fiscal year, performance ratings for individual projects met or exceeded the expectations for improvements established during the CPPR, and signed contracts and project disbursements accelerated and appear likely to meet agreed targets with a delay of between one and two months.

In Poland considerable progress was made during the year on implementing decisions from the previous year's country-strategy implementation review (CSIR), in particular, reallocating resources under lines of credit. The fourth annual CSIR exercise resulted in agreement on action plans to

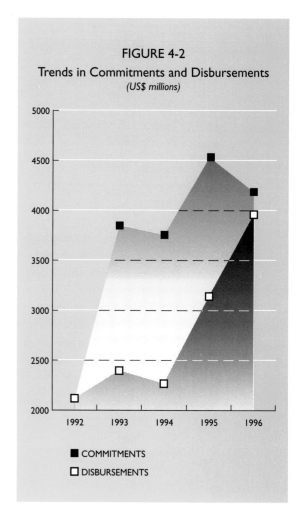

**FIGURE 4-2**

**Trends in Commitments and Disbursements**
*(US$ millions)*

■ COMMITMENTS
□ DISBURSEMENTS

address cross-cutting issues in the portfolio, including amendments and clarifications of Polish procurement regulations and extension of sovereign guarantees. The meeting also was used to advance preparations for the next country-assistance strategy, which is being prepared in a participatory program with Polish authorities.

The Turkey CPPR addressed mutual concerns of the government and the Bank, with broader participation of the core ministries and implementing agencies than in the past. The Bank's resident missions—with presence in almost all active borrowing member countries—play an increasingly prominent role in routine supervision and monitoring.

## Supporting Market Institutions

The Bank is devoting increasing resources to supporting institutions essential to the functioning of private markets and to consolidating progress in privatization and liberalization. Through a combination of new private start-ups, formal privatization, and sales of enterprise assets to the private sector, the private sector share of economic activity continues to rise. Private sector shares in GDP and employment have reached over 50 percent in all but a handful of countries in the region. Large increases in the private sector share of GDP have taken place in countries that recently have implemented comprehensive privatization programs such as Georgia and Moldova. While progress in privatization of large-scale enterprises remains slower than that of small- and medium-scale enterprises, there were several notable large-scale privatizations in 1995, including a large part of the energy sector in Russia, energy-sector utilities in Hungary, telecommunications in Hungary and the Czech Republic, and several large banks in Hungary and Poland through sales to private investors. In Romania, the Financial and Enterprise Sector Adjustment Loan supports the accelerated program of mass privatization—with the design of the cash auctions resulting in broad local private sector participation. To support the implementation of the mass privatization program in Poland, the Bank financed the fees of the national investment funds.

Banking system reforms, combined with a sound regulatory and legal environment for secured lending, are essential to ensure adequate access to credit for emerging private and privatized enterprises. These twin goals were the focus of adjustment operations in Kazakstan and Kyrgyz Republic. In the face of a banking

## TABLE 4-11. WORLD BANK COMMITMENTS, DISBURSEMENTS, AND NET TRANSFERS IN EUROPE AND CENTRAL ASIA, 1991–96

*(millions of US dollars; fiscal years)*

| Item | Russia | | | Ukraine | | | Romania | | | Total region | | |
|---|---|---|---|---|---|---|---|---|---|---|---|---|
| | start 1996 | 1996 | 1991–96 | start 1996 | 1996 | 1991–96 | start 1996 | 1996 | 1991–96 | start 1996 | 1996 | 1991–96 |
| Undisbursed commitments | 3,887 | | | 306 | | | 665 | | | 12,004 | | |
| Commitments | | 1,816 | 6,447 | | 343 | 1,016 | | 510 | 1,916 | | 4,395 | 22,474 |
| Gross disbursements | | 981 | 1,710 | | 137 | 504 | | 215 | 956 | | 3,736 | 13,238 |
| Repayments | | — | — | | — | — | | — | — | | 1,279 | 7,313 |
| Net disbursements | | 981 | 1,710 | | 137 | 504 | | 215 | 956 | | 2,457 | 5,925 |
| Interest and charges | | 88 | 162 | | 24 | 24 | | 59 | 136 | | 1,178 | 5,334 |
| Net transfer | | 893 | 1,548 | | 113 | 480 | | 156 | 820 | | 1,279 | 591 |

NOTE: *Disbursements from the IDA Special Fund are included. Regional commitment totals for fiscal 1996 and for fiscal 1991–96 include the refinanced/rescheduled overdue charges of $168 million for Bosnia and Herzegovina. The countries shown in the table are those with the largest borrowings of Bank funds during fiscal 1995–96. Details may not add to totals because of rounding.*
— *Zero.*

crisis in late 1995, the Bank provided timely advice to the Government of Latvia on how to address the underlying structural problems of the sector.

The Bank is also assisting newly privatized enterprises to adjust to the opportunities of the market economy. In Moldova, for example, where by end-June 1995, 741 medium- and large-scale enterprises and 563 small-scale enterprises had been privatized, a Bank-assisted project is focusing on measures to restructure private enterprises and build indigenous business-management skills. The project is also providing medium-term finance for private sector enterprises in the context of a strengthened regulatory and supervisory environment for banks. The Bank continues to facilitate

the sharing of experiences throughout the region. It cosponsors and supports financially the Central and Eastern European Privatization Network that brings together privatization officials from eighteen countries in the region for sharing of experiences. This experience-sharing has as its goal the transferring of the lessons learned by the more advanced transition economies to other countries. The Network's newly created Financial Forum brings together officials from finance ministries and central banks, as well as securities regulators and market participants, to share their experiences. In Budapest, the Bank organized a Pension Reform Conference in cooperation with the East-West Institute and the United States Agency for International Development, attended by officials from seven countries of Eastern and Central Europe. The purpose was to learn from the experiences of countries in implementing multipillar pension systems.

## Facilitating Social Consensus and Reducing Social Costs

Social consensus is critical to the sustainability of the economic transition in the countries of the region. As understanding of its newer member countries and rapport with its clients have grown, the Bank is increasingly listening to, and seeking advice from, nongovernmental organizations (NGOs), community groups, local governments, public service providers, trade unions, the academic community, and the growing private sector. The Armenia Social Investment Fund Project, for example, aims to promote self-help and community solidarity. The project was designed based on the lessons learned from a pilot implemented by an NGO. With financial support from the project, the communities identify eligible microprojects based on their priorities, manage the implementation of their microproject, select contractors and supervisors, and devise a plan for maintaining the facility after microproject completion. A project to support the divestiture of housing from Russian enterprises incorporated the views and concerns of tenants into both project design and the implementation process through surveys of tenant preferences and the establishment of condominium associations as the most effective way to encourage voluntary resident participation in decisions. Through the Bank's Economic Development Institute (EDI), the Bank is supporting seminars to inform parliamentarians and a broad range of civil society—in the Kyrgyz Republic and Ukraine, for example—on transition issues. The EDI, with financial support from Switzerland, also organized the Former Yugoslav Republic (FYR) of Macedonia's Forum for Senior Policymakers ("Vision of the Future"), which brought together the country's president, parliamentarians, private sector representatives, academics, journalists, and out-of-country policymakers with relevant experiences to share for a wide-ranging dicussion of the future of the country.

A critical element of the Bank's assistance program is to support the social agenda surrounding the restructuring of the enterprise sector, including facilitating the movement of workers to higher-productivity jobs. In addition to the pilot project in the coal sector in Ukraine, reported on earlier, the $500 million Russia Coal Sector Adjustment Loan and a companion implementation-assistance project will provide assistance to those affected by that country's coal sector-restructuring program. Community support and diversification programs are being supported in five coal basins (Eastern Donbass, Kisel, Kuzbass, Moscow, and Pechora). To ensure that affected communities receive adequate information, a countrywide network of major coal cities was established, and public information and social impact-monitoring activities are being supported. Elsewhere, Bank-assisted adjustment lending continues to facilitate budgetary outlays to assist workers dismissed from large, distressed enterprises. During the past fiscal year incentives and financial support were provided to more than 50,000 workers leaving troubled enterprises in Romania, as well as to workers in Kazakstan, Kyrgyz Republic, and FYR Macedonia. Projects currently under implementation that support employment services—from countries as diverse as Hungary and Kazakstan—are enabling workers not only to collect unemployment compensation but also to receive counseling to facilitate their search for other jobs. Such counseling has proven to be very cost-effective.

Given that the incidence of poverty remains high in the region, the Bank accelerated its work in this area, completing an additional five poverty assessments during the year. Eight such assessments—designed to provide the basis for a collaborative approach to poverty reduction by country officials and the Bank—have so far been completed, with several others under preparation. Restoration of growth is essential to reverse the poverty trends. At the same time, given that fiscal constraints are tight, the Bank's adjustment lending is supporting improved targeting of social safety net assistance to the poor. In Georgia, for example, the government is developing a backup program of social assistance,

## TABLE 4-12. PROJECTS APPROVED DURING FISCAL YEAR 1996, EUROPE AND CENTRAL ASIA

| Country/project name | Date of Approval | Maturities | Principal amount (millions) SDR | Principal amount (millions) US$ |
|---|---|---|---|---|
| **Albania** | | | | |
| National Roads Project | June 20, 1996 | 2006/2036 | 17.40 | 25.00 |
| Forestry Project | April 16, 1996 | 2006/2036 | 5.50 | 8.00 |
| Power Transmission and Distribution Project | March 5, 1996 | 2006/2036 | 19.70 | 29.50 |
| Agro-Processing Development Project | December 12, 1995 | 2006/2035 | 4.10 | 6.00 |
| Urban Works and Microenterprise Pilot Project | August 1, 1995 | 2005/2035 | 2.60 | 4.00 |
| **Armenia** | | | | |
| Structural Adjustment Credit | February 29, 1996 | 2006/2030 | 40.40 | 60.00 |
| Structural Adjustment Technical Assistance Credit | February 29, 1996 | 2006/2030 | 2.60 | 3.80 |
| Social Investment Fund Project | November 9, 1995 | 2006/2030 | 8.10 | 12.00 |
| Highway Project | September 14, 1995 | 2006/2030 | 10.30 | 16.00 |
| **Azerbaijan** | | | | |
| Rehabilitation Credit | August 22, 1995 | 2005/2030 | 41.60 | 65.00 |
| Institution Building Technical Assistance Project | July 25, 1995 | 2005/2030 | 11.50 | 18.00 |
| **Bosnia and Herzegovina** | | | | |
| Emergency Education Reconstruction Project | June 28, 1996 | 2006/2031 | 3.50 | 5.00 |
| War Victims Rehabilitation Project | June 28, 1996 | 2006/2031 | 3.50 | 5.00 |
| **Bulgaria** | | | | |
| Health Sector Restructuring Project | April 9, 1996 | 2001/2016 | n.a. | 26.00 |
| Railway Rehabilitation Project | July 6, 1995 | 2000/2015 | n.a. | 95.00 |
| **Croatia** | | | | |
| Capital Markets Development Project | April 4, 1996 | 2001/2013 | n.a. | 9.50 |
| Technical Assistance Project | March 26, 1996 | 2001/2013 | n.a. | 5.00 |
| Farmer Support Services Project | March 21, 1996 | 2001/2013 | n.a. | 17.00 |
| **Estonia** | | | | |
| Agriculture Project | March 5, 1996 | 2001/2012 | n.a. | 15.30 |
| **Georgia** | | | | |
| Health Project | April 25, 1996 | 2006/2031 | 9.70 | 14.00 |
| Structural Adjustment Credit | April 18, 1996 | 2006/2031 | 41.30 | 60.00 |
| Structural Adjustment Technical Assistance Project | April 18, 1996 | 2006/2031 | 3.30 | 4.80 |
| Transport Rehabilitation Project | January 18, 1996 | 2006/2030 | 8.10 | 12.00 |
| **Kazakstan** | | | | |
| Financial Sector Adjustment Loan | June 25, 1996 | 2001/2016 | n.a. | 180.00 |
| Irrigation and Drainage Improvement Project | June 18, 1996 | 2001/2016 | n.a. | 80.00 |
| **Kyrgyz Republic** | | | | |
| Financial Sector Adjustment Credit | June 25, 1996 | 2006/2031 | 31.20 | 45.00 |
| Financial Sector Technical Assistance Project | June 25, 1996 | 2006/2031 | 2.40 | 3.40 |
| Power and District Heating Rehabilitation Project | May 23, 1996 | 2006/2031 | 13.60 | 20.00 |
| Sheep Development Project | May 14, 1996 | 2006/2031 | 7.80 | 11.60 |
| Health Sector Reform Project | May 14, 1996 | 2006/2030 | 12.60 | 18.50 |
| **Latvia** | | | | |
| Municipal Services Development Project | December 14, 1995 | 2000/2012 | n.a. | 27.30 |

focusing on the most vulnerable groups—in particular, children, the elderly, and invalids—to assist destitute families who are not protected by other programs. In Armenia, child allowances, focused in particular on younger children, are being increased with assistance from the Bank. Armenia's attempt to target its humanitarian assistance better centers around a pioneering attempt to track and quantify the numbers of needy in a "social passport," and it is being

| Country/project name | Date of Approval | Maturities | Principal amount (millions) | |
|---|---|---|---|---|
| | | | SDR | US$ |
| **Lithuania** | | | | |
| Klaipeda Geothermal Demonstration Project | May 9, 1996 | 2001/2016 | n.a. | 5.90 |
| Private Agriculture Development Project | April 2, 1996 | 2001/2016 | n.a. | 30.00 |
| Siauliai Environment Project | December 5, 1995 | 1999/2011 | n.a. | 6.20 |
| **Macedonia, former Yugoslav Republic of** | | | | |
| Health Sector Transition Project | June 20, 1996 | 2006/2031 | 11.80 | 16.90 |
| Private Sector Development Project | May 16, 1996 | 2002/2016 | n.a. | 12.00 |
| Private Farmer Support Project | May 16, 1996 | 2006/2031 | 5.40 | 7.90 |
| **Moldova** | | | | |
| Energy Project | May 23, 1996 | 2001/2016 | n.a. | 10.00 |
| First Agriculture Project | May 7, 1996 | 2001/2016 | n.a. | 10.00 |
| First Private Sector Development Project | February 8, 1996 | 2001/2016 | n.a. | 35.00 |
| **Poland** | | | | |
| Bielsko-Biala Water and Wastewater Project | June 4, 1996 | 2001/2013 | n.a. | 21.50 |
| Power Transmission Project | November 18, 1995 | 2000/2012 | n.a. | 160.00 |
| **Romania** | | | | |
| Financial and Enterprise Sector Adjustment Loan | January 18, 1996 | 2001/2015 | n.a. | 280.00 |
| Railway Rehabilitation Project | January 18, 1996 | 2001/2016 | n.a. | 120.00 |
| Power Sector Rehabilitation and Modernization Project | August 29, 1995 | 2001/2015 | n.a. | 110.00 |
| **Russian Federation** | | | | |
| Coal Sector Restructuring Implementation Assistance Project | June 27, 1996 | 2001/2013 | n.a. | 25.00 |
| Coal Sector Adjustment Loan | June 27, 1996 | 2001/2013 | n.a. | 500.00 |
| Legal Reform Project | June 13, 1996 | 2001/2013 | n.a. | 58.00 |
| Medical Equipment Project | June 4, 1996 | 2001/2013 | n.a. | 270.00 |
| Capital Market Development Project | May 30, 1996 | 2001/2013 | n.a. | 89.00 |
| Enterprise Housing Divestiture Project | May 7, 1996 | 2002/2011 | n.a. | 300.00 |
| Community Social Infrastructure Project | April 30, 1996 | 2001/2013 | n.a. | 200.00 |
| Bridge Rehabilitation Project | March 28, 1996 | 2001/2013 | n.a. | 350.00 |
| Standards Development Project | November 30, 1995 | 2001/2012 | n.a. | 24.00 |
| **Slovenia** | | | | |
| Environment Project | May 28, 1996 | 2002/2011 | n.a. | 23.90 |
| **Tajikistan** | | | | |
| Institution Building Technical Assistance Project | May 16, 1996 | 2006/2036 | 3.4 | 5.00 |
| **Turkey** | | | | |
| Road Improvement and Traffic Safety Project | June 20, 1996 | 2002/2013 | n.a. | 250.00 |
| Public Financial Management Project | September 21, 1995 | 1999/2011 | n.a. | 62.00 |
| **Ukraine** | | | | |
| Enterprise Development Adjustment Loan | June 27, 1996 | 2001/2013 | n.a. | 310.00 |
| Coal Pilot Project | May 16, 1996 | 2000/2013 | n.a. | 15.81 |
| Housing Project | March 14, 1996 | 2001/2013 | n.a. | 17.00 |
| Total | | | 321.40 | 4,226.81 [a] |

n.a. = not applicable (IBRD loan).

a. Does not include the refinanced/rescheduled overdue charges of $168 million for Bosnia and Herzegovina.

reviewed as a possible vehicle for targeting general cash transfers. Again in Armenia, as well as in Albania, projects are providing employment opportunities through microprojects managed by local communities for marginalized and vulnerable groups.

**Rationalizing the Public Sector**

The Bank is also helping to facilitate the process by which the state adapts its role and priorities in the transition to a market economy, and during the past year, it expanded its nonlending support in this area. Public expenditure reviews were carried out in nine countries of the FSU, and measures were identified to improve fiscal management and reorient expenditures. In several countries of the region, underlying budgetary systems require revamping. In Turkey, for example, expenditure management and control is hampered by complex and outdated budgetary framework and systems, the plethora of agencies and funds that are effectively outside the budgetary process, and deficiencies in cash management and public sector accounting; partly as a result, government expenditures have exceeded targets in recent years. The Bank-assisted Public Financial Management Project is attempting to enhance the government budget's usefulness as a fiscal policy instrument and as a tool for managing public finances by reducing the number of sources of government spending that now operate outside budgetary channels and by introducing budgeting of public administration positions and payroll. A similar effort, also supported by the Bank, is under way in Kazakstan.

About a third of the Bank's portfolio in the region is supporting efforts to increase the effectiveness of governments' role in critical infrastructure and energy networks. Road-improvement projects currently under way in Albania and Russia have introduced competitive bidding by private contractors for awarding contracts. In Bulgaria, reforms, aimed at ensuring that the railways operate independently in a commercial manner according to market principles are being supported by the Bank and European and North American cofinanciers.

Capacity rehabilitation for both energy production and distribution needs public and private sector collaboration. Through its sector work and program of donor coordination, the Bank is assisting Ukraine to develop a competitive electricity subsector that will be an attractive target for private investments in the future.

In Kazakstan, the Bank is working on the rehabilitation of the Uzen oil field in a way that facilitates foreign investment.

### Support for Agriculture and Environmental Rehabiltation

In most countries of the region reform in agriculture has been slow. But, because most state or collective farms had been inefficient producers and because the commercial links were highly monopolistic, restructuring of farms and marketing structures are essential prerequisites to increased agricultural productivity. For example, the breakup of Kazakstan's grain monopoly during implementation of a structural adjustment loan approved in fiscal 1995 has been instrumental in dramatically improving farmgate prices. (As late as 1994, the monopoly was paying only about 50 percent of world market prices for the purchase of domestically produced grain.) While access to private plots of land has been essential in helping households across the region cope with the general economic crisis, the difficulty of reaching political and social consensus on issues of land ownership has compounded the difficulties of creating an environment in which private rural activity can flourish. The Bank continues to actively pursue reform in this area through an active dialogue and outreach program. In Georgia, it convened a series of seminars attended by officials at the highest levels of government; its agricultural sector work in Armenia is being used as a textbook published by the government; and in Romania, Bank staff, together with local officials, are analyzing problems that conspire to hinder rural entrepreneurship and are developing policy options to mitigate them.

The Bank is also supporting a number of activities aimed at the emerging class of private farmers, including operations approved during the past year supporting extension and research services in Croatia and FYR Macedonia. In Estonia, the Bank is supporting efforts to stimulate the rural economy through a project that is helping to privatize rural lands and privatize and rehabilitate select rural infrastructure.

The Bank is also working with its member countries to reverse serious environmental degradation. It continued to assist governments in developing and implementing national environmental action plans (NEAPS). One was completed in the fiscal year, adding to eleven completed earlier, with preparation under way for an additional five. Strengthening environmental institutional capacity is also receiving increasing attention.

Although Ukraine has serious environmental problems, especially in its industrial regions, local environmental agencies lack experience with modern regulatory practices. An Institutional Development Fund grant in Donetsk oblast, one of Ukraine's "hot spots," is supporting capacity building and practical training in monitoring and controlling pollution, carrying out environmental audits of main polluting plants and impact assessments of investment projects, and applying economic instruments in regulatory activities. Through innovative financing of pollution reduction in Slovenia, the Bank is demonstrating how solutions to local environmental problems—conversions from low-quality coal to gas or district heat to reduce dust and sulfur dioxide—can also address regional and global concerns over sulfur. The Global Environment Facility and the Bank are working together on another coal-to-gas conversion project in Poland to reduce greenhouse gas emissions, particularly those of carbon dioxide and methane. The Bank continued to be involved in regional programs to address degradation of economically important bodies of water—the Aral, Baltic, Black, Caspian, and Mediterranean seas, as well as the Danube river.

Mixed results characterized economic performance in the countries of Latin America and the Caribbean (LAC) in 1995. While the aggregate regional economy grew by only 0.8 percent, sharp distinctions persisted among the countries of the region. The December 1994 peso crisis in Mexico led to a substantial 6.9 percent decline in gross domestic product (GDP) in 1995. In Argentina and Uruguay, the main countries affected by "spill-over" effects from the Mexican crisis, the economies contracted by 4.4 and 2.5 percent, respectively.

However, the rest of the region weathered the effects of the Mexican crisis quite well. Figure 4-3 indicates that aggregate regional growth— excluding Argentina and Mexico—reached 4.3 percent. Brazil, the region's largest economy, with approximately 40 percent of the regional GDP, grew at a moderate 4.2 percent.

The GDP in Caribbean countries grew only slightly slower on average—3.6 percent in 1995. The two most populous countries, Haiti and the Dominican Republic, were among the fastest growing, with GDP rising above 4 percent in both.

The "containment" of the peso crisis to a relatively small group of countries was the major economic news in the region in 1995. By mid year, international capital markets were once again accessible to most countries, albeit at

higher interest rates. Substantial efforts at macroeconomic stabilization occurred in Mexico, stabilizing financial markets and helping to promote the recovery of investor and consumer confidence. In Argentina, both an adjustment of the fiscal stance and an orderly restructuring of the banking system combined to foster a climate more conducive to financial flows, which, by year's end, had returned international reserves and monetary aggregates to their pre-crisis levels. The credibility of the Real Plan in Brazil also contributed to a sharp increase in capital inflows from abroad, including strong flows of foreign direct investment. Among the other large countries, only Venezuela, where confidence in policies waned and investment stagnated, experienced a run on reserves, culminating in a devaluation of 41 percent in December.

Inflation, which in the past tended to be exacerbated by macroeconomic crises, fell in most countries in 1995, with the median inflation rate dropping to 12.3 percent from 16.8 percent in 1994. Throughout the region, countries with historically high inflation rates have sucessfully contained inflation over the past several years; that success was maintained in 1995. An exception to the regional pattern was Mexico, where the severe depreciation of the

peso contributed to a sharp rise in inflation.

Events of the past year have shown that the region's economies are now sufficiently differentiated—and world financial markets sufficiently sophisticated—that adverse developments in one country need not pull others down. This realization, if accompanied by continued pursuit of prudent macroeconomic policies, should serve to reduce volatility and increase stability in the region.

The crisis did, however, underline significant fragility and vulnerability in many of the region's financial and banking systems—not only in Mexico but also in Argentina and a number of other countries. With Bank support, countries are examining the main problems in these sectors and are formulating reform programs. Much work remains ahead, however.

In both Mexico and Argentina, the weak position of the banking system contributed to the poor GDP performance. Investors—international and domestic—feared that a collapse of important banks could result in major economic dislocations, massive and costly bailout programs, and a resurgence of inflation. In the case of Argentina, the weakness of the banking system tested the convertibility program and, in particular, the exchange-rate regime. The economic program survived the crisis intact, possibly strengthened from the government's commitment to it under adverse conditions.

In Brazil, the weakness of the banking system—and especially of state-owned banks—has added significant uncertainty to the public deficit picture. Central bank schemes to provide liquidity to private banks in distress and treasury obligations to recapitalize public banks will add significant amounts to public debt over the 1995–96 period.

An important component of the Venezuelan program is to recapitalize and strengthen the banking system. This program has a series of elements, including strengthening the regulatory framework, reprivatizing banks previously taken over by the government, and liquidating those banks deemed nonviable.

## Challenges Ahead

Looking beyond recent developments, the longer-term challenges facing the Latin America and Caribbean region include the following:

*Increasing and sustaining economic growth.* The Latin America and Caribbean region is capable of achieving a growth rate of 6 percent by the turn of the century—under reasonable assumptions about the evolution of the external environment and of appropriate domestic policies. Increased domestic savings rates will be crucial for more robust growth to occur. One of the important lessons of the Mexican crisis is that domestic savings matter greatly. They are important because they help finance the accumulation of capital and, thus, facilitate growth, and because high domestic savings are associated with lower current-account deficits. Latin America, however, has traditionally had very low saving rates: In 1980, for example, the region saved on average only 19 percent of its GDP; by 1994 this ratio was basically unaltered. This contrasts sharply with fast-growing regions of the world that save 35 percent or more of GDP. Most policymakers now recognize that raising domestic savings is one of the fundamental challenges faced by the region.

Factors enhancing the region's international competitiveness will also be important. These underline the necessity of continued and sustained trade liberalization, including through

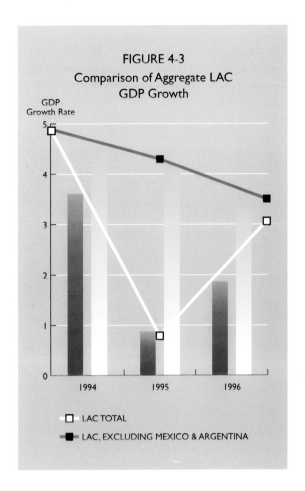

**FIGURE 4-3**
**Comparison of Aggregate LAC GDP Growth**

trade-creating regional arrangements such as MERCOSUR, the regional trade agreement between Argentina, Brazil, Paraguay, and Uruguay. MERCOSUR has been one of the more successful trade agreements in the region, if not in the developing world as a whole. It has continued to foster free trade, as marked by the recent associate membership of Chile and the anticipated associate membership of Bolivia. The region, at a minimum, must sustain the robust export performance of 1995, when the nominal value of total exports increased by 22.7 percent over 1994. In Mexico and Argentina, exports responded particularly well to the new economic circumstances, growing at 33.2 percent and 30.1 percent, respectively, in 1995. During the next eighteen months, a rapid recovery of these economies will require maintaining the momentum in export expansion, as well as a

significant increase in the level of internal demand. A more significant regional challenge is to complement traditional trade in primary products with fast growth in manufactures. There is also scope for productivity increases through port reform and privatization, as well as the application of international quality standards.

*Reducing poverty and inequality.* Poverty in Latin America and the Caribbean increased substantially during the debt crisis of the 1980s, but stabilized with the resumption of growth in the early 1990s. Robust rates of economic expansion in recent years in countries like Chile and Peru, the payoffs from economic reforms in Argentina and elsewhere, and the decrease in civil strife in parts of Central America have all helped to reduce poverty.

Nevertheless, poverty and inequality constitute the "Achilles heel" of Latin American development. About one fourth of the region's population lives on less than $1 a day. The poorest 10 percent-to-20 percent live in rural areas (and are often indigenous people). This rural poverty tends to be concentrated in remote areas with low agricultural productivity and few nonfarm jobs. Most of the increase in poverty in

the region over the past ten to fifteen years, however, has been in the cities, and as such is a relatively new and intractable phenomenon. Poverty in the region is also closely related to the distribution of income, which is still very skewed in most countries.

Reducing urban poverty will require increasing employment opportunities for the urban poor; extending access to urban services; making social safety nets more effective in urban areas; increasing the productivity of the informal economy; increasing labor-force participation rates; and reforming municipal administration. Reducing rural poverty will require eliminating regulatory barriers to enable the agricultural sector to take advantage of trade liberalization. Increasing the access of the rural poor to land and social services is another important requirement for rural poverty reduction.

*Promoting human-resource development.* Building human capital is another major challenge confronting the countries of the region. With an average of 5.2 years' education for the adult population, the region lags about two years behind countries at comparable development levels elsewhere. In addition to expanding access to educational opportunities for the poor, there is a critical need to improve the quality of education, particularly at the primary level. About 100 million people in the region are without basic health services, and about 2.2 million babies are born every year without any medical assistance. As a consequence, the occurrence of disease is significantly higher than might be expected given the region's average income level.

*Reforming and modernizing the state.* Repeated economic crises have taken a heavy toll on public sector institutions. The effects of austerity have been compounded by economic mismanagement. A number of governments in the region have recently implemented policy reforms designed to reduce the role of the state in economic activities. However, major improvements in the efficiency of government services as they affect the lives of ordinary people—particularly the quality and coverage of social services—remain to be attained. Among the challenges are strengthening the management of public finance,

TABLE 4-13.  LENDING TO BORROWERS IN LATIN AMERICA AND THE CARIBBEAN, BY SECTOR, 1987–96

*(millions of US dollars; fiscal years)*

| Sector | Annual average, 1987–91 | 1992 | 1993 | 1994 | 1995 | 1996 |
|---|---|---|---|---|---|---|
| Agriculture | 862.2 | 1,118.6 | 390.0 | 407.9 | 460.7 | 412.8 |
| Education | 181.7 | 597.1 | 588.7 | 1,083.3 | 747.1 | 493.1 |
| Electric power and other energy | 496.1 | 42.5 | 345.1 | — | 161.5 | 465.4 |
| Environment | 59.6 | 501.0 | 16.3 | 457.0 | 83.5 | 115.0 |
| Finance | 1,055.0 | 827.0 | 125.0 | 604.5 | 1,909.5 | 11.9 |
| Industry | 312.9 | — | — | — | — | 8.0 |
| Mining/Other extractive | 51.4 | — | 250.0 | 14.0 | — | 41.0 |
| Multisector | 757.1 | 782.8 | 1,318.1 | 122.2 | 328.6 | 110.9 |
| Oil and gas | 91.7 | 78.6 | 11.8 | — | 11.0 | 10.6 |
| Population, health, and nutrition | 186.6 | 37.3 | 329.0 | 331.0 | 94.6 | 1,086.4 |
| Public sector management | 322.2 | 362.2 | 443.0 | 58.3 | 596.4 | 666.4 |
| Social sector | 7.9 | 10.2 | 45.0 | 130.0 | 500.0 | 262.0 |
| Telecommunications/Informatics | 13.4 | — | — | — | — | — |
| Transportation | 485.4 | 564.2 | 1,697.5 | 595.0 | 371.0 | 530.0 |
| Urban development | 384.5 | 490.0 | 170.0 | 422.0 | 575.0 | 20.0 |
| Water supply and sanitation | 224.3 | 250.0 | 439.0 | 521.5 | 221.5 | 204.0 |
| Total | 5,492.0 | 5,661.5 | 6,168.5 | 4,746.7 | 6,060.4 | 4,437.5 |
| Of which:  IBRD | 5,328.8 | 5,256.5 | 5,851.8 | 4,434.5 | 5,715.3 | 4,047.2 |
|           IDA | 163.1 | 405.0 | 316.7 | 312.2 | 345.2 | 390.3 |
| Number of operations | 45 | 45 | 50 | 48 | 52 | 54 |

NOTE: Details may not add to totals because of rounding.
— Zero.

building effective legal and regulatory functions, reforming the judiciary, and improving the civil service. A regionwide process of governmental decentralization is already under way. This has enormous promise, but difficult questions remain concerning the modalities of fiscal decentralization and the matching of revenues and expenditures at the local level.

## Bank Operations, Fiscal 1996

As part of a coordinated effort to strengthen portfolio quality, the Bank is paying closer attention to simplifying projects, focusing conditions only on actions essential for successful project implementation, and working with clients to improve project impact and sustainability. Following a visit by Bank President James Wolfensohn to the Northeast of Brazil in July, 1995, a joint commission was established with the Government of Brazil to recommend ways of improving the effectiveness of Bank-financed operations in Brazil, with a special focus on the Northeast. The commission is identifying possible ways of addressing some of the persistent problems that have impeded the development impact of projects from being fully realized in four areas: education, health, rural development, and the environment.

In addition, business-process innovations currently under way in the Bank's Latin America and the Caribbean Regional Office are likely to enhance the development effectiveness of the region's portfolio (see Box 4-4).

*Program highlights.* In fiscal 1996, a total of fifty-four new projects, totaling $4.4 billion in new commitments, was approved. As part of an effort by the Bank's Regional Office to improve loan quality and simplify operations, the average project size declined to $82 million, down from $85 million in fiscal 1995 and $101 million in the year before that.

In addition to a substantial program of infrastructure lending, the lending program included support to strengthen financial systems, as well as a range of projects to assist in improved environmental management. The Bank lent $500 million for banking reform in Argentina, part of a program seeking to increase confidence in the banking system through a restoration of solvency and consolidation in the private banking sector. The Bolivia program included four projects to develop the regulatory and legal framework to support the country's capitalization program, including the institutional capacity to carry out financial sector reforms. To help ensure that future economic growth is also

### TABLE 4-14. WORLD BANK COMMITMENTS, DISBURSEMENTS, AND NET TRANSFERS IN LATIN AMERICA AND THE CARIBBEAN, 1991–96

*(millions of US dollars; fiscal years)*

| Item | Brazil start 1996 | Brazil 1996 | Brazil 1991–96 | Mexico start 1996 | Mexico 1996 | Mexico 1991–96 | Argentina start 1996 | Argentina 1996 | Argentina 1991–96 | Total region start 1996 | Total region 1996 | Total region 1991–96 |
|---|---|---|---|---|---|---|---|---|---|---|---|---|
| Undisbursed commitments | 4,512 | | | 5,483 | | | 2,380 | | | 18,709 | | |
| Commitments | | 875 | 5,135 | | 527 | 8,969 | | 1,509 | 6,555 | | 4,438 | 32,311 |
| Gross disbursements | | 1,082 | 4,394 | | 1,473 | 7,616 | | 733 | 4,126 | | 4,632 | 24,962 |
| Repayments | | 1,315 | 7,794 | | 1,461 | 6,548 | | 260 | 2,002 | | 4,886 | 26,145 |
| Net disbursements | | -232 | -3,400 | | 12 | 1,069 | | 472 | 2,124 | | -253 | -1,183 |
| Interest and charges | | 453 | 3,497 | | 951 | 5,463 | | 317 | 1,509 | | 2,588 | 16,742 |
| Net transfer | | -685 | -6,897 | | -939 | -4,394 | | 155 | 615 | | -2,841 | -17,925 |

NOTE: *Disbursements from the IDA Special Fund are included. The countries shown in the table are those with the largest borrowings of Bank funds during fiscal 1995–96. Details may not add to totals because of rounding.*

## BOX 4-4. PROCESS CHANGES BEGUN IN THE LATIN AMERICA AND THE CARIBBEAN REGION

*In fiscal 1996, the Latin America and the Caribbean Regional Office of the World Bank implemented a series of innovations designed to enhance implementation and effectiveness of Bank-assisted projects and responsiveness to client needs; decentralize responsibility to line managers and staff; and strengthen professional and technical expertise.*

*Highlights of the process innovations undertaken during the fiscal year include:*

***Revised country-assistance strategy.*** *Performance benchmarks will be spelled out in advance for individual countries and important sectors. In helping countries to attain the development objectives, greater decisionmaking authority and accountability have been delegated to country departments and managers within the Region.*

***Changes in country departments.*** *Effective April 1, 1996, the former Country Department II (LA 2) was replaced by separate departments for Mexico and Central America. The bulk of the Mexico department staff, including the department director, is being transferred to the field (in an expanded resident mission based in Mexico City). This is intended to improve the Bank's ability to tailor its lending and nonlending services to Mexico's evolving needs; quicken response time for both projects and analytical work; facilitate better management of existing projects; and draw upon local expertise. In addition, a Sector Leadership Group has been created to serve both new departments. This group will bring techni-*

*cal resources (with the exception of those housed in the Human Capital Development Group) to bear on specific initiatives at the request of country departments.*

***Human Capital Development Group.*** *The Human Capital Development Group is a Regionwide pilot initiative that involves pooling the Region's human-resource staff—in the areas of education, health and nutrition, poverty reduction, and gender concerns—into one discrete unit. The goal is to integrate better the Regional human-resource sector knowledge and technical skills with the work of all the country departments. As with staff in the Sector Leadership Group, staff in the Human Capital Development Group will be deployed on an as-needed basis for project and analytical work in specific countries.*

*NGO **liaison.*** *The Region held two regional Bank-NGO meetings to strengthen collaboration, particularly in the areas of poverty reduction. One outcome of the first meeting was the establishment of NGO liaison officers in resident missions. Liaison officers are responsible for facilitating closer relations between the Bank and grassroots organizations on all aspects of the Bank's country activities. In particular, they will work to improve the flow of information between the Bank and grassroots groups, help increase NGO participation in Bank projects and economic and sector work, and explore new avenues for collaboration.*

environmentally sustainable, Bank projects are incorporating innovative approaches to environmental assessments, such as regional and sectoral studies, and participation by nongovernmental organizations (NGOs). Some infrastructure projects include support for technical assistance and training to improve environmental assessment capabilities of borrowers.

The Regional Office is also undertaking an extensive program of lending for both education and health. Several of these operations were in Argentina, including the Decentralization and Improvement of Secondary Education and Polymodal Education Development Project, which facilitated the decentralization of secondary education to the provinces, and the Higher

Education Reform Project, which aimed at improving the quality of higher education through a new resource-allocation system, and by strengthening planning and managerial capacities. The Health Sector Reform Project in Brazil seeks to assist with policy reforms and improve the delivery of care under the national healthcare program, the sole source of publicly supported care for the poor. A series of basic education projects was undertaken in Dominica, the Dominican Republic, Grenada, Guyana, Panama, and Trinidad and Tobago, which includes initiatives to enhance access and quality, strengthen institutional capacities for management reform, improve teacher training, refurbish facilities, and develop curricula. In Haiti, the

## TABLE 4-15. PROJECTS APPROVED DURING FISCAL YEAR 1996, LATIN AMERICA AND THE CARIBBEAN

| Country/project name | Date of Approval | Maturities | Principal amount (millions) SDR | Principal amount (millions) US$ |
|---|---|---|---|---|
| **Argentina** | | | | |
| Health Insurance Reform Loan | April 25, 1996 | 2002/2011 | n.a. | 350.00 |
| Health Insurance Technical Assistance Project | April 25, 1996 | 2002/2011 | n.a. | 25.00 |
| Decentralization and Improvement of Secondary Education and Polymodal Education Development Project | December 21, 1995 | 2001/2015 | n.a. | 115.50 |
| Enterprise Export Development Project | November 28, 1995 | 2001/2010 | n.a. | 38.50 |
| Social Protection Project | November 21, 1995 | 2001/2011 | n.a. | 152.00 |
| Public Investment Strengthening Technical Assistance Project | November 21, 1995 | 1999/2011 | n.a. | 16.00 |
| Forestry Development Project | October 24, 1995 | 2001/2010 | n.a. | 16.00 |
| Provincial Health Sector Development Project | August 3, 1995 | 2001/2010 | n.a. | 101.40 |
| Mining Development Technical Assistance Project | July 25, 1995 | 2001/2010 | n.a. | 30.00 |
| Bank Reform Loan | July 25, 1995 | 2001/2010 | n.a. | 500.00 |
| Higher Education Reform Project | July 6, 1995 | 2001/2010 | n.a. | 165.00 |
| **Bolivia** | | | | |
| Rural Water and Sanitation Project | January 16, 1996 | 2006/2035 | 13.40 | 20.00 |
| Environment, Industry, and Mining Project | December 21, 1995 | 2006/2035 | 7.40 | 11.00 |
| Capitalization Program Adjustment Credit | July 6, 1995 | 2005/2035 | 34.00 | 50.00 |
| Capitalization Program Adjustment Credit (IDA reflows) | December 12, 1995 | 2005/2035 | 5.30 | 8.00 |
| Financial Markets and Pension Reform Technical Assistance Project | November 30, 1995 | 2006/2035 | 6.10 | 9.00 |
| Power Sector Reform Technical Assistance Project | November 30, 1995 | 2006/2035 | 3.50 | 5.10 |
| Rural Communities Development Project | August 3, 1995 | 2005/2035 | 9.60 | 15.00 |
| Hydrocarbon Sector Reform and Capitalization Technical Assistance Project | July 6, 1995 | 2005/2035 | 6.80 | 10.64 |
| **Brazil** | | | | |
| Rural Poverty Alleviation and Natural Resources Management Project | June 27, 1996 | 2001/2011 | n.a. | 175.00 |
| Health Sector Reform Project-REFORSUS | June 20, 1996 | 2001/2011 | n.a. | 300.00 |
| Federal Railways Restructuring and Privatization Project | June 20, 1996 | 2002/2011 | n.a. | 350.00 |
| Environmental Conservation and Rehabilitation Project | July 11, 1995 | 2001/2010 | n.a. | 50.00 |
| **Chile** | | | | |
| Secano Rural Poverty Alleviation and Natural Resource Management Project | January 16, 1996 | 2001/2011 | n.a. | 15.00 |
| **Colombia** | | | | |
| Bogotá Urban Transport Project | May 23, 1996 | 2001/2013 | n.a. | 65.00 |
| Urban Environment Management Project | January 16, 1996 | 2001/2013 | n.a. | 20.00 |
| Santa Fe I Water Supply and Sewerage Rehabilitation Project | November 16, 1995 | 2001/2012 | n.a. | 145.00 |
| Power Market Development Project | November 16, 1995 | 1999/2011 | n.a. | 249.30 |
| **Dominica** | | | | |
| Basic Education Reform Project[a] | December 21, 1995 | 2006/2030 | 2.10 | 3.07 |
| Basic Education Reform Project[a] | December 21, 1995 | 1999/2011 | n.a. | 3.07 |
| **Dominican Republic** | | | | |
| Second Basic Education Development Project | November 9, 1995 | 2001/2015 | n.a. | 37.00 |
| **Ecuador** | | | | |
| Environmental Management Technical Assistance Project | April 4, 1996 | 2000/2009 | n.a. | 15.00 |
| **El Salvador** | | | | |
| Land Administration Project | March 5, 1996 | 2000/2013 | n.a. | 50.00 |
| Basic Education Modernization Project | September 28, 1995 | 2001/2012 | n.a. | 34.00 |
| Competitiveness Enhancement Technical Assistance Project | September 28, 1995 | 2001/2012 | n.a. | 16.00 |
| Energy Sector Modernization Project | July 6, 1995 | 2000/2015 | n.a. | 65.00 |

| Country/project name | Date of Approval | Maturities | Principal amount (millions) | |
|---|---|---|---|---|
| | | | SDR | US$ |
| **Grenada** | | | | |
| Basic Education Reform Project[a] | December 21, 1995 | 2006/2030 | n.a. | 3.83 |
| Basic Education Reform Project[a] | December 21, 1995 | 1999/2011 | 2.60 | 3.83 |
| **Guyana** | | | | |
| Secondary School Reform Project | June 11, 1996 | 2006/2036 | 11.80 | 17.30 |
| Private Sector Development Adjustment Credit (IDA reflows) | December 12, 1995 | 2005/2035 | 2.00 | 2.90 |
| **Haiti** | | | | |
| Employment Generation Project | July 11, 1995 | 2005/2035 | 31.80 | 50.00 |
| **Honduras** | | | | |
| Public Sector Modernization Technical Assistance Credit | February 8, 1996 | 2006/2035 | 6.40 | 9.60 |
| Public Sector Modernization Structural Adjustment Credit | February 8, 1996 | 2006/2035 | 36.60 | 55.00 |
| Public Sector Modernization Structural Adjustment Credit (IDA reflows) | February 8, 1996 | 2006/2035 | 17.60 | 26.40 |
| Third Social Investment Fund Project | July 11, 1995 | 2005/2035 | 19.10 | 30.00 |
| **Jamaica** | | | | |
| Generation Recovery and Improvement Project | September 28, 1995 | 1999/2010 | n.a. | 21.00 |
| **Mexico** | | | | |
| Water Resources Management Project | June 20, 1996 | 2000/2011 | n.a. | 186.50 |
| Second Basic Health Care Project | September 26, 1995 | 1999/2011 | n.a. | 310.00 |
| Privatization Technical Assistance Project | August 29, 1995 | 1999/2010 | n.a. | 30.00 |
| **Nicaragua** | | | | |
| Road Rehabilitation and Maintenance Project | May 30, 1996 | 2006/2036 | 17.20 | 25.00 |
| Second Economic Recovery Credit (IDA reflows) | December 12, 1995 | 2004/2034 | 3.90 | 5.80 |
| Second Social Investment Fund Project | July 11, 1995 | 2005/2035 | 19.10 | 30.00 |
| **Panama** | | | | |
| Debt and Debt Service Reduction Loan | March 28, 1996 | 2000/2011 | n.a. | 30.00 |
| Basic Education Project | March 28, 1996 | 2000/2011 | n.a. | 35.00 |
| **Paraguay** | | | | |
| Secondary Education Improvement Project | September 14, 1995 | 1999/2011 | n.a. | 24.50 |
| **Peru** | | | | |
| Rural Road Rehabilitation and Maintenance Project | December 5, 1995 | 2001/2012 | n.a. | 90.00 |
| **St. Lucia** | | | | |
| Watershed and Environmental Management Project[a] | July 11, 1995 | 2001/2010 | n.a. | 2.65 |
| Watershed and Environmental Management Project[a] | July 11, 1995 | 2005/2030 | 1.70 | 2.65 |
| **Trinidad and Tobago** | | | | |
| Basic Education Project | November 16, 1995 | 1999/2011 | n.a. | 51.00 |
| **Uruguay** | | | | |
| Power Transmission and Distribution Project | October 31, 1995 | 2001/2010 | n.a. | 125.00 |
| **Venezuela** | | | | |
| Water and Sewerage Decentralization Project in the State of Monagas | June 4, 1996 | 2002/2013 | n.a. | 39.00 |
| Total | | | 258.00 | 4,437.54 |

n.a. = not applicable (IBRD loan).

a. "Blend" loan/credit.

Bank's accelerated program in response to the economic crisis included an employment-generation project.

One recent innovation in lending is taking place in Brazil, where the Bank is supporting fiscal adjustment, privatization and concessioning, and administrative reforms at the subnational level—particularly in states with strong fiscal management and project-implementation capacities. Honduras received a loan supporting the implementation of its public sector reform program. This program includes modernizing public management systems and strengthening financial management. Several projects devoted substantial attention to strengthening the regulatory frameworks of specific sectors, particularly with respect to recent privatizations. They included the Power Market Development Project (Colombia), the Railroads Restructuring and Privatization Project (Brazil), the Private Sector Development Project (Guyana), and the Second Basic Health Care Project and the Water Resources Project (Mexico).

The regional lending program includes a large amount of cofinancing activity—$2.1 billion for twenty-six projects. The Inter-American Development Bank (IDB) provided the largest amount of cofinancing—$1.6 billion. The Health Sector Reform Project (Brazil) provides a vivid example of close collaboration between the Bank and the IDB. This $750 million project (supported by $300 million in Bank funds and $350 million from the IDB) was jointly identified and appraised by the two institutions. It is being managed by one administrative unit (composed of Bank and IDB personnel), with joint supervisory efforts. Even the loan agreements by the two institutions are essentially identical, with corresponding conditionality matrices and procurement procedures.

## Economic and Sector Work

The Regional Office maintained its efforts to improve the impact of the Bank's program of economic and sector studies as instruments of analysis and dialogue with governments, adopting a range of formats and styles as appropriate. The trend has been away from general country economic memoranda toward more issue-focused analyses of economywide and sectoral topics. A recurring theme is the challenge of efficient management at the subnational level, both provincial and state (in the cases of Argentina, Brazil, and Mexico, for example), as well as the regional and municipal levels. An assessment of state creditworthiness in Brazil was undertaken as a basis for assisting with fiscal adjustment and structural reform programs at the state level. In Argentina's Tucuman province and in Mexico's Chiapas state, the Bank undertook studies (in the case of Tucuman jointly with the IFC, and in the case of Chiapas together with the IFC and Inter-American Development Bank) to design strategies for stronger private sector involvement in these regions. In Tucuman, the resulting action plan is now being implemented with support from the Bank and the IFC. Again in Argentina, another study in cooperation with the IFC was carried out to identify reforms for Cordoba province. Substantial work has also been undertaken on the managerial implications of democratization and decentralization, particularly in the case of Colombia.

The program of poverty assessments continued, bringing the total number completed to twenty-five. These documents have helped to provide a framework for the design of country-specific poverty-reduction strategies. Unemployment has become a serious political and social issue in several countries. Thus, in Argentina, a detailed quantitative look at the structure of unemployment was carried out, and the links between unemployment and collective bargaining arrangements were explored. Work is under way on labor-market characteristics at both the national and regional levels in a number of countries.

As is customary every second year, the Bank hosted the Consultative Group for Caribbean Economic Development. In preparation for this June 1996 meeting, a program of analytic work was undertaken, focusing on growth, trade, public sector management, and poverty. Following the successful format of the previous meeting of the group, representatives from the private sector were again invited to participate in all aspects of the meeting, which ranged from individual country sessions to Caribbean Business Forum and Tourism and Informatics Promotion conferences.

The Middle East and North Africa (MENA) region achieved a modest upswing in growth of gross domestic product (GDP) in 1995. Among the economies in which the Bank is active, Algeria, Egypt, Iran, Tunisia, and the West Bank and Gaza all achieved GDP growth ranging from 2.5 percent to 5 percent. Jordan and Lebanon both continued to do well, with growth in excess of 6 percent. Others fared less well. Morocco, hard hit by severe drought, suffered an estimated decline in GDP of over 6 percent. Yemen's GDP grew by just over 1 percent.

*Recent developments.* Restoring rapid, widely shared, and environmentally sustainable growth remains a top priority for the region. In addition, further progress toward a just and comprehensive peace will be crucial for securing region-wide stability and security on which increased investment flows and more rapid growth in turn demand. The past year has offered both opportunities and challenges in this respect.

Agreement was reached on the establishment of the new Middle East Development Bank, which would provide an additional development funding source for the region. The second Middle East/North Africa Economic Summit was held in Amman, Jordan; at the Summit, the Bank called for initiatives to develop the region's water resources to stave off the prospect of growth-threatening water scarcity. And the European Union (EU) launched a potentially far-reaching initiative for a Euro-Mediterranean Partnership and Economic Area, which envisages complete free trade in industrial goods between the EU and eight Arab countries by 2010. Tunisia and Morocco have already signed free trade agreements with the EU; negotiations are under way with Egypt, Jordan, and Lebanon, while preliminary discussions have been completed with Algeria and have begun with Syria.

*The challenge of global integration.* Accelerating regional and national growth rates will depend above all on MENA countries' capacity to match external opportunities with domestic policies and programs that ready them for greater integration into the wider global economy. The Bank's *Global Economic Prospects* for 1996 clearly indicate that the "fast integrators" among the developing countries have reaped substantial rewards from their participation in this process, while the slow or lagging integrators have fallen behind—and can be expected to continue to do so as the international investment flows that fuel growth increasingly reward the fast integrators and penalize the slow ones.[10] The MENA region today faces the challenge of securing rapid integration based on maintaining macroeconomic stability; undertaking sometimes difficult outward-looking, private sector-oriented, and competitiveness-enhancing economic reform; and making complementary investments in the physical and human capital required for rapid and balanced growth.

## The Bank's Operational Response

In recent years, MENA countries have increasingly turned towards the path of openness, reform, and private sector-based competitiveness, although some are moving faster than others or have gained from starting the process earlier than others. During the year under review, as in the past, the Bank has supported country efforts with both lending and nonlending services.

*Promoting preconditions for rapid growth.* Almost half of the year's $1,595 million of Bank and IDA commitments to MENA countries was devoted to macroeconomic stabilization and private sector and export-oriented reform. A $300 million Structural Adjustment Loan to Algeria is supporting the government's determined efforts to turn towards a market-oriented economy. These efforts include measures to further cut the budget deficit and move forward with

10. World Bank. 1996. *Global Economic Prospects and the Developing Countries 1996.* Washington, D.C.

privatization and public enterprise and financial sector reform. The Government of Yemen has responded to problems of inflation, unemployment, and budgetary and balance-of-payments deficits with a comprehensive stabilization and adjustment program, to be assisted by an $80 million IDA Economic Recovery Credit that will support macroeconomic stabilization; privatization; and trade, regulatory, and public enterprise reform—all essential building blocks for balanced private sector-led development.

Morocco and Tunisia were the earliest economic reformers in the region. Lending during the year has further deepened the Bank's commitment to both countries' reform efforts. In Tunisia, a $38.7 million loan for the Industry Support Institutions Upgrading Project will help Tunisian firms to integrate into the proposed Euro-Med Economic Area by strengthening the technical services provided to industry, including sectorally oriented technical centers and national metrology services. Morocco has a strong and diversified private sector, but its rapid further expansion is inhibited by a shortage of resources to finance private investment. A $250 million Financial Markets Development

TABLE 4-16.  LENDING TO BORROWERS IN MIDDLE EAST AND NORTH AFRICA, BY SECTOR, 1987–96

*(millions of US dollars; fiscal years)*

| Sector | Annual average, 1987–91 | 1992 | 1993 | 1994 | 1995 | 1996 |
|---|---|---|---|---|---|---|
| Agriculture | 275.0 | 299.2 | 463.0 | 601.7 | 231.6 | 100.0 |
| Education | 132.7 | 75.0 | 115.2 | 33.0 | 158.3 | 138.3 |
| Electric power and other energy | 122.9 | 220.0 | 165.0 | 80.0 | — | — |
| Environment | — | — | — | 6.0 | 113.0 | 78.0 |
| Finance | 127.2 | 250.0 | — | 120.0 | — | 408.7 |
| Industry | 101.7 | — | — | — | — | — |
| Mining/Other extractive | 11.2 | — | — | — | — | — |
| Multisector | 270.0 | 275.0 | — | — | 150.0 | 380.0 |
| Oil and gas | 17.9 | 160.0 | — | — | — | 35.0 |
| Population, health, and nutrition | 76.4 | 26.8 | 188.0 | — | 35.7 | 85.2 |
| Public sector management | 35.8 | 9.0 | — | 19.9 | — | 20.0 |
| Social sector | — | — | — | — | — | 223.0 |
| Telecommunications/Informatics | 32.2 | — | 100.0 | 20.0 | — | — |
| Tourism | — | — | 130.0 | — | — | — |
| Transportation | 135.0 | — | 35.0 | — | 239.1 | 37.0 |
| Urban development | 98.0 | 110.0 | 684.0 | — | 51.0 | 50.0 |
| Water supply and sanitation | 87.1 | 57.0 | — | 270.0 | — | 40.0 |
| Total | 1,523.1 | 1,482.0 | 1,880.2 | 1,150.6 | 978.7 | 1,595.2 |
| Of which: IBRD | 1,433.4 | 1,324.0 | 1,756.4 | 1,050.6 | 925.4 | 1,276.7 |
| IDA | 89.6 | 158.0 | 123.8 | 100.0 | 53.3 | 318.5 |
| Number of operations | 20 | 17 | 19 | 16 | 14 | 21 |

NOTE: Details may not add to totals because of rounding.
— Zero.

Loan, the first element of a proposed multiyear private sector-development lending program, is supporting a government policy package that will help liberate the financial system to serve private sector expansion needs more effectively.

Two loans to Jordan during the year will help underpin the government's strategy for increasing the economy's outward orientation and integration into the global economy. Recognizing the constraints on growth represented by Jordan's small domestic market, the government plans to intensify its efforts to pursue a policy of private sector-led, export-oriented development. The $80 million Economic Reform and Development Loan is supporting a government policy package designed to promote new foreign and domestic investment and foster greater integration into world markets. To help speed this process, the government has also prepared an Export Sector Development Program, whose aim is to enhance the international competitiveness of Jordanian firms. The $40 million Bank-assisted Export Development Project will help to finance this program.

*Supporting human development.* Human development, broadly defined, is simultaneously an essential complement to, and a core component of, a national strategy for balanced growth and global competitiveness. Projects to support human development accounted for slightly more than one third of the value of lending to MENA countries during the year. An IBRD loan to Algeria and an IDA credit to Yemen are helping offset the adverse effects of these countries' adjustment programs on the poor by providing temporary employment in small public works activities. In Yemen, the $25 million Public Works Project is expected to create up to 10,000 manyears of labor-intensive employment in a large number of small-scale maintenance or extension programs. In Algeria, a $50 million Bank loan for the Social Safety Net Support Project is helping to launch an innovative pilot public works program that is expected to create nearly 20,000 manyears of temporary work in poorly served areas with high unemployment. The project has also been designed to strengthen Algeria's existing social safety net and support community-level testing of a new Social Fund

and a possible microenterprise program. In Egypt, an IDA credit of $120 million is providing a second tranche of support to that country's Social Fund for Development (SFD), which is expected to create about 50,000 permanent jobs and about 20,000 temporary jobs annually between 1997 and the year 2000.

Worker training was the focus of two operations during the year, in Tunisia and Yemen. A $60 million loan to Tunisia for the Second Training and Employment Project is helping to make training services more demand-driven and responsive to employers' needs by moving to a system emphasizing enterprise-based training. Yemen's vocational training (VT) system is being upgraded and expanded with the help of a $24.3 million IDA credit, which is also supporting adult education and training programs focusing on women, special VT programs for the handicapped, and establishment of a largely employer-financed Skills Development Fund.

Despite heavy past investment, MENA countries' education and health services are still struggling to deliver high levels of literacy and adequate health care, especially to rural populations and women—and, in several cases, current provision can barely keep pace with rapid population growth. These issues were directly addressed in lending to Morocco and Egypt during the year. The Bank is supporting Morocco's innovative, multisectoral Social Priorities Program (SPP) with three linked loans—a $68 million loan for health (focusing on basic health care and safe motherhood/family planning); a $54 million loan for education (focusing on primary schooling, especially in rural areas and for girls); and a $28 million loan for rural employment-promotion through labor-intensive public works. The SPP is targeted at Morocco's poorest provinces, and will be implemented on a coordinated basis at the same sites so as to maximize its synergistic effects. In Egypt, the aim of a $17.2 million IDA credit is to strengthen the operational and strategic leadership capacity of the new Ministry of Population and Family Planning and promote family-planning services in currently underserved areas, particularly rural areas of Upper Egypt, where fertility remains high.

One other operation during the year was designed to ameliorate the lives of less well-off or vulnerable groups. The $100 million Emergency Drought Recovery Project in Morocco will address the devastating effects of last year's drought on the (largely poor) rural population by providing seeds and livestock feed, and by improving rural water supply. Over the longer run, the project is expected to begin the process of reducing the vulnerability of the rural population to severe drought through greater preparedness, better rural infrastructure, and improved management of natural resources.

*Investing in infrastructure and environmental protection.* The remainder of the year's lending focused on two other aspects of rapid growth—providing the infrastructure needed to support it and cleaning up the industrial pollution that can be one of its unintended consequences. Infrastructure investments included one transportation operation—a $37 million IDA credit for the Transport Rehabilitation Project in Yemen. This operation focuses on highway and airport rehabilitation works of high priority for the economy. It also includes assistance to the government in devising financial mechanisms to make the roads network self-supporting.

Efficient water-resource management and service delivery to consumers is a top priority for the region. Water scarcity not only creates severe health hazards and costs, but also has the potential to cripple economic growth prospects in many MENA countries. A $50 million loan to Lebanon is providing supplementary financing for the water and wastewater-rehabilitation components of the Emergency Reconstruction and Rehabilitation Project, approved in fiscal 1994. The supplementary loan will help reduce the health risks associated with contaminated water and is expected to encourage refugees to return to their towns and villages. The $40 million Second Sewerage and Water Reuse Project in Morocco will also have substantial health benefits—especially among the poor, since most sewerage extensions financed are to be in low-income neighborhoods—as well as help to ease water constraints by treating wastewater for safe reuse. Administrative capacity building and

reform was the focus of the $20 million loan in support of the Administrative Rehabilitation Project to Lebanon, where restoring the basic capacity of public administration to function effectively is a national priority.

Finally, two of the year's operations addressed the need to clean up environmental "hot spots" where industrial pollution is threatening human health and essential natural resources. A $78 million loan to Algeria is addressing industrial air and water pollution by supporting hazardous emissions reduction and treatment of industrial wastewater. In Egypt, a $20 million IBRD loan and a $15 million IDA credit are supporting the

Pollution Abatement Project, whose centerpiece is a Pollution Abatement Fund—to be established in the National Bank of Egypt acting as an Apex bank—that would finance loans and grants through selected local participating banks for industrial cleanup. (In the past, local financial institutions had not provided medium- and long-term financing for environmental investments because of a lack of technical capacity and familiarity with environmental lending.)

## Nonlending Services Are Diversified

Operational lending across the increasingly broad front exemplified by the year's record remains at the core of the Bank's support for strong and balanced economic growth in MENA countries. But just as the lending program itself is broadening to accommodate new needs, it is also being complemented by an increasingly diverse "product mix" of nonlending services, designed to expand the effectiveness of Bank support for governments' development efforts.

An innovative example of broadening the product mix of Bank services during the year was the first use of the Bank's guarantee function in connection with a MENA government bond issue on international markets. The bond, issued by the Government of Jordan with a

World Bank partial risk guarantee in September 1995, was successfully oversubscribed, generating new private investment for the improvement of telecommunications services in Jordan. This was also the Bank's first guarantee operation in the telecommunications sector worldwide.

An increasingly important and diverse component of nonlending services to MENA countries is Bank policy and analytical work aimed at helping governments refine and implement their national and sectoral development strategies. This work is of two main kinds. The first involves the preparation of broad-based country-assistance strategy (CAS) reports for each active borrowing country in the region, which form the basis of subsequent operational work and the ongoing policy dialogue between the Bank and national authorities. The second type of analytical work consists of policy and action-oriented reports on topics of priority concern to MENA governments. While this category of output still includes important traditional products such as country economic memoranda (two of which were prepared during the year, in a new series of MENA Economic Studies), it now embraces an increasingly diverse range of topical areas. Examples from the past year

TABLE 4-17. WORLD BANK COMMITMENTS, DISBURSEMENTS, AND NET
TRANSFERS IN MIDDLE EAST AND NORTH AFRICA, 1991–96

(millions of US dollars; fiscal years)

| Item | Algeria start 1996 | Algeria 1996 | Algeria 1991–96 | Morocco start 1996 | Morocco 1996 | Morocco 1991–96 | Tunisia start 1996 | Tunisia 1996 | Tunisia 1991–96 | Total region start 1996 | Total region 1996 | Total region 1991–96 |
|---|---|---|---|---|---|---|---|---|---|---|---|---|
| Undisbursed commitments | 1,111 | | | 1,485 | | | 752 | | | 5,545 | | |
| Commitments | | 428 | 1,785 | | 540 | 2,510 | | 99 | 1,236 | | 1,595 | 9,106 |
| Gross disbursements | | 505 | 2,001 | | 485 | 2,238 | | 142 | 1,122 | | 1,585 | 7,553 |
| Repayments | | 249 | 1,166 | | 344 | 1,724 | | 199 | 961 | | 1,095 | 5,813 |
| Net disbursements | | 256 | 836 | | 141 | 514 | | -57 | 161 | | 490 | 1,740 |
| Interest and charges | | 145 | 692 | | 275 | 1,556 | | 125 | 716 | | 743 | 4,249 |
| Net transfer | | 111 | 144 | | -134 | -1,042 | | -182 | -555 | | -253 | -2,509 |

NOTE: Disbursements from the IDA Special Fund are included. The countries shown in the table are those with the largest borrowings of Bank funds during fiscal 1995–96. Details may not add to totals because of rounding.

include reports on a framework for private sector development in Algeria, on private participation in infrastructure in Morocco, on transport strategy in Tunisia, and on issues arising for Egypt with respect to a European Union-Egypt Free Trade Agreement—along with an Environmental Action Plan for Lebanon, a Water Sector Review and a report on women in the labor force for Jordan, and a poverty assessment for Yemen.

Maximizing the development impact of operations in terms of timely results on the ground is critical for the credibility and grassroots effectiveness of the work of a development institution such as the Bank. Improving portfolio management, and conducting it in increasingly close partnership with (especially grassroots) local counterparts, therefore continued to be a top priority. Features of this effort included further acceleration of the pace and level of disbursements (as in Algeria), support for more effective implementation (as in Yemen), and portfolio restructuring and rationalization in several countries, both as a result of formal Country Portfolio

## TABLE 4-18. PROJECTS APPROVED DURING FISCAL YEAR 1996, MIDDLE EAST AND NORTH AFRICA

| Country/project name | Date of Approval | Maturities | Principal amount (millions) SDR | Principal amount (millions) US$ |
|---|---|---|---|---|
| **Algeria** | | | | |
| Industrial Pollution Control Project | June 11, 1996 | 2001/2013 | n.a. | 78.00 |
| Structural Adjustment Loan | April 25, 1996 | 2001/2013 | n.a. | 300.00 |
| Social Safety Net Support Project | April 25, 1996 | 2001/2013 | n.a. | 50.00 |
| **Egypt** | | | | |
| Pollution Abatement Project[a] | May 21, 1996 | 2002/2016 | n.a. | 20.00 |
| Pollution Abatement Project[a] | May 21, 1996 | 2006/2031 | 10.3 | 15.00 |
| Second Social Fund Project | May 21, 1996 | 2006/2031 | 82.3 | 120.00 |
| Population Project | March 21, 1996 | 2006/2030 | 11.9 | 17.20 |
| **Jordan** | | | | |
| Export Development Project | March 28, 1996 | 2001/2016 | n.a. | 40.00 |
| Economic Reform and Development Loan | October 24, 1995 | 2001/2015 | n.a. | 80.00 |
| **Lebanon** | | | | |
| Emergency Reconstruction and Rehabilitation Project (supplement) | May 30, 1996 | 2000/2013 | n.a. | 50.00 |
| Administrative Rehabilitation Project | August 3, 1995 | 2001/2012 | n.a. | 20.00 |
| **Morocco** | | | | |
| Basic Education Project | May 30, 1996 | 2001/2016 | n.a. | 54.00 |
| Basic Health Project | May 30, 1996 | 2001/2016 | n.a. | 68.00 |
| Coordination and Monitoring of Social Programs and Labor Promotion Project | May 30, 1996 | 2001/2016 | n.a. | 28.00 |
| Second Sewerage and Water Re-Use Project | April 30, 1996 | 2001/2016 | n.a. | 40.00 |
| Emergency Drought Recovery Project | August 29, 1995 | 1999/2011 | n.a. | 100.00 |
| Financial Markets Development Loan | July 27, 1995 | 1999/2010 | n.a. | 250.00 |
| **Tunisia** | | | | |
| Second Training and Employment Project | June 13, 1996 | 2002/2013 | n.a. | 60.00 |
| Industry Support Institutions Upgrading Project | June 13, 1996 | 2001/2013 | n.a. | 38.70 |
| **Yemen** | | | | |
| Public Works Project | June 11, 1996 | 2006/2036 | 17.00 | 25.00 |
| Economic Recovery Credit | April 9, 1996 | 2006/2035 | 53.70 | 80.00 |
| Transport Rehabilitation Project | February 20, 1996 | 2006/2035 | 24.70 | 37.00 |
| Vocational Training Project | December 12, 1995 | 2006/2035 | 15.70 | 24.30 |
| **Total** | | | 215.60 | 1,595.20 |

n.a. = not applicable (IBRD loan).

a. "Blend" loan/credit.

Performance Reviews and on a project-by-project basis. As a result, the percentage of poorly performing projects in the portfolio is on the decline, and the percentage of projects completed on time in line with their objectives is on the rise. The Bank considers enhanced portfolio management as central to the most fundamental development indicator of all—concrete welfare gains for the citizens of MENA countries.

Other steps taken to improve portfolio performance, and thus on-the-ground results, include insistence on policy improvements before executive board approval (actions on key policy measures are normally required prior to project appraisal, for example), use of "cluster" supervision to increase the cost-effectiveness of supervision (for example, in Yemen), more extensive use of local consultants (Tunisia), strengthening compliance with audit covenants (Morocco), and continued strengthening of resident missions and a shift of supervision responsibility to them (West Bank and Gaza, Egypt, and Yemen).

Finally, the Bank has continued to play an important role as a connector and catalyst of international partnerships for economic development in MENA. Partnership-promoting activities during the past year included traditional aid coordination work, involving convening and chairing consultative groups that bring together MENA governments and their donor supporters; newer aid-coordination functions, such as acting as the Secretariat for the Ad Hoc Liaison Committee for the West Bank and Gaza, and for the Joint Israeli-Jordan Steering Committee for the Jordan Rift Valley Development Program; continued active sponsorship of bodies as diverse as the multinational Mediterranean Environmental Technical Assistance Program and the Economic Research Forum (an intraregional network of economists and development practitioners); and working increasingly closely with bilateral and multilateral extraregional partners on activities ranging from cofinancing individual lending operations to supporting major initiatives that address critical problems (such as the MENA Water Partnership referred to earlier) or build potentially transforming new linkages between MENA countries and the outside world (such as the

proposed Euro-Mediterranean Economic Area). As the region increasingly gains a foothold in the wider international economy, fostering productive partnerships will become increasingly central to MENA countries' prospects. The Bank expects to support partnership-building for prosperity in the MENA region still further in the years to come.

# Summaries of Projects Approved for IBRD, IDA, Trust Fund for Bosnia and Herzegovina, and Trust Fund for Gaza Assistance in Fiscal 1996

## AGRICULTURE

| | |
|---|---|
| ‡◊ Albania | IDA—$8 million. Degraded state-owned forest and pasture areas will be restored, and their sustainable use promoted. Total cost: $21.6 million. |
| ◊§ Albania | IDA—$6 million. The agroprocessing sector will be developed, and the marketing of farm products will be improved, thereby improving the income of poorer farmers and increasing the availability of food products to urban consumers. Total cost: $7.1 million. |
| ‡◊§ Argentina | IBRD—$16 million. Efficient and sustainable growth of forest plantation and timber-processing institutions will be supported; in addition, some 3,000 poor rural families will benefit from a program that targets, through technical assistance and grants, groups of small farmers for whom agroforestry can play a central role in improving farmer practices. Total cost: $26.2 million. |
| ‡◊§ Bangladesh | IDA—$121.9 million. Between 2 million and 3 million people living along the right bank of the Brahmaputra river at Mathurapara-Sariakandi, mostly poor, marginal farmers, will benefit from a project that will help finance construction works to prevent the river from breaching its bank and flooding the hinterland and to secure the Jamuna bridge. Total cost: $156 million. |
| ‡◊§ Bangladesh | IDA—$53 million. Some 1.2 million people will benefit from implementation of coastal embankment rehabilitation works that will provide partial protection from cyclones of crops, infrastructure, and of human lives. Since the poor are least able to recover from cyclone damage and the construction works under this project will use their labor intensively, the poor will disproportionately benefit. Total cost: $87.8 million. |
| ◊ Bangladesh | IDA—$50 million. An agricultural research-management project designed to assist the government in generating and transferring agricultural technology to producers, thereby increasing income and employment, will be supported. Total cost: $59.1 million. |
| ‡◊§ Bolivia | IDA—$15 million. Rural poverty should be reduced and the incomes of the rural poor increased through a project that will execute rural investments identified and formulated following a participatory planning process. Total cost: $31 million. |
| Bosnia and Herzegovina | Trust Fund for Bosnia and Herzegovina—$20 million. An emergency farm-reconstruction project seeks to jump-start agricultural production, improve food security, and create employment and income for the war-affected rural population. Total cost: $50.4 million. |

Note: Data used in this section have been compiled from documentation provided at the time of project approval. Projects marked by (§) are included in the Program of Targeted Interventions, and those marked by (†) are poverty-focused adjustment operations. Projects employing at least a mechanism for joint assessment, marked by (‡), include the participation of directly affected stakeholders. Projects marked by (◊) indicate NGO involvement, from information-sharing and consultation to active participation.

‡◊§ Brazil | IBRD—$175 million. More than 255,000 subsistence and smallholder families, as well as migrant agricultural laborers, will benefit from a project in Paraná state that will finance small-scale investment activities with demonstrable technical and economic viability proposed by beneficiaries, social infrastructure, and on- and off-farm small-scale income-generation activities. Total cost: $353.5 million.

‡◊§ Chile | IBRD—$15 million. Some 2,400 small-scale farm families will benefit directly from a program of off-farm poverty-reduction investments and another that will introduce the benefits of irrigation to them, and improve rainfed cultivation practices, as well as pasture and livestock management. Total cost: $35 million.

China | IBRD—$150 million. The modernization and capacity expansion of China's animal-feed industry will be supported and facilitated. Total cost: $310.3 million.

‡◊§ China | IDA—$100 million. The incomes and living standards of some 3 million people in two poor areas of Shanxi province will be raised through terracing and irrigation improvements, improvements to rural roads, expansion of livestock and horticultural production, and support for income-producing enterprises and activities for poor and disadvantaged women. Total cost: $182.8 million.

China | IBRD—$80 million; IDA—$20 million. The government will be assisted in developing a viable, modern, and commercialized seed sector. Total cost: $185.5 million.

◊§ China | IBRD—$60 million; IDA—$90 million. Incomes and living standards of 200,000 people now living in absolute poverty will be raised through voluntary emigration and settlement on newly developed irrigated land in Gansu province. Total cost: $259.2 million.

† Côte d'Ivoire | IDA—$150 million. The government's agricultural reform program, designed to benefit the poor and which includes cocoa, coffee, and rice-sector reform, trade and domestic price reform, and public investment and divestiture, will be supported.

Côte d'Ivoire | IDA—$73.6 million. Funds from IDA reflows will be made available to help finance the government's agricultural reform program *(see above)*.

‡◊ Croatia | IBRD—$17 million. Technology-related services that are relevant to private farmers will be supported, thereby improving farmer incomes and increasing agricultural productivity. Total cost: $30 million.

‡◊ Estonia | IBRD—$15.3 million. Rural incomes will increase and the rural economy will be stimulated through a program of rural entrepreneurship (privatization of rural lands and selected rural infrastructure, improvement of human-resource skills for entrepreneurship, introduction of new farming technologies). Total cost: $30.9 million.

‡◊ Guinea | IDA—$35 million. The scope of agricultural services—agricultural extension, agricultural research, and livestock and animal health in particular—will be expanded throughout the country. Total cost: $90.5 million.

| ‡◊§ India | IDA—$290.9 million. The planning, management, and development process for Orissa state's water resources will be improved, while agricultural productivity will increase through investments to improve existing irrigation schemes and complete other viable schemes. A tribal development plan, enhanced employment opportunities for the landless, and adequate access to water will benefit the state's poorer population. Total cost: $345.5 million. |
|---|---|
| ‡◊ India | IDA—$142 million. A six-year time-slice of a program to improve India's institutional and technical capacity to measure, collate, analyze, and disseminate data concerning all aspects of surface water and groundwater resources will be supported. Total cost: $162.4 million. |
| ◊§ Indonesia | IBRD—$27 million. Some 75,000 rural households living in two of the country's poorest provinces will benefit directly from a project that seeks to raise smallholder incomes through agriculture-based area development, strengthen local-level institutions, and foster broad-based participation at the grassroots level. Total cost: $41.1 million. |
| ‡◊§ Indonesia | IBRD—$26.8 million. Some 90,000 households are to benefit directly from a project designed to help the government reduce the incidence of poverty in Central and Southeast Sulawesi provinces through agriculture-based area development, a strengthening of the capacity of local agricultural support services, and support for farming systems and fisheries research. Total cost: $42.6 million. |
| ‡◊§ Indonesia | IBRD—$19.1 million. The 1.3 million-hectare Kerinci Seblat National Park in Sumatra will be protected through the preparation of a management and zoning plan, and some 1.5 million people living in the park's buffer zone, including tribal communities and other disadvantaged groups, will benefit from income-generating benefits and improved soil and water quality. Total cost: $46 million. |
| ‡◊ Kazakstan | IBRD—$80 million. Agricultural irrigation and drainage systems will be improved. |
| ‡◊§ Kenya | IDA—$22 million. Community-driven initiatives to reduce widespread poverty and enhance food security and conserve the natural resource base in eight arid districts and parts of another will be supported, thereby benefiting a population of about 1 million who have poor linkages to the rest of the economy. Total cost: $25.1 million. |
| ‡◊§ Kyrgyz Republic | IDA—$11.6 million. The sheep industry will be transformed into an efficient and sustainable market-based production system, thereby increasing the incomes of private sheep producers, who are among the poorest groups in the country. Total cost: $16.7 million. |
| ◊ Lao People's Democratic Republic | IDA—$20.7 million. More than a quarter of a million parcels of land will be registered, thereby improving tenure security, raising the possibility of landholders selling their land-use rights, and improving the ability to use land as collateral. Total cost: $28.4 million. |

◊§  Lithuania                    IBRD—$30 million. The government will be assisted in developing a vi-
                                 able, private agriculture sector and in fostering economic growth in rural
                                 areas. In addition, alternative income opportunities will be identified for
                                 those affected by a dramatic decline in rural employment, women in par-
                                 ticular, and help will be given them in starting their own businesses
                                 through increased access to credit. Total cost: $54.8 million.

‡◊  Macedonia, Former            IDA—$7.9 million. The provision of technology-related services to private
    Yugoslav Republic of         farmers will be supported in order to improve their production and
                                 income. Total cost: $10.2 million.

‡◊  Mexico                       IBRD—$186.5 million. Conditions for environmentally sustainable, eco-
                                 nomically efficient, and equitably allocated use of water resources will be
                                 promoted. Total cost: $342 million.

‡◊  Moldova                      IBRD—$10 million. Agricultural research for key export commodities, as
                                 well as related research institutions' farmer-outreach programs, will be
                                 supported. In addition, agroenterprise restructuring and investment plan-
                                 ning will be promoted. Total cost: $18.5 million.

◊   Morocco                      IBRD—$100 million. Specific components of the government's Emer-
                                 gency Drought Relief and Recovery Program, which primarily benefits
                                 poorer farmers, will be financed. Total cost: $333.8 million.

‡◊§ Niger                        IDA—$26.7 million. The quality of life of more than 200,000 people
                                 living in some 380 rural communities will be substantially improved
                                 through the design and implementation of community-based natural
                                 resource-management plans. Total cost: $42.7 million.

‡◊§ Pakistan                     IDA—$26.7 million. Balochistan's community-irrigation schemes will be
                                 developed—especially those in small, remote communities—together
                                 with farmer organizations to operate and maintain them efficiently. Total
                                 cost: $38.5 million.

    Philippines                  IBRD—$150 million. The volume of commercial credit for agriculture and
                                 rural development will be expanded, and the policy framework of the
                                 rural financial sector will be enhanced. Total cost: $262.7 million.

    Senegal                      IDA—$2.8 million. Funds from IDA reflows will be provided to help
                                 finance the Agricultural Sector Adjustment Credit, approved in fiscal
                                 1995.

‡◊  St. Lucia                    IBRD—$2.6 million; IDA—$2.7 million. Priority river and drainage-reha-
                                 bilitation works will be executed, and a plan for integrated watershed-
                                 development and pilot watershed-management projects will be prepared.
                                 Total cost: $7.1 million.

‡◊  Uganda                       IDA—$17.9 million. Analytic capacity for policy formulation in the agri-
                                 cultural sector will be enhanced. Total cost: $19.9 million.

◊§  Vietnam                      IDA—$122 million. Efforts to improve living conditions in rural areas
                                 will be supported by a project that will provide finance for investment in
                                 rural areas and increase the access of the rural poor to financial services.
                                 Total cost: $139.7 million.

# EDUCATION

**Argentina**  IBRD—$165 million. A more competitive environment for the improvement of higher education will be established, and incentives will be provided for continuous educational efficiency gains and quality enhancement. Total cost: $273 million.

‡ **Argentina**  IBRD—$115.5 million. Institutional capacity in the provincial ministries of education will be strengthened, the quality and efficiency of secondary education will be increased, and physical capacity enhanced so as to serve secondary school students more effectively. Total cost: $164.4 million.

‡◊§ **Bangladesh**  IDA—$10.5 million. The government will be helped in establishing a nonformal education system that is capable of delivering effective, large-scale affordable literacy programs to low-literacy districts and females in particular. Total cost: $51 million.

‡ **Bosnia and Herzegovina**  Trust Fund for Bosnia and Herzegovina—$5 million. Through a program of primary school rehabilitation and of textbook printing and distribution, classroom conditions permitting effective teaching and learning will be restored. Total cost: $32.8 million.

‡ **Bosnia and Herzegovina**  IDA—$5 million. Additional funds will be provided to help finance the school-rehabilitation project (see above).

‡◊§ **China**  IDA—$100 million. About 5 million of the poorest school children in some of the economically most disadvantaged counties of China's poorer provinces will benefit from a project designed to support the attainment of universal primary education and expansion of coverage of lower secondary education. Total cost: $191.8 million.

**Dominica**  IBRD—$3.1 million; IDA—$3.1 million. The first stage of a major reform of basic education, including quality improvement, expansion of access, and strengthened sector management, will be supported. Total cost: $7.9 million.

‡◊§ **Dominican Republic**  IBRD—$37 million. The government's development and investment program for basic education, designed to improve its quality and increase enrollment and completion rates—with priority directed to children from low-income families—will be supported. Total cost: $100 million.

‡◊§ **El Salvador**  IBRD—$34 million. Some 32,000 preschool children and 64,000 children in grades 1–6 living in 135 towns most in need of social services will benefit from a project designed to improve access to, and the quality of, the education system—with emphasis on preschool and basic education. Total cost: $80.2 million.

‡◊§ **Ghana**  IDA—$50 million. Access to basic education, especially of girls, the poor, and other disadvantaged segments of the population, will be improved, and pedagogic effectiveness will be enhanced by improving the teaching process and learning outcomes. Total cost: $241.6 million.

**Grenada**  IBRD—$3.8 million; IDA—$3.8 million. The first stage of a major reform of basic education, designed to ensure the existence of a needed mix of skills, will be supported. Total cost: $9.9 million.

| ‡ Guinea | IDA—$6.6 million. Support for development and implementation of a new policy framework in higher education, as well as for institutional capacity building, will be provided. Total cost: $7.4 million. |
| ‡ Guyana | IDA—$17.3 million. The government will be helped in initiating a long-term, multiphased reform program to improve quality, relevance, equity, and efficiency in secondary education. Total cost: $19.3 million. |
| ‡◊§ India | IDA—$425.2 million. The quality of instruction and learning achievement for approximately 10 million children annually—most of whom are poor, and, in particular, children with mild to moderate disabilities, girls, and Scheduled Caste/Scheduled Tribe students—will be increased in seventy districts in eleven project states. Total cost: $534.4 million. |
| ‡◊§ Indonesia | IBRD—$99 million. Geographical and financial obstacles barring poorer children from attending junior secondary education (JSE) schools will be offset through a project that will increase access to JSE by adding classrooms to existing schools and building new schools in poor and remote areas. Total cost: $146.4 million. |
| Indonesia | IBRD—$65 million. Improvements in higher education will focus on six less well-established public universities, where the needs for improved quality, efficiency, and relevance are the greatest. Total cost: $102.1 million. |
| Indonesia | IBRD—$60.4 million. The quality of teaching-learning processes in secondary schools will be enhanced through improvements in teacher education in thirty-one teacher-training institutions. Total cost: $87.1 million. |
| ‡◊§ Malawi | IDA—$22.5 million. A primary education project will increase effective access to education through the construction of classrooms to provide shelter and adequate learning conditions for about 100,000 children currently taking their lessons in the open air. Total cost: $25.2 million. |
| ◊§ Mali | IDA—$13.4 million. A vocational education and training project will focus particularly on developing skills among relatively poor individuals—especially women—working in the informal sector, thereby improving their productivity and earnings. Total cost: $22.9 million. |
| ‡§ Morocco | IBRD—$54 million. The construction, rehabilitation, and equipping of schools in targeted rural areas of the country's thirteen most deprived provinces is expected to allow the school system to accommodate about 65,000 new pupils each year by the end of the project and raise primary enrollment rates to 85 percent. Total cost: $97.7 million. |
| ‡◊§ Panama | IBRD—$35 million. The quality, efficiency, and equity of the Panamanian system of basic education will be improved through a project that focuses benefits on the poorest of the country's townships containing 41 percent of the school population in grades 1–9. Total cost: $58 million. |
| ‡◊ Paraguay | IBRD—$24.5 million. The government's initiatives to improve the quality, efficiency, and coverage of secondary education will be supported. Total cost: $40.5 million. |

| ‡ | Senegal | IDA—$26.5 million. The government will be helped in refocusing the activities of the country's two universities around their pedagogic mission, while reinforcing management capacity and quality control. Total cost: $30.9 million. |

‡◊§ Senegal IDA—$12.6 million. About 300,000 people, three quarters of whom are women, are expected to benefit from a project that supports the first phase of the government's ten-year program to reduce in half illiteracy among people ages ten to thirty-nine. Total cost: $14 million.

§ Sri Lanka IDA—$64.1 million. Cost-effective and quality preservice and in-service teacher education for primary and secondary teachers will be put into place, thereby enhancing the quality of education for all children, but, in particular, the poor, since their schools currently have the most untrained teachers. Total cost: $79.3 million.

Thailand IBRD—$81.9 million. The quality of secondary education in science and mathematics will be raised through strengthening teacher education in those subjects. Total cost: $140.2 million.

Thailand IBRD—$31.6 million. The government's strategy to modernize and improve the country's vocational and technical education program will be supported. Total cost: $52.7 million.

‡◊§ Trinidad and Tobago IBRD—$51 million. The cognitive and social development of preschool children, mainly from low-income families, will be enhanced; the quality of teaching and academic achievement in primary education will be increased; and the physical infrastructure of facilities in poor areas will be upgraded. Total cost: $103 million.

Tunisia IBRD—$60 million. Efforts to modernize training services with a view to increasing the competitiveness of the Tunisian economy will be supported. Total cost: $104 million.

◊ Yemen IDA—$24.3 million. The country's capacity to train skilled manpower in line with present and emerging needs of the economy will be strengthened. Total cost: $59.8 million.

## ELECTRIC POWER AND OTHER ENERGY

Albania IDA—$29.5 million. The overall standard, reliability, and efficiency of the country's electricity-transmission and distribution systems will be improved. Total cost: $117 million.

Bolivia IDA—$5.1 million. Technical assistance will be provided to help the Secretary of Energy and Ministry of Capitalization carry out key reform-transition activities and complete various reform and capitalization programs. Total cost: $7 million.

Bosnia and Herzegovina Trust Fund for Bosnia and Herzegovina—$20 million. District heating will be restored in Sarajevo by reconstructing the district heat-supply system and building internal heating installations; project preparatory work for the same will be initiated in Banja Luka. Total cost: $58 million.

| ‡◊ Cambodia | IDA—$40 million. Urgently needed rehabilitation of Phnom Penh's power-distribution system will be supported, as will government efforts to strengthen sector institutions. Total cost: $45.7 million. |
| China | IBRD—$440 million. Acute power shortages will be reduced and integrated development of the power system in Henan province will be fostered through a program of investments, power-sector reforms, and institutional development. Total cost: $1,161.1 million. |
| ‡ China | IBRD—$400 million. Construction of the Ertan hydroelectric development scheme, which includes a 240 meter-high dam and an underground powerhouse complex with an installed capacity of 3,300 mw, will be completed. Total cost: $2,200.2 million. |
| Colombia | IBRD—$249.3 million. Power-sector reform will be supported by facilitating the operation of a competitive bulk supply market for electricity. Total cost: $410 million. |
| El Salvador | IBRD—$65 million. The government's objectives for the power sector—improve service reliability and coverage, sector restructuring, and regulatory reform—will be supported. Total cost: $101.2 million. |
| India | IBRD—$350 million. Orissa state will be assisted in implementing a program of regulatory, institutional, and tariff reforms in its power sector. Total cost: $997.2 million. |
| Indonesia | IBRD—$373 million. The physical capacity, efficiency, and reliability of the Java-Bali power-transmission system and distribution network will be increased. Total cost: $649 million. |
| Jamaica | IBRD—$21 million. Lost generating capacity will be replaced, generation costs reduced through upgrading existing facilities, system reliability enhanced, electricity tariff reforms supported, and environmental damage reduced and controlled. Total cost: $76.5 million. |
| ‡◊ Kyrgyz Republic | IDA—$20 million. Economic growth will be supported by rehabilitating and upgrading the country's electricity and heat-supply infrastructure. Total cost: $87.5 million. |
| ◊ Lithuania | IBRD—$5.9 million. The feasibility and value of using low-temperature geothermal water as a renewable indigenous energy resource for use in district heating systems will be demonstrated. Total cost: $18 million. |
| Madagascar | IDA—$46 million. The bulk of the investment program of the national utility will be financed, thereby ensuring an adequate supply of electricity; in addition, power-sector reforms will be supported. Total cost: $132.5 million. |
| Mali | IDA—$27.3 million. The Selingue hydropower facilities—the country's largest—will be repaired and rehabilitated to ensure that a major source of electricity supply is not lost. Total cost: $42.1 million. |
| ‡◊ Pakistan | IBRD—$350 million. A power complex and its ancillary works with an installed capacity of about 1,450 mw will be constructed near the village of Barotha, and the country's power-sector reform program will be consolidated. Total cost: $1,863.5 million. |

| ◊ | Philippines | IBRD—$250 million. Transfer capacity will increase, and the reliability of the extra high-voltage transmission of bulk power to the major load centers in central Luzon will be improved. Total cost: $750 million. |
| | Poland | IBRD—$160 million. Investments in rehabilitation and upgrading of key substations, as well as modernization of high-voltage transmission lines, will be made. Total cost: $275.7 million. |
| | Romania | IBRD—$110 million. The government's power sector-reform program will be supported, and about 1,445 mw of existing thermal generating capacity will be rehabilitated. Total cost: $363.9 million. |
| | Uruguay | IBRD—$125 million. The first of four phases of the modernization of the power-distribution system of Montevideo will be supported. Total cost: $228 million. |
| ‡ | Vietnam | IDA—$180 million. Help will be provided in meeting the rapid growth in electricity demand in the south of the country. Total cost: $242 million. |

## ENVIRONMENT

| ◊ | Algeria | IBRD—$78 million. The government will be assisted in reducing industrial pollution. Total cost: $118.1 million. |
| | Brazil | IBRD—$50 million. The entire environmental program of the Companhia Vale do Rio Doce, a major mixed state-private company with mining, industrial, transport, and port operations, will be supported. Total cost: $109.9 million. |
| | China | IBRD—$125 million; IDA—$25 million. A sustainable environmental framework will be developed for the long-term economic and social development of Yunnan province. Total cost: $307.6 million. |
| ‡◊ | Ecuador | IBRD—$15 million. Support for the ongoing process of strengthening the capacity of the Environmental Advisory Commission (CAAM) to undertake environmental policy analysis and environmental program design and management will be provided. Total cost: $20 million. |
| § | El Salvador | IBRD—$50 million. Land registration for the country's estimated 1.6 million parcels of rural and urban land will be regularized, thereby enhancing land security—and value—and contributing to better land use and enhanced collateral. Land registration will provide landowners, most of whom are smallholders, with security of tenure. Total cost: $70 million. |
| ‡ | Lithuania | IBRD—$6.2 million. The first steps toward reducing pollution from the Upper Lielupe river basin, a major water-pollution source into the Gulf of Riga portion of the Baltic sea, will be taken. Total cost: $22.9 million. |
| ◊ | Slovenia | IBRD—$23.9 million. Ambient concentrations of particulates and sulfur dioxide, along with health damage associated with exposure to air pollution in Slovenian cities, will be reduced. |
| ‡◊ | Uganda | IDA—$11.8 million. Capacity for environmental management will be built at the national, district, and community levels, and participatory rural appraisals will identify microprojects and enable local governments to base their plans on needs and priorities as identified by communities. Total cost: $15.2 million. |

| | |
|---|---|
| **Bolivia** | IDA—$9 million. The institutional framework and capacity for (a) pension-funds operation and regulation, (b) the regulation and operating norms for securities markets, and (c) strong banking regulation and supervision will be established. Total cost: $19.3 million. |
| **Croatia** | IBRD—$9.5 million. The regulatory and policy framework of the capital markets will be strengthened, as will the infrastructure to support securities transactions. Total cost: $20.6 million. |
| **Ghana** | IDA—$23.9 million. The growth of an efficient, competitive, well-regulated, nonbank financial sector and an effective payments system will be promoted. Total cost: $24.9 million. |
| **Guyana** | IDA—$2.9 million. Funds from IDA reflows will be provided to help finance the Private Sector Development Credit, approved in fiscal 1995. |
| ‡◊ **India** | IBRD—$200 million; IDA—$5 million. Infrastructure Leasing and Financial Services Limited, one of the country's top five nonbanking financial companies, will be assisted in financing infrastructure subprojects to be implemented on a build-operate-and-transfer basis and expected to be started within the next three years. Total cost: $1,600 million. |
| **Jordan** | IBRD—$80 million. The constraints on Jordan's long-term growth imposed by the limitation of a small domestic market will be addressed through close integration with international markets and the establishment of an investment-friendly environment. |
| **Jordan** | IBRD—$40 million. The government's Export Sector Development Program, which aims at enhancing the international competitiveness of the country's exports, will be supported. Total cost: $60 million. |
| **Kazakstan** | IBRD—$180 million. The financial sector reform program of the government and the national bank will be supported. |
| **Kyrgyz Republic** | IDA—$45 million. The policy and regulatory environment conducive to the sound growth of a competitive and efficient banking system will be created. |
| **Kyrgyz Republic** | IDA—$3.4 million. Technical assistance, designed to implement reforms in the financial sector, will be provided. Total cost: $7.3 million. |
| **Macedonia, Former Yugoslav Republic of** | IBRD—$12 million. Private sector finance will be provided to creditworthy private enterprises and farmers to improve their profitability (by increasing output or improving efficiency) and agricultural output. |
| **Morocco** | IBRD—$250 million. The temporary cost to the Moroccan Treasury of implementing a program of financial markets reforms over a three-year period will be financed. |
| ◊§ **Russia** | IBRD—$300 million. The divestiture of enterprise housing will be accelerated and made sustainable through housing privatization, cost recovery of housing maintenance and utility fees from tenants, a system of targeted housing allowances to protect vulnerable groups in the context of increased cost recovery, and an increase in private sector participation in the provision of services in the housing sector. Total cost: $551 million. |

| Russia | IBRD—$89 million. Advisory services, training, and information technology will be provided to help build the regulatory infrastructure and market architecture needed for capital market development. Total cost: $132.2 million. |

Tanzania — IDA—$10.9 million. The downsizing and restructuring of government-owned banks, the strengthening of bank supervision, and the implementation of a strategy to promote the gradual evolution of a capital market will be supported. Total cost: $13.4 million.

Tunisia — IBRD—$38.7 million. An efficient and market-responsive system of support agencies that provides assistance to the industrial sector will be put into place. Total cost: $62.1 million.

Uganda — IDA—$12.3 million. The Ugandan private sector will be made more competitive so that it can expand sales on both domestic and international markets. Total cost: $20.9 million.

Vietnam — IDA—$49 million. The development of a modern banking sector will be assisted through improving payment services and institutional strengthening. Total cost: $60.5 million.

Zambia — IDA—$12.1 million. Funds from IDA reflows will be made available to help finance the Economic Recovery and Investment Promotion Credit.

## INDUSTRY

Bangladesh — IDA—$3.4 million. Funds from IDA reflows will be made available to help finance the Jute Sector Adjustment Credit, approved in fiscal 1994.

Bolivia — IDA—$8 million. Funds from IDA reflows will be made available to help finance the Capitalization Program Adjustment Credit.

Cape Verde — IDA—$11.4 million. The government will be assisted in its efforts to promote private sector development and modernize the financial sector. Total cost: $12.7 million.

◊ China — IBRD—$170 million. Chongqing municipality will be helped to reduce pollution and restructure and increase the efficiency of production facilities in its most polluting industry—iron and steel. Total cost: $478.1 million.

Indonesia — IBRD—$47 million. The competitiveness of Indonesian industry, particularly of small and medium industries, will be enhanced. Total cost: $60.9 million.

## MINING/OTHER EXTRACTIVE

◊ Argentina — IBRD—$30 million. The government's policy, regulatory, and institutional reforms, designed to encourage the expansion of private investment in mining in an environmentally sound way, will be supported. Total cost: $40 million.

‡ Bolivia — IDA—$11 million. Implementation and refinement of a regulatory framework to assure that privately led mining and industrial activities grow in a more environmentally friendly fashion will be supported. Total cost: $22 million.

| ‡◊§ India | IDA—$63 million. Coal India will be assisted in achieving its objective of making coal production more socially and environmentally sustainable. The implementation of Indigenous Peoples Development Plans for twenty-five mines that are slated to receive financial assistance is expected to improve the lives of some 186,000 people, most of whom are poor. Total cost: $84 million. |

**Mongolia**
IDA—$35 million. Sustainable production levels at the country's major open-pit coal mine will be increased through the modernization of technology. Total cost: $60.4 million.

**‡◊† Russia**
IBRD—$500 million. The effective implementation of a far-reaching restructuring program in the coal sector, including reduction (and eventual elimination) of subsidies, provision of safety-net support, and sector commercialization, will be supported.

**§ Russia**
IBRD—$25 million. Efforts to provide support for the implementation of the coal sector-restructuring program—including assistance in addressing the inadequacies of the existing social safety net—will be supported. Total cost: $30.8 million.

**‡◊§ Ukraine**
IBRD—$15.8 million. The social and environmental consequences that arise from the government's decision to close uneconomic coal mines, as part of the restructuring program for the sector, will be mitigated. Total cost: $28.5 million.

## MULTISECTOR

**† Algeria**
IBRD—$300 million. The government's program of structural reform and privatization will be supported, as will further improvements in the social safety net.

**Argentina**
IBRD—$38.5 million. An Enterprise Assistance Program will be established to develop export competencies of the private sector in manufacturing and service industries. Total cost: $74.2 million.

**† Armenia**
IDA—$60 million. The government's reform program to stabilize the economy and create the conditions for a resumption of growth and an improvement in living standards, including better targeting of social benefits, will be supported.

**† Azerbaijan**
IDA—$65 million. The government's program of economic stabilization and structural reform, including improved coverage of social safety net programs, will be supported.

**Bosnia and Herzegovina**
Trust Fund for Bosnia and Herzegovina—$45 million. Bosnia and Herzegovina's severely damaged productive capacity and infrastructure facilities will be rehabilitated and restored, and production and economic activities will be initiated. Total cost: $160 million.

**† Cambodia**
IDA—$40 million. Cambodia's recovery program, which includes increasing public expenditures for social programs and its continued transition to a market economy, will be assisted.

**† Chad**
IDA—$30 million. A structural adjustment program will restore critical public sector capacity and improve public finances, increase the development and poverty impact of public expenditures, and create a favorable environment for private sector growth.

| ‡ | Chad | IDA—$9.5 million. The government's efforts to enhance revenue mobilization, improve the quality of public expenditures, strengthen capacity in economic policymaking, implement its divestiture program, and design and implement a program of civil service reform will be supported. Total cost: $10 million. |
|---|---|---|
| | El Salvador | IBRD—$16 million. The government's program to accelerate outward-oriented private sector development and raise productivity will be supported. Total cost: $20 million. |
| † | Georgia | IDA—$60 million. Structural adjustment assistance aims at consolidating stabilization, sustaining growth recovery, and reducing poverty (through support for improvements in the targeting of social benefits to the poorest groups). |
| | Ghana | IDA—$4.8 million. Funds from IDA reflows will be made available to help finance the Private Sector Adjustment Credit, approved in fiscal 1995. |
| | Honduras | IDA—$26.4 million. Funds from IDA reflows will be provided to supplement the Public Sector Modernization Adjustment Credit. |
| | Kenya | IDA—$90 million. Government reforms in the areas of public resource management, public enterprise reform, and civil service reform will be supported. |
| | Kenya | IDA—$36.8 million. Funds from IDA reflows will be used to finance the Structural Adjustment Credit *(see above)*. |
| † | Lao People's Democratic Republic | IDA—$40 million. Economic reforms, focusing on the private sector enabling environment and public resource management, will be supported, thereby assisting the government in shifting its focus towards social issues and the reduction of poverty. |
| † | Malawi | IDA—$102 million. The country's emerging macroeconomic reform program, aimed at ensuring the macroeconomic essentials to allow growth and a fundamental restructuring of programs that address the country's pervasive poverty, will be supported. |
| | Malawi | IDA—$4.4 million. Funds from IDA reflows will be used to finance the Fiscal Restructuring and Deregulation Program Credit *(see above)*. |
| | Mali | IDA—$60 million. The government's efforts to deepen fiscal adjustment and provide a stable macroeconomic environment will be supported. |
| | Mauritania | IDA—$20 million. The government will be helped to improve economic management capacity, strengthen and deepen recent fiscal gains, and improve the efficiency of the allocation and management of public expenditure. |
| | Panama | IBRD—$30 million. Support will be provided the government in the implementation of its debt and debt-service reduction agreement with its commercial creditors. |
| † | Papua New Guinea | IBRD—$50 million. The first phase of the government's economic reform program, which, among other things, will address poverty issues by restructuring public expenditures so as to refocus them on basic social services, will be supported. |

| Romania | IBRD—$280 million. Balance of payments support will be provided to help the government pursue its stabilization and structural reform program. |
| --- | --- |
| Russia | IBRD—$24 million. Russia's accession to the World Trade Organization will be supported by ensuring that its requirements in the area of product and process standards are met; Russian standards will be harmonized with international standards; and testing and certification capacity will be upgraded and strengthened. Total cost: $34 million. |
| Sierra Leone | IDA—$300,000. Funds from IDA reflows will be made available to help finance the Structural Adjustment Credit, approved in fiscal 1994. |
| † Togo | IDA—$50 million. Support will be provided for (a) policies designed to restore a predictable and stable macroeconomic environment and (b) the reallocation of public expenditures towards basic services and physical infrastructure, both of which are expected to be particularly beneficial for the poorest segments of the population. |
| West Bank and Gaza | Trust Fund for Gaza—$20 million. A second Emergency Rehabilitation Project will finance broad-based improvements in the general quality of life for the population in neighborhoods and villages, as well as remove constraints on economic activity. |
| † Yemen | IDA—$80 million. Support will be provided in support of the initial phase of the government's structural reform program, which includes protecting social sector expenditures. |

## OIL AND GAS

| Bolivia | IDA—$10.6 million. The government will be assisted in the analysis, planning, design, and execution of its hydrocarbon-sector adjustment program and in the capitalization of the state-owned oil company. Total cost: $13.3 million. |
| --- | --- |
| ◊ Egypt | IBRD—$20 million; IDA—$15 million. The government will be assisted in reducing industrial pollution causing adverse health effects and/or ecological degradation. Total cost: $48.7 million. |
| Moldova | IBRD—$10 million. Maintenance of a combined heat and power plant, repair of leaky gas-distribution points, and a pilot program of gas-meter installation form part of a first step program that aims at moving the energy sector toward better financial and economic management. Total cost: $20.5 million. |

## POPULATION, HEALTH, AND NUTRITION

| † Argentina | IBRD—$350 million. The process that will improve the efficiency and equity of Argentina's health-insurance system and contain the already high level of health spending in the country will be initiated. |
| --- | --- |
| § Argentina | IBRD—$101.4 million. The government's objective of rationalizing health-sector spending by strengthening policymaking and improving service-delivery capacity will be supported, thereby increasing the efficiency and quality of services of public hospitals, which are primarily used by the poor. Total cost: $144.7 million. |

| | | |
|---|---|---|
| | Argentina | IBRD—$25 million. Technical assistance will be provided to the government in the design and implementation of health-insurance reforms. Total cost: $29.8 million. |
| ◊ | Bosnia and Herzegovina | Trust Fund for Bosnia and Herzegovina—$5 million. People with war-related disabilities will be integrated into productive life through a program of community-based rehabilitation and orthopedic and reconstructive surgery. Total cost: $30 million. |
| ◊ | Bosnia and Herzegovina | IDA—$5 million. Additional funds will be provided to help finance the War Victims Rehabilitation Project (see above). |
| ‡◊ | Brazil | IBRD—$300 million. The delivery of care under the country's Unified Health System (SUS), the sole source of publicly subsidized care for the poor, will be improved through the rehabilitation and equipping of SUS hospitals. Total cost: $750 million. |
| § | Bulgaria | IBRD—$26 million. Restructuring of the health sector will be supported, and the population at large—vulnerable groups, in particular— protected by ensuring continued provision of essential health services during the transition period and beyond. Total cost: $47.1 million. |
| § | China | IDA—$100 million. About 6 million infants born each year in ten of the country's poorest provinces will benefit by being immunized against mortality and morbidity caused by measles, polio, pertussis, diphtheria, tetanus, and tuberculosis. Total cost: $162.6 million. |
| ‡◊§ | Côte d'Ivoire | IDA—$40 million. The foundation for universal access to health services, which would be a great achievement in the country's fight against poverty, will be created. Total cost: $52 million. |
| ‡◊§ | Egypt | IDA—$17.2 million. The conditions and status of women and children in areas where fertility remains high—mainly in rural Upper Egypt—will improve though the stimulation of additional demand for smaller family size and for family-planning services. Total cost: $20.7 million. |
| ◊§ | Georgia | IDA—$14 million. The government's health-sector reform program, which increases total spending on health, ensures coverage of essential health services to the entire population, improves the quality of health-care services, and increases efficiency of the system, will be supported. Total cost: $19.7 million. |
| ‡◊§ | India | IDA—$350 million. About 10 million outpatients and 700,000 inpatients—about two thirds of whom belong to the lowest 40 percent of the population in terms of income distribution—currently using hospital services in Karnataka, Punjab, and West Bengal are to benefit from a project that will assist the three state governments in putting into place a first-referral health-care system. Total cost: $416.7 million. |
| ◊ | Indonesia | IBRD—$24.8 million. The first phase of the government's strategy aimed at slowing the transmission of HIV and sexually transmitted diseases will be supported. Total cost: $35.2 million. |
| | Indonesia | IBRD—$20 million. The government will be helped in formulating clear sector strategies for improving the performance of the social sectors. Total cost: $25 million. |

| | |
|---|---|
| ‡◊§ Kyrgyz Republic | IDA—$18.5 million. The capacity of the health system to deliver efficient and cost-effective primary health services will be improved, thereby significantly improving the health status of the population, especially among women and children, through improvements in the areas of women's reproductive health, acute respiratory infections, diarrheal diseases, and tuberculosis. Total cost: $20.1 million. |
| § Macedonia, Former Yugoslav Republic of | IDA—$16.9 million. The health of the population will be enhanced through investments in strengthening primary health care—especially in rural areas, where the poor disproportionately live—and in disease prevention. Total cost: $19.4 million. |
| ‡◊§ Mexico | IBRD—$310 million. Significant improvements in the health status of about 15.5 million uninsured people in the eleven poorest states will be engendered through the implementation of a cost-effective basic health-care package. Total cost: $443.4 million. |
| ‡§ Morocco | IBRD—$68 million. Improved primary health care is being targeted to the needy and is expected to benefit some 27 percent of the population, including 1.05 million women of childbearing age and 1.4 million children under age five. Total cost: $118.8 million. |
| ◊§ Mozambique | IDA—$98.7 million. A five-year time-slice of the National Health Strategy, which will increase coverage and quality of health services and increase equity in access to services, with a shift of resources toward rural areas and a basic package of health care, will be financed. Total cost: $355.7 million. |
| ‡◊§ Pakistan | IDA—$26.7 million. The health status of the population—with emphasis on women and young children—in the northern areas and in Azad Jammu and Kashmir—will be improved through cost-effective improvements in primary health care. Total cost: $57.7 million. |
| Russia | IBRD—$270 million. Medical equipment will be made available to primary and secondary health-care facilities in thirty-four selected oblasts. |
| ‡◊ Sierra Leone | IDA—$20 million. The health status of the people of the country will be improved by increasing access to and improving the quality of a basic package of better-managed and increasingly decentralized health services. Total cost: $138.1 million. |
| § Vietnam | IDA—$101.2 million. The health status of the rural population in the poorer areas of the country will be improved through provision of good, reliable primary health care, a reduction of mortality and morbidity due to diseases that disproportionately affect the poor, and a program of capacity building. Total cost: $127.3 million. |
| ‡◊§ Vietnam | IDA—$50 million. Family health and family-planning services at the grassroots level will be improved through public sector programs, thereby contributing to poverty reduction. In addition, access to services for disadvantaged and isolated ethnic minorities will be improved. Total cost: $129.6 million. |

# PUBLIC-SECTOR MANAGEMENT

‡§ Albania

IDA—$4 million. A five-year program to boost employment (more than 5,000 manmonths) and small-scale economic activity in urban areas will be developed. Total cost: $4.4 million.

Argentina

IBRD—$500 million. The government's ambitious bank-reform program will be supported.

Argentina

IBRD—$16 million. The effectiveness and efficiency of the government's public expenditure management will be enhanced. Total cost: $25 million.

Armenia

IDA—$3.8 million. Technical support for privatization, as well as for financial and civil service reforms, will be funded. Total cost: $4.1 million.

Azerbaijan

IDA—$18 million. Support will be provided to the government in formulating and implementing reforms to move to a market-oriented system. Total cost: $20.3 million.

Bolivia

IDA—$50 million. An appropriate legal and regulatory framework to attract private investment and spur growth will be established, and the government's program to divest six major public enterprises through the capitalization process will be supported.

† Cameroon

IDA—$150 million. The government's adjustment program in the areas of public finance management (including reforms aimed at increasing the share of key development sectors), domestic debt settlement, and financial sector reform will be supported.

Cameroon

IDA—$30.3 million. Funds from IDA reflows will be used to supplement the Structural Adjustment Credit, approved in fiscal 1994.

Cameroon

IDA—$12.6 million. Financing to complete public enterprise privatization work in the agriculture and financial sectors will be provided. Total cost: $16.7 million.

Congo

IDA—$9 million. The government's capacity to prepare and implement the second phase of its reform program will be supported. Total cost: $11 million.

Côte d'Ivoire

IDA—$180 million. The government's private sector development program, designed to increase external and internal competitiveness and promote investment and exports, will be supported.

Croatia

IBRD—$5 million. Studies and advisory services to help design and implement reforms supported by the Enterprise and Financial Sector Adjustment Loan will be financed. Total cost: $6.2 million.

Georgia

IDA—$4.8 million. Technical assistance necessary for the implementation of the government's reform program will be financed. Total cost: $5.2 million.

Ghana

IDA—$26.5 million. The government will be helped in implementing its public enterprise reform and privatization program. Total cost: $36.3 million.

Guinea

IDA—$12.2 million. The government's ability to act as a facilitator and regulator of mining activities will be strengthened, thus helping to attract private investment. Total cost: $16.8 million.

| | | |
|---|---|---|
| | **Honduras** | IDA—$55 million. The government's public sector modernization program will be supported. |
| | **Honduras** | IDA—$9.6 million. Technical assistance will be provided the government to help it implement its public sector modernization program. Total cost: $16.6 million. |
| | **Lebanon** | IBRD—$20 million. The public administration will be rehabilitated, while the process of administrative reform will be launched. Total cost: $29.5 million. |
| | **Mauritania** | IDA—$800,000. Funds from IDA reflows will be made available to help finance the Private Sector Development Credit, approved in fiscal 1995. |
| | **Mexico** | IBRD—$30 million. Technical assistance will be provided to the government to assist it in the privatization of infrastructure. Total cost: $46 million. |
| | **Moldova** | IBRD—$35 million. The government's reform program in the enterprise and financial sectors will be supported and accelerated. Total cost: $49 million. |
| | **Nicaragua** | IDA—$5.8 million. Funds from IDA reflows will be made available to provide additional finance for the Economic Recovery Credit II, approved in fiscal 1994. |
| ◊ | **Russia** | IBRD—$58 million. The performance of the Russian legal system in areas key to the effective functioning of market institutions will be improved. Total cost: $89.4 million. |
| | **Sri Lanka** | IDA—$77 million. A long-term debt facility will be established, and associated technical assistance furnished, so as to promote significant participation by the private sector in infrastructure investments. Total cost: $232 million. |
| | **Sri Lanka** | IDA—$15 million. Technical assistance will be provided in support of continued reform and efficient development of the telecommunications sector, as well as to help promote private investments, operation, and competition in the sector. Total cost: $21.6 million. |
| | **Tajikistan** | IDA—$5 million. Tajikistan's transition toward a market economy will be supported by helping the government design and implement a comprehensive reform program. Total cost: $5.5 million. |
| | **Turkey** | IBRD—$62 million. Technical assistance will be provided to address problems in taxation, government spending, and customs administration. Total cost: $94.2 million. |
| | **Ukraine** | IBRD—$310 million. The government's trade and price liberalization, privatization, capital markets development, and post-privatization restructuring programs will be supported. |
| † | **Zambia** | IDA—$140 million. Support will be provided for continuing macroeconomic and structural policy reforms, including the reform of social security and the financial and mining sector and the protection of social sector spending. |
| | **Zambia** | IDA—$23 million. The implementation of the government's reform program, and of reforms that were the focus of previous adjustment operations, will be supported. Total cost: $27.2 million. |

| | |
|---|---|
| Zimbabwe | IDA—$70 million. Efforts to increase the growth of export-based output and to broaden participation in economic activity, in particular by indigenous firms, will be supported. |

## SOCIAL SECTOR

| | |
|---|---|
| ‡◊§ Algeria | IBRD—$50 million. Twenty thousand manyears of temporary employment will be created though creation of jobs for the underemployed, the country's social safety net system will be strengthened, and social development programs based on increased community participation will be tested. Total cost: $70.4 million. |
| ‡◊§ Angola | IDA—$24 million. A social action fund, designed to improve access to basic services and to generate employment for the poor in rural and urban areas through rehabilitating and equipping community infrastructure in health, education, and water and sanitation will be financed. Total cost: $52 million. |
| ‡◊§ Argentina | IBRD—$152 million. Health and nutrition services for millions of people now living in poverty or facing unemployment will be preserved, while through a small social fund, ways to provide more basic social services and stimulate the economic production of poor households will be tested. Total cost: $417.9 million. |
| ‡◊§ Armenia | IDA—$12 million. The Armenian Social Investment Fund, which finances the rehabilitation of basic social and economic infrastructure on a grant basis, will be supported, thus generating substantial benefits for the poor through the implementation of hundreds of microprojects. Total cost: $20 million. |
| China | IBRD—$10 million; IDA—$20 million. A pilot effort to test the impact on labor-market development and labor mobility of improved employment and training services and an enhanced policy and legal framework for workers and employers will be implemented. Total cost: $51.8 million. |
| ‡◊§ Egypt | IDA—$120 million. Some 200,000 permanent jobs are expected to be created through support for small enterprises and labor-intensive works. In addition, community infrastructure and services, in partnership with NGOs and local groups, will be supported. Total cost: $775 million. |
| ‡◊§ Eritrea | IDA—$17.5 million. Community-initiated subprojects will be financed that will support the rehabilitation and development of basic social and economic infrastructure—especially in rural and war-torn areas—and improve the income-generating capacity of poor people and households. Total cost: $49.7 million. |
| ‡◊§ Ethiopia | IDA—$120 million. The Ethiopian Social Rehabilitation Development Fund, which provides financial and technical support to poor, mainly rural communities to launch small projects aimed at creating the assets and services needed to upgrade their economic and social standards and strengthen self-reliance, will be supported. Total cost: $242.4 million. |
| ‡◊§ Haiti | IDA—$50 million. Short-term employment will be provided to people in extreme poverty in support of the government's program to reduce poverty. Total cost: $56.4 million. |

| | |
|---|---|
| ‡◊§ Honduras | IDA—$30 million. A Third Social Investment Project seeks to help reduce poverty through improved access to basic infrastructure and social services in poor areas and for poor communities. Total cost: $112.6 million. |
| ‡◊§ Madagascar | IDA—$40 million. The nationwide expansion of the activities of a social fund currently engaged in poverty-reduction activities in two of the country's six provinces will be supported. Total cost: $45.4 million. |
| ‡◊§ Malawi | IDA—$56 million. The country's Social Action Fund, targeted at rural communities in the poorest areas of the country, will be supported through the financing of subprojects aimed at increasing access to safe water, construction of primary schools, and provision of primary health infrastructure. Total cost: $71.3 million. |
| ‡◊§ Mongolia | IDA—$10 million. The social costs of adjustment will be mitigated through a project that seeks to create gainful employment and income for the poor and absolute poor, raise enrollment in basic education, reduce mortality and morbidity rates, and provide assistance to the handicapped, mentally retarded, and disabled. Total cost: $10.5 million. |
| ‡§ Morocco | IBRD—$28 million. About 30,000 manyears of work in basic infrastructure improvements will be created for underemployed persons in deprived rural areas of the country's thirteen poorest provinces. Total cost: $49.5 million. |
| ‡◊§ Nicaragua | IDA—$30 million. Poverty—especially among women—will be reduced through the provision of economic and social infrastructure and improved social services in poor areas. Total cost: $102.4 million. |
| ‡◊§ Yemen | IDA—$25 million. Between 75,000 and 96,000 manmonths of new employment will be created through small-scale civil works investments in sectors with benefits accruing mainly to the poor. Total cost: $28 million. |

## TELECOMMUNICATIONS

| | |
|---|---|
| Pakistan | IBRD—$35 million. The reform and efficient development of the country's telecommunications sector will be supported. Total cost: $53.6 million. |

## TRANSPORTATION

| | |
|---|---|
| Albania | IDA—$25 million. A key infrastructural bottleneck to economic development will be overcome by rehabilitating and constructing national roads. Total cost: $66 million. |
| Armenia | IDA—$16 million. The level of maintenance for the country's road network will be expanded, and the institutional capacity to carry out future road-maintenance activities will be strengthened. Total cost: $36.9 million. |
| Bosnia and Herzegovina | Trust Fund for Bosnia and Herzegovina—$35 million. Urgent high-priority links and services in the transport system will be reconstructed and repaired. Total cost: $152 million. |
| Brazil | IBRD—$350 million. The cost of freight transport in Brazil's main corridors will be reduced by restructuring and privatizing the federal railways. Total cost: $700 million. |

| | | |
|---|---|---|
| Bulgaria | IBRD—$95 million. The restructuring process begun by the Bulgarian State Railways and the government will be supported and deepened by financing investments that are in line with the restructuring concept. Total cost: $126 million. | |

‡◊§ **Cameroon** IDA—$60.7 million. A three-year time-slice of the country's road-rehabilitation and maintenance program will be financed, directly impacting on the poor through the promotion of local small and medium enterprises and use of labor-based methods and local materials. Total cost: $722.7 million.

‡ **China** IBRD—$260 million. Highway capacity in the Shanghai-Hangzhou corridor will be increased, and road safety in northern Zhejiang province improved. Total cost: $729 million.

**China** IBRD—$210 million. Continued support will be provided for the development of road infrastructure in Shaanxi province. Total cost: $556.5 million.

◊ **China** IBRD—$210 million. Continued support will be provided for the development of road infrastructure in Henan province so as to relieve congestion, facilitate mobility, and increase the efficiency of road transport. Total cost: $606 million.

‡§ **Colombia** IBRD—$65 million. About 630,000 low-income residents of Bogotá will benefit from a project that will help facilitate public transport access to low-income settlements. In addition, more efficient use will be made of the city's street system by improving vehicle flows in a major transport corridor. Total cost: $141 million.

**Côte d'Ivoire** IDA—$20 million. Part of the Ivorian component of a larger program for the rehabilitation of the Abidjan/Ouagadougou/Kaya railway will be financed. Total cost: $48 million.

**Georgia** IDA—$12 million. Policy reform in the transport sector will be supported, its institutions restructured, and some of the system's most critical elements repaired and maintained. Total cost: $20 million.

◊ **Ghana** IDA—$100 million. Funds will be provided to help maintain, rehabilitate, and reconstruct the country's entire road network. Total cost: $111.5 million.

**Indonesia** IBRD—$86.9 million. Traffic bottlenecks on the national roads in selected urban areas in the North Java corridor will be reduced. Total cost: $167.6 million.

**Kenya** IDA—$115 million. The economic efficiency of the road network in twenty-six urban centers will be increased, and a sustainable road-maintenance capacity will be built. Total cost: $155 million.

**Kenya** IDA—$50 million. The primary transport link between Nairobi and Mombasa will be rehabilitated and widened, while maintenance financing, planning, and execution will be strengthened. Total cost: $122 million.

‡◊† **Lesotho** IDA—$40 million. Some 2 million mandays of work will be generated over a five-year period through a project that seeks to develop the government's capacity to regularly maintain the whole classified road network. Total cost: $129 million.

| ‡ Nicaragua | IDA—$25 million. The condition of selected trunk roads will be improved to enhance the country's export competitiveness. Total cost: $28.4 million. |

‡◊§ Peru — IBRD—$90 million. Investments—targeted to the poorest rural communities—in the maintenance and rehabilitation of rural roads, as well as secondary and primary roads connecting to the primary road network, will help reduce poverty and raise living standards of rural communities. Total cost: $250.3 million.

Romania — IBRD—$120 million. The restructuring program of Romanian National Railways, designed to improve efficiency and make it more commercially oriented, will be supported. Total cost: $383 million.

Russia — IBRD—$350 million. A four-year program of urgently needed bridge works on federal roads will be supported. Total cost: $466.3 million.

Sierra Leone — IDA—$35 million. A four-year time-slice of the government's ten-year transportation-sector investment and maintenance program will be supported. Total cost: $41 million.

‡◊ Thailand — IBRD—$150 million. The government's various Highway Plans, which aim to increase network capacity by widening the country's major interurban road links to four-lane standard, will be supported. Total cost: $325.5 million.

Turkey — IBRD—$250 million. Road-transport costs will be reduced through infrastructure improvements, and past investments will be protected through rehabilitation and strengthening of paved highways. Total cost: $389.3 million.

Yemen — IDA—$37 million. Urgent rehabilitation needs in the roads and civil aviation sectors will be undertaken, and institutional capacity for maintenance of the road network will be improved. Total cost: $51.8 million.

## URBAN DEVELOPMENT

‡ China — IBRD—$250 million. An investment program of environmentally oriented capital works and institutional measures to support management and operational capacity building of the Shanghai Municipal Sewerage Company will be supported. Total cost: $633.3 million.

China — IBRD—$125 million; IDA—$25 million. Environmental conditions in cities in Hubei province will be improved through wastewater collection and treatment investments and by improvements in solid waste and nightsoil handling. Total cost: $385.2 million.

‡◊ Colombia — IBRD—$20 million. Technical assistance will be provided to national, regional, and local institutions for improving environmental management in the country's urban areas. Total cost: $40 million.

‡◊§ Ghana — IDA—$71 million. Productivity and living standards in the country's five major cities will increase, especially for lower-income people, through provision of drainage, sanitation, solid waste, and community-upgrading infrastructure. Total cost: $89.3 million.

| ‡◊ Indonesia | IBRD—$142.7 million. A three-year program of high-priority expenditures and subproject investments in 102 urban areas of East Java will be supported. Total cost: $357.3 million. |
| Latvia | IBRD—$27.3 million. Riga's urban transport system will be rehabilitated, as will the water and wastewater-treatment plant in Daugavpils. In addition, through the financing of the Municipal Development Fund, funds will be channeled for a number of small-scale investments in municipal services elsewhere in the country. Total cost: $45.4 million. |
| Lebanon | IBRD—$50 million. Supplementary funds are being provided to help finance additional components of the Emergency Reconstruction and Rehabilitation Project, approved in March 1993. |
| ‡◊§ Mauritania | IDA—$14 million. A program of poverty-oriented, labor-intensive works subprojects, consisting of rehabilitation or construction of urban facilities, will be supported. Total cost: $24 million. |
| ‡◊§ Pakistan | IDA—$21.5 million. The productivity and well-being of low-income groups in North-West Frontier Province will be increased through improvement of living conditions by the provision of basic urban and rural infrastructure. Total cost: $38.8 million. |
| ‡◊ Tanzania | IDA—$105 million. Basic infrastructure will be rehabilitated and expanded into high-priority, underserved urban areas. Total cost: $138.5 million. |
| ◊ Ukraine | IBRD—$17 million. The development of a housing market to meet the needs of the people of Ukraine will be supported. Total cost: $27.9 million. |
| West Bank and Gaza | Trust Fund for Gaza—$40 million. High-priority urban infrastructure will be rehabilitated, reconstructed, extended, and maintained, and the local government system will be strengthened. Total cost: $45 million. |

## WATER SUPPLY AND SANITATION

| ‡◊§ Bolivia | IDA—$20 million. Some 800,000 rural dwellers, most of whom are indigenous and poor, will enjoy enhanced productivity through a project that, by providing for a rural water- and sanitation-infrastructure program, will improve health conditions and reduce the time spent collecting water. Total cost: $48 million. |
| Bosnia and Herzegovina | Trust Fund for Bosnia and Herzegovina—$20 million. Water, sanitation, and solid waste services will be restored to a level that would mitigate public health risk in priority areas. Total cost: $70 million. |
| § Colombia | IBRD—$145 million. More than a million urban poor living in marginal neighborhoods of Bogotá will benefit from a project that will finance investments in water, sewerage, and flood control/drainage systems and provide technical assistance for institutional strengthening. Total cost: $717.9 million. |
| ‡◊ Ethiopia | IDA—$35.7 million. The long-term viability of water supply and sanitation operations in line with the government's regionalization policies will be ensured through provision of institutional support, engineering consultancies, and physical works. Total cost: $65.5 million. |

| ‡◊ India | IBRD—$167 million; IDA—$25 million. First-stage works to partially treat and dispose of sewage effluent in the greater Bombay area will be completed, and slum-sanitation schemes will be implemented. Total cost: $295.6 million. |
| --- | --- |
| ◊ India | IBRD—$59.6 million. Some 1.2 million people living in 1,000 communities in Uttar Pradesh will benefit from a package of investments in rural water and environmental sanitation. Total cost: $71 million. |
| Morocco | IBRD—$40 million. Operational efficiency of sewerage-system operations will be improved, and adequate sewerage service provided to the inhabitants of Fès. Total cost: $97 million. |
| ◊§ Philippines | IBRD—$57 million. Finance will be provided for the rehabilitation of Metro Manila's separate sewerage network and of the Ayala treatment plant, as well as implementation of the first phase of the septage-management plan. Low-income households will benefit disproportionately from the project. Total cost: $76.2 million. |
| Poland | IBRD—$21.5 million. Bielsko-Biala's water and wastewater systems will be rehabilitated and expanded, thus providing consumers with more reliable, safer, and better-quality services. Total cost: $35.4 million. |
| ‡ Russia | IBRD—$200 million. Decentralization of federal responsibilities will be supported by strengthening the ability of local governments to provide essential community services that are fundamental to social well-being. Total cost: $288.1 million. |
| ‡◊ Venezuela | IBRD—$39 million. The efficiency and quality of water supply and sewerage services will be increased through the development of a model for decentralization, institutional strengthening, and expanded private sector participation. Total cost: $71.1 million. |

## Economic Development Institute (EDI)

Knowledge is often the key ingredient in advancing social and economic development. Among the World Bank's greatest contributions in the coming years will be to help countries strengthen their capacities to manage change and economic reform by sharing knowledge about best practices in policy design and implementation. The EDI supports this goal by helping government officials share policy lessons and exchange experiences, by imparting skills needed to use resources effectively, and by helping to build an informed and engaged civil society committed to sustaining economic reform. The EDI pursues this mission by working with a growing network of Bank and external partners to deliver seminars and training programs, train trainers, produce and disseminate publications, and reach broader audiences through new technologies. During fiscal 1996, the EDI conducted 358 conferences, seminars, and workshops in all regions of the world, reaching nearly 7,000 people directly. More than 600 trainers, who, in turn, reached an additional 20,000, were trained. EDI audiences expanded to include parliamentarians, journalists, educators, staff of nongovernmental organizations (NGOs), labor and business leaders, as well as government officials. In fiscal 1996, the EDI worked with partners from over 150 organizations, including the Bank, other multilateral and bilateral agencies, foundations, NGOs, government agencies, and in-country training institutions.

EDI resources were concentrated in sub-Saharan Africa and the former Soviet Union in fiscal 1996, with the remainder distributed among other developing regions. Within the Europe and Central Asia region, the Institute moved to place more emphasis on the lower-income countries and the new transition economies. Its program in the Middle East and North Africa, South Asia, and Latin America grew during the year and is expected to be larger in fiscal 1997. The EDI also provided programs to countries in post-conflict reconstruction, including Angola, Bosnia and Herzegovina, Cambodia, and Haiti.

EDI curriculum covered four broad areas:

• macroeconomic management and policy, emphasizing decentralization and fiscal policy;

• environment and natural resources, focusing on management and valuation of natural assets;

• human resources and poverty, particularly girls' education and reproductive health; and

• regulatory reform of private and public sectors.

In addition, EDI began development of distance learning and mass media products that will extend its reach from the thousands to the millions in the years ahead.

EDI is building its future on innovative programs that have proven to meet client needs and demand. Its goal is to increase the number and quality of high-impact programs it can offer clients. These programs include those that:

• *Create national vision and consensus.* EDI has developed a number of programs to promote national vision and consensus. Two successful examples include a joint EDI–Latin America and the Caribbean Regional Office seminar to facilitate a development vision for El Salvador that involved 300 leaders of the government, parliament, labor organizations, academia, the media, and private sector as well as ex-guerrilla leaders. The program was organized by Salvadorians who had participated in an EDI study tour in Malaysia. In the Former Yugoslav Republic of Macedonia, EDI conducted a senior policymakers forum attended by the president, prime minister, government officials, parliamentarians, and private sector and NGO representatives. Macedonia's newspapers and television gave wide coverage to the program, sparking broad public engagement in the process of building a shared vision.

• *Strengthen regional cooperation.* With the support of

France and Canada, EDI held a workshop on Integrating Africa into the World Economy for ministers, CEOs, central bank governors, and other leaders from Burkina Faso, Cameroon, Cape Verde, Côte d'Ivoire, Ghana, Uganda, and Zambia. The objectives were to develop a long-term vision for the region; facilitate collaboration between public and private sectors; and provide feedback to the donor community on assistance to Africa. Experts from Chile, Malaysia, Mauritius, and Tunisia shared their experiences in meeting similar objectives.

• *Aid post-conflict reconstruction.* Post-conflict countries face huge challenges of demobilizing soldiers, repatriating refugees, rebuilding institutions, restoring trust, and revitalizing their economies. To support these needs in Angola, EDI held a five-day policy seminar in February to clarify next steps on the path to normalcy. EDI brought officials from Uganda and Ethiopia who had guided those countries' recoveries from war to share their experiences with Angolan officials. A similar program was launched in Gaza and the West Bank. EDI is also collaborating with the Austrian Peace Institute on a program for Bosnia.

• *Integrate sector policies in the macroeconomy.* EDI conducted a seminar series designed to help mainstream the environment in country-assistance strategies. For example, working closely with the Bank's South Asia and East Asia and Pacific Regional Offices, EDI conducted a three-day ministerial level seminar in Manila in June for senior policymakers from Indonesia, the Philippines, Sri Lanka, and Thailand. The seminar promoted better understanding among government policymakers of the links between the economy and the environment.

• *Build capacity at the grassroots.* EDI's highly effective six-year-old Grassroots Management Training program, which began as a pilot program in Malawi and Tanzania, was expanded to include Burkina Faso, India, Mali, Nepal, Nigeria, Senegal, and Tunisia. This program trains poor village women who manage tiny businesses, women farmers, traders, and artisans. EDI assisted local NGOs and training institutes to design the program and materials to meet the needs of illiterate learners. Assessments have shown that the training has helped make microenterprises more profitable and credit-worthy.

• *Increase impact through technology.* In fiscal 1996, EDI began several pilot projects to improve access to knowledge within developing countries, particularly where local capacity is absent or weak. Working with the African Economic Research Consortium and seven African universities, EDI began to build an electronic network of training institutions that will have access to courses in subjects where the World Bank has unique competence. This will start a process to build their own capacity to offer such courses. Similarly, in Russia and elsewhere in the former Soviet Union, EDI started building a network of collaborating institutions. As a first step, it began operating a Russian language World Wide Web site with information about EDI training opportunities, policy forums, and teaching aids.

*Joint Vienna Institute.* The Joint Vienna Institute, cosponsored by the Bank, the Bank for International Settlements, the European Bank for Reconstruction and Development, and the Organisation for Economic Co-operation and Development, conducted courses for public officials in skills needed to implement reforms, as well as introductory courses in market economics through its regional centers in Kiev, Moscow, Prague, and Tashkent.

*Scholarship and Fellowship Programs.* The Joint Japan/World Bank Graduate Scholarship Program, which supports graduate studies for mid career officials of member countries, provided funding to 310 students in fiscal 1996. Twenty-five students were enrolled in a two-year Economic Policy Management program under a special master's degree program funded by the Government of Japan. Under a program initiated jointly with the African Capacity Building Foundation, eight students each were studying at McGill University and the Université d'Auvergne in economic policy management. Thirty students pursued advanced studies in Japan through the policy-management program at Tsukuba University, the infrastructure-management and public policy and taxation programs at Yokohama National University, and the taxation-policy and management program at Keio University.

## Research at the World Bank

The Bank's research activities are intended to enhance understanding of development and policy. The success of the Bank's work as it tackles new and critical problems often depends on the reliability and depth of the research conducted and on the effectiveness of communicating what has been learned to the development community.

The Bank's research budget has dropped by 30 percent in recent years—from a peak of $36 million in fiscal 1992 to less than $25 million in fiscal 1996. As part of an effort to assess how best to use fewer resources, an assessment of the influence of the Bank's research program was undertaken during the fiscal year. It included an assessment by internationally renowned experts of quantitative performance indicators and qualitative approaches, using surveys, structured interviews, case studies, and evaluations of research products.

The assessments showed that Bank research is broad in coverage, influential among policymakers, well-regarded by researchers, heavily used as teaching material, and widely read. However, the assessment also identified that the scope of research needs to be expanded and the exposition of findings improved. The Bank is revising its research processes and format accordingly.

More than 3,400 readers from 113 countries responded to a survey about World Bank publications and the Bank's broader dissemination efforts. The results indicate that Bank research is among the most extensively distributed of Bank publications: *World Development Report* continues as the Bank's flagship publication,[1] and the research journal, *The World Bank Economic Review,* is most widely read in borrowing countries. Bank products are commonly used for research: More than three quarters of government organizations and more than half of commercial firms reported that they use them for this purpose. In addition, more than half of respondents from government agencies and

nearly three quarters of policymakers reported using Bank publications in the process of formulating policy.

The World Bank's "Policy Research Bulletin" documents the Bank's current and recently completed research. It reaches 18,000 subscribers, 16,000 in developing countries. Some 2,100 "Bulletin" readers responded to a survey indicating that the "Bulletin" is a much-valued and unique source of information about World Bank research and what is being learned in development studies generally. Based on the survey results, the "Bulletin" was revised to meet respondents' desires for changes in timing, format, and substance. A column on electronic information was added, and a calendar and research briefs were discontinued. The "Bulletin" is now distributed quarterly.

A measure of the influence of a research publication is how many people cite it in their own publications. Data on citations of articles in 1,400 professional journals published in thirty-five countries were analyzed to estimate the reach and influence of Bank research publications. Articles in *The World Bank Research Observer* and *The World Bank Economic Review* are cited more than articles in any other development economic journal, and, based on this measure, the two Bank journals rank in the top third of all economic journals. Citation rates of papers from the Bank's major research conference, published in the *Proceedings of the World Bank Annual Conference on Development Economics,* is even higher.

World Bank research is also disseminated through many non-Bank publications. Bank staff published nearly 300 articles in professional journals in each of the past two fiscal years. The quality of this work is high: Bank-authored journal articles are cited from 10 percent-to-50 percent

---

1. *World Development Report 1996: From Plan to Market* observes that with consistent and sustained reforms, economies in transition can achieve successful long-term economic growth; it also warns that many challenges and risks—among them long-term stagnation and rising poverty—still lie ahead for some countries. The report concludes that consistent liberalization and stabilization pay off, even when the institutional underpinnings of a market system are weak, and notes that individual country circumstances are important.

more than the average economics article. Bank research also receives wide press coverage, further extending its dissemination. Bank research findings have been reviewed at an increasing rate over the past two years, averaging thirteen reviews a month in newspapers, magazines, and journals.

Bank-authored studies are also well represented on reading lists in university courses in economic development. In a recently published collection of twenty-five course reading lists (mostly at the graduate level), one sixth of the entries were by Bank authors. The Bank's Economic Development Institute draws heavily on Bank studies in its courses, workshops, and seminars—reaching thousands of participants in the Bank's client countries.

Research funded by the central Research Support Budget are periodically evaluated by international experts in the relevant fields to improve the selection process, project design, management, and dissemination of results. Evaluation of the two research journals, the Annual Bank Conference on Development Economics, and more than sixty research projects was completed in fiscal 1996. The evaluation reports were circulated to the Research Committee and the editorial boards of the journals as a basis for decisions on policy and procedure revisions.

Reviewers generally lauded the Bank's journals, noting the increased diversity in topic and viewpoint in articles over the past five years. They praised the quality, exposition, and relevance of the *Research Observer*. While the journals were considered to be unparalleled in the quality and stature of their authors and their focus on the policy relevance of research, the articles in the *Economic Review* were often found to be "dull," and reviewers called for efforts to moderate the technical language used by authors to meet the needs of policy-analyst readers. Because readership in developing countries is so large and because the needs are so great—given the scarcity of research information in many countries—the Bank was urged to further expand dissemination of the journals.

The Annual Bank Conference on Development Economics was held in April 1996 and

was judged by reviewers to have met its goal of facilitating communication among academics, economists, policy analysts, and World Bank staff and to have dealt with crucial and timely issues. But reviewers asked for more work on political economy and institutional issues and more airing of controversial approaches and varying points of view in the future. The quality of presentations and papers was seen to be high, but reviewers recommended stricter reviews before presentation. Finally, evaluators suggested wide dissemination of the *Proceedings* in the Bank's client countries.

Evaluations of recent large research projects on international economics, poverty and human resources, macroeconomics and the transition economies, and agriculture and the environment were completed in fiscal 1996. The reviewers were impressed by the emphasis on empirical and policy-relevant topics, as well as with the many multicountry studies, which policymakers find most interesting and useful. Generally, they found the level of analysis to be appropriate to the topics and data and praised many projects for their contributions to policy formulation and the broader store of information. Success in targeting dissemination was more mixed, and, although many projects involved local researchers, only a small number were seen to have enhanced research capacity in the Bank's member countries.

The World Bank's policy and best-practice papers, as well as economic and sector work, are often based on Bank research. They shape the Bank's lending program and policy advice. Case studies of policy change in pension reform, road maintenance in Africa, and emissions-reduction programs in several countries, for example, provide evidence of the linkages of research to policy formulation and illustrate a broad and continuous process of learning and diffusion.

The linkages work in both directions. The Bank's research agenda responds to emerging policy problems because research staff are actively engaged in operational work. And Bank research also draws expertise from the external research community. One third of Bank research projects involves local counterpart research institutes and consultants. And in the Bank's vice presidencies responsible for sectoral advice and research, half of the consultant time recently spent on research was provided by nationals of developing countries.

The various evaluations of the World Bank's research program are encouraging. They indicate that it plays a significant role in expanding understanding about development, while suggesting where further efforts can be directed to focus and improve World Bank research.

## The Administrative Budget, Corporate Planning, and Resource Management

The Bank's total administrative budget for fiscal 1996, as approved by the executive directors in fiscal 1995, was $1,382.2 million. Late in fiscal 1996, the directors approved a total administrative budget of $1,374.7 million, a drop of 3.6 percent in real terms (0.5 percent in nominal terms) *(see Appendix 6)*.

The net administrative budget, which takes into account reimbursements and fee revenues that offset the costs of programs not financed from the regular budget, was set at $1,193.8 milllion for fiscal year 1996; for fiscal 1997, it is $1,177.1 million. Fiscal 1997 will mark the third consecutive year of a decline in the Bank's net administrative expenditures in real terms.

The priority of the various units that comprise the Bank's corporate planning and resource-management services is to support the Bank's emerging change agenda, with programs focused on upgrading professional skills, adjusting personnel policies to support key business objectives, and providing support for changes toward a more results-oriented Bank culture. Efforts in different units have focused on the following:

*Human Resources (HR)*. The human resources function was streamlined and realigned to provide more efficient and professional services to management and staff, with a 15 percent savings in resources in the period fiscal 1996–97. In the process, the HR vice presidency became an important agent in the institutional change process. Concerted efforts were made to enhance managerial skills and potential through new approaches to assessment, more transparent selection procedures, and succession planning. An upward feedback program from staff to managers was also introduced, and performance evaluations made more rigorous.

*Learning and Leadership Center (LLC)*. A revamped and expanded education and training effort, coordinated and managed by the LLC, includes: (a) upgrading of professional skills for staff at all levels through strengthened in-house training programs; (b) expanding training for the Bank's technical staff in major sectors and promoting the sharing of best practices, cross-fertilization, and selective secondments to relevant organizations; (c) executive education, involving sending selected managers and staff to leading international management and business schools; (d) staff exchange and secondment programs, involving private sector organizations and autonomous agencies in selected countries; and (e) a Presidential Fellows program to bring eminent scholars and leaders to the Bank.

*Information and Technology Services (ITS)*. Through a concerted and collaborative effort between ITS and the vice presidential units throughout the Bank, the Enterprise Network— a basic technology platform—was implemented across the entire headquarters and in many field offices. Another important program during the year focused on managing information through an automated filing (imageBank) program, with some 10,000 reports already imaged and accessible over the network at the desktop. In addition, improvements were made in customer support, governance, computing technology, and the management of Bank information and knowledge. In the coming year, technology tools that will enhance collaboration in virtual teams, regardless of location, will be aggressively implemented across the Bank. Such tools will also help to drive institutional change toward more openness and sharing of information and knowledge within the Bank and with its clients.

*General Services (GSD)*. In adapting successfully to the institution's new directions, the "cost-per-workplace" of GSD services has been reduced by about 11 percent in the past two years. At headquarters, with the upcoming completion of the second and final phase of the Main Complex, the medium-term strategy for space has been updated in light of new organizational changes. So far, more than 100,000 square feet in net office space have been surrendered, thereby enabling the redeployment of $3.5 million in savings. Field-facilities projects also were completed in Armenia, Brazil, China, the former Yugoslav Republic of Macedonia, Mexico, Moldova, Nigeria, Uganda, and the West Bank and Gaza.

*Health Services (HSD).* The Health Services Department (HSD) provided a variety of clinical and occupational health services that included a comprehensive Breast Care Program with an in-house mammography screening and an on-site clinic to assist staff with episodic, acute illnesses. Utilization of HSD services is high and continues to increase.

*Headquarters construction.* The headquarters construction project continued its steady progress towards completion of the Phase Two new building in the middle of the next fiscal year, within the approved budget of $314 million.

*Staffing.* As projected at the beginning of fiscal 1996, the number of new appointments was lower than in previous years. The Bank Group recruited 188 staff, of whom 33 percent were from developing countries and 31 percent were women. Regular and fixed-term staff on board at the end of fiscal 1996—excluding staff on special leave and leave without pay—numbered 5,681, down from 6,059 as of June 30, 1995. During fiscal year 1996, the Bank completed the implementation of a special staff-redundancy program. In February 1995, the Bank's executive directors approved a special authorization to fund 568 staff redundancies for a total amount of $153 million. As the program unfolded, the total number increased, while the average cost turned out to be lower. In total, 608 staff left the Bank under the special program, at a total cost of about $112 million. Included in this cost are expenses associated with job-search assistance, training, outplacement consulting, pension-plan contributions, and related tax allowances.

## International Finance Corporation (IFC)

The IFC sought to enhance the developmental impact of its activities in fiscal 1996 by continuing to expand and diversify its investment, mobilization, and advisory activities.[2] The Corporation focused on areas of demonstrated comparative advantage such as the development of capital markets, the promotion of private sector infrastructure, privatization, the exploration of new markets for investment finance and advisory services, and the direct mobilization of funds. Where the climate for private investment was uncertain, the IFC concentrated on advisory services to build the capacity for private sector development, with investment to follow. Through this process, it responded in a comprehensive way to client needs in developing countries.

In November 1995 IFC clarified and strengthened its traditional cooperation with private financial institutions through the development and application of policies outlined in "Collaboration with Private International Financial Institutions—Practices and Policies." The underlying principles contained in the statement clearly define IFC's role: to support investments and advisory projects with a strong developmental impact, and in situations where others could not have played a similar role.

The Corporation also further refined its disclosure policy during the year to better ensure that its activities are undertaken with transparency and accountability. It continued to expand its advisory work, seeking to leverage its experience through technical assistance and dissemination of knowledge. A new publication series, focusing on lessons of experience in the areas of privatization, infrastructure, capital markets, investment funds, and leasing, was launched. The Corporation will continue to focus on dissemination as a tool in achieving results on the ground and as a means for broadening its developmental impact. The IFC also continued its

2. Details of the IFC's investment and mobilization activities during fiscal 1996 may be found on page 61.

work in support of environmental sustainability through joint projects with the Global Environment Facility, the Montreal Protocol, and other donors.

The IFC realized record net income of $346 million, reflecting improved profitability of its loan portfolio and strong capital gains performance. It earned a return of 8.9 percent on its average net worth, which reached $4.2 billion at June 30, 1996. New commitments signed during the year totaled $2.1 billion, down from $2.4 billion in fiscal 1995. Disbursements were up, to $2.1 billion, and the IFC's total disbursed portfolio reached $7.8 billion as of June 30, 1996. The Corporation borrowed $3.0 billion in the international markets and $8 million from the IBRD. The IFC issued bonds in twelve currencies.

In fiscal 1996, the Corporation's membership increased to 170 countries with the additions of Azerbaijan, Bahrain, Eritrea, St. Kitts and Nevis, as well as of Bosnia and Herzegovina, which suceeded to the membership of the former Socialist Federal Republic of Yugoslavia.

Details of the IFC's fiscal year can be found in its *Annual Report*, published separately.

## Multilateral Investment Guarantee Agency (MIGA)

During fiscal 1996, MIGA's board of executive directors concurred with the president's decision on all forty-four insurance projects conveyed to it. Since MIGA's inception, the board has considered 215 projects. MIGA's net income before provisioning increased 62 percent to $20.7 million in fiscal 1996.

Six additional countries became members of the Agency in fiscal 1996, increasing the number of MIGA member countries to 134. An additional twenty-one developing countries and economies in transition are in the process of fulfilling membership requirements; MIGA has 155 signatories to its Convention.

During fiscal 1996:

• MIGA issued sixty-eight contracts for $862 million in coverage, raising the outstanding maximum contingent liability to $2.3 billion;

• MIGA issued its first guarantees in Kuwait, Kyrgyz Republic, Mali, Nepal, and Papua New Guinea;

• MIGA's risk-to-assets ratio was raised from 2.5 to 1 to a new level of 3.5 to 1; and

• country limits for guarantees were raised from $175 million to $225 million.[3]

*Technical assistance activities.* MIGA offers technical assistance, through its Investment Marketing Services Department, to help developing countries promote private investment opportunities more effectively. This support includes assistance in dissemination of information on investment opportunities and business operating conditions; organization or support of specific promotion activities; and training and other initiatives designed to enhance the institutional capacity of host-country investment-promotion agencies (IPAs). Wherever possible, MIGA seeks to support promotion activities that can be organized on a multicountry and/or sectoral basis.

MIGA is also pioneering the use of new marketing and communications technologies as vehicles for dissemination of information. During fiscal 1996, MIGA formally launched its Investment Promotion Agency Electronic Network (IPAnet). The product of two and a half years of research and development efforts that has tapped user feedback and information from over seventy countries, IPAnet is an on-line, marketing, communications, and information network that links private investors with investment intermediaries and technology providers worldwide to share information and promote foreign direct investment (FDI) via the Internet. IPAnet was opened in November 1995 to the world investment community for a free trial period while content and functionalities were being added. Concurrently, MIGA initiated marketing efforts worldwide to demonstrate the facility to gatherings of IPA officials and private businesses. Favorable press coverage from major business publications in North America, Asia, and Europe helped boost registration to more than 1,000 organizations in more than eighty countries by May 1996.

---

3. Details of MIGA's fiscal 1996 guarantee program may be found on page 61.

MIGA also continued its support of more traditional forms of investment promotion during fiscal 1996, organizing two major investment-promotion conferences focused on mining in Africa and Central Asia, respectively. MIGA also continued efforts to promote investment between developing countries, organizing in Malaysia a symposium designed to promote increased flow of "south-south" investment. Representatives from more than thirty countries attended this symposium, which provided a forum for IPAS and firms seeking to attract business collaboration from Asia to learn about government policies and business strategies of leading companies from Japan, the Republic of Korea, Malaysia, and Singapore.

During fiscal 1996 MIGA expanded the scope of its IPA capacity-building program, conducting several orientation/training programs on investment-promotion "best practices" for diplomatic officials of individual countries or groups of countries, as well as an executive management workshop for chief executives and their deputies from seven African IPAS.

MIGA also provides technical assistance through its Legal Department which helps member countries to develop appropriate legislation to facilitate FDI inflows.

Details of MIGA's activities during fiscal 1996 appear in its *Annual Report*, which is published separately.

## International Centre for Settlement of Investment Disputes (ICSID)

The International Centre for Settlement of Investment Disputes is a separate international organization established under the Convention of the Settlement of Investment Disputes between States and Nationals of Other States (the Convention), which was opened for signature in 1965 and entered into force the following year.

ICSID seeks to encourage greater flows of international investment by providing facilities for the conciliation and arbitration of disputes between governments and foreign investors. In addition, ICSID undertakes research, publications, and advisory activities in the area of foreign investment law.

During fiscal 1996, ICSID's membership continued to grow with the ratification of the Convention by Algeria, the Bahamas, Bahrain, Oman, Panama, St. Kitts and Nevis, and Uzbekistan. As of June 30, 1966, 126 countries had become members of ICSID; an additional thirteen countries had signed but not yet ratified the Convention.

During the same period, five new requests for arbitration were registered. As of June 30, 1996, ten cases were pending before the Centre.

ICSID's publications include a semiannual law journal, "ICSID Review—Foreign Investment Law Journal" and multivolume collections of "Investment Laws of the World and Investment Treaties." Two issues of the law journal and four releases of the investment laws and treaties collections were published in fiscal 1996.

Details of ICSID's activities during fiscal 1996 appear in its *Annual Report*, which is published separately.

## IBRD Financial Highlights

In the fiscal year ending June 30, 1996, the IBRD achieved strong financial performance, the highlights of which include:

• healthy net income of $1,187 million, despite a falling interest-rate environment and continuing strengthening of the United States dollar (the IBRD's reporting currency) against other major currencies.

• strong growth in loan disbursements to member countries, up by 5.5 percent to $13,372 million, from $12,672 million in fiscal 1995;

• an 8 percent reduction in the cost of new medium- and long-term borrowings, after swaps, to 5.28 percent from 6.31 percent in fiscal 1995;

• a healthy reserves-to-loan ratio of 14.1 percent;

• a 12 percent reduction in administrative expenses to $846 million, down from $961 million in fiscal 1995; and

• the retention of a 25 basis points interest waiver for eligible borrowers and a 50 basis point commitment fee waiver to all borrowers.

The board of governors agreed at the September 1995 annual meetings to allocate net income earned during fiscal 1995 as follows:

• $280 million to the general reserve to increase the reserves-to-loan ratio and prefund partial waivers of interest charges;

• $90 million, by way of grant, to the Trust Fund for Gaza;

• $100 million, by way of grant, to the Debt-reduction Facility for IDA-only Countries;

• $250 million equivalent in SDRs as of June 30, 1995, as an immediate grant to IDA; and

• the remainder, $634 million, to surplus.

## Financial Policies

*Conversion from 1982 loan terms to 1989 loan terms.* The program approved by the executive directors in November 1994 to encourage borrowers to convert the lending terms of their IBRD loans from the variable lending-rate system in effect from July 1, 1982 until July 1, 1989 (VLR 1982) to the variable lending-rate system in effect since July 1, 1989 (VLR 1989) has been very effective. Of the $38.8 billion equivalent of VLR 1982 loans outstanding at December 31, 1994, approximately $36.9 billion equivalent had been converted to VLR 1989 loans by the end of fiscal 1996. The successful implementation of the VLR 1982 loan and conversion program enabled the IBRD to improve the interest-risk management of its liquid portfolio and enhance its ability to expand the currency and interest choices it can offer to its borrowers on new and existing loans.

*Debt-funding liquidity.* In accordance with the IBRD's policies on currency and interest-rate risk management, the executive directors approved on May 7, 1996 a proposal to achieve full funding of the IBRD liquidity portfolio on a currency-by-currency basis

with floating debt by July 1, 1996. This will expose the IBRD's net income to less interest-rate risk.

*Review of single currency loans.* On June 25, 1996 the executive directors reviewed the single currency-loan program and agreed to remove the lending volume limitation on new single currency-loan commitments, effective immediately. When the single currency-loan program was expanded in May 1995, directors felt it prudent to limit borrowing countries' access to new single currency loans to 50 percent of their lending program or $100 million, whichever was greater. The single currency-loan program has proved popular with borrowers, with about 50 percent of all new commitments in fiscal 1996 made on single currency-loan terms. The decision to remove the volume limitation was a response to borrower interest for increased currency choice, and follows the successful conversion of VLR 1982 loans to VLR 1989 loan terms, and the IBRD's progress in promoting informed decision making by borrowers during fiscal 1996.

*Review of currency-pool loans.* The currency-management system approved in January 1989 established target ratios for the currency composition of currency-pool loans. Under the currency-pooling system, each loan is a share of the currency pool and has the same currency composition as all other currency-pool loans. On June 25, 1996, the executive directors reviewed the targeted currency-pool loans. In response to borrower demand, they agreed to establish new single currency-pool loans in four currencies (United States dollars, yen, deutsche mark, and Swiss francs) and to offer borrowers a choice of currencies for the undisbursed and disbursed outstanding balances of their existing currency-pool loans. Borrowers can select among three choices: (a) convert undisbursed balances to single currency-loan terms; (b) convert undisbursed balances to single currency-loan terms and disbursed and outstanding balances to single currency-pool terms; and (c) convert the entire loan (disbursed and undisbursed balances) to one of the four new single currency-pool loans.

Borrowers may also choose to remain with the existing currency-pool loans. The IBRD will continue to maintain at least 90 percent of the United States-dollar equivalent value of the currency pool in fixed currency ratios of 1 United States dollar to 125 yen to 2 deutsche mark equivalent (comprising deutsche mark, Swiss francs, and Netherlands guilders). These targets will be reviewed in five years.

The currency composition of the single currency-pool loans under options (b) and (c) will initially be the same as the original currency-pool loans. Over time, the IBRD will shift the currency composition of each of the four single currency-pool loans to 100 percent in the designated currency and, at least, to 90 percent by July 1, 1999. Starting from September 1, 1996, borrowers can make their choices known to the IBRD. The deadline for choosing is June 30, 1998. The conversions to single currency-pool loans will take place on July 1, 1997, January 1, 1998, and July 1, 1998. Except for the single currency-pool loan converted from fixed rate currency-pool loan, the lending rate for each single currency-pool loan will be variable, reset semiannually, and equal to the semester average cost of IBRD borrowing allocated to fund that pool plus the 0.50 percent contractual lending spread. The single currency-pool loan converted from fixed rate currency-pool loan will continue to carry the same fixed lending rate as in the original loan agreement. The single

currency-pool terms will not be available for new loans.

*Accumulated provisions for loan losses.* The level of loan-loss provision is based on an assessment of the collectibility of loans in nonaccrual status, together with an evaluation of collectibility risks in the remainder of the portfolio. For fiscal year 1996, loan-loss provisions were maintained at a level equal to 3 percent of total loans disbursed and outstanding plus the present value of callable guarantees for an amount equivalent to $3,340 million at the end of the fiscal year.

### Loans

*Disbursements.* The IBRD's gross disbursements to countries during fiscal 1996 were $13,372 million, up $700 million from fiscal 1995's total of $12,672 million. Net disbursements, excluding prepayments, to current borrowers were $2,882 million, an increase of $664 million over the previous year's total of $2,238 million.

*Lending rate.* For loans made under, or converted to, the IBRD's new variable lending rate (VLR) system, established in 1989, the interest rate was 7.07 percent for the first semester and 6.98 percent for the second semester of fiscal 1996. By comparison, the interest rates for older variable rate loans (established in 1982) that have not been converted to the current system were 7.09 percent and 6.97 percent for the first and second semesters, respectively.

The single currency lending rates ranged from 5.38 percent to 6.13 percent in United States dollars and from 4.41 percent to 6.85 percent in French francs (the only currencies outstanding on loans). These rates are based on the IBRD's cost of LIBOR-based funding (PIBOR for French francs) in these currencies.

*Interest waivers.* During fiscal 1996, the IBRD continued to waive 25 basis points of the semester interest rate of loans to all borrowers that had made all loan-service payments within thirty days of their due date. (Approximately 90 percent of the IBRD's total volume of outstanding loans is currently eligible for the interest-spread waiver.) This waiver was in addition to the continuation during the year of a waiver of part of the IBRD's commitment fee on undisbursed balances that resulted in a reduction of that fee from 75 to 25 basis points. Together, the partial waivers on loan charges amounted to $521 million in fiscal 1996.

*Loans in nonaccrual status.* At the end of fiscal 1996, six member countries (Bosnia and Herzegovina, Iraq, Liberia, Sudan, Syria, and Zaire), as well as one successor republic of the former Socialist Federal Republic of Yugoslavia, the Federal Republic of Yugoslavia (Serbia and Monetengro), were in nonaccrual status. Loans in nonaccrual amounted to 2.3 percent of the total IBRD portfolio at the end of fiscal 1996. In June 1996, the IBRD approved a loan-consolidation package that ensured Bosnia and Herzegovina's continued access to IBRD lending resources while maintaining the financial integrity of the IBRD. For further details on the agreement, see the box on page 101.

## Liquid Assets Management

In fiscal 1996, the IBRD once again abided by its underlying stability-oriented liquid assets-management policy by maintaining its liquidity at 43 percent of its next three years' estimated cash requirements. The policy helps the IBRD to ensure the flexibility in the timing of its borrowings should borrowing ability be adversely affected by temporary conditions in the capital markets. At the end of the fiscal year, the IBRD's liquidity totaled $15,898 million, of which $1,168 million was segregated as "held-to-maturity." Further, to ensure reduction in interest rate risks, on July 1, 1996, the IBRD will begin funding its liquidity portfolio by floating debt on a currency-by-currency basis.

The IBRD's liquid assets are invested exclusively in fixed-income markets and are actively traded, with the exception of the pound sterling holdings, which have been matched to the duration of underlying liabilities. The sterling portfolio is classified as held-to-maturity. Portfolio-management activities are fully supported by comprehensive risk-management and monitoring procedures covering both credit risk and interest-rate risk. Trading performance of actively managed portfolios is measured daily against detailed benchmark portfolios.

During fiscal 1996, the IBRD's financial return on its portfolio was 4.43 percent. The financial return on investments in fiscal 1995 was 5.69 percent. The portfolio was managed in relation to a benchmark strategy of one year duration except for the held-to-maturity portfolio, which had an average duration of 5.55 years as of June 30, 1996.

## Borrowings and Liability Management

The objectives of the IBRD's borrowing and liability-management strategy are to ensure the long-term availability of funds to the IBRD for lending and liquidity and to minimize the costs of funds for the IBRD and its borrowers. The IBRD seeks to ensure the availability of funds by developing borrowing capacity in a range of markets and by diversifying its borrowings by currency, country, source, and maturity to provide maximum flexibility in funding. It also seeks to enhance the continuing appeal of its securities by offering features tailored to satisfy investors' asset preferences and by positioning its securities advantageously in each capital market (for example, from a regulatory, tax, and investment-classification perspective).

Within the framework of the currency composition of borrowings required to fund its lending products, the IBRD seeks to minimize the cost of borrowed funds by using, among other things, currency swaps to obtain savings over the cost of direct borrowings in target currencies; structured financings converted to conventional liabilities using over-the-counter financial derivatives; short-term and variable rate instruments; and prepayments or market repurchase of borrowings, which, by varying margins, exceed the costs of refinancing.

*Medium-term and long-term funding.* During fiscal 1996, the IBRD raised $10.9 billion through MLT borrowings in fifteen currencies *(see Table 6-1)*. In connection with these borrowings, the Bank also contracted $4.7 billion of currency swaps and a notional par volume of $6.1 billion of interest-rate swaps. After swaps, most of the year's funding was denominated in United States dollars and deutsche mark, with minor amounts in French and Luxembourg francs. The average maturity of all this

## TABLE 6-1. IBRD MEDIUM- AND LONG-TERM BORROWINGS, FISCAL YEAR 1996

*(amounts in millions)*

| Type | Issue | Currency | Currency amount | US dollar equivalent [a] |
|------|-------|----------|----------------|--------------------------|
| Global | 6.125% seven-year bond, due 2002 | DM | 2,975 | 2,005.7 |
| | 6.375% ten-year bond, due 2005 | US$ | 1,490 | 1,489.9 |
| | 6.375% five-year bond, due 2001 | US$ | 995 | 994.9 |
| | 5% two-year bonds due 1998 | ¥ | 29,550 | 269.7 |
| | Capped floater seven-year bonds due 2003 | Lit | 299,640 | 194.5 |
| Structured | 10.6% three-year callable bonds due 1998 | Lit | 149,820 | 93.1 |
| | 10.6% two-year callable bond due 1997 | Lit | 250,060 | 157.1 |
| | 6% five-year extendable step-up notes due 2000 | US$ | 30 | 30.0 |
| | 9.375% three-year callable bonds due 1999 | Lit | 299,440 | 189.5 |
| | 8.70% ten-year callable bonds due 2006 | Ptas | 9,988 | 65.1 |
| | 9.65% three-year callable bond due 1999 | Lit | 199,800 | 128.1 |
| | Floating seven-year callable bond due 2003 | Lit | 299,690 | 190.5 |
| | 3% ten-year callable bond due 2005 | ¥ | 10,000 | 99.7 |
| | 3.25% ten-year callable double-up bond due 2006 | ¥ | 5,000 | 47.5 |
| | Investor puttable reverse dual currency note with multicurrency coupon option due 2029 | ¥ | 20,000 | 184.4 |
| | Step-up seven-year callable notes due 2003 | DM | 99 | 65.1 |
| | 8.50% three-year callable notes due 1999 | Lit | 299,570 | 193.1 |
| | 6.6% two-year dual currency bonds due 1998 | ¥ | 6,890 | 63.9 |
| | Zero-coupon ten-year callable bonds due 2006 | Lit | 399,786 | 255.1 |
| | Floating rate five-year callable notes due 2001 | Lit | 199,810 | 128.7 |
| | 8.25% four-year notes due 2000 | $A | 100 | 78.9 |
| Conventional | Loan due 1998 | LuxF | 1,000 | 34.9 |
| | 8-3/4% DM bonds due August 28, 2001 | DM | 45 | 31.0 |
| | 8 1/4% two-year bonds due 1998 | Ptas | 14,990 | 119.5 |
| | 7.75% three-year bond due 1999 | Ptas | 9,975 | 79.1 |
| | 7.5% four-year bonds due 1999 | $A | 199 | 151.8 |
| | Zero-coupon four-year bonds due 1999 | $A | 297 | 226.6 |
| | three-year FRN due 1998 | Dr | 19,980 | 84.7 |
| | 4% three-year bond due 1998 | US$ | 192 | 191.7 |
| | 5% five-year bond due 2000 | US$ | 49 | 48.8 |
| | 7.6% three-year bond due 1998 | $A | 198 | 153.2 |
| | 4% three-year bond due 1998 | DM | 198 | 139.5 |
| | 10.2% two-year bond due 1998 | Kč | 2,496 | 93.6 |
| | 5.35% seven-year note due 2003 | DM | 148 | 103.1 |
| | Zero coupon three-year bond due 1999 | US$ | 260 | 260.4 |
| | 4.625% 3.8-year notes due 1999 | DM | 299 | 202.5 |
| | 8.25% three-year bond due 1999 | $NZ | 99 | 68.2 |
| | 7.05% five-year LAF-eligible notes due 2001 | HK$ | 1,000 | 129.4 |
| | Zero coupon two-year bond due 1998 | Lit | 166,900 | 106.4 |
| | 5.25% five-year notes due 2001 | DM | 299 | 199.4 |
| | 5% three-year bond due 1998 | $A | 140 | 103.0 |
| | 7.65% three-year bond due 1999 | $A | 247 | 197.8 |
| | 8.75% three-year bond due 1999 | $NZ | 100 | 68.2 |
| | 7% two-and-a-half-year bonds due 1998 | £ | 200 | 304.6 |
| | 5.6% two-year bonds due 1998 | Can$ | 100 | 72.8 |
| | 8.25% three-year bonds due 1999 | $A | 100 | 79.4 |
| | 7% three-year bonds due 1999 | HK$ | 1,000 | 129.3 |
| | 9% three-year bonds due 1999 | $NZ | 199 | 135.2 |
| | 6.25% two-and-a half-year bonds due 1998 | US$ | 199 | 199.2 |
| | 4.55% three-year bond due 1999 | US$ | 99 | 99.0 |
| | 3.20% 12-year loan due 2008 | ¥ | 5,000 | 47.6 |
| | 5.75% six-year bonds due 2002 | F | 495 | 97.6 |
| Total | | | | 10,883 |

*Note: Borrowing amounts are based on net proceeds. United States dollar equivalents are expressed at the exchange rate prevailing at the time of launch.*

## TABLE 6-2.  IBRD BORROWINGS, AFTER SWAPS, FISCAL YEAR 1996

*(amounts in millions of US dollars equivalent)*

| Item | Before swaps | | | Currency swaps (amount) | After swaps | | | Cost (%) |
| | Amount | % | Maturity (years) | | Amount | % | Maturity (years) | |
|---|---|---|---|---|---|---|---|---|
| *Medium- and long-term borrowings* | | | | | | | | |
| U.S. dollars | 3,313.9 | 30 | 6.8 | 2,605.8 | 5,919.7 | 54 | 5.7 | 5.71 |
| Deutsche mark | 2,746.2 | 25 | 6.3 | 2,084.5 | 4,830.7 | 44 | 4.4 | 4.75 |
| Japanese yen | 712.9 | 7 | 5.8 | (712.0) | — | — | — | — |
| Others | 4,109.0 | 38 | 2.9 | (3,976.5) | 132.5 | 1 | 5.1 | 5.11 |
| Total[a] | 10,882.0 | 100 | 5.1 | 1.8 | 10,882.9 | 100 | 5.1 | 5.28 |
| *Short-term borrowings outstanding* | | | | | | | | |
| Central bank facility | 2,586.3 | 59 | 0.5 | | | | | 5.40 |
| Discount notes (U.S. dollars) | 1,400.0 | 32 | 0.4 | | | | | 5.46 |
| Other[b] | | | | | | | | |
| U.S. dollars | 300.0 | 7 | 0.9 | | | | | 5.52 |
| Deutsche mark | 73.6 | 2 | 0.7 | | | | | 3.02 |
| Total[c] | 4,359.9 | 100 | 0.5 | | | | | 5.43 |

NOTE: *Details may not add to totals because of rounding.*

*a. Excludes the cost of Liability Management Funding and the volume, maturity, and cost of Contingent Funding.*

*b. Executed under the IBRD's Global Multicurrency Note Program.*

*c. Short-term borrowings outstanding on June 30, 1995, totaled $3,917 million.*

funding, including the MLT funding held at floating rates, was 5.1 years, and the after-swap cost was 5.28 percent *(see Table 6-2)*.

Noteworthy among the vehicle-currency transactions executed by the IBRD during the past year was the launching of its first Czech koruna operation in December 1995, a two-year maturity, euro-Czech koruna 2.5 billion issue, the largest of its kind at the time. With a revival of investor interest in structured financings, the IBRD also took the opportunity to issue $2.4 billion of such financings during the year. Strong demand from Japanese investors, especially from retail, for non-yen paper offering a yield pick-up over historically low domestic Japanese interest rates, also enabled the IBRD to raise about $2.5 billion in Japanese targeted issues.

*Liability management.* During the past fiscal year, the IBRD prepaid an aggregate volume of $216 million of borrowings in United States dollars and Luxembourg francs. In addition, it redeemed $25 million equivalent of outstanding Swiss franc borrowings through market repurchases. To improve interest rate matching between the IBRD's liquid assets and its debt reallocated to fund such assets, the IBRD also transformed a notional principal amount of $9.3 billion in such existing debt from a fixed rate- into a floating rate-basis during the year.

At the end of the fiscal year, MLT funding outstanding amounted to $92.4 billion, or 95 percent ($93.8 billion, or 96 percent after swaps) of total debt outstanding. As of June 30, 1996, the average maturity of total MLT debt was 5.3 years, and its average cost, after swaps, was 6.26 percent.

*Short-term funding.* As of June 30, 1996, short-term borrowings outstanding were $4.3 billion, an increase of $0.4 billion over June 30, 1995. These comprised $2.6 billion from official sources through the IBRD's central bank facility, $1.4 billion from market funding in United States dollar discount notes, and $0.4 billion from short-term notes issued under the IBRD's global multicurrency note program. The cost of these borrowings was 5.4 percent, compared with 5.85 percent at the end of fiscal 1995.

## Capital

The IBRD seeks to avoid exchange risks by matching its liabilities in various currencies with assets in those same currencies and by matching the currencies of its retained earnings and accumulated provision for loan losses with those of its outstanding loans.

The IBRD presents its financial statements in United States dollars. Accordingly, changes in the value of the United States dollar vis-à-vis other currencies have an effect on the reported balances for assets and liabilities. For the June 30, 1996 financial statements, expressed in United States dollar terms, the loan portfolio was reduced by $14.4 billion, the borrowing portfolio by $11.7 billion, and accumulated provision for loan losses by $0.4 billion. In total, expressed in United States dollar terms, the total assets fell by $17.0 billion and total liabilities by $14.0 billion.

On June 30, 1996, the total subscribed capital of the IBRD was $180.6 billion, or 96 percent of authorized capital of $188 billion. During fiscal year 1996, subscriptions to the $74.8 billion 1988 general capital increase (GCI) continued on schedule. Twenty-six countries subscribed an aggregate $4.0 billion. A total of 20,584 GCI shares ($2.5 billion, or 3 percent of total allocations), including GCI shares allocated to new members that joined the IBRD after April 1988, remain to be subscribed. At the end of fiscal 1996, the permissible increase of net disbursements ("headroom") was $90.8 billion, or 45 percent of the IBRD's lending limit.

On June 14, 1996 the board of governors of the IBRD approved a Special Capital Increase of 33,230 shares for Japan, in recognition of a serious discrepancy that had developed over time

---

### BOX 6-1. A REVIEW OF THE FIRST TWO YEARS OF IDA-10

*In October 1995, the executive directors of the Bank discussed a review that reported on the use of resources during the first two years of IDA-10 (fiscal years 1994 and 1995).*

*The review covered IDA's progress in the light of the objectives agreed with donors. IDA's primary aim, poverty reduction, is reflected in country-assistance programs, as are the supporting objectives of economic growth and environmental sustainability. The focus in these country-specific programs is on the effectiveness of IDA-funded development programs and projects, since improved results are needed if IDA is to help accelerate the reduction of poverty so widespread in IDA-eligible countries. Country programs are increasingly tailored to each country situation on the basis of the results of poverty assessments, national environmental action plans, and other country-specific analytical work.*

*In the second year of IDA-10, the executive board discussed nineteen country-assistance strategy documents (CASS) after having discussed thirty-five CASS in the previous year. During the two years, the executive directors have reviewed CAS documents for about two thirds of the seventy-eight countries that were eligible to borrow from IDA. An increased focus on stakeholder participation resulted in substantial improvements in these documents. In addition, more than half of all IDA projects approved in fiscal 1995 benefited from beneficiary participation in their design.*

*The directors took note of the report and endorsed the implementation of poverty-reduction strategies through country-specific assistance strategies, while suggesting that these could be more firmly grounded in the analytical results of poverty assessments. They also encouraged a clearer evaluation of the linkages between IDA programs and results on the ground. The report, "IDA-10: The First Two Years—Review of the FY94-95 IDA Program," was made available to the public.*

between Japan's IBRD shareholding and its economic position. This increased the share of Japan from 6.17 percent of the total allocated shares to 8.18 percent.

*Reserves.* On June 30, 1996, reserves amounted to $17.1 billion, and the reserves-to-loan ratio stood at 14.1 percent.

## IDA Finances

*IDA's commitment authority.* IDA is mainly funded by donor contributions, and such funds are "replenished" by an agreement among donors every three years. Fiscal year 1996 was the third and final year of the tenth replenishment of IDA (IDA-10), the agreed size of which was SDR13 billion (see Box 6-1). IDA's commitment authority is based on these donor contributions, which are made available in three annual tranches, and other resources available to IDA (mainly repayments from past credits and net income transfers from the IBRD).

As of June 30, 1996, the donor funds made available for the IDA-10 period (fiscal 1994-96) totaled SDR11,036 million. During fiscal 1996, about SDR2,591 million was derived from the release of the third annual tranche of IDA-10 commitments. However, part of the third tranche of IDA-10 contributions is not yet available, as the United States' contribution was not made on the agreed schedule, and one donor, Germany, exercised its right to withhold its contribution proportionately to the shortfall in the United States' payment. The Association did receive a small final payment from the United States for its IDA-9 contribution, which triggered a release of some funds from Germany that had been blocked because of the delay in the United States' payment. These IDA-9 payments increased IDA's commitment authority by about SDR84 million. Also during fiscal 1996, the Association received formal notifications from Greece and Italy that they would contribute to IDA-10, thereby increasing its commitment authority by an additional SDR273 million. Only one donor, Kuwait, had not yet notified the Association of its participation in IDA-10 by the end of fiscal 1996.

Other resources made available during the year included the transfer of SDR161 million from the IBRD's fiscal 1995 net income and SDR 942 million of commitment authority against current and future repayments of past credits. Of the latter amount, SDR800 million is for ordinary credits, and another SDR142 million is for the Fifth Dimension Program. Therefore, the total available resoures for the entire IDA-10 period increased to SDR14,895 million in fiscal 1996.

Against these resources, the Association made IDA-10 commitments of SDR4,616 million during fiscal 1996. Of this amount, 40 percent went to Africa, 26 percent to South Asia, 17 percent to East Asia and Pacific, 7 percent to Europe and Central Asia, 6 percent to Latin America and the Caribbean, and 5 percent to the Middle East and North Africa.

*IDA's commitment fee.* Every year, the level of commitment fee is set by the executive directors based on an annual review of IDA's financial position. The commitment fee for fiscal 1997 was set at 0 percent for all IDA credits. IDA's commitment fee has been 0 percent from fiscal 1989 through fiscal 1996.

*Special Fund termination.* In May 1996, the executive directors approved the termination of the Special Fund, set up in 1982 to supplement IDA funding for fiscal 1984. As a result of the termination, all credits, as well as all liquid assets, were transferred to IDA.

# Financial Statements of the
## International Bank for Reconstruction and Development

# BALANCE SHEET

*June 30, 1996 and June 30, 1995*
*Expressed in millions of U.S. dollars*

|  | 1996 | 1995 |
|---|---:|---:|
| **Assets** | | |
| ***Due from Banks*** | | |
| Unrestricted currencies | $ 27 | $ 40 |
| Currencies subject to restrictions—Note A | 612 | 549 |
| | 639 | 589 |
| ***Investments—Notes B and E*** | | |
| Trading | 15,001 | 19,821 |
| Held-to-maturity | 1,169 | 1,203 |
| | 16,170 | 21,024 |
| ***Securities Purchased Under Resale Agreements—Note B*** | 1,282 | 246 |
| ***Nonnegotiable, Noninterest-bearing Demand Obligations on Account of Subscribed Capital —Note A*** | 1,765 | 1,610 |
| ***Amounts Receivable to Maintain Value of Currency Holdings—Note A*** | 732 | 1,106 |
| ***Other Receivables*** | | |
| Amounts receivable from currency swaps—Notes D and E | 18,010 | 16,735 |
| Amounts receivable from investment securities traded | 2,365 | 1,762 |
| Amounts receivable from covered forwards—Notes B and E | 204 | 1,307 |
| Accrued income on loans | 2,127 | 2,538 |
| Accrued interest on investments | 92 | 159 |
| | 22,798 | 22,501 |
| ***Loans Outstanding*** | | |
| ***(see Summary Statement of Loans—Note C)*** | | |
| Total loans | 164,766 | 179,453 |
| Less loans approved but not yet effective | 9,500 | 11,982 |
| Less undisbursed balance of effective loans | 45,020 | 43,972 |
| Loans outstanding | 110,246 | 123,499 |
| Less accumulated provision for loan losses | 3,340 | 3,740 |
| Loans outstanding net of accumulated provision | 106,906 | 119,759 |
| ***Other Assets*** | | |
| Unamortized issuance costs of borrowings | 412 | 485 |
| Miscellaneous | 1,300 | 1,259 |
| | 1,712 | 1,744 |
| **Total assets** | $152,004 | $168,579 |

|  | 1996 | 1995 |
|---|---|---|
| **Liabilities** | | |
| ***Borrowings (see Summary Statement of Borrowings—Notes D and E)*** | | |
| Short-term | $ 4,328 | $ 3,898 |
| Medium- and long-term | 92,391 | 104,392 |
| | 96,719 | 108,290 |
| ***Securities Sold Under Agreements to Repurchase and*** | | |
| ***Payable For Cash Collateral Received—Note B*** | 2,439 | 2,567 |
| ***Amounts Payable to Maintain Value of Currency Holdings—Note A*** | 4 | 24 |
| ***Other Liabilities*** | | |
| Amounts payable for currency swaps—Notes D and E | 19,427 | 19,985 |
| Amounts payable for investment securities purchased | 1,508 | 2,231 |
| Amounts payable for covered forwards—Notes B and E | 202 | 1,306 |
| Accrued charges on borrowings | 2,352 | 2,857 |
| Payable for Board of Governors-approved transfers—Note F | 205 | 135 |
| Accounts payable and miscellaneous liabilities | 848 | 723 |
| | 24,542 | 27,237 |
| **Total liabilities** | 123,704 | 138,118 |
| **Equity** | | |
| ***Capital Stock (see Statement of Subscriptions to Capital Stock and Voting Power—Note A)*** | | |
| Authorized capital (1,558,478 shares—June 30, 1996; 1,525,248 shares—June 30, 1995) | | |
| Subscribed capital (1,497,325 shares—June 30, 1996; 1,462,574 shares—June 30, 1995) | 180,630 | 176,438 |
| Less uncalled portion of subscriptions | 169,636 | 165,580 |
| | 10,994 | 10,858 |
| ***Deferred Amounts to Maintain Value of Currency Holdings—Note A*** | 136 | 770 |
| ***Payments on Account of Pending Subscriptions—Note A*** | 15 | 23 |
| ***Retained Earnings (see Statement of Changes in Retained Earnings—Note F)*** | 16,099 | 15,502 |
| ***Cumulative Translation Adjustment (see Statement of Changes in Cumulative Translation Adjustment)*** | 1,056 | 3,308 |
| **Total equity** | 28,300 | 30,461 |
| **Total liabilities and equity** | $152,004 | $168,579 |

*The Notes to Financial Statements are an integral part of these Statements.*

## STATEMENT OF INCOME

*For the fiscal years ended June 30, 1996 and June 30, 1995*
*Expressed in millions of U.S. dollars*

| | 1996 | 1995 |
|---|---|---|
| **Income** | | |
| Income from loans—Note C | | |
| Interest | $7,804 | $8,069 |
| Commitment charges | 118 | 118 |
| Income from investments—Note B | | |
| Trading | | |
| Interest | 673 | 881 |
| Net gains/(losses) | | |
| Realized | 31 | (23) |
| Unrealized | (83) | 168 |
| Held-to-maturity | | |
| Interest | 100 | 78 |
| Income from securities purchased under resale agreements | 66 | 61 |
| Other income | 11 | 10 |
| Total income | 8,720 | 9,362 |
| **Expenses** | | |
| Borrowing expenses—Note D | | |
| Interest | 6,455 | 6,832 |
| Prepayment costs | 9 | 7 |
| Amortization of issuance costs and other borrowing costs | 106 | 105 |
| Interest on securities sold under agreements to repurchase and payable for cash collateral received | 67 | 83 |
| Administrative expenses—Notes G, H, I and J | 733 | 842 |
| Provision for loan losses—Note C | 42 | 12 |
| Other expenses | 8 | 8 |
| Total expenses | 7,420 | 7,889 |
| **Operating Income** | 1,300 | 1,473 |
| Less contributions to special programs—Note G | 113 | 119 |
| **Net Income** | $1,187 | $1,354 |

## STATEMENT OF CHANGES IN RETAINED EARNINGS

*For the fiscal years ended June 30, 1996 and June 30, 1995*
*Expressed in millions of U.S. dollars*

| | 1996 | 1995 |
|---|---|---|
| Retained earnings at beginning of the fiscal year | $15,502 | $14,468 |
| Board of Governors-approved transfers—Note F | | |
| To International Development Association | (250) | (300) |
| To Debt Reduction Facility for IDA-Only Countries | (100) | — |
| To Trust Fund for Gaza and West Bank | (90) | — |
| For Emergency Assistance for Rwanda | — | (20) |
| To Trust Fund for Bosnia and Herzegovina | (150) | — |
| Net income for the fiscal year | 1,187 | 1,354 |
| Retained earnings at end of the fiscal year | $16,099 | $15,502 |

## STATEMENT OF CHANGES IN CUMULATIVE TRANSLATION ADJUSTMENT

*For the fiscal years ended June 30, 1996 and June 30, 1995*
*Expressed in millions of U.S. dollars*

| | 1996 | 1995 |
|---|---|---|
| Cumulative translation adjustment at beginning of the fiscal year | $3,308 | $1,394 |
| Translation adjustment for the fiscal year | (2,252) | 1,914 |
| Cumulative translation adjustment at end of the fiscal year | $1,056 | $3,308 |

*The Notes to Financial Statements are an integral part of these Statements.*

## STATEMENT OF CASH FLOWS

*For the fiscal years ended June 30, 1996 and June 30, 1995*
*Expressed in millions of U.S. dollars*

|  | 1996 | 1995 |
|---|---|---|
| Cash flows from lending and investing activities | | |
| Loans | | |
| Disbursements | $(13,321) | $(12,803) |
| Principal repayments | 11,494 | 11,301 |
| Principal prepayments | 812 | 625 |
| Investments: Held-to-maturity | | |
| Purchases | (5,417) | (8,160) |
| Maturities | 5,422 | 6,952 |
| Net cash used in lending and investing activities | (1,010) | (2,085) |
| Cash flows from Board of Governors-approved transfers to | | |
| International Development Association | (250) | (1,427) |
| Debt Reduction Facility for IDA-Only Countries | (86) | (25) |
| Trust Fund for Gaza and West Bank, Trust Fund for Bosnia and Herzegovina and for Emergency Assistance for Rwanda | (179) | (45) |
| Net cash used in Board of Governors-approved transfers | (515) | (1,497) |
| Cash flows from financing activities | | |
| Medium- and long-term borrowings | | |
| New issues | 9,851 | 9,979 |
| Retirements | (10,330) | (11,579) |
| Net short-term borrowings | 340 | 563 |
| Net currency swaps | (649) | (413) |
| Net capital stock transactions | 111 | 107 |
| Net cash used in financing activities | (677) | (1,343) |
| Cash flows from operating activities | | |
| Net income | 1,187 | 1,354 |
| Adjustments to reconcile net income to net cash provided by operating activities | | |
| Depreciation and amortization | 399 | 281 |
| Provision for loan losses | 42 | 12 |
| Changes in other assets and liabilities | | |
| Decrease (increase) in accrued income on loans and investments | 176 | (59) |
| Increase in miscellaneous assets | (80) | (98) |
| Decrease in accrued charges on borrowings | (214) | (186) |
| (Decrease) increase in accounts payable and miscellaneous liabilities | (18) | 109 |
| Net cash provided by operating activities | 1,492 | 1,413 |
| Effect of exchange rate changes on unrestricted cash and liquid investments | (1,632) | 1,489 |
| Net decrease in unrestricted cash and liquid investments | (2,342) | (2,023) |
| Unrestricted cash and liquid investments at beginning of the fiscal year | 17,072 | 19,095 |
| Unrestricted cash and liquid investments at end of the fiscal year | $ 14,730 | $ 17,072 |
| Composed of | | |
| Investments held in trading portfolio | $ 15,001 | $ 19,821 |
| Unrestricted currencies | 27 | 40 |
| Net receivable (payable) for investment securities traded/purchased | 857 | (469) |
| Net receivable from covered forwards | 2 | 1 |
| Net payable for securities purchased/sold under resale/repurchase agreements and payable for cash collateral received | (1,157) | (2,321) |
|  | $ 14,730 | $ 17,072 |
| Supplemental disclosure | | |
| Increase (decrease) in ending balances resulting from exchange rate fluctuations | | |
| Loans outstanding | $(14,436) | $ 13,331 |
| Borrowings | (11,731) | 10,269 |
| Currency swaps | (1,184) | 1,553 |
| Investments: Held-to-maturity | (29) | (5) |

*The Notes to Financial Statements are an integral part of these Statements.*

# Summary Statement of Loans

*June 30, 1996*
*Expressed in millions of U.S. dollars*

| Borrower or guarantor | Total loans | Loans approved but not yet effective[1] | Undisbursed balance of effective loans[2] | Loans outstanding[3] | Percentage of total loans outstanding |
|---|---|---|---|---|---|
| Algeria | $  2,987 | $  128 | $  793 | $  2,066 | 1.87 |
| Argentina | 7,964 | 561 | 2,591 | 4,812 | 4.36 |
| Armenia | 12 | — | 5 | 7 | 0.01 |
| Bahamas, The | 11 | — | — | 11 | 0.01 |
| Bangladesh | 50 | — | — | 50 | 0.05 |
| Barbados | 39 | — | 22 | 17 | 0.02 |
| Belarus | 169 | — | 48 | 121 | 0.11 |
| Belize | 54 | — | 24 | 30 | 0.03 |
| Bolivia | 77 | — | — | 77 | 0.07 |
| Bosnia and Herzegovina[4] | 621 | — | — | 621 | 0.56 |
| Botswana | 80 | — | — | 80 | 0.07 |
| Brazil | 10,037 | 927 | 3,309 | 5,801 | 5.26 |
| Bulgaria | 844 | 26 | 389 | 429 | 0.39 |
| Cameroon | 603 | — | 31 | 572 | 0.52 |
| Chile | 1,746 | 50 | 442 | 1,254 | 1.14 |
| China | 15,082 | 1,820 | 5,930 | 7,332 | 6.65 |
| Colombia | 3,323 | 85 | 897 | 2,341 | 2.12 |
| Congo | 95 | — | 3 | 92 | 0.08 |
| Costa Rica | 355 | — | 86 | 269 | 0.24 |
| Côte d'Ivoire | 1,442 | — | 21 | 1,421 | 1.29 |
| Croatia | 350 | 31 | 175 | 144 | 0.13 |
| Cyprus | 124 | — | 55 | 69 | 0.06 |
| Czech Republic | 561 | — | 139 | 422 | 0.38 |
| Dominica | 4 | 4 | — | — | — |
| Dominican Republic | 352 | 65 | 27 | 260 | 0.24 |
| Ecuador | 1,396 | 15 | 347 | 1,034 | 0.94 |
| Egypt | 1,502 | 47 | 274 | 1,181 | 1.07 |
| El Salvador | 491 | 115 | 86 | 290 | 0.26 |
| Estonia | 123 | 14 | 55 | 54 | 0.05 |
| Fiji | 51 | — | 19 | 32 | 0.03 |
| Gabon | 120 | — | 21 | 99 | 0.09 |
| Ghana | 50 | — | — | 50 | 0.05 |
| Grenada | 4 | — | 4 | — | — |
| Guatemala | 252 | — | 52 | 200 | 0.18 |
| Guyana | 30 | — | — | 30 | 0.03 |
| Honduras | 389 | — | — | 389 | 0.35 |
| Hungary | 2,556 | — | 523 | 2,033 | 1.84 |
| Iceland | 3 | — | — | 3 | * |
| India | 13,842 | 804 | 3,440 | 9,598 | 8.71 |
| Indonesia | 16,658 | 460 | 4,423 | 11,775 | 10.68 |
| Iran, Islamic Republic of | 851 | — | 509 | 342 | 0.31 |
| Iraq | 50 | — | — | 50 | 0.05 |
| Jamaica | 689 | — | 142 | 547 | 0.50 |
| Jordan | 917 | — | 218 | 699 | 0.63 |
| Kazakstan | 807 | 260 | 161 | 386 | 0.35 |
| Kenya | 367 | — | — | 367 | 0.33 |
| Korea, Republic of | 2,581 | — | 628 | 1,953 | 1.77 |
| Latvia | 148 | — | 88 | 60 | 0.05 |
| Lebanon | 419 | 105 | 196 | 118 | 0.11 |
| Lesotho | 110 | — | 55 | 55 | 0.05 |
| Liberia | 152 | — | — | 152 | 0.14 |
| Lithuania | 161 | 42 | 58 | 61 | 0.06 |
| Macedonia, Former Yugoslav Republic of | 101 | 12 | 3 | 86 | 0.08 |
| Madagascar | 9 | — | — | 9 | 0.01 |
| Malawi | 48 | — | — | 48 | 0.04 |
| Malaysia | 1,146 | — | 195 | 951 | 0.86 |
| Mauritania | 9 | — | — | 9 | 0.01 |
| Mauritius | 209 | 7 | 74 | 128 | 0.12 |
| Mexico | 16,716 | 187 | 3,706 | 12,823 | 11.63 |

| Borrower or guarantor | Total loans | Loans approved but not yet effective[1] | Undisbursed balance of effective loans[2] | Loans outstanding[3] | Percentage of total loans outstanding |
|---|---|---|---|---|---|
| Moldova | $ 229 | $ 54 | $ 30 | $ 145 | 0.13 |
| Morocco | 5,101 | 190 | 1,140 | 3,771 | 3.42 |
| Nicaragua | 51 | — | — | 51 | 0.05 |
| Nigeria | 3,616 | — | 642 | 2,974 | 2.70 |
| Oman | 22 | — | — | 22 | 0.02 |
| Pakistan | 4,432 | — | 1,441 | 2,991 | 2.71 |
| Panama | 355 | 65 | 110 | 180 | 0.16 |
| Papua New Guinea | 403 | — | 117 | 286 | 0.26 |
| Paraguay | 384 | — | 244 | 140 | 0.13 |
| Peru | 2,370 | — | 713 | 1,657 | 1.50 |
| Philippines | 6,200 | 307 | 1,099 | 4,794 | 4.35 |
| Poland | 3,479 | 21 | 1,201 | 2,257 | 2.05 |
| Portugal | 96 | — | 2 | 94 | 0.09 |
| Romania | 1,924 | 120 | 838 | 966 | 0.88 |
| Russia | 6,413 | 1,899 | 2,824 | 1,690 | 1.53 |
| St. Kitts and Nevis | 3 | 2 | — | 1 | * |
| St. Lucia | 10 | 2 | 5 | 3 | * |
| St. Vincent and the Grenadines | 3 | 2 | 1 | — | — |
| Senegal | 28 | — | — | 28 | 0.03 |
| Seychelles | 7 | — | 2 | 5 | * |
| Sierra Leone | 2 | — | — | 2 | * |
| Slovak Republic | 293 | — | 37 | 256 | 0.23 |
| Slovenia | 202 | 23 | 12 | 167 | 0.15 |
| Sri Lanka | 44 | — | — | 44 | 0.04 |
| Sudan | 6 | — | — | 6 | 0.01 |
| Swaziland | 43 | — | 27 | 16 | 0.01 |
| Syrian Arab Republic | 399 | — | — | 399 | 0.36 |
| Tanzania | 69 | — | — | 69 | 0.06 |
| Thailand | 2,401 | 114 | 603 | 1,684 | 1.53 |
| Trinidad and Tobago | 170 | 51 | 44 | 75 | 0.07 |
| Tunisia | 2,320 | 99 | 609 | 1,612 | 1.46 |
| Turkey | 6,228 | 250 | 1,382 | 4,596 | 4.17 |
| Turkmenistan | 25 | — | 23 | 2 | * |
| Ukraine | 982 | 375 | 137 | 470 | 0.43 |
| Uruguay | 772 | 125 | 178 | 469 | 0.43 |
| Uzbekistan | 234 | — | 81 | 153 | 0.14 |
| Venezuela | 2,552 | 39 | 1,008 | 1,505 | 1.37 |
| Yugoslavia, Federal Republic of (Serbia/Montenegro)[4] | 1,204 | — | — | 1,204 | 1.09 |
| Zaire | 88 | — | — | 88 | 0.08 |
| Zambia | 131 | — | — | 131 | 0.12 |
| Zimbabwe | 698 | — | 164 | 534 | 0.48 |
| Subtotal** | 163,924 | 9,500 | 44,978 | 109,446 | 99.27 |
| Caribbean Development Bank[5] | 39 | — | 30 | 9 | 0.01 |
| International Finance Corporation | 803 | — | 12 | 791 | 0.72 |
| Total—June 30, 1996** | $164,766 | $ 9,500 | $45,020 | $110,246 | 100.00 |
| Total—June 30, 1995 | $179,453 | $11,982 | $43,972 | $123,499 | |

*Indicates amounts less than 0.005 percent. ** May differ from the sum of individual figures shown because of rounding.

NOTES

1. Loans totaling $5,170 million ($5,198 million—June 30, 1995) have been approved by IBRD, but the related agreements have not been signed. Loan agreements totaling $4,330 million ($6,784 million—June 30, 1995) have been signed, but the loans do not become effective and disbursements thereunder do not start until the borrowers and guarantors, if any, take certain actions and furnish certain documents to IBRD.

2. Of the undisbursed balance, IBRD has entered into irrevocable commitments to disburse $2,258 million ($1,834 million—June 30, 1995).

3. Total loans outstanding at June 30, 1996 include $98,047 million ($106,371 million—June 30, 1995) at variable interest rates and $12,199 million ($17,128 million—June 30, 1995) at fixed interest rates.

4. See Notes to Financial Statements—Notes A and C.

5. These loans are for the benefit of The Bahamas, Barbados, Grenada, Guyana, Jamaica, Trinidad and Tobago, and territories of the United Kingdom (Associated States and Dependencies) in the Caribbean Region, who are severally liable as guarantors to the extent of subloans made in their territories.

## Summary of Currencies Repayable on Loans Outstanding

| Currency | 1996 | 1995 |
|---|---:|---:|
| Austrian schillings | $ 196 | $ 216 |
| Belgian francs | 242 | 268 |
| Canadian dollars | 167 | 165 |
| Danish kroner | 80 | 87 |
| Deutsche mark | 29,949 | 30,053 |
| European currency units | 13 | 16 |
| Finnish markkaa | 54 | 59 |
| French francs | 847 | 861 |
| Indian rupees | 23 | 26 |
| Irish pounds | 28 | 29 |
| Italian lire | 187 | 176 |
| Japanese yen | 34,353 | 44,722 |
| Kuwaiti dinars | 52 | 52 |
| Luxembourg francs | 14 | 41 |
| Malaysian ringgit | 45 | 46 |
| Netherlands guilders | 2,170 | 3,016 |
| Norwegian kroner | 67 | 72 |
| Portuguese escudos | 23 | 25 |
| Pounds sterling | 255 | 263 |
| Saudi Arabian riyals | 90 | 90 |
| South African rand | 34 | 41 |
| Spanish pesetas | 118 | 126 |
| Swedish kronor | 83 | 75 |
| Swiss francs | 9,018 | 13,068 |
| U.S. dollars | 32,121 | 29,886 |
| Other currencies | 17 | 20 |
| Loans outstanding | $110,246 | $123,499 |

## Maturity Structure of Loans Outstanding

| Period | |
|---|---:|
| July 1, 1996 through June 30, 1997 | $ 12,705 |
| July 1, 1997 through June 30, 1998 | 11,675 |
| July 1, 1998 through June 30, 1999 | 11,839 |
| July 1, 1999 through June 30, 2000 | 11,534 |
| July 1, 2000 through June 30, 2001 | 10,761 |
| July 1, 2001 through June 30, 2006 | 37,095 |
| July 1, 2006 through June 30, 2011 | 13,275 |
| July 1, 2011 through June 30, 2016 | 1,108 |
| July 1, 2016 through June 30, 2021 | 124 |
| July 1, 2021 through June 30, 2026 | 124 |
| July 1, 2026 through June 30, 2031 | 6 |
| Total | $110,246 |

*The Notes to Financial Statements are an integral part of these Statements.*

# Summary Statement of Borrowings

*June 30, 1996 and June 30, 1995*
*Expressed in millions of U.S. dollars*

## Medium- and Long-term Borrowings and Swaps

| | Medium- and long-term borrowings | | | Swap agreements [a,c] | | | Net currency obligations [f] | |
|---|---|---|---|---|---|---|---|---|
| | Principal outstanding [b,d] | | Weighted average cost (%) | Currency swap payables (receivables) | | Weighted average cost (return) (%) | | |
| | 1996 | 1995 | 1996 | 1996 | 1995 | 1996 | 1996 | 1995 |
| Australian dollars | $ 1,041 | $ 322 | 7.69 | $(1,029) | $ (319) | (7.70) | $ 12 | $ 3 |
| Austrian schillings | 186 | 205 | 7.81 | — | — | — | 186 | 205 |
| Belgian francs | 159 | 353 | 7.42 | (153) | (339) | (7.80) | 6 | 14 |
| Canadian dollars | 1,394 | 1,549 | 8.28 | (1,196) | (1,348) | (7.93) | 198 | 201 |
| Czech koruny | 91 | — | 10.02 | (90) | — | (10.02) | 1 | — |
| Deutsche mark | 14,516 | 14,456 | 6.72 | 11,919 | 11,826 | 5.97 | 26,435 | 26,282 |
| European currency units | 1,277 | 1,701 | 5.13 | (1,257) | (1,518) | (5.28) | 20 | 183 |
| Finnish markkaa | — | 141 | — | — | (139) | — | — | 2 |
| French francs | 966 | 1,169 | 8.81 | (526) | (821) | (8.52) | 440 | 348 |
| Greek drachmas | 144 | 66 | 14.59 | (144) | (66) | (14.59) | — | — |
| Hong Kong dollars | 323 | 336 | 6.44 | (320) | (333) | (6.42) | 3 | 3 |
| Irish pounds | 63 | 65 | 7.75 | (63) | (65) | (7.75) | — | — |
| Italian lire | 4,917 | 3,642 | 10.25 | (4,876) | (3,615) | (10.26) | 41 | 27 |
| Japanese yen | 30,698 | 42,039 | 5.11 | 406 | 690 | 3.27 | | |
| | | | | (1,056) | (1,246) | (5.61) | 30,048 | 41,483 |
| Luxembourg francs | 95 | 140 | 7.09 | (95) | (105) | (7.46) | — | 35 |
| Netherlands guilders | 2,837 | 3,259 | 7.23 | 91 | 500 | 6.31 | | |
| | | | | (1,447) | (1,597) | (7.70) | 1,481 | 2,162 |
| New Zealand dollars | 306 | 168 | 10.67 | (304) | (167) | (10.67) | 2 | 1 |
| Norwegian kroner | — | 40 | — | — | — | — | — | 40 |
| Portuguese escudos | 341 | 296 | 10.36 | (337) | (293) | (10.51) | 4 | 3 |
| Pounds sterling | 2,404 | 2,308 | 9.12 | (1,241) | (1,130) | (8.08) | 1,163 | 1,178 |
| Spanish pesetas | 816 | 866 | 10.16 | (808) | (856) | (10.16) | 8 | 10 |
| Swedish kronor | 76 | 124 | 9.84 | (75) | (123) | (9.84) | 1 | 1 |
| Swiss francs | 4,996 | 6,077 | 6.04 | 3,415 | 4,729 | 5.36 | | |
| | | | | (873) | — | (6.47) | 7,538 | 10,806 |
| U.S. dollars | 24,758 | 25,053 | 7.66 | 3,522 | 2,146 | 5.44 | | |
| | | | | (2,046) | (2,569) | (7.32) | 26,234 | 24,630 |
| At face value | 92,404 | 104,375 | 6.80 [e] | | | | 93,821 | 107,617 |
| Net unamortized (discounts) premiums | (13) | 17 | | | | | (13) | 17 |
| Total | $92,391 | $104,392 | | $1,417 | $ 3,242 | | $93,808 | $107,634 |

a. See Notes to Financial Statements—Notes D and E.
b. Includes zero-coupon borrowings that have been recorded at their discounted values. The aggregate face amounts and discounted values of these borrowings at June 30, 1996 and June 30, 1995 are:

In millions of U.S. dollars equivalent

| Currency | Aggregate face amount | | Discounted value | |
|---|---|---|---|---|
| | 1996 | 1995 | 1996 | 1995 |
| Australian dollars | $ 317 | $ — | $ 249 | $ — |
| Canadian dollars | — | 145 | — | 132 |
| Deutsche mark | 2,092 | 2,303 | 471 | 486 |
| Italian lire | 847 | 184 | 443 | 167 |
| Japanese yen | 916 | 1,189 | 822 | 1,033 |
| Swiss francs | 968 | 1,130 | 278 | 310 |
| U.S. dollars | 2,894 | 2,634 | 750 | 476 |

Summary Statement of Borrowings *(continued)*
*June 30, 1996 and June 30, 1995*
*Expressed in millions of U.S. dollars*

## Medium- and Long-term Borrowings and Swaps *(continued)*

c. Includes income and expense from interest rate swaps. At June 30, 1996, IBRD has entered into interest rate swap agreements with respect to notional principal amounts as follows:

In millions

| Currency | Currency amount | | U.S. dollars equivalent | |
|---|---|---|---|---|
| | 1996 | 1995 | 1996 | 1995 |
| Canadian dollars | — | 149 | $  — | $  109 |
| Deutsche mark | 16,436 | 14,293 | 10,744 | 10,289 |
| French francs | 1,669 | 984 | 322 | 202 |
| Italian lire | 200,000 | 200,000 | 130 | 123 |
| Japanese yen | 420,979 | 155,038 | 3,857 | 1,843 |
| Pounds sterling | — | 100 | — | 158 |
| Swiss francs | 1,124 | 1,124 | 892 | 977 |
| U.S. dollars | 10,451 | 2,435 | 10,451 | 2,435 |

d. Includes the following variable rate borrowings at June 30, 1996 and June 30, 1995, before swaps:

In millions

| Currency | Currency amount | | U.S. dollars equivalent | |
|---|---|---|---|---|
| | 1996 | 1995 | 1996 | 1995 |
| Canadian dollars | 100 | 100 | $  73 | $  73 |
| Deutsche mark | 550 | 550 | 360 | 396 |
| European currency units | 640 | 640 | 802 | 857 |
| Greek drachmas | 20,000 | — | 82 | — |
| Italian lire | 650,000 | 550,000 | 423 | 337 |
| Japanese yen | 134,500 | 144,500 | 1,232 | 1,718 |
| Pounds sterling | 25 | 25 | 39 | 40 |
| U.S. dollars | 1,452 | 1,563 | 1,452 | 1,563 |

e. The weighted average cost of medium- and long-term borrowings outstanding at June 30, 1996, after adjustment for swap activities, was 6.26 percent (6.53 percent—June 30, 1995).

f. Includes the following variable rate borrowings after interest rate swaps at June 30, 1996 and June 30, 1995:

In millions

| Currency | Currency amount | | U.S. dollars equivalent | |
|---|---|---|---|---|
| | 1996 | 1995 | 1996 | 1995 |
| Deutsche mark | 5,645 | — | $3,690 | $ — |
| French francs | 316 | — | 61 | — |
| Japanese yen | 265,941 | — | 2,436 | — |
| U.S. dollars | 6,309 | 408 | 6,309 | 408 |

## Maturity Structure of Medium- and Long-term Borrowings

| Period | |
| --- | ---: |
| July 1, 1996 through June 30, 1997 | $12,467 |
| July 1, 1997 through June 30, 1998 | 13,949 |
| July 1, 1998 through June 30, 1999 | 9,526 |
| July 1, 1999 through June 30, 2000 | 14,262 |
| July 1, 2000 through June 30, 2001 | 7,529 |
| July 1, 2001 through June 30, 2006 | 25,886 |
| July 1, 2006 through June 30, 2011 | 2,490 |
| July 1, 2011 through June 30, 2016 | 2,622 |
| July 1, 2016 through June 30, 2021 | 1,660 |
| July 1, 2021 through June 30, 2026 | 1,693 |
| Thereafter | 320 |
| Total | $92,404 |

## Short-term Borrowings and Swaps

| | Principal outstanding | | Currency swap payables (receivables) [a] | | Weighted average cost (after swaps) (%) | Net currency obligations | |
| --- | ---: | ---: | ---: | ---: | ---: | ---: | ---: |
| | 1996 | 1995 | 1996 | 1995 | 1996 | 1996 | 1995 |
| Short-term Notes (U.S. dollars) | $1,369 | $1,192 | $ — | $ — | 5.46 | $1,369 | $1,192 |
| Global Multicurrency Notes | | | | | | | |
| Czech koruny | 54 | — | (54) | — | — | — | — |
| Deutsche mark | — | — | 74 | 94 | 3.06 | 74 | 94 |
| Italian lire | 20 | 86 | (20) | (86) | — | — | — |
| U.S. dollars | 299 | 20 | — | — | 5.52 | 299 | 20 |
| Subtotal | 373 | 106 | — | 8 | 5.03 | 373 | 114 |
| Central Bank Facility (U.S. dollars) | 2,586 | 2,600 | — | — | 5.47 | 2,586 | 2,600 |
| Total | $4,328 | $3,898 | $ — | $ 8 | 5.43 | $4,328 | $3,906 |

a. See Notes to Financial Statements—Notes D and E.

*The Notes to Financial Statements are an integral part of these Statements.*

# STATEMENT OF SUBSCRIPTIONS TO
# CAPITAL STOCK AND VOTING POWER

*June 30, 1996*
*Expressed in millions of U.S. dollars*

| Member | Shares | Subscriptions Percentage of total | Total amounts | Amounts paid in (Note A) | Amounts subject to call (Note A) | Voting power Number of votes | Percentage of total |
|---|---|---|---|---|---|---|---|
| Afghanistan | 300 | 0.02 | $ 36.2 | $ 3.6 | $ 32.6 | 550 | 0.04 |
| Albania | 830 | 0.06 | 100.1 | 3.6 | 96.5 | 1,080 | 0.07 |
| Algeria | 9,252 | 0.62 | 1,116.1 | 67.1 | 1,049.0 | 9,502 | 0.62 |
| Angola | 2,676 | 0.18 | 322.8 | 17.5 | 305.4 | 2,926 | 0.19 |
| Antigua and Barbuda | 520 | 0.03 | 62.7 | 1.3 | 61.5 | 770 | 0.05 |
| Argentina | 17,911 | 1.20 | 2,160.7 | 132.2 | 2,028.4 | 18,161 | 1.18 |
| Armenia | 1,139 | 0.08 | 137.4 | 5.9 | 131.5 | 1,389 | 0.09 |
| Australia | 21,610 | 1.44 | 2,606.9 | 171.4 | 2,435.5 | 21,860 | 1.42 |
| Austria | 11,063 | 0.74 | 1,334.6 | 80.7 | 1,253.9 | 11,313 | 0.73 |
| Azerbaijan | 1,646 | 0.11 | 198.6 | 9.7 | 188.8 | 1,896 | 0.12 |
| Bahamas, The | 1,071 | 0.07 | 129.2 | 5.4 | 123.8 | 1,321 | 0.09 |
| Bahrain | 1,103 | 0.07 | 133.1 | 5.7 | 127.4 | 1,353 | 0.09 |
| Bangladesh | 4,854 | 0.32 | 585.6 | 33.9 | 551.6 | 5,104 | 0.33 |
| Barbados | 948 | 0.06 | 114.4 | 4.5 | 109.9 | 1,198 | 0.08 |
| Belarus | 3,323 | 0.22 | 400.9 | 22.3 | 378.5 | 3,573 | 0.23 |
| Belgium | 28,983 | 1.94 | 3,496.4 | 215.8 | 3,280.6 | 29,233 | 1.90 |
| Belize | 586 | 0.04 | 70.7 | 1.8 | 68.9 | 836 | 0.05 |
| Benin | 487 | 0.03 | 58.7 | 2.5 | 56.2 | 737 | 0.05 |
| Bhutan | 479 | 0.03 | 57.8 | 1.0 | 56.8 | 729 | 0.05 |
| Bolivia | 1,785 | 0.12 | 215.3 | 10.8 | 204.5 | 2,035 | 0.13 |
| Bosnia and Herzegovina | 549 | 0.04 | 66.2 | 5.8 | 60.4 | 799 | 0.05 |
| Botswana | 615 | 0.04 | 74.2 | 2.0 | 72.2 | 865 | 0.06 |
| Brazil | 24,946 | 1.67 | 3,009.4 | 185.1 | 2,824.2 | 25,196 | 1.63 |
| Brunei Darussalam | 2,373 | 0.16 | 286.3 | 15.2 | 271.1 | 2,623 | 0.17 |
| Bulgaria | 5,215 | 0.35 | 629.1 | 36.5 | 592.6 | 5,465 | 0.35 |
| Burkina Faso | 868 | 0.06 | 104.7 | 3.9 | 100.8 | 1,118 | 0.07 |
| Burundi | 716 | 0.05 | 86.4 | 3.0 | 83.4 | 966 | 0.06 |
| Cambodia | 214 | 0.01 | 25.8 | 2.6 | 23.2 | 464 | 0.03 |
| Cameroon | 857 | 0.06 | 103.4 | 6.6 | 96.8 | 1,107 | 0.07 |
| Canada | 44,795 | 2.99 | 5,403.8 | 334.9 | 5,068.9 | 45,045 | 2.92 |
| Cape Verde | 508 | 0.03 | 61.3 | 1.2 | 60.1 | 758 | 0.05 |
| Central African Republic | 484 | 0.03 | 58.4 | 2.5 | 55.9 | 734 | 0.05 |
| Chad | 484 | 0.03 | 58.4 | 2.5 | 55.9 | 734 | 0.05 |
| Chile | 6,931 | 0.46 | 836.1 | 49.6 | 786.6 | 7,181 | 0.47 |
| China | 44,799 | 2.99 | 5,404.3 | 335.0 | 5,069.3 | 45,049 | 2.92 |
| Colombia | 6,352 | 0.42 | 766.3 | 45.2 | 721.1 | 6,602 | 0.43 |
| Comoros | 282 | 0.02 | 34.0 | 0.3 | 33.7 | 532 | 0.03 |
| Congo | 520 | 0.03 | 62.7 | 2.9 | 59.9 | 770 | 0.05 |
| Costa Rica | 233 | 0.02 | 28.1 | 1.9 | 26.2 | 483 | 0.03 |
| Côte d'Ivoire | 2,516 | 0.17 | 303.5 | 16.4 | 287.1 | 2,766 | 0.18 |
| Croatia | 2,293 | 0.15 | 276.6 | 17.3 | 259.3 | 2,543 | 0.16 |
| Cyprus | 1,461 | 0.10 | 176.2 | 8.4 | 167.9 | 1,711 | 0.11 |
| Czech Republic | 6,308 | 0.42 | 761.0 | 45.9 | 715.0 | 6,558 | 0.43 |
| Denmark | 10,251 | 0.68 | 1,236.6 | 74.6 | 1,162.0 | 10,501 | 0.68 |
| Djibouti | 314 | 0.02 | 37.9 | 0.7 | 37.2 | 564 | 0.04 |
| Dominica | 504 | 0.03 | 60.8 | 1.1 | 59.7 | 754 | 0.05 |
| Dominican Republic | 1,174 | 0.08 | 141.6 | 9.8 | 131.8 | 1,424 | 0.09 |
| Ecuador | 2,771 | 0.19 | 334.3 | 18.2 | 316.1 | 3,021 | 0.20 |
| Egypt | 7,108 | 0.47 | 857.5 | 50.9 | 806.6 | 7,358 | 0.48 |
| El Salvador | 141 | 0.01 | 17.0 | 1.7 | 15.3 | 391 | 0.03 |
| Equatorial Guinea | 401 | 0.03 | 48.4 | 1.6 | 46.8 | 651 | 0.04 |
| Eritrea | 593 | 0.04 | 71.5 | 1.8 | 69.7 | 843 | 0.05 |
| Estonia | 923 | 0.06 | 111.3 | 4.3 | 107.1 | 1,173 | 0.08 |
| Ethiopia | 978 | 0.07 | 118.0 | 4.7 | 113.3 | 1,228 | 0.08 |
| Fiji | 987 | 0.07 | 119.1 | 4.8 | 114.3 | 1,237 | 0.08 |

| Member | Shares | Subscriptions Percentage of total | Total amounts | Amounts paid in (Note A) | Amounts subject to call (Note A) | Voting power Number of votes | Percentage of total |
|---|---|---|---|---|---|---|---|
| Finland | 8,560 | 0.57 | $1,032.6 | $ 61.9 | $ 970.8 | 8,810 | 0.57 |
| France | 69,397 | 4.63 | 8,371.7 | 520.4 | 7,851.3 | 69,647 | 4.52 |
| Gabon | 554 | 0.04 | 66.8 | 3.6 | 63.3 | 804 | 0.05 |
| Gambia, The | 305 | 0.02 | 36.8 | 0.7 | 36.1 | 555 | 0.04 |
| Georgia | 1,584 | 0.11 | 191.1 | 9.3 | 181.8 | 1,834 | 0.12 |
| Germany | 72,399 | 4.84 | 8,733.9 | 542.9 | 8,190.9 | 72,649 | 4.71 |
| Ghana | 856 | 0.06 | 103.3 | 10.3 | 92.9 | 1,106 | 0.07 |
| Greece | 945 | 0.06 | 114.0 | 11.4 | 102.6 | 1,195 | 0.08 |
| Grenada | 531 | 0.04 | 64.1 | 1.4 | 62.7 | 781 | 0.05 |
| Guatemala | 2,001 | 0.13 | 241.4 | 12.4 | 229.0 | 2,251 | 0.15 |
| Guinea | 725 | 0.05 | 87.5 | 5.0 | 82.4 | 975 | 0.06 |
| Guinea-Bissau | 303 | 0.02 | 36.6 | 0.6 | 36.0 | 553 | 0.04 |
| Guyana | 1,058 | 0.07 | 127.6 | 5.3 | 122.3 | 1,308 | 0.08 |
| Haiti | 1,067 | 0.07 | 128.7 | 5.4 | 123.3 | 1,317 | 0.09 |
| Honduras | 641 | 0.04 | 77.3 | 2.3 | 75.0 | 891 | 0.06 |
| Hungary | 8,050 | 0.54 | 971.1 | 58.0 | 913.1 | 8,300 | 0.54 |
| Iceland | 1,258 | 0.08 | 151.8 | 6.8 | 144.9 | 1,508 | 0.10 |
| India | 44,795 | 2.99 | 5,403.8 | 333.7 | 5,070.1 | 45,045 | 2.92 |
| Indonesia | 14,981 | 1.00 | 1,807.2 | 110.3 | 1,697.0 | 15,231 | 0.99 |
| Iran, Islamic Republic of | 23,686 | 1.58 | 2,857.4 | 175.8 | 2,681.5 | 23,936 | 1.55 |
| Iraq | 2,808 | 0.19 | 338.7 | 27.1 | 311.6 | 3,058 | 0.20 |
| Ireland | 5,271 | 0.35 | 635.9 | 37.1 | 598.8 | 5,521 | 0.36 |
| Israel | 4,750 | 0.32 | 573.0 | 33.2 | 539.8 | 5,000 | 0.32 |
| Italy | 44,795 | 2.99 | 5,403.8 | 334.8 | 5,069.0 | 45,045 | 2.92 |
| Jamaica | 2,578 | 0.17 | 311.0 | 16.8 | 294.2 | 2,828 | 0.18 |
| Japan | 93,770 | 6.26 | 11,311.9 | 703.5 | 10,608.5 | 94,020 | 6.10 |
| Jordan | 1,388 | 0.09 | 167.4 | 7.8 | 159.6 | 1,638 | 0.11 |
| Kazakstan | 2,985 | 0.20 | 360.1 | 19.8 | 340.3 | 3,235 | 0.21 |
| Kenya | 2,461 | 0.16 | 296.9 | 15.9 | 281.0 | 2,711 | 0.18 |
| Kiribati | 465 | 0.03 | 56.1 | 0.9 | 55.2 | 715 | 0.05 |
| Korea, Republic of | 9,372 | 0.63 | 1,130.6 | 67.9 | 1,062.7 | 9,622 | 0.62 |
| Kuwait | 13,280 | 0.89 | 1,602.0 | 97.4 | 1,504.6 | 13,530 | 0.88 |
| Kyrgyz Republic | 1,107 | 0.07 | 133.5 | 5.7 | 127.9 | 1,357 | 0.09 |
| Lao People's Democratic Republic | 178 | 0.01 | 21.5 | 1.5 | 20.0 | 428 | 0.03 |
| Latvia | 1,384 | 0.09 | 167.0 | 7.8 | 159.2 | 1,634 | 0.11 |
| Lebanon | 340 | 0.02 | 41.0 | 1.1 | 39.9 | 590 | 0.04 |
| Lesotho | 663 | 0.04 | 80.0 | 2.3 | 77.6 | 913 | 0.06 |
| Liberia | 463 | 0.03 | 55.9 | 2.6 | 53.3 | 713 | 0.05 |
| Libya | 7,840 | 0.52 | 945.8 | 57.0 | 888.8 | 8,090 | 0.52 |
| Lithuania | 846 | 0.06 | 102.1 | 6.3 | 95.8 | 1,096 | 0.07 |
| Luxembourg | 1,652 | 0.11 | 199.3 | 9.8 | 189.5 | 1,902 | 0.12 |
| Macedonia, Former Yugoslav Republic of | 427 | 0.03 | 51.5 | 3.2 | 48.3 | 677 | 0.04 |
| Madagascar | 1,422 | 0.09 | 171.5 | 8.1 | 163.5 | 1,672 | 0.11 |
| Malawi | 1,094 | 0.07 | 132.0 | 5.6 | 126.4 | 1,344 | 0.09 |
| Malaysia | 8,244 | 0.55 | 994.5 | 59.5 | 935.0 | 8,494 | 0.55 |
| Maldives | 469 | 0.03 | 56.6 | 0.9 | 55.7 | 719 | 0.05 |
| Mali | 1,162 | 0.08 | 140.2 | 6.1 | 134.1 | 1,412 | 0.09 |
| Malta | 1,074 | 0.07 | 129.6 | 5.4 | 124.1 | 1,324 | 0.09 |
| Marshall Islands | 469 | 0.03 | 56.6 | 0.9 | 55.7 | 719 | 0.05 |
| Mauritania | 505 | 0.03 | 60.9 | 2.7 | 58.2 | 755 | 0.05 |
| Mauritius | 1,242 | 0.08 | 149.8 | 6.7 | 143.1 | 1,492 | 0.10 |
| Mexico | 18,804 | 1.26 | 2,268.4 | 139.0 | 2,129.4 | 19,054 | 1.24 |
| Micronesia, Federated States of | 479 | 0.03 | 57.8 | 1.0 | 56.8 | 729 | 0.05 |
| Moldova | 1,368 | 0.09 | 165.0 | 7.6 | 157.4 | 1,618 | 0.10 |
| Mongolia | 466 | 0.03 | 56.2 | 2.3 | 53.9 | 716 | 0.05 |

*June 30, 1996*
*Expressed in millions of U.S. dollars*

| Member | Shares | Subscriptions Percentage of total | Total amounts | Amounts paid in (Note A) | Amounts subject to call (Note A) | Voting power Number of votes | Percentage of total |
|---|---|---|---|---|---|---|---|
| Morocco | 4,973 | 0.33 | $ 599.9 | $ 34.8 | $ 565.1 | 5,223 | 0.34 |
| Mozambique | 930 | 0.06 | 112.2 | 4.8 | 107.4 | 1,180 | 0.08 |
| Myanmar | 2,484 | 0.17 | 299.7 | 16.1 | 283.6 | 2,734 | 0.18 |
| Namibia | 1,523 | 0.10 | 183.7 | 8.8 | 174.9 | 1,773 | 0.11 |
| Nepal | 968 | 0.06 | 116.8 | 4.6 | 112.1 | 1,218 | 0.08 |
| Netherlands | 35,503 | 2.37 | 4,282.9 | 264.8 | 4,018.1 | 35,753 | 2.32 |
| New Zealand | 7,236 | 0.48 | 872.9 | 51.9 | 821.0 | 7,486 | 0.49 |
| Nicaragua | 608 | 0.04 | 73.3 | 2.1 | 71.3 | 858 | 0.06 |
| Niger | 478 | 0.03 | 57.7 | 2.4 | 55.2 | 728 | 0.05 |
| Nigeria | 12,655 | 0.85 | 1,526.6 | 92.7 | 1,433.9 | 12,905 | 0.84 |
| Norway | 9,982 | 0.67 | 1,204.2 | 72.6 | 1,131.6 | 10,232 | 0.66 |
| Oman | 1,561 | 0.10 | 188.3 | 9.1 | 179.2 | 1,811 | 0.12 |
| Pakistan | 9,339 | 0.62 | 1,126.6 | 67.8 | 1,058.9 | 9,589 | 0.62 |
| Panama | 385 | 0.03 | 46.4 | 3.2 | 43.2 | 635 | 0.04 |
| Papua New Guinea | 726 | 0.05 | 87.6 | 5.0 | 82.5 | 976 | 0.06 |
| Paraguay | 1,229 | 0.08 | 148.3 | 6.6 | 141.6 | 1,479 | 0.10 |
| Peru | 5,331 | 0.36 | 643.1 | 37.5 | 605.6 | 5,581 | 0.36 |
| Philippines | 6,844 | 0.46 | 825.6 | 48.9 | 776.7 | 7,094 | 0.46 |
| Poland | 10,908 | 0.73 | 1,315.9 | 79.6 | 1,236.3 | 11,158 | 0.72 |
| Portugal | 5,460 | 0.36 | 658.7 | 38.5 | 620.2 | 5,710 | 0.37 |
| Qatar | 1,096 | 0.07 | 132.2 | 9.0 | 123.3 | 1,346 | 0.09 |
| Romania | 4,011 | 0.27 | 483.9 | 30.5 | 453.4 | 4,261 | 0.28 |
| Russia | 44,795 | 2.99 | 5,403.8 | 333.9 | 5,070.0 | 45,045 | 2.92 |
| Rwanda | 587 | 0.04 | 70.8 | 3.6 | 67.2 | 837 | 0.05 |
| St. Kitts and Nevis | 275 | 0.02 | 33.2 | 0.3 | 32.9 | 525 | 0.03 |
| St. Lucia | 552 | 0.04 | 66.6 | 1.5 | 65.1 | 802 | 0.05 |
| St. Vincent and the Grenadines | 278 | 0.02 | 33.5 | 0.3 | 33.2 | 528 | 0.03 |
| São Tomé and Principe | 278 | 0.02 | 33.5 | 0.3 | 33.2 | 528 | 0.03 |
| Saudi Arabia | 44,795 | 2.99 | 5,403.8 | 335.0 | 5,068.9 | 45,045 | 2.92 |
| Senegal | 2,072 | 0.14 | 250.0 | 13.0 | 237.0 | 2,322 | 0.15 |
| Seychelles | 263 | 0.02 | 31.7 | 0.2 | 31.6 | 513 | 0.03 |
| Sierra Leone | 403 | 0.03 | 48.6 | 1.8 | 46.8 | 653 | 0.04 |
| Singapore | 320 | 0.02 | 38.6 | 3.9 | 34.7 | 570 | 0.04 |
| Slovak Republic | 3,216 | 0.21 | 388.0 | 23.0 | 365.0 | 3,466 | 0.22 |
| Slovenia | 1,261 | 0.08 | 152.1 | 9.5 | 142.6 | 1,511 | 0.10 |
| Solomon Islands | 513 | 0.03 | 61.9 | 1.2 | 60.7 | 763 | 0.05 |
| Somalia | 552 | 0.04 | 66.6 | 3.3 | 63.3 | 802 | 0.05 |
| South Africa | 13,462 | 0.90 | 1,624.0 | 98.8 | 1,525.2 | 13,712 | 0.89 |
| Spain | 23,686 | 1.58 | 2,857.4 | 175.6 | 2,681.7 | 23,936 | 1.55 |
| Sri Lanka | 3,817 | 0.25 | 460.5 | 26.1 | 434.3 | 4,067 | 0.26 |
| Sudan | 850 | 0.06 | 102.5 | 7.2 | 95.3 | 1,100 | 0.07 |
| Suriname | 412 | 0.03 | 49.7 | 2.0 | 47.7 | 662 | 0.04 |
| Swaziland | 440 | 0.03 | 53.1 | 2.0 | 51.1 | 690 | 0.04 |
| Sweden | 14,974 | 1.00 | 1,806.4 | 110.2 | 1,696.2 | 15,224 | 0.99 |
| Switzerland | 26,606 | 1.78 | 3,209.6 | 197.2 | 3,012.4 | 26,856 | 1.74 |
| Syrian Arab Republic | 1,236 | 0.08 | 149.1 | 10.5 | 138.6 | 1,486 | 0.10 |
| Tajikistan | 1,060 | 0.07 | 127.9 | 5.3 | 122.5 | 1,310 | 0.08 |
| Tanzania | 727 | 0.05 | 87.7 | 7.9 | 79.8 | 977 | 0.06 |
| Thailand | 6,349 | 0.42 | 765.9 | 45.2 | 720.7 | 6,599 | 0.43 |
| Togo | 620 | 0.04 | 74.8 | 3.9 | 70.9 | 870 | 0.06 |
| Tonga | 277 | 0.02 | 33.4 | 0.3 | 33.1 | 527 | 0.03 |
| Trinidad and Tobago | 2,664 | 0.18 | 321.4 | 17.6 | 303.7 | 2,914 | 0.19 |
| Tunisia | 719 | 0.05 | 86.7 | 5.7 | 81.1 | 969 | 0.06 |
| Turkey | 7,379 | 0.49 | 890.2 | 52.9 | 837.2 | 7,629 | 0.49 |
| Turkmenistan | 526 | 0.04 | 63.5 | 2.9 | 60.5 | 776 | 0.05 |

| Member | Shares | Subscriptions Percentage of total | Total amounts | Amounts paid in (Note A) | Amounts subject to call (Note A) | Voting power Number of votes | Percentage of total |
|---|---|---|---|---|---|---|---|
| Uganda | 617 | 0.04 | $ 74.4 | $ 4.4 | $ 70.1 | 867 | 0.06 |
| Ukraine | 10,908 | 0.73 | 1,315.9 | 79.3 | 1,236.6 | 11,158 | 0.72 |
| United Arab Emirates | 2,385 | 0.16 | 287.7 | 22.6 | 265.1 | 2,635 | 0.17 |
| United Kingdom | 69,397 | 4.63 | 8,371.7 | 539.5 | 7,832.2 | 69,647 | 4.52 |
| United States | 264,969 | 17.70 | 31,964.5 | 1,998.4 | 29,966.2 | 265,219 | 17.20 |
| Uruguay | 2,812 | 0.19 | 339.2 | 18.6 | 320.7 | 3,062 | 0.20 |
| Uzbekistan | 2,493 | 0.17 | 300.7 | 16.1 | 284.7 | 2,743 | 0.18 |
| Vanuatu | 586 | 0.04 | 70.7 | 1.8 | 68.9 | 836 | 0.05 |
| Venezuela | 20,361 | 1.36 | 2,456.2 | 150.8 | 2,305.5 | 20,611 | 1.34 |
| Vietnam | 968 | 0.06 | 116.8 | 8.1 | 108.7 | 1,218 | 0.08 |
| Western Samoa | 298 | 0.02 | 35.9 | 0.5 | 35.4 | 548 | 0.04 |
| Yemen, Republic of | 2,212 | 0.15 | 266.8 | 14.0 | 252.8 | 2,462 | 0.16 |
| Zaire | 2,643 | 0.18 | 318.8 | 25.4 | 293.5 | 2,893 | 0.19 |
| Zambia | 2,810 | 0.19 | 339.0 | 20.0 | 319.0 | 3,060 | 0.20 |
| Zimbabwe | 3,325 | 0.22 | 401.1 | 22.4 | 378.7 | 3,575 | 0.23 |
| Total—June 30, 1996* | 1,497,325 | 100.00 | $180,630 | $10,993.7 | $169,636 | 1,542,325 | 100.00 |
| Total—June 30, 1995 | 1,462,574 | 100.00 | $176,438 | $10,857.5 | $165,580 | 1,507,074 | |

* May differ from the sum of individual figures due to rounding.

The Notes to Financial Statements are an integral part of these Statements.

## PURPOSE AND AFFILIATED ORGANIZATIONS

The International Bank for Reconstruction and Development (IBRD) is an international organization that commenced business in 1946. The principal purpose of IBRD is to promote economic development in its member countries, primarily by providing loans and related technical assistance for specific projects and for programs of economic reform in developing member countries. The activities of IBRD are complemented by those of three affiliated organizations, the International Development Association (IDA), the International Finance Corporation (IFC), and the Multilateral Investment Guarantee Agency (MIGA). IDA's purpose is to promote economic development in the less developed areas of the world included in IDA's membership by providing financing on concessional terms. IFC's purpose is to encourage the growth of productive private enterprises in its member countries through loans and equity investments in such enterprises without a member's guarantee. MIGA was established to encourage the flow of investments for productive purposes among member countries and, in particular, to developing member countries by providing guarantees against noncommercial risks for foreign investment in its developing member countries.

## SUMMARY OF SIGNIFICANT ACCOUNTING AND RELATED POLICIES

IBRD's financial statements are prepared in conformity with the accounting principles generally accepted in the United States and with International Accounting Standards.

The preparation of financial statements in conformity with generally accepted accounting principles requires management to make estimates and assumptions that affect the reported amounts of assets and liabilities and disclosure of contingent assets and liabilities at the date of the financial statements and the reported amounts of revenue and expenses during the reporting period. Actual results could differ from these estimates. Significant judgments have been used in the computation of estimated and fair values of loans and borrowings respectively, the adequacy of the accumulated provision for loan losses, and the present value of obligations under the Staff Retirement and Retired Staff Benefits Plans.

Certain reclassifications of the prior year's information have been made to conform to the current period's presentation.

*Translation of Currencies*: IBRD's financial statements are expressed in terms of U.S. dollars solely for the purpose of summarizing IBRD's financial position and the results of its operations for the convenience of its members and other interested parties.

IBRD is an international organization that conducts its business in the currencies of all of its members. IBRD's resources are derived from its capital, borrowings, and accumulated earnings in those various currencies. IBRD

has a number of general policies aimed at minimizing exchange-rate risk in a multicurrency environment. IBRD matches its borrowing obligations in any one currency (after swap activities) with assets in the same currency, as prescribed by its Articles of Agreement, primarily by holding or lending the proceeds of its borrowings (after swaps) in the same currencies in which they are borrowed. In addition, IBRD periodically undertakes currency conversions to match more closely the currencies underlying its Retained Earnings with those of the outstanding loans.

Assets and liabilities are translated at market exchange rates at the end of the year. Income and expenses are translated at the market exchange rate on the dates on which they are recognized or at average market exchange rates in effect during each month. Translation adjustments are charged or credited to Equity.

*Valuation of Capital Stock:* In the Articles of Agreement, the capital stock of IBRD is expressed in terms of "U.S. dollars of the weight and fineness in effect on July 1, 1944" (1944 dollars). Following the abolition of gold as a common denominator of the monetary system and the repeal of the provision of the U.S. law defining the par value of the U.S. dollar in terms of gold, the pre-existing basis for translating 1944 dollars into current dollars or into any other currency disappeared. The Executive Directors of IBRD have decided, until such time as the relevant provisions of the Articles of Agreement are amended, that the words "U.S. dollars of the weight and fineness in effect on July 1, 1944" in Article II, Section 2(a) of the Articles of Agreement of IBRD are interpreted to mean the Special Drawing Right (SDR) introduced by the International Monetary Fund, as the SDR was valued in terms of U.S. dollars immediately before the introduction of the basket method of valuing the SDR on July 1, 1974, such value being $1.20635 for one SDR.

*Retained Earnings:* Retained Earnings consists of allocated amounts (Special Reserve, General Reserve, and Surplus) and unallocated Net Income.

The Special Reserve consists of loan commissions set aside pursuant to Article IV, Section 6 of the Articles of Agreement which are to be held in liquid assets. These assets may be used only for the purpose of meeting liabilities of IBRD on its borrowings and guarantees in the event of defaults on loans made, participated in, or guaranteed by IBRD. The Special Reserve assets are included under Investments held in the Trading portfolio, comprising obligations of the United States Government, its agencies, and other official entities. The allocation of such commissions to the Special Reserve was discontinued in 1964 with respect to subsequent loans, and no further additions are being made to it.

The General Reserve consists of earnings from prior fiscal years that in the judgment of the Executive Directors should be retained in IBRD's business.

Surplus consists of earnings from prior fiscal years that are retained by IBRD until a further decision is made on their disposition or the conditions of transfer for specified uses have been met.

Unallocated Net Income consists of earnings in the current fiscal year. Commencing in 1950, a portion or all of the unallocated Net Income has been allocated to the General Reserve. The Board of Governors, consisting of one Governor appointed by each member, periodically approves transfers out of Retained Earnings, after an assessment by the Executive Directors of IBRD's reserve needs, to various entities for development purposes consistent with IBRD's Articles of Agreement. Transfers have been made out of unallocated Net Income and Surplus to IDA (or facilities administered by IDA), for Emergency Assistance for Rwanda, the Global Environment Trust Fund, the Technical Assistance Trust Fund for the Union of Soviet Socialist Republics, the Trust Fund for Bosnia and Herzegovina, and the Trust Fund for Gaza and West Bank.

*Loans:* All of IBRD's loans are made to or guaranteed by members, except loans to IFC. The majority of IBRD's loans have repayment obligations in various currencies determined on the basis of a currency pooling system, which is designed to equalize exchange-rate risks among borrowers. IBRD also offers single currency loans. Except for certain loans that were converted to the currency pooling system, loans negotiated prior to July 1980 and all single currency loans are repayable in the currencies disbursed.

Incremental direct costs associated with originating loans are expensed as incurred as such amounts are considered immaterial.

IBRD's policy is not to reschedule interest or principal payments on its loans or participate in debt rescheduling agreements with respect to its loans. In exceptional cases, however, such as when implementation of a financed project has been delayed, the loan amortization schedule may be modified to avoid substantial repayments prior to project completion. In addition, in the special case of Bosnia and Herzegovina, IBRD has refinanced/rescheduled, through three new IBRD consolidation loans, certain loans made to the former Socialist Federal Republic of Yugoslavia (SFRY) for which Bosnia and Herzegovina has accepted liability. IBRD's special treatment in this case was based on the following criteria: the country (i) has emerged from a current, or former, member of IBRD, (ii) is assuming responsibility for a share of the debt of that member, (iii) has limited creditworthiness for servicing the debt that it assumes because of a major armed conflict in its territory involving extensive destruction of physical assets, and (iv) can improve significantly its repayment capacity through refinancing/rescheduling if appropriate supporting measures are taken. At the Balance Sheet date no other country met these criteria.

It is the policy of IBRD to place in nonaccrual status all loans made to or guaranteed by a member of IBRD if principal, interest, or other charges with respect to any such loan are overdue by more than six months, unless IBRD management determines that the overdue amount will be collected in the immediate future. In addition, if development credits made by IDA to a member government are placed in nonaccrual status, all loans to that member government will also be placed in nonaccrual status by IBRD. On the date a member's loans are placed in nonaccrual status, unpaid interest and other charges accrued on loans outstanding to the member are deducted from the income of the current period. Interest and other charges on nonaccruing loans are included in income only to the extent that payments have actually been received by IBRD. If collectibility risk is considered to be particularly high at the time of arrears clearance or if IBRD refinances/reschedules nonaccruing loans to a member so that no debt-service payments remain overdue, its loans would not automatically emerge from nonaccrual status, even though its eligibility for new loans would have been restored. The previously overdue interest and other charges would not be recognized as income in the period the refinancing/rescheduling occurs. After a suitable period of payment performance has passed from the time of arrears clearance, a decision on the restoration of accrual status would be made on a case-by-case basis.

IBRD determines the Accumulated Provision for Loan Losses based on an assessment of collectibility risk in the total loan portfolio, including loans in nonaccrual status. The accumulated provision is periodically adjusted based on a review of the prevailing circumstances and would be used to meet actual losses on loans. Adjustments to the accumulated provision are recorded as a charge or credit to income.

During the first quarter of fiscal year 1996, IBRD adopted a new accounting standard that prescribes the methodology for calculating the accumulated provision for loan losses for impaired loans. The adoption of the new accounting standard had no impact on IBRD's Accumulated Provision for Loan Losses or on its results of operations. In the context of determining the adequacy of the accumulated provision for loan losses, IBRD considers the present value of expected cash flows relative to the contractual cash flows for loans in making the required assessment.

*Investments:* In fiscal year 1995, IBRD began holding certain securities to maturity to align the investment portfolio with the debt funding these investments in specific currencies. Remaining investment securities are held in a trading portfolio and classified as an element of liquidity in the Statement of Cash Flows due to their nature and IBRD's policies governing the level and use of such investments.

IBRD carries its investment securities and related financial instruments classified as its trading portfolio at market value and investment securities in the held-to-maturity portfolio at amortized cost. From time to time, IBRD enters into forward contracts for the sale or purchase of investment securities; these transactions are recorded at the time of commitment.

*Fair Value Disclosures:* Financial instruments for which market quotations are available have been valued at the prevailing market value. Financial instruments for which market quotations are not readily available have been valued using methodologies and assumptions that necessarily require the use of subjective judgments. Accordingly, the actual value at which such financial instruments could be exchanged in a current transaction or whether they are actually exchangeable is not determinable.

## NOTE A—CAPITAL STOCK, RESTRICTED CURRENCIES, MAINTENANCE OF VALUE, AND MEMBERSHIP

*Capital Stock:* At June 30, 1996, IBRD's capital comprised 1,558,478 (1,525,248—June 30, 1995) authorized shares, of which 1,497,325 (1,462,574—June 30, 1995) shares had been subscribed. Each share has a par value of 0.1 million 1974 SDRs, valued at the rate of $1.20635 per 1974 SDR. Of the subscribed capital, $10,994 million ($10,858 million—June 30, 1995) has been paid in, and the remaining $169,636 million ($165,580 million—June 30, 1995) is subject to call only when required to meet the obligations of IBRD created by borrowing or guaranteeing loans. As to $144,504 million ($141,150 million—June 30, 1995) the restriction on calls is imposed by the Articles of Agreement and as to $25,132 million ($24,430 million—June 30, 1995) by resolutions of the Board of Governors.

*Restricted Currencies:* The portion of capital subscriptions paid in to IBRD is divided into two parts: (1) $1,100 million ($1,086 million—June 30, 1995) initially paid in gold or U.S. dollars and (2) $9,894 million ($9,772 million—June 30, 1995) paid in cash or noninterest-bearing demand obligations denominated either in the currencies of the respective members or in U.S. dollars. The amounts mentioned in (1) above, and (i) $777 million ($774 million—June 30, 1995), which were repurchased by members with U.S. dollars, and (ii) $419 million ($364 million—June 30, 1995), which were the proceeds from encashments of U.S. dollar-denominated notes that are included in the amounts mentioned in (2) above, are freely usable by IBRD in any of its operations. The portion of the amounts paid in U.S. dollar-denominated notes are encashed by IBRD in accordance with the schedules agreed between the members and IBRD. The remaining amounts paid in the currencies of the members, referred to as restricted currencies, are usable by IBRD in its lending operations only with the consent of the respective members, and for administrative expenses. The equivalent of $5,522 million ($5,967 million—

June 30, 1995) has been used for lending purposes, with such consent.

*Maintenance of Value:* Article II, Section 9 of the Articles of Agreement provides for maintenance of the value, at the time of subscription, of such restricted currencies, requiring (1) the member to make additional payments to IBRD in the event that the par value of its currency is reduced or the foreign exchange value of its currency has, in the opinion of IBRD, depreciated to a significant extent in its territories and (2) IBRD to reimburse the member in the event that the par value of its currency is increased.

Since currencies no longer have par values, maintenance of value amounts are determined by measuring the foreign exchange value of a member's currency against the standard of value of IBRD capital based on the 1974 SDR. Members are required to make payments to IBRD if their currencies depreciate significantly relative to the standard of value. Furthermore, the Executive Directors have adopted a policy of reimbursing members whose currencies appreciate significantly in terms of the standard of value.

The net maintenance of value amounts relating to restricted currencies out on loan are included in Deferred Amounts to Maintain Value of Currency Holdings and shown as a component of Equity since maintenance of value becomes effective only as such currencies are repaid to IBRD.

*Membership:* In February 1993 IBRD's Executive Directors decided that the SFRY had ceased to be a member of IBRD and that the Republic of Bosnia and Herzegovina (now called Bosnia and Herzegovina), the Republic of Croatia, the former Yugoslav Republic of Macedonia, the Republic of Slovenia and the Federal Republic of Yugoslavia (Serbia and Montenegro) (FRY) are authorized to succeed to the SFRY's membership when certain requirements are met including entering into a final agreement with IBRD on IBRD's loans made to or guaranteed by the SFRY which the particular successor Republic would assume. Four of the five successor Republics—Bosnia and Herzegovina, the Republic of Croatia, the Republic of Slovenia and the former Yugoslav Republic of Macedonia—have become members of IBRD. The paid-in portion of the SFRY's subscribed capital allocated to the FRY is included under Payments on Account of Pending Subscriptions until the requirements of succession are met.

## NOTE B—INVESTMENTS

As part of its overall portfolio management strategy, IBRD invests in government and agency obligations, time deposits and related financial instruments with off-balance sheet risk including futures, forward contracts, covered forward contracts, options, and short sales.

*Government and Agency Obligations:* These obligations include marketable bonds, notes and other obligations. Obligations issued or unconditionally guaranteed by governments of countries require a minimum credit rating of AA, if denominated in a currency other than the home currency of the issuer; otherwise no rating is required. Obligations issued by an agency or instrumentality of a government of a country, a multilateral organization or any other official entity require a credit rating of AAA.

**Time Deposits:** Time deposits include certificates of deposit, bankers' acceptances, and other obligations issued or unconditionally guaranteed by banks and other financial institutions.

**Futures and Forwards:** Futures and forward contracts are contracts for delayed delivery of securities or money market instruments in which the seller agrees to make delivery at a specified future date of a specified instrument, at a specified price or yield. Futures contracts are traded on regulated United States and international exchanges. IBRD generally closes out most open positions in futures contracts prior to maturity. Therefore, cash receipts or payments are mostly limited to the change in market value of the futures contracts. Futures contracts generally entail daily settlement of the net cash margin.

**Covered Forwards:** Covered forwards are agreements in which cash in one currency is converted into a different currency and, simultaneously, a forward exchange agreement is executed providing for a future exchange of the two currencies in order to recover the currency converted.

**Options:** Options are contracts that allow the holder of the option to purchase or sell a financial instrument at a specified price within a specified period of time from or to the seller of the option. The purchaser of an option pays a premium at the outset to the seller of the option, who then bears the risk of an unfavorable change in the price of the financial instrument underlying the option. IBRD only invests in exchange-traded options. The initial price of an option contract is equal to the premium paid by the purchaser and is significantly less than the contract or notional amount. IBRD does not write uncovered option contracts.

**Short Sales:** Short sales are sales of securities not held in IBRD's portfolio at the time of the sale. IBRD must purchase the security at a later date and bears the risk that the market value of the security will move adversely between the time of the sale and the time the security must be delivered.

**Repurchase and Resale Agreements and Securities Loans:** Repurchase agreements are contracts under which a party sells securities and simultaneously agrees to repurchase the same securities at a specified future date at a fixed price. The reverse of this transaction is called a resale agreement. Securities loans are contracts under which securities are lent up to a future specified date at a fixed price.

**Trading Portfolio:** A summary of IBRD's position in trading instruments at June 30, 1996 and June 30, 1995 is as follows:

In millions of U.S. dollars equivalent

| | Deutsche mark | | Japanese yen | | U.S. dollars | | Other currencies | | All currencies | |
|---|---|---|---|---|---|---|---|---|---|---|
| | FY96 | FY95 | FY96 | FY95 | FY96 | FY95 | FY96 | FY95 | FY96 | FY95 |
| **Investments** | | | | | | | | | | |
| Trading: | | | | | | | | | | |
| Government and agency obligations: | | | | | | | | | | |
| Carrying value | 524 | 1,118 | 1,119 | 5,642 | 3,536 | 4,280 | 238 | 265 | 5,417 | 11,305 |
| Average balance during period | 879 | 1,019 | 2,738 | 4,198 | 3,473 | 4,263 | 257 | 529 | 7,347 | 10,009 |
| Net gains (losses) for the period | 19 | 5 | (45) | 106 | (41) | 69 | 7 | (5) | (60) | 175 |
| Average yield (%) | 4.60 | 5.43 | 1.35 | 1.43 | 5.03 | 5.95 | 4.82 | 5.65 | 4.12 | 3.75 |
| Average maturity (years) | 5.10 | 4.16 | 2.94 | 1.93 | 3.80 | 2.80 | 8.40 | 1.70 | 3.87 | 2.55 |
| Time deposits: | | | | | | | | | | |
| Carrying value | 1,041 | 520 | 1,775 | 1,221 | 5,822 | 6,055 | 942 | 711 | 9,580 | 8,507 |
| Average balance during period | 411 | 316 | 1,562 | 2,305 | 3,793 | 4,819 | 1,035 | 1,259 | 6,801 | 8,699 |
| Net gains (losses) for the period | — | — | — | — | — | (*) | (*) | — | (*) | (*) |
| Average yield (%) | 3.38 | 4.73 | 0.50 | 1.26 | 5.52 | 6.28 | 3.96 | 6.01 | 4.21 | 5.45 |
| Average maturity (years) | 0.02 | 0.03 | 0.07 | 0.04 | 0.01 | 0.03 | 0.02 | 0.02 | 0.03 | 0.03 |

*(table continued on next page)*

*(table continued)*

In millions of U.S. dollars equivalent

| | Deutsche mark | | Japanese yen | | U.S. dollars | | Other currencies | | All currencies | |
|---|---|---|---|---|---|---|---|---|---|---|
| | FY96 | FY95 | FY96 | FY95 | FY96 | FY95 | FY96 | FY95 | FY96 | FY95 |
| **Futures and forwards:** | | | | | | | | | | |
| Carrying value | 1 | * | 3 | 9 | — | — | * | * | 4 | 9 |
| Average balance during period | 1 | 1 | 3 | 9 | — | — | * | 1 | 4 | 11 |
| Net gains (losses) for the period | (2) | (2) | (3) | (26) | 15 | (1) | (*) | 2 | 10 | (27) |
| **Options:** | | | | | | | | | | |
| Carrying value | — | — | * | * | (*) | — | * | * | * | * |
| Average balance during period | — | — | * | * | * | * | * | * | * | * |
| Net gains (losses) for the period | (*) | (*) | (*) | (1) | (2) | (2) | (*) | (*) | (2) | (3) |
| **Total Trading Investments** | | | | | | | | | | |
| Carrying value | 1,566 | 1,638 | 2,897 | 6,872 | 9,358 | 10,335 | 1,180 | 976 | 15,001 | 19,821 |
| Average balance during period | 1,291 | 1,336 | 4,303 | 6,512 | 7,266 | 9,082 | 1,292 | 1,789 | 14,152 | 18,719 |
| Net gains (losses) for the period | 17 | 3 | (48) | 79 | (28) | 66 | 7 | (3) | (52) | 145 |
| **Repurchase agreements and Securities loans:** | | | | | | | | | | |
| Carrying value | — | (167) | — | — | (2,394) | (2,400) | (45) | — | (2,439) | (2,567) |
| Average balance during period | (142) | (81) | — | — | (1,406) | (1,525) | (27) | (6) | (1,575) | (1,612) |
| Average yield (%) | — | 3.60 | — | — | 5.20 | 6.12 | 4.06 | — | 5.18 | 5.95 |
| Average maturity (years) | — | 0.08 | — | — | 0.02 | 0.01 | 0.02 | — | 0.02 | 0.02 |
| **Resale agreements:** | | | | | | | | | | |
| Carrying value | 571 | 122 | — | — | 655 | 88 | 56 | 36 | 1,282 | 246 |
| Average balance during period | 463 | 637 | — | — | 775 | 557 | 68 | 21 | 1,306 | 1,215 |
| Average yield (%) | 3.49 | 4.44 | — | — | 5.17 | 6.17 | 4.40 | 7.40 | 4.39 | 5.49 |
| Average maturity (years) | 0.01 | 0.03 | — | — | 0.03 | 0.01 | ** | 0.02 | 0.02 | 0.02 |
| **Short sales** | | | | | | | | | | |
| Carrying value | (25) | (77) | — | — | (54) | (*) | (*) | — | (79) | (77) |
| Average balance during period | (44) | (37) | (5) | (55) | (133) | (349) | (12) | (3) | (194) | (444) |
| **Net covered forwards:** | | | | | | | | | | |
| Carrying value | 60 | 587 | (91) | (106) | (17) | (763) | 50 | 283 | 2 | 1 |
| Average balance during period | 162 | 301 | (88) | 8 | (423) | (611) | 348 | 303 | (1) | 1 |
| Average yield (%) | 3.33 | 4.62 | 0.43 | 1.42 | 5.40 | 6.05 | 3.17 | 5.14 | 3.69 | 4.83 |
| Average maturity (years) | 0.01 | 0.06 | 0.04 | 0.16 | 0.02 | 0.06 | 0.01 | 0.02 | 0.02 | 0.05 |

\* *Less than $0.5 million.* \*\* *Less than 0.005 years.*

***Held-to-maturity portfolio:*** The carrying and fair values of investment securities in the Held-to-maturity portfolio at June 30, 1996 and June 30, 1995 are as follows:

*In millions*

| | June 30, 1996 | | | | |
|---|---|---|---|---|---|
| | Carrying Value | Average Yield (%) | Gross Unrealized Gains | Gross Unrealized Losses | Fair Value |
| Government and agency obligations | $1,055 | 8.74 | $56 | $— | $1,111 |
| Time deposits | 114 | 5.81 | — | — | 114 |
| Total | $1,169 | 8.46 | $56 | $— | $1,225 |

| | June 30, 1995 | | | | |
|---|---|---|---|---|---|
| | Carrying Value | Average Yield (%) | Gross Unrealized Gains | Gross Unrealized Losses | Fair Value |
| Government and agency obligations | $1,085 | 8.75 | $19 | $— | $1,104 |
| Time deposits | 118 | 6.50 | — | — | 118 |
| Total | $1,203 | 8.53 | $19 | $— | $1,222 |

At June 30, 1996 and June 30, 1995 the Held-to-maturity portfolio comprised investments in pounds sterling only. The annualized rate of return on average investments in the Held-to-maturity portfolio, held during the fiscal year ended June 30, 1996, was 8.35 percent (8.11 percent—June 30, 1995).

The expected maturities of investment securities in the Held-to-maturity portfolio at June 30, 1996 are summarized below

*In millions*

| | June 30, 1996 | | |
|---|---|---|---|
| | Carrying Value | Fair Value | Net Unrealized Gains |
| July 1, 1996 through June 30, 1997 | $ 114 | $ 114 | $— |
| July 1, 1997 through June 30, 2001 | 162 | 170 | 8 |
| July 1, 2001 through June 30, 2006 | 236 | 252 | 16 |
| Thereafter | 657 | 689 | 32 |
| Total | $1,169 | $1,225 | $56 |

## NOTE C—LOANS, COFINANCING AND GUARANTEES

**Loans:** On August 1, 1995, IBRD's Executive Directors approved a one-year interest waiver of 25 basis points on disbursed and outstanding loans for all payment periods commencing in the fiscal year ending June 30, 1996 for all eligible borrowers. A similar waiver was in effect for the fiscal year ended June 30, 1995. In fiscal year 1995, IBRD's Executive Directors approved a one-time 10 basis point interest waiver, for two consecutive six-month interest periods, on currency pool loans, which a borrower converts from loan terms in effect between 1982 and 1989 to loan terms in effect since 1989. For the fiscal year ended June 30, 1996 the combined effect of these waivers was to reduce Net Income by $286 million ($251 million—June 30, 1995).

Also, on August 1, 1995, the Executive Directors approved a one-year commitment fee waiver of 50 basis points on undisbursed loans to all borrowers for all payment periods commencing in the fiscal year ending June 30, 1996. A similar waiver was in effect for the fiscal year ended June 30, 1995. For the fiscal year ended June 30, 1996 the effect of the commitment fee waiver was to reduce Net Income by $235 million ($233 million—June 30, 1995).

In connection with the cessation of the membership of the SFRY discussed in Note A, in February 1993 IBRD reached an agreement with the FRY for the apportionment and service of debt due to IBRD on loans made to or guaranteed by the SFRY and assumed by the FRY, which confirmed a February 1992 interim agreement between the SFRY (then consisting of the Republics of Bosnia and Herzegovina, Macedonia, Montenegro and Serbia) and IBRD pertaining, among other things, to such loans. As of the date hereof, no debt-service payments have been received by IBRD from the FRY.

On June 14, 1996, the accumulated arrears on loans to the former SFRY assumed by Bosnia and Herzegovina were cleared through three new consolidation loans extended by IBRD. These new loans consolidated all outstanding principal and overdue interest on the loans assumed by Bosnia and Herzegovina. This resulted in an increase in loans outstanding of $168 million and the deferral of the recognition of the related interest income. The first consolidation loan is a currency pool loan of $29 million carrying IBRD's adjustable lending rate for such loans, currently 6.98 percent, plus 41 basis points. The second consolidation loan is also a currency pool loan in the amount of $285 million carrying IBRD's adjustable lending rate for such loans, currently 6.98 percent, plus 4 basis points. The third consolidation loan is a U. S. dollar LIBOR-based single currency loan of $307 million carrying IBRD's lending rate for such loans, currently 5.38 percent. All three consolidation loans have a final maturity of 30 years, which includes a five-year grace period. The consolidation loans aggregated the existing assumed loans, which had final maturities ranging from April 1, 1992 to May 15, 2001 and a combined weighted-average interest rate of 7.95 percent.

At June 30, 1996, no loans payable to IBRD other than those referred to in the following paragraphs were overdue by more than three months.

At June 30, 1996, the loans made to or guaranteed by certain member countries and the FRY with an aggregate principal balance outstanding of $2,520 million ($2,618 million—June 30, 1995), of which $1,227 million

($1,411 million—June 30, 1995) was overdue, were in nonaccrual status. At such date, overdue interest and other charges in respect of these loans totaled $808 million ($864 million—June 30, 1995). If these loans had not been in nonaccrual status, income from loans for the fiscal year ended June 30, 1996 would have been higher by $188 million ($156 million—June 30, 1995). A summary of countries with loans or guarantees in nonaccrual status follows:

In millions

| | June 30, 1996 | | |
|---|---|---|---|
| Borrower | Principal Outstanding | Principal and Charges Overdue | Nonaccrual Since |
| **With Overdues** | | | |
| Federal Republic of Yugoslavia | $1,204 | $1,143 | September 1992 |
| Iraq | 50 | 66 | December 1990 |
| Liberia | 152 | 250 | June 1987 |
| Sudan | 6 | 3 | January 1994 |
| Syrian Arab Republic | 399 | 514 | February 1987 |
| Zaire | 88 | 59 | November 1993 |
| Total | $1,899 | $2,035 | |
| **Without Overdues** | | | |
| Bosnia and Herzegovina | 621 | — | September 1992 |
| Total | $2,520 | $2,035 | |

The average recorded investment in nonaccruing loans during the fiscal year ended June 30, 1996 was $2,453 million ($2,474 million—June 30, 1995).

During the fiscal years ended June 30, 1996 and June 30, 1995, no loans came out of nonaccrual status.

An analysis of the changes to the Accumulated Provision for Loan Losses for the fiscal years ended June 30, 1996 and June 30, 1995 appears below:

In millions

| | 1996 | 1995 |
|---|---|---|
| Balance, beginning of the fiscal year | $3,740 | $3,324 |
| Provision for loan losses | 42 | 12 |
| Translation adjustment | (442) | 404 |
| Balance, end of the fiscal year | $3,340 | $3,740 |

Under an IDA program established in September 1988, a portion of principal repayments to IDA are allocated on an annual basis to provide supplemental IDA credits to IDA-eligible countries that are no longer able to borrow on IBRD terms, but have outstanding IBRD loans approved prior to September 1988 and have in place an IDA-supported structural adjustment program. Such supplemental IDA credits are allocated to countries that meet specified conditions, in proportion to each country's interest payments due that year on its pre-September 1988 IBRD loans. To be eligible for such IDA supplemental credits, a member country must meet IDA's eligibility criteria for lending, must be ineligible for IBRD lending and must not have had an IBRD loan approved within the last twelve months. To receive a supplemental credit from the program, a member country cannot be more than 60 days overdue on its debt-service payments to IBRD or IDA. At June 30, 1996, IDA had approved credits of $1,379 million ($1,179 million—June 30, 1995) under this program from inception, of which $1,327 million ($1,128 million—June 30, 1995) had been disbursed to the eligible countries.

*Cofinancing and Guarantees:* IBRD has taken direct participations in, or provided partial guarantees of, loans syndicated by other financial institutions for projects or programs also financed by IBRD through regular loans. IBRD also has provided partial guarantees of securities issued by an entity eligible for IBRD loans. IBRD's partial guarantees of bond issues are included in the guarantees amount mentioned below. IBRD's direct participations in syndicated loans are included in reported loan balances.

Guarantees of loan principal of $1,537 million at June 30, 1996 ($1,610 million—June 30, 1995) were not included in reported loan balances. $122 million of these guarantees were subject to call at June 30, 1996 ($173 million—June 30, 1995). IBRD has partially guaranteed the timely payment of interest amounts on certain loans that have been sold. At June 30, 1996, these guarantees, approximating $1 million ($4 million—June 30, 1995), were subject to call.

*Estimated value of loans:* All of IBRD's loans are made to or guaranteed by countries that are members of IBRD, except for those loans made to IFC. IBRD does not currently sell its loans, nor is there a market of loans comparable to those made by IBRD. IBRD has never suffered a loss on any of its loans, although from time to time certain borrowers have found it difficult to make timely payments for protracted periods, resulting in their loans being placed in nonaccrual status. Several borrowers have emerged from nonaccrual status after a period of time by bringing up-to-date all principal payments and all interest payments, including interest and other charges on overdue principal payments. In an attempt to recognize the risk inherent in these overdue payments, IBRD maintains a provision for loan losses. The balance of the Accumulated Provision for Loan Losses at June 30, 1996 was $3,340 million ($3,740 million—June 30, 1995).

*Fixed rate loans:* On loans negotiated prior to July 1982, IBRD charges interest at fixed rates. The estimated value of these loans has been based on discounted future cash flows using the rate at which IBRD could undertake borrowings of comparable maturities at June 30, 1996 plus a 50 basis point spread.

*Adjustable rate loans:* In 1982 IBRD mitigated its interest rate risk by moving from fixed rate to adjustable rate lending. This rate, reset twice a year, is based on IBRD's own cost of qualified borrowings plus a 50 basis point spread, resulting in a pass-through of its average borrowing costs to those members that benefit from IBRD loans. Since the interest rate for adjustable rate loans is based on the interest rate of the qualified borrowings, the estimated value of adjustable rate loans has been based on the relationship of the fair value to the carrying value of the underlying borrowings.

*Single currency loans:* IBRD introduced variable rate single currency loans in 1993 and fixed rate single currency loans in 1995.

The rates charged on variable rate single currency loans are a direct pass-through of IBRD's cost of funding for these loans, and are reset semi-annually. They comprise a base rate equal to the six-month reference interbank offered rate for the applicable currency on the rate reset date and a total spread consisting of (a) IBRD's average funding cost margin for these loans and (b) a spread of 50 basis points. The estimated value of variable rate single currency loans has been based on the relationship of the fair value to the carrying value of the underlying borrowings.

The rates charged on fixed rate single currency loans are set on semi-annual rate fixing dates for loan amounts disbursed during the preceding six-month period and remain fixed for such disbursed amounts until they are repaid. For the interim period from the date each disbursement is made until its rate fixing date, interest accrues at a rate equal to the rate on variable rate single currency loans applicable for such interim period. The fixed lending rate comprises a base rate reflecting medium- to long-term market rates on the rate fixing date, plus a total spread consisting of (a) IBRD's funding cost margin for these loans, (b) a risk premium (intended to compensate IBRD for market risks incurred in funding these loans), and (c) a spread of 50 basis points. The estimated value of these loans has been based on discounted future cash flows using the rate at which IBRD could make similar loans of comparable maturities at June 30, 1996.

In addition to its other loan products, beginning on September 1, 1996, IBRD will offer its borrowers the option to convert undisbursed currency pool loan amounts to single currency loan terms. Further, borrowers will be given the option to convert disbursed and undisbursed currency pool loan balances to single currency pool loans. Borrowers selecting single currency pool loans will have their choice of four different pools (U. S. dollars, Japanese yen, Deutsche mark or Swiss francs) each of which will be a multi-currency pool at inception, but will be adjusted to reach a level of at least 90 percent in the designated currency by July 1, 1999 and will be maintained at or above that level thereafter.

The following table reflects the carrying and estimated values of the loan portfolio based on current borrowing rates net of the Accumulated Provision for Loan Losses at June 30, 1996 and June 30, 1995:

**In millions**

| | 1996 | | 1995 | |
|---|---|---|---|---|
| | Carrying Value | Estimated Value | Carrying Value | Estimated Value |
| Fixed rate loans | $ 11,126 | $ 12,469 | $ 17,128 | $ 19,065 |
| Adjustable rate loans | 96,856 | 102,994 | 106,137 | 114,141 |
| Single currency loans | 2,264 | 2,175 | 234 | 235 |
| Total | 110,246 | 117,638 | 123,499 | 133,441 |
| Less accumulated provision for loan losses | 3,340 | 3,340 | 3,740 | 3,740 |
| | $106,906 | $114,298 | $119,759 | $129,701 |

**Statutory Lending Limit:** Under the Articles of Agreement, the total amount outstanding of guarantees, participations in loans, and direct loans made by IBRD may not be increased to an amount exceeding 100 percent of the sum of Subscribed Capital, reserves, and surplus. At June 30, 1996 and June 30, 1995, the status of the statutory lending limit is as follows:

In millions

|  | 1996 | 1995 |
|---|---|---|
| **Statutory Lending Limit** | | |
| Subscribed capital | $180,630 | $176,438 |
| Retained earnings | 16,099 | 15,502 |
| Cumulative translation adjustment | 1,056 | 3,308 |
| Accumulated provision for loan losses | 3,340 | 3,740 |
|  | $201,125 | $198,988 |
| **Loans and Guarantees Outstanding** | | |
| Loans outstanding | $110,246 | $123,499 |
| Principal guarantees callable | 122 | 173 |
| Interest guarantees callable | 1 | 4 |
|  | $110,369 | $123,676 |
| Loans and guarantees outstanding as a percentage of statutory lending limit | 55% | 62% |

## NOTE D—BORROWINGS

Providing liquidity and minimizing the cost of funds are key objectives to IBRD's overall borrowing strategy. IBRD uses swaps in its borrowing strategy to lower the overall cost of its borrowings for those members who benefit from IBRD loans. IBRD undertakes swap transactions with a list of authorized counterparties. Credit and maturity limits have been established for each counterparty.

Swaps are used to modify the interest rate and/or currency characteristics of the borrowing portfolio and are linked to the related borrowings at inception and remain so throughout the terms of their contracts. The interest component of a swap is recognized as an adjustment to the borrowing cost over the life of the contract. Upon termination, the change in a swap's market value is recorded as an adjustment to the carrying value of the underlying borrowing and recognized as an adjustment of the borrowing cost over the expected remaining life of the borrowing. In instances where the underlying borrowing is prepaid, the change in the associated swap's market value is recognized immediately as an adjustment to the cost of the underlying borrowing instrument.

**Currency swaps:** Currency swaps are agreements in which proceeds of a borrowing are converted into a different currency and, simultaneously, a forward exchange agreement is executed providing for a schedule of future exchanges of the two currencies in order to recover the currency converted. The combination of a borrowing and a currency swap produces the financial equivalent of substituting a borrowing in the currency obtained in the initial conversion for the original borrowing.

**Interest rate swaps:** Interest rate swaps are agreements that transform a fixed rate payment obligation in a particular currency into a floating rate obligation in that currency and vice-versa.

**Forward interest rate swaps:** A forward interest rate swap is an agreement under which the cash flow exchanges of the underlying interest rate swaps would begin to take effect from a specified date.

**Swaptions:** A swaption is an option that gives the holder the right to enter into an interest rate or currency swap at a certain future date.

**Deferred rate setting agreements:** IBRD enters into deferred rate setting agreements in conjunction with some of its bond issues. These agreements provide for payments to be made to or by IBRD reflecting gain or loss on one or more government securities or related financial instruments. These agreements allow IBRD to fix the effective interest cost to IBRD of all or a portion of the issues over a specified period of time after the issue date of the respective bond. The potential credit loss to IBRD from nonperformance is limited to any amounts due, but unsettled, from the financial intermediary. However, periodic mark-to-market settlements on these agreements limit this risk. At June 30, 1996 and June 30, 1995 the effective interest cost of all principal amounts had been fixed.

The following table reflects the carrying and estimated fair values of the borrowing portfolio at June 30, 1996 and June 30, 1995:

In millions

|  | 1996 | | 1995 | |
|---|---|---|---|---|
|  | Carrying Value | Estimated Fair Value | Carrying Value | Estimated Fair Value |
| Short-term | $ 4,328 | $ 4,371 | $ 3,898 | $ 3,898 |
| Medium- and long-term | 92,391 | 99,250 | 104,392 | 112,977 |
| Swaps | | | | |
|   Currency | | | | |
|     Payable | 19,427 | 19,841 | 19,985 | 20,495 |
|     Receivable | (18,010) | (19,203) | (16,735) | (17,717) |
|   Interest rate | — | 1,064 | — | 1,059 |
|   Forward interest rate | — | — | — | 23 |
|   Swaptions | — | 1 | — | — |
| Total | $98,136 | $105,324 | $111,540 | $120,735 |

The estimated fair values are based on quoted market prices where such prices are available. Where no quoted market price is available, the fair value is estimated based on the cost at which IBRD could currently undertake borrowings with similar terms and remaining maturities, using the secondary market yield curve. The fair value of swaps represents the estimated cost of replacing these contracts on that date.

The average cost of borrowings outstanding during the fiscal year ended June 30, 1996 was 6.44 percent (6.62 percent—June 30, 1995), reflecting a reduction in interest expense of $170 million ($157 million—June 30, 1995) as a result of swaps.

## NOTE E—CREDIT RISK

*Country Credit Risk:* Country credit risk is risk of loss including loss due to protracted arrears on payments from borrowers. IBRD manages country credit risk through individual country exposure limits according to creditworthiness. These exposure limits are tied to performance on macroeconomic and structural policies. In addition, IBRD establishes absolute limits on the share of outstanding loans to any individual borrower. The country credit risk is further managed by financial incentives such as pricing loans using IBRD's own cost of borrowing and partial interest charge waivers conditioned on timely payment that give bor-

rowers self-interest in IBRD's continued strong intermediation capacity. Collectibility risk is covered by the Accumulated Provision for Loan Losses. IBRD also uses a simulation model to assess the adequacy of its reserves in the case a major borrower, or group of borrowers, stops servicing its loans for an extended period of time.

*Commercial Credit Risk:* For the purpose of risk management, IBRD is party to a variety of financial instruments, certain of which involve elements of credit risk in excess of the amount recorded on the balance sheet. Credit risk exposure represents the maximum potential accounting loss due to possible nonperformance by obligors and counterparties under the terms of the contracts. Additionally, the nature of the instruments involves contract value and notional principal amounts that are not reflected in the basic financial statements. For both on- and off-balance sheet securities, IBRD limits trading to a list of authorized dealers and counterparties. Credit limits have been established for each counterparty by type of instrument and maturity category.

The contract value/notional amounts and credit risk exposure, as applicable, of these financial instruments at June 30, 1996 and June 30, 1995 are given below:

In millions

|  | 1996 | 1995 |
|---|---|---|
| **INVESTMENTS—TRADING PORTFOLIO** | | |
| Futures and forwards | | |
|   Long position | $ 1,499 | $ 4,039 |
|   Short position | 5,875 | 8,051 |
|   Credit exposure due to potential nonperformance by counterparties | 2 | 6 |
| Options | | |
|   Long position | 679 | 19 |
|   Short position | 429 | — |
| Covered forwards | | |
|   Credit exposure due to potential nonperformance by counterparties | 2 | 7 |

*(table continued on next page)*

*(table continued)*

**In millions**

| | 1996 | 1995 |
|---|---|---|
| **BORROWINGS** | | |
| Currency swaps | | |
| Credit exposure due to potential nonperformance by counterparties | 728 | 713 |
| Interest rate swaps | | |
| Notional principal | 26,396 | 16,136 |
| Credit exposure due to potential nonperformance by counterparties | 96 | 57 |
| Forward interest rate swaps | | |
| Notional principal | — | 300 |
| Credit exposure due to potential nonperformance by counterparties | — | — |
| Swaptions | | |
| Notional principal | 30 | — |
| Credit exposure due to potential nonperformance by counterparties | — | — |

## NOTE F—RETAINED EARNINGS, ALLOCATIONS AND TRANSFERS

***Retained Earnings:*** Retained Earnings comprised the following elements at June 30, 1996 and June 30, 1995:

**In millions**

| | 1996 | 1995 |
|---|---|---|
| Special Reserve | $ 293 | $ 293 |
| General Reserve | 13,909 | 13,629 |
| Surplus | 710 | 226 |
| Unallocated Net Income | 1,187 | 1,354 |
| Total | $16,099 | $15,502 |

On August 1, 1995, the Executive Directors allocated $280 million of the net income earned in the fiscal year ended June 30, 1995 to the General Reserve. On October 12, 1995, the Board of Governors approved the following transfers, by way of grant, out of Unallocated Net Income: $250 million in an equivalent amount in SDRs to IDA, $100 million to the Debt Reduction Facility for IDA-Only Countries, and $90 million to the Trust Fund for Gaza and West Bank. On the same day, the Board of Governors also approved a transfer of $634 million to Surplus. On February 23, 1996, the Board of Governors approved a transfer from Surplus, by way of grant, of $150 million to a trust fund administered by IDA to finance an emergency reconstruction program in Bosnia and Herzegovina.

***Transfers to International Development Association:*** The Board of Governors has approved aggregate transfers to IDA totaling $4,573 million from Unallocated Net Income through June 30, 1994. On October 12, 1995, the Board of Governors approved a transfer to IDA, by way of grant, of $250 million in an equivalent amount in SDRs out of Unallocated Net Income. At June 30, 1996 and June 30, 1995, all transfers to IDA had been paid.

***Transfers to Debt Reduction Facility for IDA-Only Countries:*** The Board of Governors has approved aggregate transfers to the Debt Reduction Facility for IDA-Only Countries (DRF) totaling $200 million through June 30, 1994. On October 12, 1995, the Board of Governors approved a transfer to the DRF, by way of grant, of $100 million out of Unallocated Net Income. At June 30, 1996, $119 million ($105 million—June 30, 1995) remained payable.

***Transfer to Trust Fund for Gaza and West Bank:*** The Board of Governors has approved aggregate transfers to the Trust Fund for Gaza and West Bank (TFG), totaling $50 million through June 30, 1994. On October 12, 1995, the Board of Governors approved a transfer to the TFG, by way of grant, of $90 million out of Unallocated Net Income. At June 30, 1996, $70 million ($25 million—June 30, 1995) remained payable.

***Transfer for Emergency Assistance for Rwanda:*** In November 1994 the Board of Governors approved a transfer of $20 million for Emergency Assistance for Rwanda out of Surplus. At June 30, 1996, the transfer for the Emergency Assistance for Rwanda had been made. At June 30, 1995, $5 million remained payable.

***Transfer to Trust Fund for Bosnia and Herzegovina:*** On February 23, 1996, the Board of Governors approved a transfer from Surplus, by way of grant, of $150 million to a trust fund administered by IDA to finance an emergency reconstruction program in Bosnia and Herzegovina. At June 30, 1996, $16 million remained payable.

## NOTE G—ADMINISTRATIVE EXPENSES AND CONTRIBUTIONS TO SPECIAL PROGRAMS

In February 1995, the Executive Directors authorized expenditures for costs associated with planned staff reductions. During fiscal year 1995, IBRD charged to expense $131 million for these reductions, of which $53 million was charged to IDA. The reductions are designed to improve IBRD's and IDA's efficiency, adjust the staffing skills mix and thereby better meet client demands. The planned staff reductions are expected to lower future years' administrative expenses by an amount greater than the associated cost. On October 31, 1995, the program for planned staff reductions was brought to a close when all affected staff had been identified and informed. Under this program, 608 staff were identified as redundant at a total cost of $112 million. The difference of $19 million has been taken back as a reduction of administrative expenses, of which $8 million has been allocated to IDA as a reduction to the management fee charged to IDA. At June 30, 1996, $26 million ($1 million—June 30, 1995) has been charged against the accrual of $112 million. This accrual included costs associated with job search assistance, training, outplacement consulting, pension plan contributions, medical insurance contributions and related tax allowances.

Administrative Expenses are net of the management fee of $508 million ($571 million—June 30, 1995) charged to IDA and $102 million ($111 million—June 30, 1995) charged to reimbursable programs. Included in the amounts charged to reimbursable programs are allocated charges of $22 million ($21 million—June 30, 1995) charged to IFC and $1 million ($1 million—June 30, 1995) charged to MIGA.

Contributions to special programs represent grants for agricultural research, the control of onchocerciasis, and other developmental activities.

## NOTE H—TRUST FUNDS

IBRD, alone or jointly with IDA, administers on behalf of donors, including members, their agencies and other entities, funds restricted for specific uses which include the cofinancing of IBRD lending projects, debt reduction operations, technical assistance for borrowers, including feasibility studies and project preparation, global and regional programs and research and training programs. These funds are placed in trust and are not included in the assets of IBRD. The distribution of trust fund assets by executing agent at June 30, 1996 and June 30, 1995 is as follows:

|  | 1996 | | 1995 | |
|---|---|---|---|---|
|  | Total Fiduciary Assets (in millions) | Number of Trust Fund Accounts | Total Fiduciary Assets (in millions) | Number of Trust Fund Accounts |
| IBRD executed | $ 548 | 1,314 | $ 645 | 1,294 |
| Recipient executed | 1,308 | 935 | 1,270 | 684 |
| Total | $1,856 | 2,249 | $1,915 | 1,978 |

The responsibilities of IBRD under these arrangements vary and range from services normally provided under its own lending projects to full project implementation including procurement of goods and services. During the fiscal year ended June 30, 1996, IBRD received $15 million ($19 million—June 30, 1995) as fees for administering trust funds. These fees have been recorded as a reduction of administrative expenses.

## NOTE I—STAFF RETIREMENT PLAN

IBRD has a defined benefit retirement plan (the Plan) covering substantially all of its staff. The Plan also covers substantially all the staff of IFC and MIGA. Under the Plan, benefits are based on the years of contributory service and the highest three-year average of pensionable remuneration as defined in the Plan, with the staff contributing a fixed percentage of pensionable remuneration, and IBRD contributing the remainder of the actuarially determined cost of future Plan benefits. The actuarial present values of Plan obligations throughout the fiscal year are determined at the beginning of the fiscal year by the Plan's actuary. All contributions to the Plan and all other assets and income held for the purposes of the Plan are held by IBRD separately from the other assets and income of IBRD, IDA, IFC and MIGA and can be used only for the benefit of the participants in the Plan and their beneficiaries, until all liabilities to them have been paid or provided for. Plan assets consist primarily of equity and fixed income securities, with smaller holdings of cash, real estate and other investments.

Net periodic pension cost for IBRD participants for the fiscal years ended June 30, 1996 and June 30, 1995 consisted of the following components:

In millions

|  | 1996 | 1995 |
|---|---|---|
| Service cost—benefits earned during the fiscal year | $216 | $186 |
| Interest cost on projected benefit obligation | 360 | 348 |
| Actual return on plan assets | (917) | (428) |
| Net amortization and deferral | 437 | (3) |
| Net periodic pension cost | $ 96 | $103 |

The portion of this cost that relates to IBRD and is included in Administrative Expenses for the fiscal year ended June 30, 1996 is $60 million ($65 million—June 30, 1995). The balance has been included in the management fee charged to IDA.

The following table sets forth the Plan's funded status at June 30, 1996 and June 30, 1995:

In millions

|  | 1996 | 1995 |
|---|---|---|
| Actuarial present value of benefit obligations | | |
| Accumulated benefit obligation | | |
| Vested | $(3,543) | $(3,551) |
| Nonvested | (36) | (22) |
| Subtotal | (3,579) | (3,573) |
| Effect of projected compensation levels | (1,718) | (1,866) |
| Projected benefit obligation | (5,297) | (5,439) |
| Plan assets at fair value | 7,033 | 5,925 |
| Plan assets in excess of projected benefit obligation | 1,736 | 486 |
| Remaining unrecognized net transition asset | (91) | (104) |
| Unrecognized prior service cost | 74 | 82 |
| Unrecognized net gain from past experience different from that assumed and from changes in assumptions | (1,719) | (464) |
| Prepaid pension cost | $   — | $   — |

The weighted-average discount rate used in determining the actuarial present value of the projected benefit obligation was 7.5 percent (7.5 percent—June 30, 1995). The effect of projected compensation levels was calculated based on a scale that provides for a decreasing rate of salary increase depending on age, beginning with 13.3 percent at age 20 and decreasing to 6.8 percent at age 64. The expected long-term rate of return on assets was 9 percent (9 percent—June 30, 1995).

## NOTE J—RETIRED STAFF BENEFITS PLAN

IBRD has a Retired Staff Benefits Plan (RSBP) that provides certain health care and life insurance benefits to retirees. All staff who are enrolled in the insurance programs while in active service and who meet certain requirements are eligible for benefits when they reach early or normal retirement age while working for IBRD. The RSBP also covers the staff of IFC and MIGA.

Retirees contribute a level amount toward life insurance based on the amount of coverage. Retiree contributions toward health care are based on length of service and age at retirement. IBRD annually contributes the remainder of the actuarially determined cost for future benefits. The actuarial present values of RSBP obligations throughout the fiscal year are determined at the beginning of the fiscal year by the RSBP's actuary. All contributions to the RSBP and all other assets and income held for purposes of the RSBP are held by IBRD separately from the other assets and income of IBRD, IDA, IFC, and MIGA and can be used only for the benefit of the participants in the RSBP and their beneficiaries until all liabilities to them have been paid or provided

for. RSBP assets consist primarily of fixed income and equity securities.

Net periodic postretirement benefits cost for IBRD participants for the fiscal years ended June 30, 1996 and June 30, 1995 consisted of the following components:

In millions

|  | 1996 | 1995 |
|---|---|---|
| Service cost—benefits earned during the fiscal year | $ 32 | $ 28 |
| Interest cost on accumulated postretirement benefit obligation | 45 | 48 |
| Actual return on plan assets | (130) | (40) |
| Net amortization and deferral | 87 | 1 |
|  | $ 34 | $ 37 |

The portion of this cost that relates to IBRD and is included in Administrative Expenses for the fiscal year ended June 30, 1996 is $22 million ($23 million—June 30, 1995). The balance has been included in the management fee charged to IDA.

The following table sets forth the RSBP's funded status at June 30, 1996 and June 30, 1995:

In millions

|  | 1996 | 1995 |
|---|---|---|
| Accumulated postretirement benefit obligation | | |
| Retirees | $(293) | $(257) |
| Fully eligible active plan participants | (128) | (125) |
| Other active plan participants | (285) | (292) |
|  | (706) | (674) |
| Plan assets at fair value | 937 | 770 |
| Plan assets in excess of accumulated postretirement benefit obligation | 231 | 96 |
| Unrecognized prior service costs | (12) | (14) |
| Unrecognized net loss from past experience different from that assumed and from changes in assumptions | 107 | 250 |
| Prepaid postretirement benefit cost | $ 326 | $ 332 |

Of the $326 million prepaid at June 30, 1996 ($332 million—June 30, 1995), $295 million is attributable to IBRD ($301 million—June 30, 1995) and is included in Miscellaneous Assets on the Balance Sheet. The remainder has been attributed to IFC and MIGA.

For June 30, 1996, the accumulated plan benefit obligation (APBO) was determined using health care cost trend rates of 14.4 percent to 11.2 percent, decreasing gradually to 5.5 percent in 2010 and thereafter. The health care cost trend rate used for June 30, 1995 was

15.1 percent to 11.2 percent decreasing gradually to 5.1 percent in 2010 and thereafter.

The health care cost trend rate assumption has a significant effect on the amounts reported. To illustrate, increasing the assumed health care cost trend rates by one percentage point would increase the APBO at June 30, 1996 by $145 million and the net periodic postre-tirement benefit cost for the fiscal year then ended by $20 million.

The weighted average discount rate used in determining the APBO was 8 percent (7.5 percent—June 30, 1995). The expected long-term rate of return on plan assets was 8 percent (8.25 percent—June 30, 1995).

| Price Waterhouse | The Hague | New York |
|---|---|---|
| (International Firm) | Beijing | Tokyo |
| | Hong Kong | Washington |
| | London | |

## *Price Waterhouse*

July 31, 1996

President and Board of Governors
 International Bank for Reconstruction
 and Development

In our opinion, the financial statements appearing on pages 168 through 195 of this Report present fairly, in all material respects, in terms of United States dollars, the financial position of the International Bank for Reconstruction and Development at June 30, 1996 and 1995, and the results of its operations and its cash flows for the years then ended in conformity with generally accepted accounting principles in the United States and with International Accounting Standards. These financial statements are the responsibility of management of the International Bank for Reconstruction and Development; our responsibility is to express an opinion on these financial statements based on our audits. We conducted our audits of these statements in accordance with generally accepted auditing standards, including International Standards on Auditing, which require that we plan and perform the audit to obtain reasonable assurance about whether the financial statements are free of material misstatement. An audit includes examining, on a test basis, evidence supporting the amounts and disclosures in the financial statements, assessing the accounting principles used and significant estimates made by management, and evaluating the overall financial statement presentation. We believe that our audits provide a reasonable basis for the opinion expressed above.

*Price Waterhouse*
*(International Firm)*

# SPECIAL PURPOSE FINANCIAL STATEMENTS OF THE INTERNATIONAL DEVELOPMENT ASSOCIATION

# STATEMENT OF SOURCES AND APPLICATIONS OF DEVELOPMENT RESOURCES

*June 30, 1996 and June 30, 1995*
*Expressed in millions of U.S. dollars*

|  | 1996 | 1995[a] |
|---|---:|---:|
| **Applications of Development Resources** | | |
| *Net Resources Available For Development Activities* | | |
| Cash and investments immediately available for disbursement | | |
|    Due from banks | $     15 | $     44 |
|    Obligations of governments and other official entities— | | |
|      Notes B and F | 2,487 | 1,851 |
|    Obligations of banks and other financial institutions— | | |
|      Notes B and F | 2,257 | 2,590 |
|    Net payable on investment securities transactions— | | |
|      Notes B and F | (307) | (128) |
| | 4,452 | 4,357 |
| Cash and investments not immediately available for disbursement | | |
|    Due from banks | 8 | 3 |
|    Obligations of governments and other official entities— | | |
|      Notes B and F | 1,413 | 938 |
|    Obligations of banks and other financial institutions— | | |
|      Notes B and F | 273 | 402 |
| | 1,694 | 1,343 |
| Restricted cash and notes | 69 | 73 |
| Nonnegotiable, noninterest-bearing demand obligations | 21,232 | 23,677 |
| Other resources, net | 166 | 153 |
|    Total net resources available for development activities | 27,613 | 29,603 |
| *Resources Used For Development Credits* | | |
| **(see Summary Statement of Development Credits, Notes E and F)** | | |
|    Total development credits | 97,450 | 98,285 |
|    Less undisbursed balance | 24,629 | 26,253 |
|      Total resources used for development credits | 72,821 | 72,032 |
| **Total applications of development resources** | **$100,434** | **$101,635** |

# STATEMENT OF CASH FLOWS

*For the fiscal years ended June 30, 1996 and June 30, 1995*
*Expressed in millions of U.S. dollars*

|  | 1996 | 1995[a] |
|---|---|---|
| Cash flows from development activities | | |
| Development credit disbursements | $(5,884) | $(5,703) |
| Development credit principal repayments | 563 | 498 |
| Net cash used in development activities | (5,321) | (5,205) |
| | | |
| Cash flows from member subscriptions and contributions | 5,087 | 5,191 |
| | | |
| Cash flows from IBRD transfers | 250 | 1,427 |
| | | |
| Cash flows from operating activities | | |
| Changes from operations | 340 | 217 |
| Less: Income from restricted investments | 80 | 99 |
| Adjustments to reconcile changes from operations to net cash provided by operating activities | | |
| Amortization of discount on subscription advances | 9 | 12 |
| Net changes in other development resources | 240 | (171) |
| | | |
| Net cash provided by (used in) operating activities | 509 | (41) |
| | | |
| Effect of exchange rate changes on cash and investments immediately available for disbursement | (430) | 286 |
| Net increase in cash and investments immediately available for disbursement | 95 | 1,658 |
| | | |
| Cash and investments immediately available for disbursement at beginning of the fiscal year | 4,357 | 2,699 |
| | | |
| Cash and investments immediately available for disbursement at end of the fiscal year | $ 4,452 | $ 4,357 |
| | | |
| Supplemental disclosure | | |
| Increase (Decrease) in ending balances resulting from exchange rate fluctuations | | |
| Development credits outstanding | $(4,532) | $ 4,017 |
| Receivable from the International Bank for Reconstruction and Development | — | 90 |

a. Restated to include Special Fund activity for the fiscal year ended June 30, 1995; see Note A.

**The Notes to Special Purpose Financial Statements are an integral part of these Statements.**

# Summary Statement of Development Credits

June 30, 1996
Expressed in millions of U.S. dollars

| Borrower or guarantor | Total development credits | Undisbursed development credits[1] | Development credits outstanding | Percentage of development credits outstanding |
|---|---|---|---|---|
| Afghanistan | $ 75 | $ — | $ 75 | 0.10 |
| Albania | 276 | 153 | 123 | 0.17 |
| Angola | 282 | 184 | 98 | 0.14 |
| Armenia | 233 | 105 | 128 | 0.18 |
| Azerbaijan | 153 | 91 | 62 | 0.08 |
| Bangladesh | 7,010 | 1,402 | 5,608 | 7.70 |
| Benin | 656 | 143 | 513 | 0.70 |
| Bhutan | 28 | 6 | 22 | 0.03 |
| Bolivia | 1,211 | 422 | 789 | 1.08 |
| Bosnia and Herzegovina | 10 | 10 | — | — |
| Botswana | 11 | — | 11 | 0.02 |
| Burkina Faso | 806 | 185 | 621 | 0.85 |
| Burundi | 722 | 137 | 585 | 0.80 |
| Cambodia | 174 | 81 | 93 | 0.13 |
| Cameroon | 733 | 218 | 515 | 0.71 |
| Cape Verde | 69 | 34 | 35 | 0.05 |
| Central African Republic | 466 | 53 | 413 | 0.57 |
| Chad | 547 | 127 | 420 | 0.58 |
| Chile | 10 | — | 10 | 0.01 |
| China | 9,787 | 2,544 | 7,243 | 9.95 |
| Colombia | 11 | — | 11 | 0.01 |
| Comoros | 79 | 13 | 66 | 0.09 |
| Congo | 178 | 7 | 171 | 0.23 |
| Costa Rica | 2 | — | 2 | * |
| Côte d'Ivoire | 1,292 | 406 | 886 | 1.22 |
| Djibouti | 50 | 4 | 46 | 0.06 |
| Dominica | 16 | 4 | 12 | 0.02 |
| Dominican Republic | 17 | — | 17 | 0.02 |
| Ecuador | 26 | — | 26 | 0.04 |
| Egypt | 1,495 | 446 | 1,049 | 1.44 |
| El Salvador | 20 | — | 20 | 0.03 |
| Equatorial Guinea | 56 | 4 | 52 | 0.07 |
| Eritrea | 43 | 18 | 25 | 0.03 |
| Ethiopia | 2,119 | 585 | 1,534 | 2.11 |
| Gambia, The | 184 | 22 | 162 | 0.22 |
| Georgia | 192 | 73 | 119 | 0.16 |
| Ghana | 3,490 | 1,082 | 2,408 | 3.31 |
| Grenada | 11 | 4 | 7 | 0.01 |
| Guinea | 1,068 | 224 | 844 | 1.16 |
| Guinea-Bissau | 249 | 39 | 210 | 0.29 |
| Guyana | 293 | 90 | 203 | 0.28 |
| Haiti | 567 | 150 | 417 | 0.57 |
| Honduras | 623 | 218 | 405 | 0.56 |
| India | 22,672 | 5,263 | 17,409 | 23.91 |
| Indonesia | 746 | — | 746 | 1.02 |
| Jordan | 68 | — | 68 | 0.09 |
| Kenya | 2,596 | 557 | 2,039 | 2.80 |
| Korea, Republic of | 80 | — | 80 | 0.11 |
| Kyrgyz Republic | 312 | 143 | 169 | 0.23 |
| Lao People's Democratic Republic | 486 | 189 | 297 | 0.41 |
| Lesotho | 241 | 87 | 154 | 0.21 |
| Liberia | 109 | 3 | 106 | 0.15 |
| Macedonia, Former Yugoslav Republic of | 159 | 74 | 85 | 0.12 |
| Madagascar | 1,445 | 332 | 1,113 | 1.53 |
| Malawi | 1,725 | 396 | 1,329 | 1.83 |
| Maldives | 50 | 14 | 36 | 0.05 |
| Mali | 1,157 | 277 | 880 | 1.21 |
| Mauritania | 475 | 130 | 345 | 0.47 |
| Mauritius | 16 | — | 16 | 0.02 |
| Mongolia | 132 | 69 | 63 | 0.09 |

| Borrower or guarantor | Total development credits | Undisbursed development credits[1] | Development credits outstanding | Percentage of development credits outstanding |
|---|---|---|---|---|
| Morocco | $ 33 | $ — | $ 33 | 0.04 |
| Mozambique | 1,619 | 692 | 927 | 1.27 |
| Myanmar | 770 | — | 770 | 1.06 |
| Nepal | 1,318 | 286 | 1,032 | 1.42 |
| Nicaragua | 468 | 152 | 316 | 0.43 |
| Niger | 702 | 113 | 589 | 0.81 |
| Nigeria | 825 | 518 | 307 | 0.42 |
| Pakistan | 4,680 | 1,333 | 3,347 | 4.60 |
| Papua New Guinea | 106 | — | 106 | 0.15 |
| Paraguay | 35 | — | 35 | 0.05 |
| Philippines | 277 | 92 | 185 | 0.25 |
| Rwanda | 676 | 155 | 521 | 0.71 |
| St. Kitts and Nevis | 2 | — | 2 | * |
| St. Lucia | 14 | 6 | 8 | 0.01 |
| St. Vincent and the Grenadines | 10 | 2 | 8 | 0.01 |
| São Tomé and Principe | 69 | 12 | 57 | 0.08 |
| Senegal | 1,449 | 319 | 1,130 | 1.55 |
| Sierra Leone | 414 | 168 | 246 | 0.34 |
| Solomon Islands | 37 | 9 | 28 | 0.04 |
| Somalia | 423 | — | 423 | 0.58 |
| Sri Lanka | 1,931 | 453 | 1,478 | 2.03 |
| Sudan | 1,247 | — | 1,247 | 1.71 |
| Swaziland | 6 | — | 6 | 0.01 |
| Syrian Arab Republic | 44 | — | 44 | 0.06 |
| Tajikistan | 5 | 5 | — | — |
| Tanzania | 2,978 | 787 | 2,191 | 3.01 |
| Thailand | 101 | — | 101 | 0.14 |
| Togo | 672 | 102 | 570 | 0.78 |
| Tonga | 5 | — | 5 | 0.01 |
| Tunisia | 48 | — | 48 | 0.07 |
| Turkey | 127 | — | 127 | 0.17 |
| Uganda | 2,420 | 623 | 1,797 | 2.47 |
| Vanuatu | 17 | 4 | 13 | 0.02 |
| Vietnam | 1,280 | 1,027 | 253 | 0.35 |
| Western Samoa | 47 | 4 | 43 | 0.06 |
| Yemen, Republic of | 1,191 | 361 | 830 | 1.14 |
| Zaire | 1,288 | — | 1,288 | 1.77 |
| Zambia | 1,686 | 360 | 1,326 | 1.82 |
| Zimbabwe | 507 | 177 | 330 | 0.45 |
| Subtotal members | 97,336 | 24,578 | 72,758 | 99.92 |
| West African Development Bank[2] | 63 | 29 | 34 | 0.05 |
| Caribbean Development Bank[3] | 44 | 21 | 23 | 0.03 |
| Subtotal regional development banks | 107 | 50 | 57 | 0.08 |
| Other[4] | 7 | — | 7 | 0.01 |
| Total—June 30, 1996 ** | $97,450 | $24,629 | $72,821 | 100.00 |
| Total—June 30, 1995[5] | $98,285 | $26,253 | $72,032 | |

* Indicates amounts less than 0.005 percent.
** May differ from the sum of individual figures shown because of rounding.

NOTES

1. Of the undisbursed balance at June 30, 1996, IDA has entered into irrevocable commitments to disburse $349 million ($270 million—June 30, 1995).
2. These development credits are for the benefit of Benin, Burkina Faso, Côte d'Ivoire, Mali, Niger, Senegal, and Togo.
3. These development credits are for the benefit of Grenada and territories of the United Kingdom (Associated States and Dependencies) in the Caribbean region.
4. Represents development credits made at a time when the authorities on Taiwan represented China in IDA (prior to May 15, 1980).
5. See Notes to Special Purpose Financial Statements—Note A for reclassifications.

## Maturity Structure of Development Credits Outstanding

| Period | |
|---|---:|
| July 1, 1996 through June 30, 1997 | $ 753 |
| July 1, 1997 through June 30, 1998 | 739 |
| July 1, 1998 through June 30, 1999 | 898 |
| July 1, 1999 through June 30, 2000 | 1,052 |
| July 1, 2000 through June 30, 2001 | 1,269 |
| | |
| July 1, 2001 through June 30, 2006 | 9,524 |
| July 1, 2006 through June 30, 2011 | 12,485 |
| July 1, 2011 through June 30, 2016 | 14,156 |
| July 1, 2016 through June 30, 2021 | 12,854 |
| July 1, 2021 through June 30, 2026 | 10,086 |
| | |
| July 1, 2026 through June 30, 2031 | 6,537 |
| July 1, 2031 through June 30, 2036 | 2,388 |
| July 1, 2036 through June 30, 2041 | 80 |
| | |
| Total | $72,821 |

*The Notes to Special Purpose Financial Statements are an integral part of these Statements.*

# Statement of Voting Power, and Subscriptions and Contributions

*June 30, 1996*
*Expressed in millions of U.S. dollars*

| Member[1] | Number of votes | Percentage of total | Subscriptions and contributions committed |
|---|---|---|---|
| **Part I Members** | | | |
| Australia | 141,883 | 1.32 | $ 1,560.8 |
| Austria | 71,910 | 0.67 | 758.7 |
| Belgium | 126,316 | 1.18 | 1,553.9 |
| Canada | 325,422 | 3.03 | 3,987.0 |
| Denmark | 104,317 | 0.97 | 1,204.5 |
| Finland | 68,091 | 0.63 | 611.6 |
| France | 451,054 | 4.20 | 6,446.3 |
| Germany | 747,221 | 6.97 | 10,466.2 |
| Iceland | 24,561 | 0.23 | 16.6 |
| Ireland | 30,401 | 0.28 | 104.5 |
| Italy | 295,641 | 2.76 | 3,767.0 |
| Japan | 1,154,286 | 10.76 | 20,218.6 |
| Kuwait | 69,834 | 0.65 | 649.1 |
| Luxembourg | 25,959 | 0.24 | 48.8 |
| Netherlands | 234,735 | 2.19 | 3,387.2 |
| New Zealand | 30,575 | 0.28 | 105.0 |
| Norway | 105,156 | 0.98 | 1,147.1 |
| Portugal | 24,702 | 0.23 | 23.0 |
| Russian Federation | 28,202 | 0.26 | 143.8 |
| South Africa | 30,365 | 0.28 | 82.8 |
| Spain | 58,166 | 0.54 | 421.8 |
| Sweden | 214,153 | 2.00 | 2,376.4 |
| Switzerland[2] | 95,430 | 0.89 | 1,009.5 |
| United Arab Emirates | 1,367 | 0.01 | 5.6 |
| United Kingdom | 540,211 | 5.04 | 6,529.7 |
| United States | 1,607,213 | 14.98 | 21,831.5 |
| Subtotal Part I Members[3] | 6,607,171 | 61.59 | $88,457.0 |
| **Part II Members** | | | |
| Afghanistan | 13,557 | 0.13 | 1.3 |
| Albania | 24,389 | 0.23 | 0.3 |
| Algeria | 27,720 | 0.26 | 5.1 |
| Angola | 45,662 | 0.43 | 7.9 |
| Argentina | 112,879 | 1.05 | 58.0 |
| Armenia | 584 | 0.01 | 0.5 |
| Azerbaijan | 644 | 0.01 | 0.9 |
| Bangladesh | 61,951 | 0.58 | 7.2 |
| Belize | 1,788 | 0.02 | 0.2 |
| Benin | 5,297 | 0.05 | 0.6 |
| Bhutan | 12,272 | 0.11 | 0.1 |
| Bolivia | 30,397 | 0.28 | 1.4 |
| Bosnia and Herzegovina | 17,871 | 0.17 | 2.3 |
| Botswana | 23,815 | 0.22 | 0.2 |
| Brazil | 176,169 | 1.64 | 92.4 |
| Burkina Faso | 19,466 | 0.18 | 0.7 |
| Burundi | 23,006 | 0.21 | 1.0 |

June 30, 1996
*Expressed in millions of U.S. dollars*

| Member[1] | Number of votes | Percentage of total | Subscriptions and contributions committed |
|---|---|---|---|
| Cambodia | 7,826 | 0.07 | $ 1.3 |
| Cameroon | 19,459 | 0.18 | 1.3 |
| Cape Verde | 5,012 | 0.05 | 0.1 |
| Central African Republic | 10,920 | 0.10 | 0.6 |
| Chad | 10,990 | 0.10 | 0.6 |
| Chile | 31,782 | 0.30 | 4.5 |
| China | 217,996 | 2.03 | 39.7 |
| Colombia | 34,350 | 0.32 | 22.5 |
| Comoros | 13,141 | 0.12 | 0.1 |
| Congo | 6,685 | 0.06 | 0.6 |
| Costa Rica | 12,480 | 0.12 | 0.3 |
| Côte d'Ivoire | 18,669 | 0.17 | 1.3 |
| Croatia | 29,526 | 0.28 | 5.5 |
| Cyprus | 28,236 | 0.26 | 1.1 |
| Czech Republic | 40,537 | 0.38 | 23.7 |
| Djibouti | 532 | ** | 0.2 |
| Dominica | 15,049 | 0.14 | 0.1 |
| Dominican Republic | 25,658 | 0.24 | 0.6 |
| Ecuador | 23,800 | 0.22 | 0.8 |
| Egypt | 49,528 | 0.46 | 6.7 |
| El Salvador | 6,244 | 0.06 | 0.4 |
| Equatorial Guinea | 6,167 | 0.06 | 0.4 |
| Eritrea | 23,363 | 0.22 | 0.1 |
| Ethiopia | 21,353 | 0.20 | 0.7 |
| Fiji | 7,206 | 0.07 | 0.7 |
| Gabon | 2,093 | 0.02 | 0.6 |
| Gambia, The | 15,366 | 0.14 | 0.3 |
| Georgia | 22,523 | 0.21 | 0.9 |
| Ghana | 22,131 | 0.21 | 3.0 |
| Greece | 45,138 | 0.42 | 25.7 |
| Grenada | 18,999 | 0.18 | 0.1 |
| Guatemala | 25,634 | 0.24 | 0.5 |
| Guinea | 28,087 | 0.26 | 1.3 |
| Guinea-Bissau | 5,090 | 0.05 | 0.2 |
| Guyana | 18,160 | 0.17 | 1.0 |
| Haiti | 17,143 | 0.16 | 1.0 |
| Honduras | 21,570 | 0.20 | 0.4 |
| Hungary | 80,902 | 0.75 | 34.3 |
| India | 338,901 | 3.16 | 54.9 |
| Indonesia | 103,697 | 0.97 | 14.8 |
| Iran, Islamic Republic of | 15,455 | 0.14 | 5.7 |
| Iraq | 9,407 | 0.09 | 1.0 |
| Israel | 21,954 | 0.20 | 2.5 |
| Jordan | 24,865 | 0.23 | 0.4 |
| Kazakstan | 806 | 0.01 | 1.8 |
| Kenya | 27,105 | 0.25 | 2.2 |
| Kiribati | 4,777 | 0.04 | 0.1 |
| Korea, Republic of | 43,668 | 0.41 | 114.5 |
| Kyrgyz Republic | 580 | 0.01 | 0.5 |
| Lao People's Democratic Republic | 11,723 | 0.11 | 0.6 |
| Latvia | 614 | 0.01 | 0.7 |

| Member[1] | Number of votes | Percentage of total | Subscriptions and contributions committed |
|---|---|---|---|
| Lebanon | 8,562 | 0.08 | $    0.6 |
| Lesotho | 23,874 | 0.22 | 0.2 |
| Liberia | 23,379 | 0.22 | 1.1 |
| Libya | 7,771 | 0.07 | 1.3 |
| Macedonia, Former Yugoslav Republic of | 15,759 | 0.15 | 1.0 |
| Madagascar | 11,600 | 0.11 | 1.2 |
| Malawi | 27,960 | 0.26 | 1.0 |
| Malaysia | 41,061 | 0.38 | 3.6 |
| Maldives | 22,916 | 0.21 | * |
| Mali | 22,407 | 0.21 | 1.2 |
| Marshall Islands | 4,914 | 0.05 | * |
| Mauritania | 10,885 | 0.10 | 0.6 |
| Mauritius | 29,011 | 0.27 | 1.2 |
| Mexico | 78,854 | 0.74 | 123.7 |
| Micronesia, Federated States of | 18,424 | 0.17 | * |
| Moldova | 612 | 0.01 | 0.7 |
| Mongolia | 24,389 | 0.23 | 0.3 |
| Morocco | 48,482 | 0.45 | 4.9 |
| Mozambique | 6,815 | 0.06 | 1.7 |
| Myanmar | 37,470 | 0.35 | 2.9 |
| Nepal | 26,166 | 0.24 | 0.7 |
| Nicaragua | 24,865 | 0.23 | 0.4 |
| Niger | 16,541 | 0.15 | 0.7 |
| Nigeria | 8,257 | 0.08 | 4.2 |
| Oman | 24,870 | 0.23 | 0.4 |
| Pakistan | 97,461 | 0.91 | 13.6 |
| Panama | 5,657 | 0.05 | * |
| Papua New Guinea | 13,050 | 0.12 | 1.1 |
| Paraguay | 11,419 | 0.11 | 0.4 |
| Peru | 13,524 | 0.13 | 2.2 |
| Philippines | 16,583 | 0.15 | 6.5 |
| Poland | 249,421 | 2.32 | 52.1 |
| Rwanda | 17,979 | 0.17 | 1.0 |
| St. Kitts and Nevis | 5,082 | 0.05 | 0.2 |
| St. Lucia | 22,535 | 0.21 | 0.2 |
| St. Vincent and the Grenadines | 514 | ** | 0.1 |
| São Tomé and Principe | 4,714 | 0.04 | 0.1 |
| Saudi Arabia | 377,100 | 3.52 | 2,033.2 |
| Senegal | 28,447 | 0.27 | 2.2 |
| Sierra Leone | 12,667 | 0.12 | 1.0 |
| Slovak Republic | 20,893 | 0.19 | 7.0 |
| Slovenia | 18,956 | 0.18 | 3.0 |
| Solomon Islands | 518 | ** | 0.1 |
| Somalia | 10,506 | 0.10 | 1.0 |
| Sri Lanka | 44,784 | 0.42 | 4.0 |
| Sudan | 23,689 | 0.22 | 1.3 |
| Swaziland | 11,073 | 0.10 | 0.4 |
| Syrian Arab Republic | 7,651 | 0.07 | 1.2 |
| Tajikistan | 20,568 | 0.19 | 0.5 |
| Tanzania | 34,943 | 0.33 | 2.1 |

| Member[1] | Number of votes | Percentage of total | Subscriptions and contributions committed |
|---|---|---|---|
| Thailand | 44,784 | 0.42 | $      4.3 |
| Togo | 22,455 | 0.21 | 1.0 |
| Tonga | 11,380 | 0.11 | 0.1 |
| Trinidad and Tobago | 770 | 0.01 | 1.6 |
| Tunisia | 2,793 | 0.03 | 1.9 |
| Turkey | 70,837 | 0.66 | 76.3 |
| Uganda | 22,438 | 0.21 | 2.2 |
| Uzbekistan | 746 | 0.01 | 1.5 |
| Vanuatu | 13,821 | 0.13 | 0.2 |
| Vietnam | 8,889 | 0.08 | 1.9 |
| Western Samoa | 13,061 | 0.12 | 0.1 |
| Yemen, Republic of | 33,296 | 0.31 | 2.0 |
| Zaire | 12,164 | 0.11 | 3.8 |
| Zambia | 26,868 | 0.25 | 3.4 |
| Zimbabwe | 10,657 | 0.10 | 5.0 |
| Subtotal Part II Members [3] | 4,120,901 | 38.41 | 2,956.0 |
| Total—June 30, 1996 [2,3] | 10,728,072 | 100.00 | $91,413.0 |
| Total—June 30, 1995 [2,4] | 10,192,107 | | $93,487.5 |

\*  *Indicates amounts less than $0.05 million.*
\*\* *Indicates amounts less than 0.005 percent.*

**NOTES**

*1. See Notes to Special Purpose Financial Statements—Note A for an explanation of the two categories of membership.*
*2. $512 million of Switzerland's subscription and contribution have not been included in the Statements of Sources and Applications of Development Resources at June 30, 1996 and June 30, 1995 since this represents the difference between the total cofinancing grants of $580 million provided by Switzerland directly to the IDA borrowers as cofinancing grants between the fourth and the ninth replenishments of the IDA resources, and the July 1992 contribution by Switzerland of $68 million.*
*3. May differ from the sum of individual figures shown because of rounding.*
*4. See Notes to Special Purpose Financial Statements—Note A for reclassifications.*

**The Notes to Special Purpose Financial Statements are an integral part of these Statements.**

## NOTE A—ORGANIZATION, OPERATIONS AND SIGNIFICANT ACCOUNTING AND RELATED POLICIES

### PURPOSE AND AFFILIATED ORGANIZATIONS

The International Development Association (IDA) is an international organization established on September 24, 1960 to promote economic development in the less developed areas of the world included in IDA's membership by providing financing on concessionary terms. IDA has three affiliated organizations, the International Bank for Reconstruction and Development (IBRD), the International Finance Corporation (IFC), and the Multilateral Investment Guarantee Agency (MIGA). The principal purpose of the IBRD is to promote the economic development of its member countries, primarily by providing loans and related technical assistance for specific projects and for programs of economic reform in developing member countries. IFC's purpose is to encourage the growth of productive private enterprises in its member countries through loans and equity investments in such enterprises without a member's guarantee. MIGA was established to encourage the flow of investments for productive purposes among member countries and, in particular, to developing member countries by providing guarantees against noncommercial risks for foreign investment in its developing member countries.

*Special Fund:* On October 26, 1982, IDA established the Special Fund constituted by funds contributed by members of IDA and administered by IDA to supplement the regular resources available for lending by IDA. On May 31, 1996, the Special Fund was terminated and all its assets, liabilities and capital were transferred to IDA. On June 26, 1996, the Board of Governors approved the allocation of voting rights in respect of contributions to the Special Fund, to be reflected in the general voting rights adjustment of IDA's Eleventh Replenishment. Voting rights will be adjusted upon the effectiveness of IDA's Eleventh Replenishment.

### SUMMARY OF SIGNIFICANT ACCOUNTING AND RELATED POLICIES

Due to the nature and organization of IDA, these financial statements have been prepared for the specific purpose of reflecting the sources and applications of member subscriptions and are not intended to be a presentation in accordance with generally accepted accounting principles in the United States or with International Accounting Standards. These special purpose financial statements have been prepared to comply with Article VI, Section 11 (a) of the Articles of Agreement of IDA.

IDA's special purpose financial statements are prepared in accordance with the accounting policies outlined below.

### *Reclassifications*

Certain reclassifications of the prior year's information have been made to conform to the current year's presentation. In prior years, the Special Fund was presented separately in the Special Purpose Financial Statements. The prior year's IDA balances have been restated to include the Special Fund at June 30, 1995 due to the Special Fund termination during fiscal year 1996. The effect has been to increase the following in IDA's accounts:

In millions

| | Special Fund | |
| --- | --- | --- |
| | May 31, 1996 (Prior to transfer) | June 30, 1995 |
| **Statement of Sources and Applications of Development Resources** | | |
| **Applications of Development Resources** | | |
| Cash and investments immediately available for disbursement | | |
| Due from banks | $359 | $ 1 |
| Obligations of banks and other financial institutions | — | 333 |
| Net resources available for development activities | 359 | 334 |
| Total application of development resources | $359 | $334 |
| **Sources of Development Resources** | | |
| Member subscriptions and contributions | | |
| Unrestricted | $203 | $203 |
| Subscriptions and contributions committed | 203 | 203 |
| Subscriptions and contributions paid in | 203 | 203 |
| Accumulated surplus | 156 | 131 |
| Total sources of development resources | $359 | $334 |

### Basis of Accounting

IDA's special purpose financial statements are prepared on the accrual basis of accounting for development credit income, investment income, and admini-strative expenses. That is, the effects of transactions and other events are recognized when they occur (and not as cash or its equivalent is received or paid), and they are recorded in the accounting records and reported in the financial statements of the periods to which they relate.

### Translation of Currencies

IDA's special purpose financial statements are expressed in terms of U.S. dollars solely for the purpose of summarizing IDA's financial position and the results of its operations for the convenience of its members and other interested parties.

IDA is an international organization that conducts its business in the currencies of all of its members. Development resources and sources of development resources are translated at market rates of exchange at the end of the accounting period, except Member Subscriptions and Contributions, which are translated in the manner described below. Income and expenses are translated at the market rates of exchange at the dates on which they are recognized or at an average of the market rates of exchange in effect during each month. Translation adjustments relating to the revaluation of development credits denominated in Special Drawing Rights (SDRs) are charged or credited to Cumulative Translation Adjustment on Development Credits. Other translation adjustments are charged or credited to the Accumulated Surplus.

### Member Subscriptions and Contributions

#### Recognition

Member Subscriptions and Contributions for each IDA replenishment are recorded in full as Subscriptions and Contributions Committed upon effectiveness of the relevant replenishment. Replenishments become effective when IDA has received commitments from members for subscriptions and contributions of a specified portion of the full replenishment. Amounts not yet paid in, at the date of effectiveness, are recorded as Subscriptions and Contributions Receivable and shown as a reduction of Subscriptions and Contributions Committed. These receivables come due throughout the replenishment period (generally three years) in accordance with an agreed maturity schedule. The actual payment of receivables when they become due from certain members is conditional upon the respective member's budgetary appropriation processes.

The Subscriptions and Contributions Receivable are settled through payment of cash or nonnegotiable, noninterest-bearing demand notes. If the receivable is settled in cash, the cash is recorded in Cash and Investments Not Immediately Available for Disburse-

ment until such time as it becomes available in accordance with the replenishment agreement. The notes are encashed by IDA as provided in the relevant replenishment resolution over the disbursement period of the credits committed under the replenishment, and the cash received is recorded in Cash and Investments Immediately Available for Disbursement.

In certain replenishments, members have had the option of paying all of their subscription and contribution amount in cash before it becomes due and receiving a discount. In these cases, IDA and the member agree that IDA will invest the cash and retain the income. The related subscription and contribution is recorded at the full undiscounted amount. The cash and investments are recorded in Cash and Investments Not Immediately Available for Disbursement until the date when it would have become due, at which time it becomes available. The discount is recorded in Other Resources and amortized over the projected disbursement period for the replenishment's credits.

Under the Articles of Agreement and the arrangements governing replenishments, IDA must take appropriate steps to ensure that over a reasonable period of time the resources provided by donors for lending by IDA are used on an approximately pro rata basis. As discussed in the previous paragraph, donors sometimes contribute resources substantially ahead of their pro rata share. Unless otherwise agreed, IDA does not disburse these funds ahead of donors' pro rata shares. Cash and Investments Not Immediately Available for Disbursement represents the difference between the amount contributed and the amount available for disbursements on a pro rata basis.

Transfers to IDA from IBRD are recorded as Sources of Development Resources and are receivable upon approval by IBRD's Board of Governors.

For the purposes of its financial resources, the membership of IDA is divided into two categories: (1) Part I members, which make payments of subscriptions and contributions provided to IDA in convertible currencies that may be freely used or exchanged by IDA in its operations, and (2) Part II members make payments of 10 percent of their initial subscriptions in freely convertible currencies, and the remaining 90 percent of their initial subscriptions, and all additional subscriptions and contributions in their own currencies or in freely convertible currencies. Certain Part II members provide a portion of their subscriptions and contributions in the same manner as mentioned in (1) above. IDA's Articles of Agreement and subsequent replenishment agreements provide that the currency of any Part II member paid in by it may not be used by IDA for projects financed by IDA and located outside the territory of the member except by agreement between the member and IDA. These subscriptions of Part II members are recorded as Restricted Cash and Notes.

## Valuation

The subscriptions and contributions provided through the third replenishment are expressed in terms of "U.S. dollars of the weight and fineness in effect on January 1, 1960" (1960 dollars). Following the abolition of gold as a common denominator of the monetary system and the repeal of the provision of the U.S. law defining the par value of the U.S. dollar in terms of gold, the pre-existing basis for translating 1960 dollars into current dollars or any other currency disappeared. The Executive Directors of IDA have decided, with effect on that date and until such time as the relevant provisions of the Articles of Agreement are amended, that the words "U.S. dollars of the weight and fineness in effect on January 1, 1960" in Article II, Section 2(b) of the Articles of Agreement of IDA are interpreted to mean the SDR introduced by the International Monetary Fund as the SDR was valued in terms of U.S. dollars immediately before the introduction of the basket method of valuing the SDR on July 1, 1974, such value being equal to $1.20635 for one SDR (the 1974 SDR), and have also decided to apply the same standard of value to amounts expressed in 1960 dollars in the relevant resolutions of the Board of Governors.

The subscriptions and contributions provided through the third replenishment are expressed on the basis of the 1974 SDR. Prior to the decision of the Executive Directors, IDA had valued these subscriptions and contributions on the basis of the SDR at the current market value of the SDR.

The subscriptions and contributions provided under the fourth replenishment and thereafter are expressed in members' currencies or SDRs and are payable in members' currencies. Beginning July 1, 1986, subscriptions and contributions made available for disbursement in cash to IDA are translated at market rates of exchange on the dates they were made available. Prior to that date, subscriptions and contributions that had been disbursed or converted into other currencies were translated at market rates of exchange on dates of disbursement or conversion. Subscriptions and contributions not yet available for disbursements are translated at market rates of exchange at the end of the accounting period.

Article IV, Section 2(a) and (b) of IDA's Articles of Agreement provides for maintenance of value payments on account of the local currency portion of the initial subscription whenever the par value of the member's currency or its foreign exchange value has, in the opinion of IDA, depreciated or appreciated to a significant extent within the member's territories, so long as and to the extent that such currency shall not have been initially disbursed or exchanged for the currency of another member. The provisions of Article IV, Section 2(a) and (b) have by agreement been extended to cover additional subscriptions and contributions of IDA through the third replenishment, but are not applicable to those of the fourth and subsequent replenishments.

The Executive Directors decided on June 30, 1987 that settlements of maintenance of value, which would result from the resolution of the valuation issue on the basis of the 1974 SDR, would be deferred until the Executive Directors decide to resume such settlements. These amounts are shown as Deferred Amounts Receivable to Maintain Value of Currency Holdings.

### Development Credits

All development credits are made to or guaranteed by member governments or to the government of a territory of a member (except for development credits that have been made to regional development banks for the benefit of members or territories of members of IDA). In order to qualify for lending on IDA terms, a country's per capita income must be below a certain level, and the country may have only limited or no creditworthiness for IBRD lending. Development credits carry a service charge of 0.75 percent, generally have 35- or 40-year final maturities and a 10-year grace period for principal payments. Development credits are carried in the financial statements at the full face amount of the borrowers' outstanding obligations.

It is the policy of IDA to place in nonaccrual status all development credits made to a member government or to the government of a territory of a member if principal or charges with respect to any such development credit are overdue by more than six months, unless IDA management determines that the overdue amount will be collected in the immediate future. In addition, if loans by IBRD to a member government are placed in nonaccrual status, all development credits to that member government will also be placed in nonaccrual status by IDA. On the date a member's development credits are placed in nonaccrual status, charges that had been accrued on development credits outstanding to the member that remained unpaid are deducted from the income from development credits of the current period. Charges on nonaccruing development credits are included in income only to the extent that payments have actually been received by IDA. On the date a member pays in full all overdue amounts to IBRD and IDA, the member's credits emerge from nonaccrual status, its eligibility for new credits is restored, and all overdue charges (including those from prior years) are recognized as income from development credits in the current period. If collectibility risk is considered to be particularly high at the time of arrears clearance, or if IBRD or IDA refinances/reschedules nonaccruing loans or credits to a member so that no debt-service payments remain overdue, its loans or credits would not automatically emerge from nonaccrual status, even though its eligibility for new loans or credits would have been restored. The previously overdue interest and other charges would not be recognized as income in the period the refinancing/

rescheduling occurs. After a suitable period of payment performance has passed from the time of arrears clearance, a decision on the restoration of accrual status would be made on a case-by-case basis.

In fulfilling its mission, IDA makes concessional loans to the poorest countries; therefore there is significant credit risk in the portfolio of development credits. Management continually monitors this credit risk. However, no provision for credit losses has been established because it is not practicable to determine such an amount in view of the nature and maturity structure of the credit portfolio. Should actual losses occur, they would be charged against IDA's Accumulated Surplus. To date, IDA has not suffered any losses on receivables from development credits.

The repayment obligations of IDA's development credits funded from resources through the fifth replenishment are expressed in the development credit agreements in terms of 1960 dollars. In June 1987, the Executive Directors decided to value those development credits at the rate of $1.20635 per 1960 dollar on a permanent basis. Development credits funded from resources provided under the sixth replenishment and thereafter are denominated in SDRs; the principal amounts disbursed under such development credits are to be repaid in currency amounts currently equivalent to the SDRs disbursed.

### Investments

IDA carries its investment securities and related financial instruments at market value. Both realized and unrealized gains and losses are included in Income from Investments.

### NOTE B—INVESTMENTS

As part of its overall portfolio management strategy, IDA invests in government and agency obligations, time deposits, and related financial instruments with off-balance sheet risk including futures, forward contracts, covered forward contracts, options, and short sales.

*Government and Agency Obligations:* These obligations include marketable bonds, notes, and other obligations. Obligations issued or unconditionally guaranteed by governments of countries require a minimum credit rating of AA if denominated in a currency other than the home currency of the issuer; otherwise no rating is required. Obligations issued by an agency or instrumentality of a government of a country, a multilateral organization, or any other official entity require a credit rating of AAA.

*Time Deposits:* Time deposits include certificates of deposit, bankers' acceptances, and other obligations issued or unconditionally guaranteed by banks and other financial institutions.

*Futures and Forwards:* Futures and forward contracts are contracts for delayed delivery of securities or money market instruments in which the seller agrees to make delivery at a specified future date of a specified instrument, at a specified price or yield. Futures contracts are traded on regulated United States and international exchanges. IDA generally closes out most open positions in futures contracts prior to maturity. Therefore, cash receipts or payments are mostly limited to the change in market value of the futures contracts. Futures contracts generally entail daily settlement of the net cash margin.

*Covered Forwards:* Covered forwards are agreements in which cash in one currency is converted into a different currency and, simultaneously, a forward exchange agreement is executed providing for a future exchange of the two currencies in order to recover the currency converted.

*Options:* Options are contracts that allow the holder of the option to purchase or sell a financial instrument at a specified price within a specified period of time from or to the seller of the option. The purchaser of an option pays a premium at the outset to the seller of the option, who then bears the risk of an unfavorable change in the price of the financial instrument underlying the option. IDA only invests in exchange-traded options. The initial price of an option contract is equal to the premium paid by the purchaser and is significantly less than the contract or notional amount. IDA does not write uncovered option contracts.

*Short Sales:* Short sales are sales of securities not held in IDA's portfolio at the time of the sale. IDA must purchase the security at a later date and bears the risk that the market value of the security will move adversely between the time of the sale and the time the security must be delivered.

*Repurchase and Resale Agreements and Securities Loans:* Repurchase agreements are contracts under which a party sells securities and simultaneously agrees to repurchase the same securities at a specified future date at a fixed price. The reverse of this transaction is called a resale agreement. Securities loans are contracts under which securities are lent up to a future specified date at a fixed price.

A summary of IDA's investment portfolio by instrument for Investments Immediately Available for Disbursement at June 30, 1996 and June 30, 1995 is as follows:

In millions

|  | 1996 | | | 1995 | | |
|---|---|---|---|---|---|---|
|  | Carrying Value | Average Daily Balance During the Fiscal Year | Net Gains (Losses) for the Fiscal Year | Carrying Value | Average Daily Balance During the Fiscal Year | Net Gains (Losses) for the Fiscal Year |
| Government and agency obligations | $2,282 | $1,900 | $(6) | $1,642 | $1,334 | $19 |
| Time deposits | 2,257 | 2,309 | — | 2,585 | 1,906 | — |
| Futures and forwards | 1 | 1 | 4 | 1 | 1 | (1) |
| Covered forwards | * | (1) | — | 5 | 1 | — |
| Options | * | * | (1) | * | * | * |
| Resale agreements | 204 | 629 | — | 208 | 415 | — |
|  | $4,744 | $4,838 | $(3) | $4,441 | $3,657 | $18 |
| Short Sales | $ (34) | $ (32) | $— | $ (27) | $ (46) | $— |
| Repurchase agreements and Securities loans | (319) | (281) | — | (64) | (102) | — |

*Less than $0.5 million*

A summary of IDA's investment portfolio by instrument for Investments Not Immediately Available for Disbursement at June 30, 1996 and June 30, 1995 is as follows:

In millions

|  | 1996 | | | 1995 | | |
|---|---|---|---|---|---|---|
|  | Carrying Value | Average Daily Balance During the Fiscal Year | Net Gains (Losses) for the Fiscal Year | Carrying Value | Average Daily Balance During the Fiscal Year | Net Gains for the Fiscal Year |
| Government and agency obligations | $1,320 | $ 963 | $(1) | $ 937 | $562 | $48 |
| Time deposits | 272 | 327 | — | 402 | 393 | — |
| Futures and forwards | 1 | 1 | 4 | 1 | * | * |
| Covered forwards | * | * | — | — | * | — |
| Options | * | * | * | * | * | * |
| Resale agreements | 93 | 93 | — | — | 22 | — |
|  | $1,686 | $1,384 | $ 3 | $1,340 | $977 | $48 |
| Short Sales | $ (24) | $ (8) | $— | $ — | $ * | $— |
| Repurchase agreements and Securities loans | (33) | (138) | — | (145) | (63) | — |

*Less than $0.5 million*

A summary of the currency composition of Investments Immediately Available for Disbursement and Not Immediately Available for Disbursement at June 30, 1996 and June 30, 1995, is as follows:

In millions of U.S. dollar equivalents

| | 1996 | | | 1995 | | |
|---|---|---|---|---|---|---|
| | Immediately available for disbursement | Not immediately available for disbursement | Total | Immediately available for disbursement | Not immediately available for disbursement | Total |
| Canadian dollars | $ — | $ — | $ — | $ 127 | $ — | $ 127 |
| Deutsche mark | 1,739 | 321 | 2,060 | 1,587 | 236 | 1,823 |
| French francs | 387 | 167 | 554 | 381 | 123 | 504 |
| Italian lire | * | — | * | 95 | — | 95 |
| Japanese yen | 542 | 299 | 841 | 623 | 289 | 912 |
| Pound sterling | 425 | 146 | 571 | 288 | 95 | 383 |
| Swedish kronor | — | — | — | 59 | — | 59 |
| U.S. dollars | 1,651 | 753 | 2,404 | 1,243 | 597 | 1,840 |
| Other currencies | * | — | * | 38 | — | 38 |
| | $4,744 | $1,686 | $6,430 | $4,441 | $1,340 | $5,781 |

* Less than $0.5 million.

For the purpose of risk management, IDA is party to a variety of financial instruments, certain of which involve elements of credit risk in excess of the amount reflected in the Statement of Sources and Applications of Development Resources. Credit risk represents the maximum potential accounting loss due to possible nonperformance by obligors and counterparties under the terms of the contracts. Additionally, the nature of the instruments involves contract value and notional principal amounts that are not reflected in the basic financial statements. For both on- and off-balance sheet securities, IDA limits trading to a list of authorized dealers and counterparties. Credit limits have been established for each counterparty by type of instrument and maturity category.

The credit risk exposure and contract value, as applicable, of these financial instruments at June 30, 1996 and June 30, 1995 are given below:

In millions

| | 1996 | 1995 |
|---|---|---|
| Futures and Forwards | | |
| Long position | $ 759 | $359 |
| Short position | 2,840 | 561 |
| Credit exposure due to potential nonperformance by counterparties | 7 | 2 |
| Options | | |
| Long position | 179 | 35 |
| Short position | 36 | — |
| Covered forward contracts | | |
| Credit exposure due to potential nonperformance by counterparties | 1 | 5 |

## NOTE C—MEMBER SUBSCRIPTIONS AND CONTRIBUTIONS

### Subscriptions and Contributions Receivable:

The payment of subscriptions and contributions is conditional on the members' budgetary processes. At June 30, 1996, receivables from subscriptions and contributions was $1,517 million ($6,739 million—June 30, 1995) of which $945 million ($475 million—June 30, 1995) was due and $572 million ($6,264 million—June 30, 1995) was not yet due.

Subscriptions and contributions due at June 30, 1996 were as follows:

In millions

| Amounts initially due on | |
|---|---|
| July 1, 1995 through June 30, 1996 | $944 |
| July 1, 1994 through June 30, 1995 | 1 |
| July 1, 1993 through June 30, 1994 | — |
| July 1, 1993 and earlier | * |
| Total | $945 |

* Less than $0.5 million.

Subscriptions and contributions not yet due at June 30, 1996 will become due as follows:

In millions

| Period | |
|---|---|
| July 1, 1996 through June 30, 1997 | $491 |
| July 1, 1997 through June 30, 1998 | 11 |
| Thereafter | 70 |
| Total | $572 |

*Eleventh Replenishment*: On June 26, 1996, the Board of Governors of IDA adopted resolutions authorizing the Eleventh Replenishment of IDA's resources. The Eleventh Replenishment provides IDA with resources to fund credits and grants committed during the period July 1, 1996 to June 30, 1999. The total amount of donor contributions during this period, including supplementary contributions provided by certain members, is equivalent to SDR 6,894 million. The Eleventh Replenishment will become effective when IDA has received commitments for subscriptions and contributions of SDR 3,746 million. As part of the Eleventh Replenishment, an Interim Trust Fund consisting of donor contributions equivalent to SDR 2,211 million will be established and administered by IDA.

*Interim Trust Fund*: The Interim Trust Fund will be administered by IDA to help fund operations during the period July 1, 1996 to June 30, 1997 and contributions will have a separate legal, procurement and accounting status. The Interim Trust Fund will become effective when contributions totaling SDR 400 million from at least seven donors have been received. Credits financed by the Interim Trust Fund will be made on the same terms and conditions as those of IDA credits except for procurement and decision-making. Service charges paid by borrowers on Interim Trust Fund credits will be received by IDA to compensate it for its services as administrator. The Interim Trust Fund will be terminated when the credits it financed have been substantially disbursed. Upon termination, its assets and liabilities will transfer to IDA.

*Membership:* In February 1993 the Socialist Federal Republic of Yugoslavia (SFRY) ceased to be a member of IDA due to the cessation of its membership in IBRD. Four of the five successor Republics—Bosnia and Herzegovina, the Republics of Croatia and Slovenia, and the former Yugoslav Republic of Macedonia—have since become members of IDA. At June 30, 1996, the subscription and contributions allocated to the other successor country, the Federal Republic of Yugoslavia (Serbia and Montenegro), are included under Payments on Account of Pending Membership.

In May 1992 Switzerland became a member of IDA. Before that date Switzerland had contributed to IDA an equivalent of $51 million. As agreed between the Swiss Confederation and IDA, these grant contributions were converted to an IDA subscription. Further, during the commitment periods between the fourth and the ninth replenishments of IDA resources, Switzerland had cofinanced projects by making available to IDA borrowers untied grants in the aggregate amount of Swiss francs 1,055 million (historical U.S. dollar amount of $580 million). In July 1992, as agreed between the Swiss Confederation and IDA, these grant contributions were converted to an IDA subscription and contribution when Switzerland contributed a further $68 million, representing the present value of future reflows of the cofinancing grants if they had been made through IDA on IDA's repayment terms. At

June 30, 1996, $512 million ($512 million—June 30, 1995), representing the difference between the total cofinancing grants of $580 million and the present value of future reflows of $68 million, have not been included in the Member Subscriptions and Contributions in the Statement of Sources and Applications of Development Resources.

## NOTE D—TRANSFERS FROM IBRD

IDA has received from IBRD aggregate transfers totaling $4,823 million through June 30, 1996 ($4,573 million—June 30, 1995).

## NOTE E—DEVELOPMENT CREDITS

At June 30, 1996, no development credits payable to IDA other than those referred to in the following paragraphs were overdue by more than three months.

At June 30, 1996, the development credits made to or guaranteed by certain member countries with an aggregate principal balance outstanding of $3,183 million ($3,376 million—June 30, 1995), of which $95 million ($65 million—June 30, 1995) was overdue, were in nonaccrual status. At such date, overdue charges in respect of these development credits totaled $86 million ($66 million—June 30, 1995). If these development credits had not been in nonaccrual status, income from development credits for the fiscal year ended June 30, 1996 would have been higher by $24 million ($24 million—June 30, 1995), which is net of charges received from such members during the year. A summary of member countries with credits or guarantees in nonaccrual status follows:

**In millions**

| | June 30, 1996 | | |
| Borrower | Principal outstanding | Principal and charges overdue | Nonaccrual since |
|---|---|---|---|
| *With overdues* | | | |
| Afghanistan | $ 75 | $ 8 | June 1992 |
| Liberia | 106 | 15 | April 1988 |
| Somalia | 423 | 33 | July 1991 |
| Sudan | 1,247 | 59 | January 1994 |
| Syrian Arab Republic | 44 | 11 | April 1988 |
| Zaire | 1,288 | 55 | November 1993 |
| Total | 3,183 | 181 | |
| | | | |
| *Without overdues* | | | |
| Bosnia and Herzegovina[a] | — | — | September 1992 |
| Total | $3,183 | $181 | |

a. At June 30, 1996, Bosnia and Herzegovina had $10 million in undisbursed development credits.

During the fiscal year ended June 30, 1996, no development credits came out of nonaccrual status. For the fiscal year ended June 30, 1995, the increase in income from development credits due to countries coming out of nonaccrual status was $7 million.

Under a program established in September 1988, a portion of principal repayments to IDA is allocated on an annual basis to provide supplemental IDA credits to IDA-eligible countries that are no longer able to borrow on IBRD terms but have outstanding IBRD loans approved prior to September 1988 and have in place an IDA-supported structural adjustment program. Such supplemental IDA credits are allocated to countries that meet specified conditions, in proportion to each country's interest payments due that year on its pre-September 1988 IBRD loans. To be eligible for such IDA supplemental credits, a member country must meet IDA's eligibility criteria for lending, must be ineligible for IBRD lending, and must not have had an IBRD loan approved within the last twelve months. To receive a supplemental credit from the program, a member country cannot be more than sixty days overdue on its debt-service payments to IBRD or IDA.

A summary of cumulative IDA credits committed and disbursed under this program from inception at June 30, 1996 and June 30, 1995 is given below:

In millions

|  | 1996 | 1995 |
|---|---|---|
| Commitments | $1,379 | $1,179 |
| Less: Undisbursed | 52 | 51 |
| Disbursed and outstanding | $1,327 | $1,128 |

## NOTE F—FAIR VALUE OF FINANCIAL INSTRUMENTS

*Investments:* Since IDA carries its investments at market value, the carrying amount represents the fair value of the portfolio. These fair values are based on quoted market prices, where available. If quoted market prices are not available, fair values are based on quoted market prices of comparable instruments. The fair value of short-term financial instruments approximates their carrying value.

*Development Credits:* IDA development credits have a significant grant element because of the concessional nature of IDA's terms. Discounting IDA's credits using the standard 10 percent discount rate of the Development Assistance Committee (DAC) of the Organization for Economic Cooperation and Development provides an estimate for the grant element of IDA credits. Using the 10 percent DAC discount rate indicates that the typical IDA credit contains a grant element of 75 percent to 80 percent of the nominal credit amount

at the time the credit is committed. This grant element calculation considers interest rates, maturity structures, and grace periods for the credits. It does not consider credit risk, portfolio seasoning, multilateral and sovereign credit preferences, and other risks or indicators that would be relevant in calculating fair value. Estimating the impact of these factors is not practicable. However, the fair value of Total Development Credits is substantially lower than the $97,450 million reflected on the Statement of Sources and Applications of Development Resources.

## NOTE G—INCOME AND EXPENSES

IDA pays a management fee to IBRD representing its share of the administrative expenses incurred by IBRD. In February 1995, the Executive Directors authorized expenditures for costs associated with planned staff reductions. During fiscal year 1995, IBRD charged to expense $131 million of which $53 million was charged to IDA through the Management Fee Charged by IBRD for the fiscal year ended June 30, 1995. The reductions are designed to improve IBRD's and IDA's efficiency, adjust the staffing skills mix and thereby better meet client demands. The planned staff reductions are expected to lower future years' administrative expenses by an amount greater than the associated cost. On October 31, 1995, the program for planned staff reductions was brought to a close. Under this program 608 staff were identified as redundant at a total cost of $112 million. Of the difference of $19 million, $8 million has been allocated to IDA through the Management Fee Charged by IBRD for the fiscal year ended June 30, 1996.

## NOTE H—TRUST FUNDS

IDA, alone or jointly with IBRD, administers on behalf of donors, including members, their agencies, and other entities, funds restricted for specific uses, which include the cofinancing of IDA lending projects, debt reduction operations for IDA members, technical assistance for borrowers including feasibility studies and project preparation, global and regional programs, and research and training programs. These funds are placed in trust and are not included in the development resources of IDA. At June 30, 1996 and June 30, 1995, the distribution of trust fund assets by executing agent is as follows:

|  | 1996 | | 1995 | |
|---|---|---|---|---|
|  | Total Fiduciary Assets (in millions) | Number of Trust Fund Accounts | Total Fiduciary Assets (in millions) | Number of Trust Fund Accounts |
| IDA Executed | $235 | 454 | $263 | 445 |
| Recipient Executed | 537 | 384 | 404 | 280 |
| Total | $772 | 838 | $667 | 725 |

The responsibilities of IDA under these arrangements vary and range from services normally provided under its own lending projects to full project implementation including procurement of goods and services. IDA receives fees for administering trust funds as a reduction of the Management Fee Charged by IBRD. During the fiscal year ended June 30, 1996, the IDA received $10 million ($12 million—June 30, 1995) as fees for administering trust funds.

# REPORT OF INDEPENDENT ACCOUNTANTS ON SPECIAL PURPOSE FINANCIAL STATEMENTS

| Price Waterhouse | The Hague | New York |
|---|---|---|
| (International Firm) | Beijing | Tokyo |
| | Hong Kong | Washington |
| | London | |

*Price Waterhouse*

July 31, 1996

President and Board of Governors
 International Development Association

We have audited the special purpose Statement of Sources and Applications of Development Resources as of June 30, 1996 and 1995, the Summary Statement of Development Credits and the Statement of Voting Power, and Subscriptions and Contributions as of June 30, 1996, and the related special purpose Statements of Changes in Accumulated Surplus and of Cash Flows for the years ended June 30, 1996 and 1995, expressed in terms of United States dollars, of the International Development Association (IDA), which appear on pages 198 through 217 of this Report. These financial statements are the responsibility of management. Our responsibility is to express an opinion on these financial statements based on our audits.

We conducted our audits in accordance with generally accepted auditing standards, including International Standards on Auditing. Those standards require that we plan and perform the audit to obtain reasonable assurance about whether the financial statements are free of material misstatement. An audit includes examining, on a test basis, evidence supporting the amounts and disclosures in the financial statements. An audit also includes assessing the accounting principles used and significant estimates made by management, as well as evaluating the overall financial statement presentation. We believe that our audits provide a reasonable basis for our opinion.

The special purpose financial statements were prepared to reflect the sources and applications of development resources and the development credits, voting power, and subscriptions and contributions of IDA to comply with Article VI, Section 11(a) of the Articles of Agreement of IDA as described in Note A, and are not intended to be a presentation in conformity with generally accepted accounting principles in the United States or with International Accounting Standards.

In our opinion, the special purpose financial statements referred to above present fairly, in all material respects, in terms of United States dollars, the sources and applications of development resources as of June 30, 1996 and 1995, the development credits, voting power, and subscriptions and contributions of IDA at June 30, 1996 and the changes in its accumulated surplus and its cash flows for the years ended June 30, 1996 and 1995, on the basis of accounting described in Note A.

This report is intended solely for the information of the Board of Governors, management and members of IDA. However, under IDA's Articles of Agreement, this report is a matter of public record and its distribution is not limited.

*Price Waterhouse*

*( International Firm )*

| Member | Governor | Alternate |
|---|---|---|
| Afghanistan | Ahmad Rashidi | Mohammad Ehsan |
| Albania | Dylber Vrioni | Edmond Leka |
| Algeria | Ahmed Benbitour | Ali Hamdi |
| Angola | Jose Pedro de Morais | Antonio Gomes Furtado |
| Antigua and Barbuda † | Molwyn Joseph | Ludolph Brown |
| Argentina | Domingo Felipe Cavallo | Roque Benjamin Fernandez |
| Armenia | Vahram Avanessian | Bagrat Asatryan |
| Australia | Peter Costello | Andrew Thomson |
| Austria | Viktor Klima | Hans Dietmar Schweisgut |
| Azerbaijan | Elman Siradjogly Rustamov | Fuad Akhundov |
| | | |
| Bahamas, The † | Hubert A. Ingraham | Ruth Millar |
| Bahrain † | Ibrahim Abdul Karim | Zakaria Ahmed Hejres |
| Bangladesh | Shah A.M.S. Kibria | Muhammad Lutfullahil Majid |
| Barbados † | Owen S. Arthur | Erskine Griffith |
| Belarus † | Nikolai Filippovich Rumas | Nikolai K. Lisai |
| Belgium | Philippe Maystadt | Alfons Verplaetse |
| Belize | Manuel Esquivel | Yvonne S. Hyde |
| Benin | Albert Tevoedjre | Felix Adimi |
| Bhutan | Dorji Tshering | Yeshey Zimba |
| Bolivia | Juan Fernando Candia Castillo | Gonzalo Afcha |
| | | |
| Bosnia and Herzegovina | Hasan Muratovic | Kasim Omicevic |
| Botswana | Festus G. Mogae | O.K. Matambo |
| Brazil | Pedro Sampaio Malan | Gustavo J. Laboissiere Loyola |
| Brunei Darussalam † | Haji Jefri Bolkiah | Ahmad Wally Skinner |
| Bulgaria † | Dimitar Kostov | Mileti Mladenov |
| Burkina Faso | Tertius Zongo | Patrice Nikiema |
| Burundi | Toyi Salvator | Nestor Ntungwanayo |
| Cambodia | Keat Chhon | Sun Chan Thol |
| Cameroon | Justin Ndioro | Esther Dang Belibi |
| Canada | Paul Martin | Huguette Labelle |
| | | |
| Cape Verde | Antonio Gualberto do Rosario | Jose Ulisses Silva |
| Central African Republic | Dogo Nendje Bhe | Emmanuel Dokouna |
| Chad | Nassour Guelendouksia Ouaidou | Hassan Adoum Bakhit |
| Chile | Eduardo Aninat | Jose Pablo Arellano |
| China | Liu Zhongli | Liu Jibin |
| Colombia | Jose Antonio Ocampo | Juan Carlos Ramirez |
| Comoros | Said Youssouf Mondoha | Chabane Abdallah Halifa |
| Congo | Nguila Moungounga-Nkombo | Jean Christophe Boungou Bazika |
| Costa Rica | Francisco de Paula Gutierrez | Rodrigo Bolanos Zamora |
| Côte d'Ivoire | Daniel Kablan Duncan | N'Goran Niamien |

| Member | Governor | Alternate |
|---|---|---|
| Croatia | Bozo Prka | Josip Kulisic |
| Cyprus | Christodoulos Christodoulou | Antonis Malaos |
| Czech Republic | Ivan Kocarnik | Jan Vit |
| Denmark | Poul Nielson | Ellen Margrethe Loj |
| Djibouti | Mohamed Ali Mohamed | Hawa Ahmed Youssouf |
| Dominica | Julius C. Timothy | Gilbert Williams |
| Dominican Republic | Hector Valdez Albizu | Luis Manuel Piantini M. |
| Ecuador | Ivan Andrade Apunte | Jose E. Mantilla |
| Egypt, Arab Rep. of | Atef Mohamed Mohamed Ebeid | Yousef Boutros Ghali |
| El Salvador | Manuel Enrique Hinds | Jose Roberto Orellana Milla |
| | | |
| Equatorial Guinea | Baltazar Engonga Edjo | Antonio Nve Ngu |
| Eritrea | Haile Woldense | Gebreselassie Yosief |
| Estonia † | Mart Opmann | Enn Pant |
| Ethiopia | Sufian Ahmed | Girma Birru |
| Fiji | Berenado Vunibobo | Tevita K. Banuve |
| Finland | Sauli Niinisto | Pekka Haavisto |
| France | Jean Arthuis | Jean Lemierre |
| Gabon | Pierre-Claver Maganga Moussavou | Richard Onouviet |
| Gambia, The | Bala Garba Jahumpa | Alieu M. N'gum |
| Georgia | David Iakobidze | Tengiz Geleishvili |
| | | |
| Germany | Carl-Dieter Spranger | Juergen Stark |
| Ghana | Richard Kwame Peprah | Kwesi Amissah-Arthur |
| Greece | Yannos Papantoniou | Christos Pachtas |
| Grenada | Keith Mitchell | Linus Spencer Thomas |
| Guatemala | Jose Alejandro Arevalo Alburez | Willy W. Zapata Sagastume |
| Guinea | Michel Kamano | Kerfalla Yansane |
| Guinea-Bissau | Rui Dia de Sousa | Francisco Correia, Jr. |
| Guyana | Bharrat Jagdeo | Michael Sheer Chan |
| Haiti | Fred Joseph | Jean Erick Deryce |
| Honduras | Guillermo Bueso | Juan Ferrera |
| | | |
| Hungary | Peter Medgyessy | Almos Kovacs |
| Iceland | Finnur Ingolfsson | Fridrik Sophusson |
| India | P. Chidambaram | Montek Singh Ahluwalia |
| Indonesia | Mar'ie Muhammad | Boediono |
| Iran, Islamic Rep. of | Morteza Mohammad-Khan | Aliakbar Arabmazar |
| Iraq | Issam Rashid Hwaish | Hashim Ali Obaid |
| Ireland | Ruairi Quinn | Paddy Mullarkey |
| Israel | Jacob A. Frenkel | David Brodet |
| Italy | Antonio Fazio | Mario Draghi |
| Jamaica † | Omar Lloyd Davies | Wesley Hughes |

| Member | Governor | Alternate |
|---|---|---|
| Japan | Wataru Kubo | Yasuo Matsushita |
| Jordan | Rima Khalaf Hunaidi | Nabil Ammari |
| Kazakstan | Alexander S. Pavlov | Altai A. Tleuberdin |
| Kenya | W. Musalia Mudavadi | Benjamin Kipkoech Kipkulei |
| Kiribati | Beniamina Tinga | Kaburoro Ruaia |
| Korea, Republic of | Woong-Bae Rha | Kyung Shik Lee |
| Kuwait | Nasser Abdullah Al-Roudhan | Bader Meshari Al-Humaidhi |
| Kyrgyz Republic | Kemelbek Nanaev | Askar I. Sarygulov |
| Lao People's Dem. Rep. | Xaysomphone Phomvihane | Pany Yathotou |
| Latvia | Aivars Guntis Kreituss | Guntars Krasts |
| | | |
| Lebanon | Fuad A.B. Siniora | Nabil Al-Jisr |
| Lesotho | Leketekete Victor Ketso | E.M. Matekane |
| Liberia | Francis M. Carbah | Lasanah V. Kromah |
| Libya | Mohamed A. Bait El Mal | Bashir Ali Khallat |
| Lithuania † | Algimantas Krizinauskas | Jonas Niaura |
| Luxembourg | Marc Fischbach | Yves Mersch |
| Macedonia, former Yugoslav Republic of | Ljube Trpevski | Taki Fiti |
| Madagascar | Jean Claude Raherimanjato | Mamy Rabemila |
| Malawi | Aleke K. Banda | Alex C. Gomani |
| Malaysia | Anwar bin Ibrahim | Clifford Francis Herbert |
| | | |
| Maldives | Fathulla Jameel | Adam Maniku |
| Mali | Soumaila Cisse | Ibrahima Konate |
| Malta † | John Dalli | Albert A. Attard |
| Marshall Islands | Ruben R. Zackhras | Michael Konelios |
| Mauritania | Mohamed Ould Amar | Mohamed Lemine Ould Deidah |
| Mauritius | Rajkeswur Purryag | Dharam Dev Manraj |
| Mexico | Guillermo Ortiz | Jose Julian Sidaoui |
| Micronesia, Federated States of | John Ehsa | Sebastian L. Anefal |
| Moldova | Valeriu Sergiu Kitsan | Dumitru Ursu |
| Mongolia | Demchigjavyn Molomjamts | Erdeniin Byambajav |
| | | |
| Morocco | Mohamed Kabbaj | Abdelfettah Benmansour |
| Mozambique | Adriano Afonso Maleiane | Luisa Dias Diogo |
| Myanmar | Win Tin | Antt Kyaw |
| Namibia † | Saara Kuugongelwa | Godfrey Gaoseb |
| Nepal | Ram S. Mahat | Ram Binod Bhattarai |
| Netherlands | Gerrit Zalm | J.P. Pronk |
| New Zealand | Murray Horn | John Whitehead |
| Nicaragua | Emilio Pereira Alegria | Jose Evenor Taboada Arana |
| Niger | Almoustapha Soumaila | Halidou Badje |
| Nigeria | Anthony A. Ani | Gidado Idris |

| Member | Governor | Alternate |
|---|---|---|
| Norway | Sigbjoern Johnsen | Kari Nordheim-Larsen |
| Oman | Ahmed Bin Abdulnabi Macki | Mohammed Bin Musa Al Yousef |
| Pakistan | V.A. Jafarey | Javed Talat |
| Panama | Guillermo O. Chapman, Jr. | Olmedo Miranda, Jr. |
| Papua New Guinea | Christopher Haiveta | Gerea Aopi |
| Paraguay | Carlos Alberto Facetti Masulli | Jose Ernesto Buttner Limprich |
| Peru | Jorge Camet Dickmann | Alfredo Jalilie Awapara |
| Philippines | Roberto F. de Ocampo | Gabriel C. Singson |
| Poland | Hanna Gronkiewicz-Waltz | Witold Kozinski |
| Portugal | Antonio de Sousa Franco | Fernando Teixeira dos Santos |
| | | |
| Qatar † | Mohammed Bin Khalifa Al-Thani | Abdullah Bin Khalid Al-Attiyah |
| Romania † | Florin Georgescu | Vladimir Soare |
| Russian Federation | Vladimir V. Kadannikov | Yevgeni Yasin |
| Rwanda | Marc Rugenera | Pierre Claver Gashumba |
| St. Kitts and Nevis | Denzil Douglas | Timothy Harris |
| St. Lucia | Vaughan Lewis | Zenith James |
| St. Vincent and the Grenadines | James F. Mitchell | Maurice Edwards |
| São Tomé and Principe | Joaquim Rafael Branco | Maria das Neves Batista de Sousa |
| Saudi Arabia | Ibrahim A. Al-Assaf | Jobarah Al-Suraisry |
| Senegal | Papa Ousmane Sakho | Awa Thiongane |
| | | |
| Seychelles † | Danielle de St. Jorre | Emmanuel Faure |
| Sierra Leone | Thaimu Bangura | Samura Kamara |
| Singapore † | Richard Hu Tsu Tau | Ngiam Tong Dow |
| Slovak Republic | Sergej Kozlik | Vladimir Masar |
| Slovenia | Mitja Gaspari | Bozo Jasovic |
| Solomon Islands | Christopher Columbus Abe | Snyder Rini |
| Somalia | (vacant) | (vacant) |
| South Africa | Trevor Andrew Manuel | Gill Marcus |
| Spain | Rodrigo de Rato Figaredo | Cristobal Montoro Romero |
| Sri Lanka | Chandrika Bandaranaika Kamaratunga | B.C. Perera |
| | | |
| Sudan | Abdel Wahab Osman | Abdalla Hassan Ahmed |
| Suriname † | Humphrey S. Hildenberg | Stanley B. Ramsaran |
| Swaziland | Themba N. Masuku | Musa D. Fakudze |
| Sweden | Erik Asbrink | Pierre Schori |
| Switzerland | Jean-Pascal Delamuraz | Flavio Cotti |
| Syrian Arab Republic | Mohammed Khaled Al-Mahayni | Adnan Al-Satti |
| Tajikistan | Murotali M. Alimardanov | Sharif M. Rakhimov |
| Tanzania | Daniel A.N. Yona | Peter J. Ngumbullu |
| Thailand | Bodi Chunnananda | M.R. Chatu Mongol Sonakul |
| Togo | Kwassi Klutse | (vacant) |

| Member | Governor | Alternate |
|---|---|---|
| Tonga | Kinikinilau Tutoatasi Fakafanua | 'Aisake V. Eke |
| Trinidad and Tobago | Brian Kuei Tung | T. Ainsworth Harewood |
| Tunisia | Mohamed Ghannouchi | Taoufik Baccar |
| Turkey | Mehmet Kaytaz | Cuneyt Sel |
| Turkmenistan † | Hudaiberdy A. Orazov | Orazmuradov Khakmurat |
| Uganda | Jehoash Mayanja-Nkangi | Emmanuel T. Mutebile |
| Ukraine † | Ihor Mitiukov | Olexander Vesselovsky |
| United Arab Emirates | Hamdan bin Rashid Al-Maktoum | Ahmed Humaid Al-Tayer |
| United Kingdom | Kenneth Clarke | Baroness Chalker of Wallasey |
| United States | Robert E. Rubin | Joan E. Spero |
| | | |
| Uruguay † | Luis Mosca | Ariel Davrieux |
| Uzbekistan | Bakhtiyar S. Hamidov | Akram Mukhidov |
| Vanuatu | Barak Tame Sope | George Borugu |
| Venezuela † | Luis Raul Matos Azocar | Teodoro Petkoff |
| Vietnam | Cao Sy Kiem | Le Van Chau |
| Western Samoa | Tuilaepa S. Malielegaoi | Epa Tuioti |
| Yemen, Republic of | Abdul Kader Bajamal | Mutahar A. Al-Saeedi |
| Zaire | Gilbert Kiakwama Kia Kiziki | (vacant) |
| Zambia | Ronald Damson Siame Penza | James M. Mtonga |
| Zimbabwe | Herbert M. Murerwa | Leonard Ladislas Tsumba |

† Not a member of IDA

*June 30, 1996*

| Executive director | Alternate | Casting votes of | IBRD | | IDA | |
|---|---|---|---|---|---|---|
| | | | Total votes | % of total | Total votes | % of total |
| **Appointed** | | | | | | |
| Jan Piercy | Michael Marek | United States | 265,219 | 17.43 | 1,607,213 | 15.08 |
| Atsuo Nishihara | Rintaro Tamaki | Japan | 94,020 | 6.18 | 1,154,286 | 10.83 |
| Fritz Fischer[b] | Erika Wagenhöfer | Germany | 72,649 | 4.78 | 747,221 | 7.01 |
| Marc-Antoine Autheman | Arnaud Chneiweiss | France | 69,647 | 4.58 | 451,054 | 4.23 |
| Huw Evans | David Stanton | United Kingdom | 69,647 | 4.58 | 540,211 | 5.07 |
| **Elected** | | | | | | |
| Walter Rill (Austria) | Luc Hubloue (Belgium) | Austria, Belarus,[a] Belgium, Czech Republic, Hungary, Kazakstan, Luxembourg, Slovak Republic, Slovenia, Turkey | 76,720 | 5.04 | 457,116 | 4.29 |
| Eveline Herfkens (Netherlands) | Sergiy Kulyk (Ukraine) | Armenia, Bulgaria,[a] Croatia, Cyprus, Georgia, Israel, Macedonia (former Yugoslav Republic of), Moldova, Netherlands, Romania,[a] Ukraine[a] | 71,409 | 4.69 | 353,929 | 3.32 |
| Jorge Terrazas (Mexico) | Roberto Jimenez-Ortiz (El Salvador) | Costa Rica, El Salvador, Guatemala, Honduras, Mexico, Nicaragua, Panama, Spain, Venezuela[a] | 69,110 | 4.54 | 233,470 | 2.19 |
| Leonard Good (Canada) | Winston Cox (Barbados) | Antigua and Barbuda,[a] The Bahamas,[a] Barbados,[a] Belize, Canada, Dominica, Grenada, Guyana, Ireland, Jamaica,[a] St. Kitts and Nevis, St. Lucia, St. Vincent and the Grenadines | 62,217 | 4.09 | 437,950 | 4.11 |
| Bimal Jalan (India) | Mushfiqur Rahman (Bangladesh) | Bangladesh, Bhutan, India, Sri Lanka | 54,945 | 3.61 | 457,908 | 4.30 |
| Franco Passacantando (Italy) | Helena Cordeiro (Portugal) | Albania, Greece, Italy, Malta,[a] Portugal | 54,354 | 3.57 | 389,870 | 3.66 |
| Abdul Karim Lodhi (Pakistan) | Kaçim Brachemi (Algeria) | Afghanistan, Algeria, Ghana, Iran (Islamic Republic of), Morocco, Pakistan, Tunisia | 50,875 | 3.34 | 227,599 | 2.14 |
| Ruth Jacoby (Sweden) | Jorgen Varder (Denmark) | Denmark, Estonia,[a] Finland, Iceland, Latvia, Lithuania,[a] Norway, Sweden | 50,178 | 3.30 | 516,892 | 4.85 |
| Marcos Caramuru de Paiva (Brazil) | Jorge Cock-Londoño (Colombia) | Brazil, Colombia, Dominican Republic, Ecuador, Haiti, Philippines, Suriname,[a] Trinidad and Tobago | 48,230 | 3.17 | 294,473 | 2.76 |
| Jean-Daniel Gerber (Switzerland) | Jan Sulmicki (Poland) | Azerbaijan, Kyrgyz Republic, Poland, Switzerland, Tajikistan Turkmenistan,[a] Uzbekistan | 46,096 | 3.03 | 367,389 | 3.45 |

| Executive director | Alternate | Casting votes of | IBRD | | IDA | |
|---|---|---|---|---|---|---|
| | | | Total votes | % of total | Total votes | % of total |
| Peter W. E. Nicholl (New Zealand) | Christopher Y. Legg (Australia) | Australia, Cambodia, Kiribati, Korea (Republic of), Marshall Islands, Micronesia (Federated States of), Mongolia, New Zealand, Papua New Guinea, Solomon Islands, Vanuatu, Western Samoa | 45,434 | 2.99 | 316,906 | 2.97 |
| Li Yong (China) | Zhu Guangyao (China) | China | 45,049 | 2.96 | 217,996 | 2.05 |
| Khalid H. Alyahya (Saudi Arabia) | Ibrahim M. Al-Mofleh (Saudi Arabia) | Saudi Arabia | 45,045 | 2.96 | 377,100 | 3.54 |
| Andrei Bugrov (Russian Federation) | Eugene Miagkov (Russian Federation) | Russian Federation | 45,045 | 2.96 | 28,202 | 0.26 |
| Khalid M. Al-Saad (Kuwait) | Mohamed W. Hosny (Arab Republic of Egypt) | Bahrain,[a] Egypt (Arab Republic of), Jordan, Kuwait, Lebanon, Libya, Maldives, Oman, Qatar,[a] Syrian Arab Republic, United Arab Emirates, Yemen (Republic of) | 43,018 | 2.83 | 250,660 | 2.35 |
| Leonard Mseka (Malawi) | Joaquim R. Carvalho (Mozambique) | Angola, Botswana, Burundi, Eritrea, Ethiopia, The Gambia, Guinea, Kenya, Lesotho, Liberia, Malawi, Mozambique, Namibia,[a] Nigeria, Seychelles,[a] Sierra Leone, Sudan, Swaziland, Tanzania, Uganda, Zambia, Zimbabwe | 41,332 | 2.72 | 440,377 | 4.13 |
| Suwan Pasugswad (Thailand) | Khin Ohn Thant (Myanmar) | Fiji, Indonesia, Lao People's Democratic Republic, Malaysia, Myanmar, Nepal, Singapore,[a] Thailand, Tonga, Vietnam | 38,256 | 2.51 | 292,376 | 2.74 |
| Julio Nogués (Argentina) | Carlos Steneri (Uruguay) | Argentina, Bolivia, Chile, Paraguay, Peru, Uruguay[a] | 37,499 | 2.46 | 200,001 | 1.88 |
| Ali Bourhane (Comoros) | Luc-Abdi Aden (Djibouti) | Benin, Burkina Faso, Cameroon, Cape Verde, Central African Republic, Chad, Comoros, Congo, Côte d'Ivoire, Djibouti, Equatorial Guinea, Gabon, Guinea-Bissau, Madagascar, Mali, Mauritania, Mauritius, Niger, Rwanda, São Tomé and Principe, Senegal, Togo, Zaire | 25,337 | 1.67 | 299,724 | 2.81 |

In addition to the executive directors and alternates shown in the foregoing list, the following also served after June 30, 1995:

| Executive director | End of period of service | Alternate director | End of period of service |
| --- | --- | --- | --- |
| Ibrahim A. Al-Assaf (Saudi Arabia) | September 20, 1995 | Helga Jonsdottir (Iceland) | July 31, 1995 |
| Faisal A. Al-Khaled (Kuwait) | July 31, 1995 | Armando Montenegro (Colombia) | January 9, 1996 |
| Enzo Grilli (Italy) | October 31, 1995 | Philippe Peeters (Belgium) | August 27, 1995 |
| Zhang Shengman (China) | December 31, 1995 | | |

NOTE: Bosnia and Herzegovina (799 votes in IBRD and 17,871 votes in IDA) and Brunei Darussalam[a] (2,623 votes in IBRD) became members after the 1994 Regular Election of Executive Directors. Iraq (3,058 votes in IBRD and 9,407 votes in IDA), Somalia (802 votes in IBRD and 10,506 votes in IDA), and South Africa (13,712 votes in IBRD and 30,365 votes in IDA) did not participate in the 1994 Regular Election of Executive Directors.
a. Member of the IBRD only.
b. To be succeeded by Helmut Schaffer (Germany) effective July 1, 1996.

| | |
|---|---|
| President | James D. Wolfensohn |
| | |
| Vice President and Chief of Staff | Rachel Lomax |
| Managing Director, Corporate Planning & Resource Management | Sven Sandström |
| Managing Director, Finance and Resource Mobilization | Jessica P. Einhorn |
| Managing Director, Operations | Gautam S. Kaji |
| Managing Director, Operations | Caio K. Koch-Weser |
| Managing Director and Chairman, Private Sector Development Group | Richard H. Frank |
| | |
| Vice President, Africa | Callisto Madavo |
| Vice President, Africa | Jean-Louis Sarbib |
| Vice President and Controller | Jules W. Muis |
| Senior Vice President and Chief Economist, Development Economics | Michael P. Bruno |
| Vice President, East Asia and Pacific | Russell J. Cheetham |
| Vice President, Environmentally Sustainable Development | M. Ismail Serageldin |
| Vice President, Europe and Central Asia | Johannes Linn |
| Vice President, External Affairs | Mark Malloch Brown |
| Vice President, Finance and Private Sector Development | Jean-François Rischard |
| Vice President, Financial Policy and Institutional Strategy | Brian Wilson |
| Senior Vice President and General Counsel | Ibrahim F. I. Shihata |
| Vice President, Human Capital Development | Armeane M. Choksi |
| Vice President, Human Resources | Dorothy Hamachi Berry |
| Vice President, Latin America and the Caribbean | S. Javed Burki |
| Vice President, Middle East and North Africa | Kemal Dervis |
| Director-General, Operations Evaluation | Robert Picciotto |
| Vice President, Resource Mobilization and Cofinancing | Hiroo Fukui |
| Vice President and Secretary | ZHANG Shengman |
| Vice President, South Asia | D. Joseph Wood |
| Vice President and Treasurer | Gary Perlin |

*June 30, 1996*

**Headquarters:** 1818 H Street, N.W., Washington, D.C. 20433, U.S.A.

**New York Office:** The World Bank Mission to the United Nations/New York Office, 809 United Nations Plaza, Suite 900, New York, N.Y. 10017, U.S.A.

**European Office:** The World Bank, 66, avenue d'Iéna, 75116 Paris, France

**Brussels:** The World Bank, 10 rue Montoyer, B-1000 Brussels, Belgium

**London:** The World Bank, New Zealand House, 15th Floor, Haymarket, London, SW1 Y4TE, England

**Tokyo Office:** The World Bank, Kokusai Building (Room 916), 1-1, Marunouchi 3-chome, Chiyoda-ku, Tokyo 100, Japan

**Regional Mission in Eastern Africa:** The World Bank, Hill Park Building, Upper Hill, Nairobi, Kenya
(mailing address: P.O. Box 30577)

**Regional Mission in Western Africa:** The World Bank, Corner of Booker Washington and Jacques AKA Streets, Cocody, Abidjan 01, Côte d'Ivoire
(mailing address: B. P. 1850)

**Regional Mission in Thailand:** The World Bank, 14th Floor, Tower A, Diethelm Towers, 93/1 Wireless Road, Bangkok 10330, Thailand

**Regional Mission in Latvia:** The World Bank, Kalku Street 15, Riga, Latvia LV-1162

**Baltics Regional Mission Satellite in Estonia:** The World Bank, Kohtu 8, Tallinn EE0100, Estonia

**Baltics Regional Mission Satellite in Lithuania:** The World Bank, Vilniaus Str. 28, 2600 Vilnius, Lithuania

**Albania:** The World Bank, Deshmoret e 4 Shkurtit, No. 34, Tirana, Albania

**Angola:** Banco Mundial, Rua Alfredo Troni (Edificio BPC), 15° Andar, CP 1331, Luanda, Angola

**Argentina:** Banco Mundial, Avenida Leandro N. Alem 628-30, Piso 12, Buenos Aires, Argentina

**Armenia:** The World Bank, Republic Square, 2 Khorhertarani Street, Yerevan 10, Armenia

**Azerbaijan:** The World Bank, Neftchilar Avenue 65, Apartment 85, Baku, Azerbaijan

**Bangladesh:** The World Bank, 3A Paribagh, Dhaka 1000, Bangladesh
(mailing address: G.P.O. 97)

**Belarus:** The World Bank, 6A Partizansky Avenue, 5th Floor, Minsk 220033, Republic of Belarus

**Benin:** The World Bank, Zone Résidentielle de la Radio, Cotonou, Benin
(mailing address: B. P. 03-2112)

**Bolivia:** Banco Mundial, Edificio BISA, Piso 9, 16 de Julio 1628, La Paz, Bolivia
(mailing address: Casilla 8692)

**Bosnia and Herzegovina:** The World Bank, c/o National Bank of Bosnia and Herzegovina, Marsala Tita 25, 71000 Sarajevo, Bosnia and Herzegovina

**Brazil:** Banco Mundial , SCN Quadra 02—Lote A, Ed. Corporate Financial Center, Conjuntos 303/304, 70710-500 Brasília, DF, Brazil

**Brazil:** Banco Mundial, Avenida Isaac Povoas, No. 1251, Edifício Nacional Palacios, Sala 603, Centro, 78.045–640 Cuiaba, Mato Grosso (MT), Brazil

**Brazil:** Banco Mundial, Edifício SUDENE, S/IS-108 Cidade Universitária, 50670-9001 Recife PE, Brazil

**Bulgaria:** The World Bank, World Trade Center–Sofia, 36 Dragan Tsankov Boulevard, Sofia, 1057 Bulgaria

**Burkina Faso:** The World Bank, Immeuble BICIA (3ème étage), Ouagadougou, Burkina Faso
(mailing address: B. P. 622)

**Burundi:** The World Bank, Avenue du 18 Septembre, Bujumbura, Burundi
(mailing address: B. P. 2637)

**Cameroon:** The World Bank, New Bastos, Yaoundé, Cameroon
(mailing address: B. P. 1128)

**Central African Republic:** Banque Mondiale, Rue des Missions, Bangui, C.A.R.

**Chad:** The World Bank, 3244 P.67, Quartier Curvette St. Martin, N'djamena, Chad
(mailing address: B.P. 146)

**China:** World Bank Resident Mission in China, 9th floor, Building A, Fuhua Mansion, No. 8 Chaoyangmen Beidajie, Dongcheng District, Beijing 100027, China

**Colombia:** Banco Mundial, Diagonal 35 No. 5-98, Bogotá, D.E., Colombia
(mailing address: Apartado Aéreo 10229)

**Congo:** Banque Mondiale, Immeuble Arc (5ème étage), Avenue Amilcar Cabral, Brazzaville, Congo
(mailing address: B. P. 14536)

**Costa Rica:** Regional Implementation Mission—Banco Mundial, Bulevar Rohrmoser, 150 mts. Oeste Residencia Ex-Presidente Oscar Arias, San José, Costa Rica
(mailing address: C.P. 11925-1000)

**Ecuador:** Banco Mundial, Calle Juan León Mera 130 y Ave. Patria, Edificio Corporación Financiera Nacional, 6to Piso, Quito, Ecuador

**Egypt:** The World Bank, World Trade Center, 1191 Corniche El-Nil, 15th Floor, Cairo, Egypt

**Ethiopia:** The World Bank, Africa Avenue, Bole Road, Addis Ababa, Ethiopia
(mailing address: P.O. Box 5515)

**Georgia:** The World Bank, 18A Chonkadze Street, Tbilisi, Georgia

**Ghana:** The World Bank, 69 Dr. Isert Road, Northridge Residential Area, Accra, Ghana
(mailing address: P.O. Box M27)

**Guinea:** Banque Mondiale, Immeuble de l'Archevêche, Face Baie des Anges, Conakry, Guinea
(mailing address: B. P. 1420)

**Haiti:** The World Bank, c/o IDB, Bourdon 386, Port-au-Prince, Haiti
(mailing address: B.P. 1321)

**Hungary:** The World Bank, Bank Center, Granite Tower, Szabadság ter 5-7, 1944 Budapest, Hungary

**India:** The World Bank, 70 Lodi Estate, New Delhi 110 003, India
(mailing address: P.O. Box 416, New Delhi 110 001)

**Indonesia:** The World Bank, Lippolife Building, 3rd floor, J1. H. R. Rasuna Said, Kav. B-10, Kuningan, Jakarta 12940, Indonesia
(mailing address: P.O. Box 324/JKT)

**Jamaica:** The World Bank, Island Life Center, 3rd floor/north, 6 St. Lucia Avenue, Suite 8–South, Kingston 5, Jamaica

**Kazakstan:** The World Bank, Samal-1, Bldg. No. 36, 3rd Floor, Almaty, Republic of Kazakstan 480099

**Kyrgyz Republic:** The World Bank, Moskovskaya and K. Akieva Streets, Bishkek 720000, Kyrgyz Republic

**Macedonia, FYR:** The World Bank, 34 Leninova Street, 3rd floor, Skopje, Former Yugoslav Republic of Macedonia

**Madagascar:** Banque Mondiale, 1 Rue Patrice Lumumba, Antananarivo 101, Madagascar
(mailing address: B. P. 4140)

**Malawi:** The World Bank, Development House, Capital City, Lilongwe 3, Malawi
(mailing address: P.O. Box 30557)

**Mali:** Banque Mondiale, Immeuble SOGEFIH, Centre Commercial Rue 321, Quartier du Fleuve, Bamako, Mali
(mailing address: B. P. 1864)

**Mauritania:** The World Bank, Villa No. 30, Lot A, Quartier Socofim, Nouakchott, Mauritania
(mailing address: B. P. 667)

**Mexico:** Mexico Resident Mission, Insurgentes Sur 1605, Piso 24, Torre Mural Insurgentes, Col. San José Insurgentes, 03900 Mexico, D.F.

**Moldova:** The World Bank, Government Building, Room 561, Piata Marii Adunari Nationale 1, 277033 Chisinau, Moldova

**Mozambique:** The World Bank, Ave. Kenneth Kaunda, 1224, 2-Andar, Maputo, Mozambique
(mailing address: Caixa Postal 4053)

**Nepal:** World Bank, Jyoti Bhawan, Kantipath, Kathmandu, Nepal
(mailing address: P.O. Box 798)

**Niger:** Banque Mondiale, Rue des Dallols, Niamey, Niger
(mailing address: B. P. 12402)

**Nigeria:** The World Bank, 1st Floor, Plot PC-10, Engineering Close, off Idowu Taylor Street, Victoria Island, Lagos, Nigeria
(mailing address: P.O. Box 127)

**Nigeria:** The World Bank, Plot 433, Ecowas Road, Opposite Ecowas Secretariat, Assokoro District, Abuja, Nigeria
(mailing address: P.O. Box 2826, Garki)

**Pakistan:** The World Bank, 20 A , Shahra-e-Jamhuriyat, Ramna 5 G-5/1, Islamabad, Pakistan
(mailing address: P.O. Box 1025)

**Paraguay:** The World Bank, Edificio City Tercer Piso, Estrella 345, Casa Chile, Asuncion, Paraguay

**Peru:** The World Bank, Avenida Pardo y Aliaga 640, Piso 16, San Isidro, Lima, Peru

**Philippines:** The World Bank, Central Bank of the Philippines, Multi-Storey Building, Room 200, Roxas Boulevard, Manila, Philippines

**Poland:** The World Bank, INTRACO I Building, 17th Floor, 2 Stawki Street, 00-193 Warsaw, Poland

**Romania:** The World Bank, Boulevard Dacia 83, Sector 2, Bucharest, Romania

**Russia:** The World Bank, Sadovo-Kudrinskaya No. 3, Moscow 123242, Russian Federation

**Rwanda:** The World Bank, Blvd. de la Révolution, SORAS Building, Kigali, Rwanda
(mailing address: P.O. Box 609)

**Saudi Arabia:** The World Bank Resident Mission, UNDP Building, King Faisal Street, Riyadh, Saudi Arabia 11432
(mailing address: P.O. Box 5900)

**Senegal:** The World Bank, Immeuble S.D.I.H., 3 Place de l'Indépendance, Dakar, Senegal
(mailing address: B. P. 3296)

**South Africa:** The World Bank, Grosvenor Gate, First Floor, Hyde Park Lane, Hyde Park 2196, Johannesburg, South Africa
(mailing address: P.O. Box 41283, Craig Hall 2024)

**Sri Lanka:** The World Bank, Development Finance Corporation of Ceylon (DFCC) Building, 1st Floor, 73/5 Galle Road, Colombo 3, Sri Lanka
(mailing address: P.O. Box 1761)

**Tanzania:** The World Bank, N.I.C. Building (7th Floor, B), Samora Avenue, Dar-es-Salaam, Tanzania
(mailing address: P.O. Box 2054)

**Togo:** Banque Mondiale, 169 boulevard du 13 Janvier, Immeuble BTCI (8ème étage), Lomé, Togo
(mailing address: B. P. 3915)

**Turkey:** The World Bank, Ataturk Bulvari, No. 211, Gama-Guris Building Kat 6, 06683 Kavaklidere, Ankara, Turkey

**Uganda:** The World Bank, Rwenzori House, 1 Lumumba Avenue and 4 Nakasero Road, Kampala, Uganda
(mailing address: P.O. Box 4463)

**Ukraine:** The World Bank, 26, Shovkovychna St. (Ex. K Liebknecht St.), Suites Two and Three, Kiev 252024, Ukraine

**Uzbekistan:** World Bank Field Office, 43, Academician Suleimanova St., Tashkent, Uzbekistan

**Venezuela:** Banco Mundial, Edificio Parque Cristal, Torre Oeste, Piso 15, Oficína 15-05, Avenida Francisco de Miranda, Los Palos Grandes, Caracas, Venezuela

**Vietnam:** The World Bank, 53 Tran Phu Street, Hanoi, Vietnam

**West Bank and Gaza:** The World Bank, Gaza City, Gaza

**Yemen:** The World Bank, 14 Djibouti St., Sana'a, Republic of Yemen
(mailing address: P.O. Box 18152)

**Zaire:** World Bank Liaison Office, c/o UNDP, P. O. Box 7248, Kinshasa, Zaire

**Zambia:** The World Bank, Red Cross House, 2nd Floor, Long Acres, Lusaka, Zambia,
(mailing address: P.O. Box 35410)

**Zimbabwe:** The World Bank, Finsure House, 5th Floor, 84-86 Union Avenue, Harare, Zimbabwe
(mailing address: P.O. Box 2960)

*(as of June 30, 1996)*

## COUNTRIES ELIGIBLE FOR IBRD FUNDS ONLY

| Income category and country | 1995 GNP per capita (US$)[a] | Income category and country | 1995 GNP per capita (US$) |
|---|---|---|---|
| *Per capita income over $5,295* | | Peru | 2,320 |
| Slovenia | 8,070 | Russian Federation[b] | 2,230 |
| Argentina | 7,770 | Belarus[b] | 2,110 |
| Seychelles | 6,410 | Lithuania[b] | 2,050 |
| Antigua and Barbuda | n.a. | Namibia | 2,000 |
| | | Colombia | 1,900 |
| *Per capita income $3,036–$5,295* | | Tunisia | 1,860 |
| Uruguay | 5,100 | Paraguay | 1,650 |
| Hungary | 4,130 | Ukraine[b] | 1,630 |
| Malaysia | 4,000 | Algeria | 1,580 |
| Chile | 3,960 | El Salvador | 1,580 |
| Czech Republic | 3,870 | Jamaica | 1,510 |
| Gabon | 3,800 | Jordan | 1,500 |
| Trinidad and Tobago | 3,720 | Iran, Islamic Republic of | n.a. |
| Brazil | 3,620 | Marshall Islands | n.a. |
| Mexico | 3,320 | Micronesia, Fed. Sts. of | n.a. |
| Croatia | 3,280 | | |
| Mauritius | 3,280 | *Per capita income $766–$1,465* | |
| South Africa | 3,160 | Dominican Republic | 1,460 |
| St. Kitts and Nevis | n.a. | Romania | 1,450 |
| | | Ecuador | 1,390 |
| *Per capita income $1,466–$3,035* | | Bulgaria | 1,340 |
| Venezuela | 3,020 | Guatemala | 1,340 |
| Botswana | 2,940 | Papua New Guinea | 1,160 |
| Slovak Republic | 2,940 | Morocco | 1,130 |
| Estonia[b] | 2,920 | Swaziland | 1,110 |
| Poland | 2,800 | Syrian Arab Republic | 1,110 |
| Panama | 2,720 | Philippines | 1,070 |
| Thailand | 2,720 | Kazakstan[b] | 1,040 |
| Lebanon | 2,670 | Indonesia | 980 |
| Turkey | 2,670 | Uzbekistan[b] | 930 |
| Belize | 2,630 | Moldova[b] | 920 |
| Costa Rica | 2,590 | Turkmenistan[b] | 920 |
| Latvia[b] | 2,420 | Suriname | 880 |
| Fiji | 2,400 | | |

## COUNTRIES ELIGBLE FOR A BLEND OF IBRD AND IDA FUNDS[c]

| Income category and country | 1995 GNP per capita (US$)[a] | Income category and country | 1995 GNP per capita (US$) |
|---|---|---|---|
| *Per capita income $3,036–$5,295* | | *Per capita income $765 or less* | |
| St. Lucia[d] | n.a. | Kyrgyz Republic[b] | 690 |
| | | China | 620 |
| *Per capita income $1,466–$3,035* | | Armenia[b] | 570 |
| Dominica[d] | n.a. | Zimbabwe | 540 |
| Grenada[d] | n.a. | Azerbaijan[b] | 480 |
| St. Vincent and the Grenadines[d] | n.a. | Pakistan | 460 |
| | | Georgia[b] | 440 |
| | | India | 350 |
| *Per capita income $766–$1,465* | | Nigeria | 260 |
| Macedonia, FYR of | 840 | Bosnia and Herzegovina | n.a. |
| Egypt | 790 | | |

## COUNTRIES ELIGIBLE FOR IDA FUNDS ONLY[c]

| Income category and country | 1995 GNP per capita (US$)[a] | Income category and country | 1995 GNP per capita (US$) |
|---|---|---|---|
| **Per capita income $1,466–$3,035** | | Lao People's Democratic Republic | 350 |
| Tonga[d] | 1,630 | São Tomé and Principe | 340 |
| | | Central African Republic | 330 |
| **Per capita income $766–$1,465** | | Mongolia | 320 |
| Vanuatu[d] | 1,200 | Togo | 310 |
| Western Samoa[d] | 1,110 | Cambodia | 260 |
| Cape Verde | 970 | Kenya | 260 |
| Solomon Islands | 910 | Yemen | 260 |
| Bolivia | 800 | Guinea-Bissau | 250 |
| Kiribati | 780 | Haiti | 250 |
| Lesotho | 770 | Mali | 250 |
| Djibouti | n.a. | Vietnam | 250 |
| Maldives | n.a. | Bangladesh | 240 |
| | | Madagascar | 240 |
| **Per capita income $765 or less** | | Uganda | 240 |
| Albania | 690 | Burkina Faso | 230 |
| Sri Lanka | 690 | Niger | 220 |
| Congo | 650 | Nepal | 210 |
| Cameroon | 630 | Chad | 180 |
| Côte d'Ivoire | 610 | Sierra Leone | 170 |
| Honduras | 600 | Malawi | 160 |
| Guyana | 590 | Burundi | 150 |
| Senegal | 570 | Tanzania | 130 |
| Guinea | 540 | Zaire | 120 |
| Comoros | 490 | Rwanda | 110 |
| Mauritania | 460 | Ethiopia | 100 |
| Bhutan | 420 | Mozambique | 80 |
| Angola | 410 | Afghanistan | n.a. |
| Ghana | 390 | Eritrea | n.a. |
| Nicaragua | 390 | Gambia, The | n.a. |
| Equatorial Guinea | 380 | Liberia | n.a. |
| Benin | 370 | Myanmar | n.a. |
| Tajikistan[b] | 370 | Somalia | n.a. |
| Zambia | 370 | Sudan | n.a. |

n.a. Not available.
a. World Bank Atlas *methodology; per capita* GNP *figures are in 1995 U.S. dollars.*
b. *Estimates for these countries are preliminary.*
c. *Countries are eligible for* IDA *on the basis of (a) relative poverty and (b) lack of creditworthiness. The operational cutoff for* IDA *eligibility for FY97 is a 1995* GNP *per capita of $905, using* Atlas *methodology. To receive* IDA *resources, countries also meet tests of performance. In exceptional circumstances,* IDA *extends eligibility temporarily to countries that are above the operational cutoff and are undertaking major adjustment efforts but are not creditworthy for* IBRD *lending. An exception has also been made for small island economies (see footnote d).*
d. *During the* IDA-11 *period (FY97–99), an exception to the* GNP *per capita operational cutoff for* IDA *eligibility ($905 for FY97) has been made for specific small island economies, which otherwise would have little or no access to Bank Group assistance because they lack creditworthiness. For such countries,* IDA *funding is considered case by case for the financing of projects and adjustment programs designed to strengthen creditworthiness.*

*(millions of US dollars; fiscal years)*

| | Actual | | | 1997 |
|---|---|---|---|---|
| Item | 1994 | 1995 | 1996 | Program |
| | | | | |
| *Expense Category* | | | | |
| Staff costs | 851.8 | 874.8 | 835.9 | 854.7 |
| Consultants | 113.7 | 111.9 | 119.5 | 105.6 |
| Contractual services/representation | 66.3 | 62.7 | 66.2 | 55.9 |
| Operational travel | 129.8 | 127.5 | 126.1 | 127.9 |
| Overhead | 230.8 | 232.2 | 222.5 | 210.9 |
| Direct contributions to special grants program[a] | 103.4 | 110.9 | 105.2 | 112.5 |
| President's contingency[b] | n.a. | n.a. | n.a. | 10.0 |
| Reimbursements | (107.3) | (111.2) | (102.5) | (104.2) |
| Pending benefit initiatives[c] | n.a. | n.a. | 3.2 | 1.4 |
| Total | 1,388.4 | 1,409.0 | 1,376.0 | 1,374.7 |
| | | | | |
| *Administrative Program[d]* | | | | |
| Regional[e] | 646.7 | 730.2 | 712.4 | 687.5 |
| Financial | 112.3 | 113.1 | 113.4 | 111.0 |
| Development and advisory[f] | 213.9 | 136.0 | 133.9 | 128.5 |
| Administrative support | 123.7 | 133.9 | 120.4 | 107.4 |
| Corporate management, and legal services | 72.1 | 78.7 | 82.0 | 77.8 |
| Total | 1,168.7 | 1,191.9 | 1,162.1 | 1,112.2 |
| | | | | |
| Overhead/benefits | 127.6 | 119.1 | 128.1 | 132.4 |
| President's contingency | n.a. | n.a. | n.a. | 10.0 |
| New initiaitves | n.a. | n.a. | n.a. | 25.4[g] |
| Pending benefit initiatives[c] | n.a. | n.a. | 3.2 | 1.4 |
| Reimbursements | (107.3) | (111.2) | (102.5) | (104.2) |
| Net administrative programs | 1,189.0 | 1,199.8 | 1,190.9 | 1,177.1 |
| | | | | |
| Non-discretionary items | 23.0[h] | 18.5[i] | n.a. | n.a. |
| Special programs[j] | 111.2 | 119.1 | 113.0 | 120.3 |
| Boards | 50.5 | 55.8 | 56.1 | 61.1 |
| Operations evaluation | 14.8 | 15.7 | 16.0 | 16.1 |
| Total budget | 1,388.4[k] | 1,409.0 | 1,376.0 | 1,374.7 |

NOTE: *Details may not add to totals because of rounding.*
*n.a. Not applicable.*
*a. Includes Institutional Development Fund.*
*b. Allocations from president's contingency have been included in respective categories/programs for fiscal 1994–96.*
*c. Accrual/provisional allocations subject to Board approval of the policy initiatives.*
*d. Fiscal 1994–95 expenses have been modified from last year's Report to include decentralized office occupancy costs, and to show operational support under regional program.*
*e. Includes operational support from development and advisory programs.*
*f. Includes FAO Co-operative Program.*
*g. Allocations for Learning and Leadership Center ($9.2m); Change Management ($5.0 m); and EDI expansion ($11.2m).*
*h. Accrual for resettlement grants on termination due to accounting changes (Financial Accounting Standards 112).*
*i. One-time charges of $9.1 million to fund accrual for local staff termination grants for prior years, and $9.4 million to fund accruals for benefit costs of redundant staff proccessed prior to February 21, 1995.*
*j. Includes direct contributions to and administrative costs of the Special Programs.*
*k. Excludes $20.0 million for Somalia relief.*

# IBRD AND IDA PAYMENTS TO SUPPLYING ACTIVE BORROWING COUNTRIES FOR FOREIGN AND LOCAL PROCUREMENT IN FISCAL 1996

*(millions of US dollars)*

| Borrowing countries | Local procurement | Foreign procurement | Total amount | Percentage of total disbursements[a] |
|---|---|---|---|---|
| Albania | 17 | 3 | 19 | 0.10 |
| Algeria | 32 | 15 | 47 | 0.24 |
| Argentina | 222 | 28 | 250 | 1.30 |
| Armenia | 32 | † | 33 | 0.17 |
| Bangladesh | 119 | 1 | 120 | 0.62 |
| Belarus | † | 19 | 19 | 0.10 |
| Bolivia | 65 | 1 | 67 | 0.35 |
| Brazil | 962 | 120 | 1,082 | 5.62 |
| Bulgaria | 1 | 51 | 53 | 0.28 |
| Burkina Faso | 32 | 1 | 33 | 0.17 |
| Cameroon | 35 | 1 | 36 | 0.19 |
| Chile | 62 | 15 | 77 | 0.40 |
| China | 1,299 | 242 | 1,542 | 8.01 |
| Colombia | 180 | 24 | 204 | 1.06 |
| Costa Rica | 6 | 22 | 28 | 0.15 |
| Côte d'Ivoire | 23 | 27 | 49 | 0.25 |
| Croatia | 34 | 4 | 38 | 0.20 |
| Cyprus | 4 | 24 | 27 | 0.14 |
| Czech Republic | 6 | 29 | 35 | 0.18 |
| Dominican Republic | 23 | † | 23 | 0.12 |
| Ecuador | 122 | 40 | 163 | 0.85 |
| Egypt | 84 | 6 | 89 | 0.46 |
| Ghana | 92 | 1 | 93 | 0.48 |
| Guinea | 12 | 20 | 32 | 0.17 |
| Haiti | 21 | † | 21 | 0.11 |
| Honduras | 24 | 3 | 27 | 0.14 |
| Hungary | 81 | 20 | 101 | 0.52 |
| India | 1,092 | 124 | 1,217 | 6.32 |
| Indonesia | 661 | 25 | 686 | 3.56 |
| Iran, Islamic Republic of | 24 | 1 | 25 | 0.13 |
| Jamaica | 27 | 1 | 28 | 0.15 |
| Jordan | 12 | 8 | 20 | 0.10 |
| Kazakstan | 5 | 82 | 87 | 0.45 |
| Kenya | 44 | 12 | 56 | 0.29 |
| Korea, Republic of | 96 | 156 | 251 | 1.30 |
| Lebanon | 10 | 17 | 27 | 0.14 |
| Macedonia, Former Yugoslav Republic of | 20 | † | 20 | 0.10 |
| Madagascar | 39 | † | 39 | 0.20 |
| Malawi | 44 | † | 45 | 0.23 |
| Malaysia | 80 | 8 | 88 | 0.46 |
| Mali | 31 | 2 | 33 | 0.17 |
| Morocco | 208 | 16 | 224 | 1.16 |
| Mozambique | 28 | — | 28 | 0.15 |
| Nepal | 28 | — | 28 | 0.15 |
| Nigeria | 137 | 59 | 196 | 1.02 |
| Pakistan | 304 | 14 | 319 | 1.66 |
| Paraguay | 24 | 3 | 27 | 0.14 |
| Peru | 53 | 4 | 57 | 0.30 |
| Philippines | 168 | 3 | 171 | 0.89 |
| Poland | 102 | 36 | 138 | 0.72 |
| Romania | 14 | 34 | 48 | 0.25 |
| Russia | 88 | 380 | 468 | 2.43 |
| Senegal | 47 | 13 | 60 | 0.31 |
| Sri Lanka | 89 | 1 | 90 | 0.47 |
| Swaziland | † | 19 | 19 | 0.10 |
| Tanzania | 42 | 4 | 47 | 0.24 |
| Thailand | 42 | 20 | 62 | 0.32 |

| Borrowing countries | Local procurement | Foreign procurement | Total amount | Percentage of total disbursements[a] |
|---|---|---|---|---|
| Togo | 18 | 1 | 19 | 0.10 |
| Trinidad and Tobago | 14 | 3 | 16 | 0.08 |
| Tunisia | 117 | 4 | 121 | 0.63 |
| Turkmenistan | † | 21 | 21 | 0.11 |
| Uganda | 52 | † | 52 | 0.27 |
| Ukraine | † | 125 | 125 | 0.65 |
| Uruguay | 24 | 3 | 27 | 0.14 |
| Venezuela | 24 | 50 | 74 | 0.38 |
| Vietnam | 14 | 11 | 25 | 0.13 |
| Yemen | 20 | † | 20 | 0.10 |
| Zambia | 19 | 24 | 43 | 0.22 |
| Zimbabwe | 24 | 10 | 34 | 0.18 |
| Other | 112 | 47 | 160 | 0.83 |
| Total | 7,718 | 2,105 | 9,823 | 51.00 |

— Zero, † less than $0.5 million

NOTE: Amounts exclude disbursements for debt reduction, net advance disbursements, and disbursements under simplified procedures for structural and sectoral adjustment loans. Details may not add to totals because of rounding.

a. Refers to the share of all IBRD and IDA payments for fiscal 1996 which totaled $19,256 million.

*(amounts in millions of US dollars)*

| Supplying country | IBRD cumulative to June 30, 1996 | | IBRD fiscal 1996 | | IDA cumulative to June 30, 1996 | | IDA fiscal 1996 | |
|---|---|---|---|---|---|---|---|---|
| | Amount | % | Amount | % | Amount | % | Amount | % |
| Algeria | 38 | * | 14 | 0.21 | 13 | * | 2 | 0.06 |
| Argentina | 816 | 0.75 | 24 | 0.35 | 106 | 0.26 | 3 | 0.13 |
| Australia | 1,130 | 1.04 | 77 | 1.13 | 636 | 1.56 | 35 | 1.33 |
| Austria | 1,584 | 1.46 | 123 | 1.81 | 235 | 0.57 | 14 | 0.52 |
| Azerbaijan | 3 | * | 2 | * | 24 | 0.06 | 14 | 0.52 |
| Belgium | 1,562 | 1.44 | 61 | 0.90 | 1,027 | 2.52 | 47 | 1.78 |
| Brazil | 1,877 | 1.72 | 102 | 1.50 | 324 | 0.79 | 18 | 0.67 |
| Bulgaria | 40 | * | 12 | 0.18 | 51 | 0.12 | 40 | 1.50 |
| Canada | 2,496 | 2.29 | 169 | 2.48 | 738 | 1.81 | 56 | 2.13 |
| Chile | 378 | 0.35 | 10 | 0.15 | 36 | 0.09 | 5 | 0.17 |
| China | 1,381 | 1.27 | 115 | 1.69 | 1,139 | 2.79 | 128 | 4.81 |
| Colombia | 245 | 0.22 | 23 | 0.34 | 20 | * | 1 | 0.05 |
| Costa Rica | 43 | * | 6 | 0.09 | 36 | 0.09 | 16 | 0.59 |
| Côte d'Ivoire | 45 | * | 4 | 0.06 | 241 | 0.59 | 22 | 0.84 |
| Cyprus | 63 | 0.06 | 22 | 0.32 | 34 | 0.08 | 2 | 0.06 |
| Czech Republic | 75 | 0.07 | 27 | 0.40 | 7 | * | 2 | 0.09 |
| Denmark | 735 | 0.68 | 45 | 0.66 | 308 | 0.75 | 27 | 1.02 |
| Ecuador | 169 | 0.16 | 37 | 0.54 | 9 | * | 4 | 0.14 |
| Egypt | 58 | 0.05 | 4 | 0.06 | 36 | 0.09 | 2 | 0.08 |
| Finland | 511 | 0.47 | 75 | 1.10 | 123 | 0.30 | 3 | 0.11 |
| France | 7,691 | 7.06 | 403 | 5.92 | 4,295 | 10.52 | 322 | 12.12 |
| Germany | 12,304 | 11.30 | 744 | 10.93 | 3,464 | 8.48 | 118 | 4.45 |
| Ghana | 10 | * | 1 | * | 14 | * | 1 | * |
| Greece | 208 | 0.19 | 11 | 0.16 | 75 | 0.18 | 6 | 0.21 |
| Guatemala | 19 | * | † | * | 21 | 0.05 | 3 | 0.11 |
| Guinea | 4 | * | 1 | * | 40 | 0.10 | 19 | 0.70 |
| Hungary | 296 | 0.27 | 20 | 0.29 | 26 | 0.06 | 1 | * |
| India | 407 | 0.37 | 48 | 0.71 | 789 | 1.93 | 77 | 2.88 |
| Indonesia | 161 | 0.15 | 12 | 0.18 | 117 | 0.29 | 13 | 0.50 |
| Iran, Islamic Republic of | 145 | 0.13 | † | * | 195 | 0.48 | 1 | * |
| Iraq | 459 | 0.42 | — | * | 30 | 0.07 | — | * |
| Ireland | 161 | 0.15 | 22 | 0.32 | 101 | 0.25 | 14 | 0.54 |
| Israel | 253 | 0.23 | 9 | 0.13 | 101 | 0.25 | 5 | 0.18 |
| Italy | 6,468 | 5.93 | 468 | 6.88 | 1,746 | 4.28 | 110 | 4.15 |
| Japan | 14,315 | 13.13 | 358 | 5.26 | 4,124 | 10.10 | 103 | 3.89 |
| Jordan | 50 | * | † | * | 139 | 0.34 | 8 | 0.31 |
| Kazakstan | 75 | 0.07 | 58 | 0.85 | 31 | 0.08 | 24 | 0.91 |
| Kenya | 28 | * | — | * | 272 | 0.67 | 12 | 0.46 |
| Korea, Republic of | 1,620 | 1.49 | 107 | 1.57 | 747 | 1.83 | 48 | 1.82 |
| Kuwait | 268 | 0.25 | 11 | 0.16 | 257 | 0.63 | 17 | 0.63 |
| Lebanon | 94 | 0.09 | 16 | 0.24 | 24 | 0.06 | 1 | * |
| Malaysia | 335 | 0.31 | 5 | 0.07 | 233 | 0.57 | 3 | 0.13 |
| Mexico | 562 | 0.52 | 45 | 0.66 | 98 | 0.24 | † | * |
| Morocco | 176 | 0.16 | 15 | 0.22 | 51 | 0.13 | 1 | * |
| Netherlands | 2,111 | 1.94 | 148 | 2.17 | 1,150 | 2.82 | 96 | 3.62 |
| New Zealand | 178 | 0.16 | 15 | 0.22 | 103 | 0.25 | 4 | 0.15 |
| Nigeria | 389 | 0.36 | — | * | 407 | 1.00 | 59 | 2.21 |
| Norway | 379 | 0.35 | 52 | 0.76 | 140 | 0.34 | 6 | 0.23 |
| Pakistan | 119 | 0.11 | 9 | 0.13 | 173 | 0.42 | 5 | 0.20 |
| Panama | 390 | 0.36 | 11 | 0.16 | 50 | 0.12 | 1 | * |
| Paraguay | 113 | 0.10 | 1 | * | 10 | * | 3 | 0.10 |
| Peru | 128 | 0.12 | 2 | * | 19 | * | 2 | 0.09 |
| Philippines | 72 | 0.07 | 2 | * | 82 | 0.20 | 1 | 0.06 |
| Poland | 243 | 0.22 | 34 | 0.50 | 46 | 0.11 | 3 | 0.11 |
| Portugal | 65 | 0.06 | 8 | 0.12 | 281 | 0.69 | 38 | 1.42 |
| Qatar | 123 | 0.11 | — | * | 17 | * | — | * |
| Romania | 310 | 0.28 | 28 | 0.41 | 75 | 0.18 | 6 | 0.23 |
| Russia | 710 | 0.65 | 354 | 5.20 | 69 | 0.17 | 26 | 0.97 |
| Saudi Arabia | 576 | 0.53 | † | * | 225 | 0.55 | 4 | 0.16 |

| Supplying country | IBRD cumulative to June 30, 1996 | | IBRD fiscal 1996 | | IDA cumulative to June 30, 1996 | | IDA fiscal 1996 | |
|---|---|---|---|---|---|---|---|---|
| | Amount | % | Amount | % | Amount | % | Amount | % |
| Senegal | 26 | * | 3 | * | 90 | 0.22 | 10 | 0.38 |
| Singapore | 1,050 | 0.96 | 64 | 0.94 | 682 | 1.67 | 13 | 0.51 |
| Slovenia | 38 | * | 6 | 0.09 | 2 | * | 1 | 0.05 |
| South Africa | 414 | 0.38 | 15 | 0.22 | 953 | 2.33 | 117 | 4.41 |
| Spain | 1,314 | 1.21 | 166 | 2.44 | 282 | 0.69 | 23 | 0.87 |
| Swaziland | 33 | * | 15 | 0.22 | 30 | 0.07 | 4 | 0.15 |
| Sweden | 1,637 | 1.50 | 55 | 0.81 | 452 | 1.11 | 28 | 1.05 |
| Switzerland | 4,388 | 4.03 | 148 | 2.17 | 1,088 | 2.66 | 86 | 3.25 |
| Syrian Arab Republic | 38 | * | 7 | 0.10 | 15 | * | † | * |
| Tanzania | 7 | * | — | * | 28 | 0.07 | 4 | 0.17 |
| Thailand | 145 | 0.13 | 1 | * | 357 | 0.88 | 19 | 0.70 |
| Tunisia | 91 | 0.08 | 1 | * | 36 | 0.09 | 3 | 0.12 |
| Turkey | 379 | 0.35 | 109 | 1.60 | 111 | 0.27 | 46 | 1.75 |
| Turkmenistan | 5 | * | 2 | * | 51 | 0.12 | 19 | 0.73 |
| Ukraine | 158 | 0.15 | 116 | 1.70 | 47 | 0.11 | 9 | 0.35 |
| United Arab Emirates | 566 | 0.52 | 20 | 0.29 | 351 | 0.86 | 8 | 0.29 |
| United Kingdom[a] | 8,200 | 7.53 | 406 | 5.97 | 5,388 | 13.20 | 318 | 11.99 |
| United States | 21,395 | 19.63 | 1,272 | 18.69 | 4,016 | 9.83 | 208 | 7.83 |
| Uruguay | 113 | 0.10 | 3 | * | 5 | * | † | * |
| Uzbekistan | 4 | * | 3 | * | 12 | * | 6 | 0.22 |
| Venezuela | 508 | 0.47 | 35 | 0.51 | 201 | 0.49 | 15 | 0.56 |
| Vietnam | 46 | * | † | * | 51 | 0.12 | 11 | 0.40 |
| Yemen | † | * | — | * | 207 | 0.51 | † | * |
| Yugoslavia (former)[b] | 857 | 0.79 | 1 | * | 172 | 0.42 | — | * |
| Zaire | 6 | * | — | * | 41 | 0.10 | 5 | 0.18 |
| Zambia | 52 | * | 22 | 0.32 | 112 | 0.27 | 1 | 0.05 |
| Zimbabwe | 34 | * | † | * | 103 | 0.25 | 10 | 0.38 |
| Other | 2,235 | 2.05 | 365 | 5.36 | 962 | 2.36 | 82 | 3.09 |
| Total | 109,012 | 100 | 6,806 | 100 | 40,833 | 100 | 2,652 | 100 |

— Zero, † than $0.5 million, * less than 0.05 percent

NOTE: Amounts exclude disbursements for debt reduction, net advance disbursements, and disbursements under simplified procedures for structural and sectoral adjustment loans. Details may not add to totals because of rounding.

a.  United Kingdom includes Hong Kong.

b.  Figures represent payments to subcontractors in respect to contracts awarded to suppliers from Yugoslavia (former).

# IBRD AND IDA PAYMENTS TO SUPPLYING COUNTRIES FOR FOREIGN PROCUREMENT, BY DESCRIPTION OF GOODS, FISCAL 1996

*(amounts in millions of US dollars)*

| | Equipment | | Civil works | | Consultants | | All other goods | | Total disbursements | |
|---|---|---|---|---|---|---|---|---|---|---|
| | Amount | % | Amount | % | Amount | % | Amount | % | Amount | % |
| Albania | 1 | * | 1 | 0.13 | — | * | — | * | 3 | * |
| Algeria | 14 | 0.19 | — | * | 1 | 0.06 | 1 | 0.19 | 15 | 0.16 |
| Angola | † | * | — | * | — | * | 2 | 0.38 | 2 | * |
| Argentina | 26 | 0.37 | † | * | 1 | 0.13 | † | * | 28 | 0.30 |
| Australia | 79 | 1.09 | 11 | 1.35 | 19 | 2.05 | 4 | 0.75 | 112 | 1.18 |
| Austria | 123 | 1.71 | 9 | 1.13 | 3 | 0.34 | 1 | 0.19 | 137 | 1.45 |
| Azerbaijan | 16 | 0.22 | — | * | — | * | 1 | 0.19 | 16 | 0.17 |
| Bahamas, The | 1 | * | 1 | 0.16 | — | * | † | * | 3 | * |
| Barbados | 1 | * | — | * | — | * | † | * | 1 | * |
| Belarus | 14 | 0.20 | 5 | 0.57 | — | * | — | * | 19 | 0.20 |
| Belgium | 83 | 1.15 | 1 | 0.14 | 10 | 1.09 | 15 | 2.82 | 109 | 1.15 |
| Brazil | 102 | 1.42 | 14 | 1.69 | 4 | 0.46 | — | * | 120 | 1.27 |
| Bulgaria | 51 | 0.71 | † | * | † | * | † | * | 51 | 0.54 |
| Canada | 159 | 2.20 | 8 | 1.02 | 57 | 6.28 | 1 | 0.19 | 225 | 2.38 |
| Chile | 14 | 0.20 | — | * | 1 | 0.08 | — | * | 15 | 0.16 |
| China | 154 | 2.14 | 81 | 10.13 | 3 | 0.28 | 4 | 0.75 | 242 | 2.56 |
| Colombia | 23 | 0.31 | † | * | 1 | 0.14 | — | * | 24 | 0.25 |
| Costa Rica | 17 | 0.24 | — | * | 5 | 0.51 | — | * | 22 | 0.23 |
| Côte d'Ivoire | 13 | 0.18 | 9 | 1.15 | 1 | 0.07 | 4 | 0.75 | 27 | 0.29 |
| Cyprus | 2 | * | 16 | 1.94 | 3 | 0.28 | 4 | 0.75 | 24 | 0.25 |
| Czech Republic | 29 | 0.40 | — | * | † | * | † | * | 29 | 0.31 |
| Denmark | 51 | 0.71 | 3 | 0.34 | 16 | 1.76 | 2 | 0.38 | 72 | 0.76 |
| Ecuador | 25 | 0.34 | 1 | 0.15 | 14 | 1.59 | † | * | 40 | 0.42 |
| Egypt | 4 | 0.05 | 1 | 0.09 | 1 | 0.11 | † | * | 6 | 0.06 |
| Finland | 66 | 0.91 | 9 | 1.06 | 4 | 0.39 | † | * | 78 | 0.82 |
| France | 528 | 7.32 | 84 | 10.47 | 90 | 9.89 | 23 | 4.32 | 725 | 7.67 |
| Germany | 679 | 9.41 | 79 | 9.92 | 39 | 4.29 | 64 | 12.03 | 862 | 9.11 |
| Greece | 10 | 0.14 | 3 | 0.36 | 1 | 0.13 | 2 | 0.38 | 16 | 0.17 |
| Guinea | 19 | 0.26 | — | * | 1 | 0.06 | — | * | 20 | 0.21 |
| Hungary | 19 | 0.26 | † | * | † | * | † | * | 20 | 0.21 |
| Iceland | 1 | * | — | * | 1 | 0.09 | 1 | 0.19 | 2 | * |
| India | 100 | 1.39 | 17 | 2.07 | 7 | 0.77 | 1 | 0.19 | 124 | 1.31 |
| Indonesia | 25 | 0.35 | — | * | † | * | — | * | 25 | 0.26 |
| Ireland | 20 | 0.27 | † | * | 17 | 1.85 | † | * | 37 | 0.39 |
| Israel | 6 | 0.08 | — | * | 8 | 0.85 | † | * | 13 | 0.14 |
| Italy | 306 | 4.24 | 221 | 27.59 | 17 | 1.85 | 35 | 6.58 | 578 | 6.11 |
| Japan | 412 | 5.71 | 18 | 2.31 | 8 | 0.86 | 23 | 4.32 | 461 | 4.87 |
| Jordan | 8 | 0.10 | † | * | 1 | 0.08 | — | * | 8 | 0.08 |
| Kazakstan | 82 | 1.14 | — | * | † | * | — | * | 82 | 0.87 |
| Kenya | 8 | 0.11 | — | * | 5 | 0.50 | † | * | 12 | 0.13 |
| Korea, Republic of | 108 | 1.50 | 46 | 5.80 | † | * | 1 | 0.19 | 156 | 1.65 |
| Kuwait | 28 | 0.39 | — | * | — | * | — | * | 28 | 0.30 |
| Lebanon | 2 | * | 2 | 0.23 | 3 | 0.30 | 11 | 2.07 | 17 | 0.18 |
| Malaysia | 8 | 0.10 | 1 | 0.07 | † | * | † | * | 8 | 0.08 |
| Mali | † | * | † | * | † | * | 1 | 0.19 | 2 | * |
| Mexico | 43 | 0.59 | 2 | 0.26 | † | * | — | * | 45 | 0.48 |
| Morocco | 16 | 0.23 | — | * | † | * | — | * | 16 | 0.17 |
| Netherlands | 159 | 2.21 | 33 | 4.14 | 45 | 4.92 | 7 | 1.32 | 244 | 2.58 |
| New Zealand | 10 | 0.14 | — | * | 9 | 0.97 | † | * | 19 | 0.20 |
| Nigeria | 58 | 0.81 | † | * | † | * | — | * | 59 | 0.62 |
| Norway | 52 | 0.72 | — | * | 6 | 0.66 | 1 | 0.19 | 58 | 0.61 |
| Pakistan | 10 | 0.14 | 2 | 0.19 | 2 | 0.17 | 1 | 0.19 | 14 | 0.15 |
| Panama | 10 | 0.14 | 2 | 0.19 | † | * | † | * | 12 | 0.13 |
| Paraguay | † | * | 3 | 0.35 | † | * | — | * | 3 | * |
| Philippines | † | * | — | * | 3 | 0.33 | — | * | 3 | * |
| Poland | 36 | 0.49 | 1 | 0.08 | † | * | — | * | 36 | 0.38 |
| Portugal | 17 | 0.24 | 14 | 1.69 | 15 | 1.62 | † | * | 46 | 0.49 |
| Romania | 32 | 0.45 | 1 | 0.17 | — | * | — | * | 34 | 0.36 |
| Russia | 380 | 5.26 | — | * | † | * | † | * | 380 | 4.02 |

| | Equipment | | Civil works | | Consultants | | All other goods | | Total disbursements | |
|---|---|---|---|---|---|---|---|---|---|---|
| | Amount | % | Amount | % | Amount | % | Amount | % | Amount | % |
| Senegal | 6 | 0.08 | 4 | 0.49 | 1 | 0.09 | 3 | 0.56 | 13 | 0.14 |
| Singapore | 75 | 1.04 | 1 | 0.10 | 1 | 0.06 | † | * | 77 | 0.81 |
| Slovenia | 6 | 0.09 | 1 | 0.16 | — | * | † | * | 8 | 0.08 |
| South Africa | 117 | 1.62 | 3 | 0.32 | 8 | 0.83 | 5 | 0.94 | 132 | 1.40 |
| Spain | 160 | 2.21 | 22 | 2.70 | 4 | 0.45 | 3 | 0.56 | 189 | 2.00 |
| Sudan | — | * | 1 | 0.17 | 1 | 0.06 | — | * | 2 | * |
| Swaziland | 18 | 0.25 | — | * | † | * | † | * | 19 | 0.20 |
| Sweden | 70 | 0.97 | 2 | 0.26 | 9 | 1.03 | 2 | 0.38 | 83 | 0.88 |
| Switzerland | 171 | 2.37 | 4 | 0.51 | 23 | 2.47 | 37 | 6.95 | 235 | 2.48 |
| Thailand | 18 | 0.25 | † | * | 1 | 0.14 | † | * | 20 | 0.21 |
| Trinidad and Tobago | † | * | 2 | 0.24 | † | 0.05 | — | * | 3 | * |
| Tunisia | 3 | * | — | * | 2 | 0.16 | — | * | 4 | * |
| Turkey | 153 | 2.12 | 2 | 0.31 | † | * | † | * | 155 | 1.64 |
| Turkmenistan | 21 | 0.29 | — | * | — | * | — | * | 21 | 0.22 |
| Ukraine | 125 | 1.73 | — | * | — | * | † | * | 125 | 1.32 |
| United Arab Emirates | 28 | 0.38 | † | * | † | * | † | * | 28 | 0.30 |
| United Kingdom[a] | 508 | 7.04 | 33 | 4.06 | 162 | 17.78 | 21 | 3.95 | 724 | 7.66 |
| United States | 1,249 | 17.31 | 8 | 0.96 | 195 | 21.40 | 28 | 5.26 | 1,480 | 15.65 |
| Uzbekistan | 9 | 0.12 | — | * | † | * | † | * | 9 | 0.10 |
| Venezuela | 45 | 0.63 | — | * | 5 | 0.53 | † | * | 50 | 0.53 |
| Vietnam | 10 | 0.14 | † | * | † | * | — | * | 11 | 0.12 |
| Zaire | 5 | 0.07 | — | * | † | * | — | * | 5 | 0.05 |
| Zambia | 23 | 0.32 | † | 0.06 | † | * | † | * | 24 | 0.25 |
| Zimbabwe | 8 | 0.11 | 1 | 0.17 | 1 | 0.06 | † | * | 10 | 0.11 |
| Other | 126 | 1.75 | 18 | 2.25 | 76 | 8.36 | 223 | 41.92 | 445 | 4.71 |
| Total | 7,214 | 100 | 800 | 100 | 911 | 100 | 532 | 100 | 9,457 | 100 |

— Zero, † less than $0.5 million, * less than 0.05 percent.
NOTE: Amounts exclude disbursements for debt reduction, net advance disbursements, and disbursements under simplified procedures for structural and sectoral adjustment loans. Details may not add to totals because of rounding.
a. United Kingdom includes Hong Kong.

# IBRD and IDA Foreign Disbursements, by Description of Goods, for Investment Lending, Fiscal 1994–96

| Item | 1994 | | | 1995 | | | 1996 | | |
|------|------|------|------|------|------|------|------|------|------|
| | OECD | Non-OECD | Total | OECD | Non-OECD | Total | OECD | Non-OECD | Total |
| | *Millions of US dollars* | | | | | | | | |
| Civil works | 317 | 209 | 526 | 708 | 229 | 937 | 565 | 234 | 799 |
| Consultants | 615 | 124 | 739 | 626 | 140 | 766 | 720 | 159 | 879 |
| Goods | 2,519 | 593 | 3,112 | 2,758 | 424 | 3,183 | 2,800 | 422 | 3,222 |
| All other | 60 | 65 | 125 | 82 | 73 | 155 | 258 | 260 | 518 |
| Total | 3,512 | 991 | 4,502 | 4,173 | 867 | 5,040 | 4,343 | 1,075 | 5,418 |
| | *Percent[a]* | | | | | | | | |
| Civil works | 60 | 40 | 12 | 76 | 24 | 19 | 71 | 29 | 15 |
| Consultants | 83 | 17 | 16 | 82 | 18 | 15 | 82 | 18 | 16 |
| Goods | 81 | 19 | 69 | 87 | 13 | 63 | 87 | 13 | 59 |
| All other | 48 | 52 | 3 | 53 | 47 | 3 | 50 | 50 | 10 |
| Total | 78 | 22 | 100 | 83 | 17 | 100 | 80 | 20 | 100 |

NOTE: *Amounts exclude disbursements for debt reduction and net advance disbursements. Amounts also exclude disbursements for structural adjustment loans and hybrids (loans that support policy and institutional reforms in a specific sector by financing both a policy component disbursed against imports and an investment component). OECD amounts are based on current OECD membership, excluding Czech Republic and Hungary, which became OECD members in December 1995 and May 1996, respectively.*
*a. All of the percentages are based on the dollar amounts shown under the total disbursements section. These percentages show both the breakdown between OECD and non-OECD countries for individual goods categories and the share of each goods category compared with total disbursements.*

# IBRD AND IDA CUMULATIVE LENDING OPERATIONS, BY MAJOR PURPOSE AND REGION, JUNE 30, 1996

*(millions of US dollars)*

| Purpose[b] | IBRD loans to borrowers, by region[a] | | | | | | |
|---|---|---|---|---|---|---|---|
| | Africa | East Asia and Pacific | South Asia | Europe and Central Asia | Latin America and the Caribbean | Middle East and North Africa | Total |
| Agriculture | 3,574.3 | 11,598.1 | 2,751.0 | 7,146.2 | 16,255.6 | 5,053.3 | 46,378.5 |
| Education | 558.5 | 5,117.3 | 55.0 | 978.3 | 5,082.5 | 1,991.5 | 13,783.1 |
| Electric power and other energy | 1,887.1 | 14,161.2 | 10,462.6 | 5,486.0 | 12,172.5 | 2,133.8 | 46,303.2 |
| Environment | 21.9 | 771.5 | 267.0 | 245.1 | 1,415.6 | 197.0 | 2,918.1 |
| Finance | 1,299.0 | 5,025.0 | 3,658.2 | 4,898.8 | 11,454.0 | 3,319.5 | 29,654.5 |
| Industry | 659.9 | 3,573.2 | 3,155.9 | 3,630.7 | 4,717.6 | 1,700.7 | 17,438.0 |
| Mining/Other extractive | 533.5 | 484.1 | 793.5 | 540.8 | 1,073.3 | 264.2 | 3,689.4 |
| Multisector | 2,148.8 | 4,217.3 | 610.0 | 8,993.2 | 7,604.7 | 2,312.3 | 25,886.3 |
| Oil and gas | 385.2 | 1,767.9 | 3,532.0 | 2,661.1 | 1,424.5 | 711.2 | 10,481.9 |
| Population, health, and nutrition | 289.4 | 925.7 | 31.3 | 950.0 | 2,933.8 | 525.3 | 5,655.5 |
| Public-sector management | 36.7 | 200.0 | 150.0 | 1,362.0 | 3,551.5 | 218.9 | 5,519.1 |
| Social sector | — | 10.0 | — | 263.5 | 830.0 | 78.0 | 1,181.5 |
| Telecommunications/informatics | 510.2 | 1,859.7 | 747.5 | 545.3 | 530.3 | 691.5 | 4,884.5 |
| Transportation | 2,998.0 | 13,743.5 | 2,891.1 | 6,198.0 | 12,886.3 | 2,945.7 | 41,662.5 |
| Urban development | 970.3 | 3,844.0 | 294.1 | 1,211.5 | 4,838.6 | 1,626.1 | 12,784.6 |
| Water supply and sanitation | 1,147.9 | 1,919.4 | 605.4 | 1,623.3 | 4,944.7 | 2,277.5 | 12,518.2 |
| Total | 17,020.7 | 69,217.9 | 30,004.6 | 46,733.8 [c] | 91,715.4 | 26,046.5 | 280,738.8 [c] |

| Purpose[b] | IDA credits to borrowers, by region | | | | | | | Total IBRD and IDA |
|---|---|---|---|---|---|---|---|---|
| | Africa | East Asia and Pacific | South Asia | Europe and Central Asia | Latin America and the Caribbean | Middle East and North Africa | Total | |
| Agriculture | 7,798.3 | 6,411.0 | 14,010.7 | 275.4 | 475.4 | 903.7 | 29,874.5 | 76,253.0 |
| Education | 3,376.7 | 1,621.9 | 3,418.8 | 14.6 | 308.4 | 415.8 | 9,156.2 | 22,939.3 |
| Electric power and other energy | 1,974.5 | 693.8 | 3,745.5 | 93.9 | 271.4 | 252.9 | 7,032.0 | 53,335.2 |
| Environment | 14.4 | 155.0 | 100.1 | — | 55.3 | — | 324.8 | 3,242.9 |
| Finance | 2,498.2 | 351.8 | 834.0 | 183.4 | 189.1 | 74.8 | 4,131.3 | 33,785.8 |
| Industry | 832.2 | 157.2 | 1,546.5 | — | 19.4 | 97.9 | 2,653.2 | 20,091.2 |
| Mining/Other extractive | 139.0 | 51.0 | 82.0 | — | 60.5 | — | 332.5 | 4,021.9 |
| Multisector | 6,247.2 | 464.7 | 4,124.7 | 461.1 | 634.5 | 115.0 | 12,047.2 | 37,933.5 |
| Oil and gas | 571.0 | 66.0 | 492.2 | 20.8 | 94.2 | 101.0 | 1,345.2 | 11,827.1 |
| Population, health, and nutrition | 1,715.4 | 978.3 | 3,184.2 | 66.8 | 138.5 | 320.8 | 6,404.0 | 12,059.5 |
| Public-sector management | 1,685.1 | 180.7 | 283.8 | 128.7 | 246.6 | 13.7 | 2,538.6 | 8,057.7 |
| Social sector | 357.5 | 39.7 | — | 53.9 | 156.5 | 145.0 | 752.6 | 1,934.1 |
| Telecommunications/informatics | 441.2 | 101.8 | 882.2 | 18.0 | — | 83.0 | 1,526.2 | 6,410.7 |
| Transportation | 5,797.0 | 1,256.4 | 2,944.6 | 86.0 | 474.3 | 301.9 | 10,860.2 | 52,522.7 |
| Urban development | 1,512.7 | 532.4 | 1,652.8 | 63.3 | 174.2 | 66.0 | 4,001.4 | 16,786.0 |
| Water supply and sanitation | 1,288.1 | 414.2 | 1,872.6 | 72.6 | 111.1 | 203.2 | 3,961.8 | 16,480.0 |
| Total | 36,248.5 | 13,475.9 | 39,174.7 | 1,538.5 | 3,409.4 | 3,094.7 | 96,941.7 | 377,680.5 [c] |

— Zero.

a. No account is taken of cancellations subsequent to original commitment. IBRD loans to the IFC are excluded.

b. Operations have been classified by the major purpose they finance. Many projects include activity in more than one sector or subsector.

c. Does not include the refinanced/rescheduled overdue charges of $167.8 million for Bosnia and Herzegovina.

*Details may not add to totals because of rounding.*

*(amounts in millions of US dollars)*

| Borrower or guarantor | IBRD loans | | IDA credits | | Total | |
|---|---|---|---|---|---|---|
| | Number | Amount | Number | Amount | Number | Amount |
| Afghanistan | — | — | 20 | 230.1 | 20 | 230.1 |
| Africa region | 1 | 15.0 | 1 | 45.5 | 2 | 60.5 |
| Albania | — | — | 22 | 272.5 | 22 | 272.5 |
| Algeria | 60 | 5,319.5 | — | — | 60 | 5,319.5 |
| Angola | — | — | 9 | 272.8 | 9 | 272.8 |
| Argentina | 74 | 11,676.2 | — | — | 74 | 11,676.2 |
| Armenia | 1 | 12.0 | 8 | 236.5 | 9 | 248.5 |
| Australia | 7 | 417.7 | — | — | 7 | 417.7 |
| Austria | 9 | 106.4 | — | — | 9 | 106.4 |
| Azerbaijan | — | — | 4 | 164.8 | 4 | 164.8 |
| Bahamas, The | 5 | 42.8 | — | — | 5 | 42.8 |
| Bangladesh | 1 | 46.1 | 147 | 7,152.5 | 148 | 7,198.6 |
| Barbados | 11 | 103.2 | — | — | 11 | 103.2 |
| Belarus | 3 | 170.2 | — | — | 3 | 170.2 |
| Belgium | 4 | 76.0 | — | — | 4 | 76.0 |
| Belize | 7 | 64.8 | — | — | 7 | 64.8 |
| Benin | — | — | 43 | 610.1 | 43 | 610.1 |
| Bhutan | — | — | 6 | 28.2 | 6 | 28.2 |
| Bolivia | 14 | 299.3 | 51 | 1,171.5 | 65 | 1,470.8 |
| Bosnia-Herzegovina | — | — | 2 | 10.0 | 2 | 10.0 |
| Botswana | 20 | 280.7 | 6 | 15.8 | 26 | 296.5 |
| Brazil | 214 | 23,116.7 | — | — | 214 | 23,116.7 |
| Bulgaria | 10 | 839.0 | — | — | 10 | 839.0 |
| Burkina Faso | — | 1.9 | 45 | 793.3 | 45 | 795.2 |
| Burundi | 1 | 4.8 | 46 | 694.0 | 47 | 698.8 |
| Cambodia | — | — | 5 | 179.7 | 5 | 179.7 |
| Cameroon | 44 | 1,294.4 | 22 | 768.6 | 66 | 2,063.0 |
| Cape Verde | — | — | 9 | 67.8 | 9 | 67.8 |
| Caribbean region | 5 | 89.8 | 2 | 47.7 | 7 | 137.5 |
| Central African Republic | — | — | 24 | 403.5 | 24 | 403.5 |
| Chad | — | — | 33 | 551.0 | 33 | 551.0 |
| Chile | 57 | 3,425.4 | — | 19.0 | 57 | 3,444.4 |
| China | 108 | 16,618.9 | 65 | 8,905.7 | 173 | 25,524.6 |
| Colombia | 143 | 8,588.9 | — | 19.5 | 143 | 8,608.4 |
| Comoros | — | — | 12 | 73.2 | 12 | 73.2 |
| Congo | 10 | 216.7 | 10 | 183.6 | 20 | 400.3 |
| Costa Rica | 38 | 888.9 | | 5.5 | 38 | 894.4 |
| Côte d'Ivoire | 62 | 2,887.9 | 15 | 1,289.2 | 77 | 4,177.1 |
| Croatia | 6 | 279.5 | — | — | 6 | 279.5 |
| Cyprus | 30 | 418.8 | — | — | 30 | 418.8 |
| Czech Republic | 2 | 326.0 | — | — | 2 | 326.0 |
| Czechoslovakia | 1 | 450.0 | — | — | 1 | 450.0 |
| Denmark | 3 | 85.0 | — | — | 3 | 85.0 |
| Djibouti | — | — | 8 | 51.6 | 8 | 51.6 |
| Dominica | 1 | 3.1 | 3 | 14.1 | 4 | 17.1 |
| Dominican Republic | 23 | 631.9 | 3 | 22.0 | 26 | 653.9 |
| East African Community | 10 | 244.8 | — | — | 10 | 244.8 |
| Eastern Africa region | — | — | 1 | 45.0 | 1 | 45.0 |
| Ecuador | 59 | 2,239.9 | 5 | 36.9 | 64 | 2,276.8 |
| Egypt | 58 | 4,002.5 | 33 | 1,582.0 | 91 | 5,584.5 |

| Borrower or guarantor | IBRD loans | | IDA credits | | Total | |
|---|---|---|---|---|---|---|
| | Number | Amount | Number | Amount | Number | Amount |
| El Salvador | 29 | 650.6 | 2 | 25.6 | 31 | 676.2 |
| Equatorial Guinea | — | — | 9 | 45.0 | 9 | 45.0 |
| Eritrea | — | — | 1 | 17.5 | 1 | 17.5 |
| Estonia | 7 | 125.7 | — | — | 7 | 125.7 |
| Ethiopia | 12 | 108.6 | 56 | 2,158.5 | 68 | 2,267.1 |
| Fiji | 13 | 152.9 | — | — | 13 | 152.9 |
| Finland | 18 | 316.8 | — | — | 18 | 316.8 |
| France | 1 | 250.0 | — | — | 1 | 250.0 |
| Gabon | 12 | 212.0 | — | — | 12 | 212.0 |
| Gambia, The | — | — | 23 | 160.2 | 23 | 160.2 |
| Georgia | — | — | 7 | 193.9 | 7 | 193.9 |
| Ghana | 9 | 207.0 | 84 | 3,069.9 | 93 | 3,276.9 |
| Greece | 17 | 490.8 | — | — | 17 | 490.8 |
| Grenada | 1 | 3.8 | 1 | 8.8 | 2 | 12.7 |
| Guatemala | 24 | 734.5 | — | — | 24 | 734.5 |
| Guinea | 3 | 75.2 | 46 | 973.8 | 49 | 1,049.0 |
| Guinea-Bissau | — | — | 19 | 208.9 | 19 | 208.9 |
| Guyana | 12 | 80.0 | 15 | 290.1 | 27 | 370.1 |
| Haiti | 1 | 2.6 | 34 | 593.0 | 35 | 595.6 |
| Honduras | 33 | 717.3 | 18 | 626.6 | 51 | 1,343.9 |
| Hungary | 33 | 3,672.9 | — | — | 33 | 3,672.9 |
| Iceland | 10 | 47.1 | — | — | 10 | 47.1 |
| India | 160 | 23,733.6 | 213 | 23,529.9 | 373 | 47,263.5 |
| Indonesia | 211 | 22,820.4 | 46 | 931.8 | 257 | 23,752.2 |
| Iran, Islamic Republic of | 39 | 2,058.1 | — | — | 39 | 2,058.1 |
| Iraq | 6 | 156.2 | — | — | 6 | 156.2 |
| Ireland | 8 | 152.5 | — | — | 8 | 152.5 |
| Israel | 11 | 284.5 | — | — | 11 | 284.5 |
| Italy | 8 | 399.6 | — | — | 8 | 399.6 |
| Jamaica | 59 | 1,249.1 | — | — | 59 | 1,249.1 |
| Japan | 31 | 862.9 | — | — | 31 | 862.9 |
| Jordan | 42 | 1,465.0 | 15 | 85.3 | 57 | 1,550.3 |
| Kazakstan | 9 | 816.8 | — | — | 9 | 816.8 |
| Kenya | 46 | 1,200.0 | 68 | 2,581.4 | 114 | 3,781.4 |
| Korea, Republic of | 110 | 8,599.0 | 6 | 110.8 | 116 | 8,709.8 |
| Kyrgyz Republic | — | — | 11 | 313.5 | 11 | 313.5 |
| Lao People's Democratic Republic | — | — | 23 | 463.5 | 23 | 463.5 |
| Latvia | 6 | 150.3 | — | — | 6 | 150.3 |
| Lebanon | 10 | 529.4 | — | — | 10 | 529.4 |
| Lesotho | 1 | 110.0 | 24 | 264.2 | 25 | 374.2 |
| Liberia | 21 | 156.0 | 14 | 114.5 | 35 | 270.5 |
| Lithuania | 7 | 160.5 | — | — | 7 | 160.5 |
| Luxembourg | 1 | 12.0 | — | — | 1 | 12.0 |
| Macedonia, Former Yugoslav Republic of | 3 | 76.0 | 4 | 163.8 | 7 | 239.8 |
| Madagascar | 5 | 32.9 | 63 | 1,323.9 | 68 | 1,356.8 |
| Malawi | 9 | 124.1 | 60 | 1,594.7 | 69 | 1,718.8 |
| Malaysia | 83 | 3,446.6 | — | — | 83 | 3,446.6 |
| Maldives | — | — | 6 | 47.3 | 6 | 47.3 |
| Mali | — | 1.9 | 54 | 1,078.7 | 54 | 1,080.6 |
| Malta | 1 | 7.5 | — | — | 1 | 7.5 |

*(amounts in millions of US dollars)*

| Borrower or guarantor | IBRD loans | | IDA credits | | Total | |
|---|---|---|---|---|---|---|
| | Number | Amount | Number | Amount | Number | Amount |
| Mauritania | 3 | 146.0 | 36 | 427.8 | 39 | 573.8 |
| Mauritius | 29 | 400.7 | 4 | 20.2 | 33 | 420.9 |
| Mexico | 155 | 26,332.5 | — | — | 155 | 26,332.5 |
| Moldova | 7 | 231.0 | — | — | 7 | 231.0 |
| Mongolia | — | — | 6 | 130.0 | 6 | 130.0 |
| Morocco | 111 | 7,687.3 | 3 | 50.8 | 114 | 7,738.1 |
| Mozambique | — | — | 28 | 1,500.0 | 28 | 1,500.0 |
| Myanmar | 3 | 33.4 | 30 | 804.0 | 33 | 837.4 |
| Nepal | — | — | 64 | 1,394.1 | 64 | 1,394.1 |
| Netherlands | 8 | 244.0 | — | — | 8 | 244.0 |
| New Zealand | 6 | 126.8 | — | — | 6 | 126.8 |
| Nicaragua | 27 | 233.6 | 13 | 464.5 | 40 | 698.1 |
| Niger | — | — | 39 | 616.0 | 39 | 616.0 |
| Nigeria | 84 | 6,248.2 | 14 | 902.9 | 98 | 7,151.1 |
| Norway | 6 | 145.0 | — | — | 6 | 145.0 |
| Oman | 11 | 157.1 | — | — | 11 | 157.1 |
| Pakistan | 82 | 6,014.2 | 101 | 4,735.5 | 183 | 10,749.7 |
| Panama | 36 | 966.3 | — | — | 36 | 966.3 |
| Papua New Guinea | 28 | 592.0 | 9 | 113.2 | 37 | 705.2 |
| Paraguay | 34 | 746.1 | 6 | 45.5 | 40 | 791.6 |
| Peru | 73 | 3,974.1 | — | — | 73 | 3,974.1 |
| Philippines | 137 | 9,525.9 | 5 | 294.2 | 142 | 9,820.1 |
| Poland | 23 | 4,053.5 | — | — | 23 | 4,053.5 |
| Portugal | 32 | 1,338.8 | — | — | 32 | 1,338.8 |
| Romania | 45 | 4,100.3 | — | — | 45 | 4,100.3 |
| Russia | 28 | 6,447.3 | — | — | 28 | 6,447.3 |
| Rwanda | — | — | 45 | 694.4 | 45 | 694.4 |
| São Tomé and Principe | — | — | 8 | 58.9 | 8 | 58.9 |
| Senegal | 19 | 164.9 | 61 | 1,313.0 | 80 | 1,477.9 |
| Seychelles | 2 | 10.7 | — | — | 2 | 10.7 |
| Sierra Leone | 4 | 18.7 | 21 | 403.6 | 25 | 422.3 |
| Singapore | 14 | 181.3 | — | — | 14 | 181.3 |
| Slovak Republic | 2 | 135.0 | — | — | 2 | 135.0 |
| Slovenia | 2 | 103.9 | — | — | 2 | 103.9 |
| Solomon Islands | — | — | 6 | 33.9 | 6 | 33.9 |
| Somalia | — | — | 39 | 492.1 | 39 | 492.1 |
| South Africa | 11 | 241.8 | — | — | 11 | 241.8 |
| Spain | 12 | 478.7 | — | — | 12 | 478.7 |
| Sri Lanka | 12 | 210.7 | 65 | 2,057.1 | 77 | 2,267.8 |
| St. Kitts and Nevis | 1 | 1.5 | — | 1.5 | 1 | 3.0 |
| St. Lucia | 3 | 8.5 | — | 11.2 | 3 | 19.7 |
| St. Vincent and the Grenadines | 1 | 1.4 | 1 | 6.4 | 2 | 7.8 |
| Sudan | 8 | 166.0 | 48 | 1,352.9 | 56 | 1,518.9 |
| Swaziland | 12 | 104.8 | 2 | 7.8 | 14 | 112.6 |
| Syrian Arab Republic | 17 | 613.2 | 3 | 47.3 | 20 | 660.5 |
| Tajikistan | — | — | 1 | 5.0 | 1 | 5.0 |
| Tanzania | 18 | 318.2 | 84 | 2,819.9 | 102 | 3,138.1 |
| Thailand | 108 | 5,510.7 | 6 | 125.1 | 114 | 5,635.8 |
| Togo | 1 | 20.0 | 37 | 622.3 | 38 | 642.3 |
| Tonga | — | — | 2 | 5.0 | 2 | 5.0 |

| Borrower or guarantor | IBRD loans | | IDA credits | | Total | |
|---|---|---|---|---|---|---|
| | Number | Amount | Number | Amount | Number | Amount |
| Trinidad and Tobago | 20 | 298.8 | — | — | 20 | 298.8 |
| Tunisia | 99 | 3,766.2 | 5 | 74.6 | 104 | 3,840.8 |
| Turkey | 116 | 12,619.9 | 10 | 178.5 | 126 | 12,798.4 |
| Turkmenistan | 1 | 25.0 | — | — | 1 | 25.0 |
| Uganda | 1 | 8.4 | 59 | 2,240.9 | 60 | 2,249.3 |
| Ukraine | 7 | 1,015.8 | — | — | 7 | 1,015.8 |
| Uruguay | 40 | 1,372.2 | — | — | 40 | 1,372.2 |
| Uzbekistan | 3 | 247.0 | — | — | 3 | 247.0 |
| Vanuatu | — | — | 4 | 15.4 | 4 | 15.4 |
| Venezuela | 33 | 3,171.7 | — | — | 33 | 3,171.7 |
| Vietnam | — | — | 12 | 1,301.7 | 12 | 1,301.7 |
| Western Africa region | 1 | 6.1 | 3 | 52.5 | 4 | 58.6 |
| Western Samoa | — | — | 8 | 46.6 | 8 | 46.6 |
| Yemen | — | — | 103 | 1,254.7 | 103 | 1,254.7 |
| Yugoslavia | 90 | 6,114.7 | — | — | 90 | 6,114.7 |
| Zaire | 7 | 330.0 | 59 | 1,151.5 | 66 | 1,481.5 |
| Zambia | 28 | 679.1 | 37 | 1,602.3 | 65 | 2,281.4 |
| Zimbabwe | 24 | 983.2 | 7 | 513.4 | 31 | 1,496.6 |
| Other[a] | 14 | 329.4 | 4 | 15.3 | 18 | 344.7 |
| Total | 3,923 | 280,739.0 [b] | 2,680 | 96,941.8 | 6,603 | 377,680.8 [b] |

— Zero

NOTE: *Joint IBRD/IDA operations are counted only once, as IBRD operations. When more than one loan is made for a single project, the operation is counted only once. Details may not add to totals because of rounding.*

*a. Represents IBRD loans and IDA credits made at a time when the authorities on Taiwan represented China in the World Bank (prior to May 15, 1980).*

*b. Does not include the refinanced/rescheduled overdue charges of $167.8 million for Bosnia and Herzegovina.*

(amounts in millions of US dollars)

| Region and Country | IBRD loans | | IDA credits | | Total | |
|---|---|---|---|---|---|---|
| | Number | Amount | Number | Amount | Number | Amount |
| **Africa** | | | | | | |
| Angola | — | — | 1 | 24.0 | 1 | 24.0 |
| Cameroon | — | — | 3 | 253.6 | 3 | 253.6 |
| Cape Verde | — | — | 1 | 11.4 | 1 | 11.4 |
| Chad | — | — | 2 | 39.5 | 2 | 39.5 |
| Congo | — | — | 1 | 9.0 | 1 | 9.0 |
| Côte d'Ivoire | — | — | 4 | 463.6 | 4 | 463.6 |
| Eritrea | — | — | 1 | 17.5 | 1 | 17.5 |
| Ethiopia | — | — | 2 | 155.7 | 2 | 155.7 |
| Ghana | — | — | 5 | 276.2 | 5 | 276.2 |
| Guinea | — | — | 3 | 53.8 | 3 | 53.8 |
| Kenya | — | — | 4 | 313.8 | 4 | 313.8 |
| Lesotho | — | — | 1 | 40.0 | 1 | 40.0 |
| Madagascar | — | — | 2 | 86.0 | 2 | 86.0 |
| Malawi | — | — | 3 | 184.9 | 3 | 184.9 |
| Mali | — | — | 3 | 100.7 | 3 | 100.7 |
| Mauritania | — | — | 2 | 34.8 | 2 | 34.8 |
| Mozambique | — | — | 1 | 98.7 | 1 | 98.7 |
| Niger | — | — | 1 | 26.7 | 1 | 26.7 |
| Senegal | — | — | 2 | 41.9 | 2 | 41.9 |
| Sierra Leone | — | — | 2 | 55.3 | 2 | 55.3 |
| Tanzania | — | — | 2 | 115.9 | 2 | 115.9 |
| Togo | — | — | 1 | 50.0 | 1 | 50.0 |
| Uganda | — | — | 3 | 42.0 | 3 | 42.0 |
| Zambia | — | — | 2 | 175.1 | 2 | 175.1 |
| Zimbabwe | — | — | 1 | 70.0 | 1 | 70.0 |
| Total | — | — | 53 | 2,740.1 | 53 | 2,740.1 |
| **East Asia and Pacific** | | | | | | |
| Cambodia | — | — | 2 | 80.0 | 2 | 80.0 |
| China | 13 | 2,490.0 | 3 | 480.0 | 16 | 2,970.0 |
| Indonesia | 12 | 991.7 | — | — | 12 | 991.7 |
| Lao People's Democratic Republic | — | — | 2 | 60.7 | 2 | 60.7 |
| Mongolia | — | — | 2 | 45.0 | 2 | 45.0 |
| Papua New Guinea | 1 | 50.0 | — | — | 1 | 50.0 |
| Philippines | 3 | 457.0 | — | — | 3 | 457.0 |
| Thailand | 3 | 263.5 | — | — | 3 | 263.5 |
| Vietnam | — | — | 5 | 502.2 | 5 | 502.2 |
| Total | 32 | 4,252.2 | 14 | 1,167.9 | 46 | 5,420.1 |
| **South Asia** | | | | | | |
| Bangladesh | — | — | 4 | 238.8 | 4 | 238.8 |
| India | 4 | 776.6 | 5 | 1,301.1 | 9 | 2,077.7 |
| Pakistan | 2 | 385.0 | 3 | 74.9 | 5 | 459.9 |
| Sri Lanka | — | — | 3 | 156.1 | 3 | 156.1 |
| Total | 6 | 1,161.6 | 15 | 1,770.9 | 21 | 2,932.5 |
| **Europe and Central Asia** | | | | | | |
| Albania | — | — | 5 | 72.5 | 5 | 72.5 |
| Armenia | — | — | 4 | 91.8 | 4 | 91.8 |
| Azerbaijan | — | — | 2 | 83.0 | 2 | 83.0 |
| Bosnia-Herzegovina | — | — | 2 | 10.0 | 2 | 10.0 |
| Bulgaria | 2 | 121.0 | — | — | 2 | 121.0 |
| Croatia | 3 | 31.5 | — | — | 3 | 31.5 |
| Estonia | 1 | 15.3 | — | — | 1 | 15.3 |

| Region and Country | IBRD loans | | IDA credits | | Total | |
|---|---|---|---|---|---|---|
| | Number | Amount | Number | Amount | Number | Amount |
| Georgia | — | — | 4 | 90.8 | 4 | 90.8 |
| Kazakstan | 2 | 260.0 | — | — | 2 | 260.0 |
| Kyrgyz Republic | — | — | 5 | 98.5 | 5 | 98.5 |
| Latvia | 1 | 27.3 | — | — | 1 | 27.3 |
| Lithuania | 3 | 42.1 | — | — | 3 | 42.1 |
| Macedonia, Former Yugoslav Republic of | 1 | 12.0 | 2 | 24.8 | 3 | 36.8 |
| Moldova | 3 | 55.0 | — | — | 3 | 55.0 |
| Poland | 2 | 181.5 | — | — | 2 | 181.5 |
| Romania | 3 | 510.0 | — | — | 3 | 510.0 |
| Russia | 9 | 1,816.0 | — | — | 9 | 1,816.0 |
| Slovenia | 1 | 23.9 | — | — | 1 | 23.9 |
| Tajikistan | — | — | 1 | 5.0 | 1 | 5.0 |
| Turkey | 2 | 312.0 | — | — | 2 | 312.0 |
| Ukraine | 3 | 342.8 | — | — | 3 | 342.8 |
| Total | 36 | 3,750.4 [a] | 25 | 476.4 | 61 | 4,226.8 [a] |
| **Latin America and the Caribbean** | | | | | | |
| Argentina | 11 | 1,509.4 | — | — | 11 | 1,509.4 |
| Bolivia | — | — | 7 | 128.7 | 7 | 128.7 |
| Brazil | 4 | 875.0 | — | — | 4 | 875.0 |
| Chile | 1 | 15.0 | — | — | 1 | 15.0 |
| Colombia | 4 | 479.3 | — | — | 4 | 479.3 |
| Dominica | 1 | 3.1 | — | 3.1 | 1 | 6.1 |
| Dominican Republic | 1 | 37.0 | — | — | 1 | 37.0 |
| Ecuador | 1 | 15.0 | — | — | 1 | 15.0 |
| El Salvador | 4 | 165.0 | — | — | 4 | 165.0 |
| Grenada | 1 | 3.8 | — | 3.8 | 1 | 7.6 |
| Guyana | — | — | 1 | 20.2 | 1 | 20.2 |
| Haiti | — | — | 1 | 50.0 | 1 | 50.0 |
| Honduras | — | — | 3 | 121.0 | 3 | 121.0 |
| Jamaica | 1 | 21.0 | — | — | 1 | 21.0 |
| Mexico | 3 | 526.5 | — | — | 3 | 526.5 |
| Nicaragua | — | — | 2 | 60.8 | 2 | 60.8 |
| Panama | 2 | 65.0 | — | — | 2 | 65.0 |
| Paraguay | 1 | 24.5 | — | — | 1 | 24.5 |
| Peru | 1 | 90.0 | — | — | 1 | 90.0 |
| St. Lucia | 1 | 2.6 | — | 2.7 | 1 | 5.3 |
| Trinidad and Tobago | 1 | 51.0 | — | — | 1 | 51.0 |
| Uruguay | 1 | 125.0 | — | — | 1 | 125.0 |
| Venezuela | 1 | 39.0 | — | — | 1 | 39.0 |
| Total | 40 | 4,047.2 | 14 | 390.3 | 54 | 4,437.5 |
| **Middle East and North Africa** | | | | | | |
| Algeria | 3 | 428.0 | — | — | 3 | 428.0 |
| Egypt | 1 | 20.0 | 2 | 152.2 | 3 | 172.2 |
| Jordan | 2 | 120.0 | — | — | 2 | 120.0 |
| Lebanon | 1 | 70.0 | — | — | 1 | 70.0 |
| Morocco | 6 | 540.0 | — | — | 6 | 540.0 |
| Tunisia | 2 | 98.7 | — | — | 2 | 98.7 |
| Yemen | — | — | 4 | 166.3 | 4 | 166.3 |
| Total | 15 | 1,276.7 | 6 | 318.5 | 21 | 1,595.2 |
| Grand Total | 129 | 14,488.1 [a] | 127 | 6,864.1 | 256 | 21,352.2 [a] |

NOTE: Supplements are included in the amount but are not counted as separate lending operations. Joint IBRD/IDA operations are counted only once, as IBRD operations.
— Zero.
a. Does not include the refinanced/rescheduled overdue charges of $167.8 million for Bosnia and Herzegovina.

*(amounts in millions of US dollars)*

| | IBRD | IDA | Total |
|---|---|---|---|
| **Agriculture** | | | |
| Albania | — | 8.0 | 8.0 |
| Albania | — | 6.0 | 6.0 |
| Argentina | 16.0 | — | 16.0 |
| Bangladesh | — | 50.0 | 50.0 |
| Bangladesh | — | 121.9 | 121.9 |
| Bangladesh | — | 53.0 | 53.0 |
| Bolivia | — | 15.0 | 15.0 |
| Brazil | 175.0 | — | 175.0 |
| Chile | 15.0 | — | 15.0 |
| China | 150.0 | — | 150.0 |
| China | 60.0 | 90.0 | 150.0 |
| China | 80.0 | 20.0 | 100.0 |
| China | — | 100.0 | 100.0 |
| Côte d'Ivoire | — | 150.0 | 150.0 |
| Côte d'Ivoire | — | 73.6 | 73.6 [b] |
| Croatia | 17.0 | — | 17.0 |
| Estonia | 15.3 | — | 15.3 |
| Guinea | — | 35.0 | 35.0 |
| India | — | 142.0 | 142.0 |
| India | — | 290.9 | 290.9 |
| Indonesia | 27.0 | — | 27.0 |
| Indonesia | 26.8 | — | 26.8 |
| Indonesia | 19.1 | — | 19.1 |
| Kazakstan | 80.0 | — | 80.0 |
| Kenya | — | 22.0 | 22.0 |
| Kyrgyz Republic | — | 11.6 | 11.6 |
| Lao People's Democratic Republic | — | 20.7 | 20.7 |
| Lithuania | 30.0 | — | 30.0 |
| Macedonia, Former Yugoslav Republic of | — | 7.9 | 7.9 |
| Mexico | 186.5 | — | 186.5 |
| Moldova | 10.0 | — | 10.0 |
| Morocco | 100.0 | — | 100.0 |
| Niger | — | 26.7 | 26.7 |
| Pakistan | — | 26.7 | 26.7 |
| Philippines | 150.0 | — | 150.0 |
| Senegal | — | 2.8 | 2.8 |
| St. Lucia | 2.6 | 2.7 | 5.3 |
| Uganda | — | 17.9 | 17.9 |
| Vietnam | — | 122.0 | 122.0 |
| Total | 1,160.3 | 1,416.4 | 2,576.7 |
| | | | |
| **Education** | | | |
| Argentina | 115.5 | — | 115.5 |
| Argentina | 165.0 | — | 165.0 |
| Bangladesh | — | 10.5 | 10.5 |
| Bosnia and Herzegovina | — | 5.0 | 5.0 |
| China | — | 100.0 | 100.0 |
| Dominica | 3.1 | 3.1 | 6.1 |
| Dominican Republic | 37.0 | — | 37.0 |
| El Salvador | 34.0 | — | 34.0 |
| Ghana | — | 50.0 | 50.0 |
| Grenada | 3.8 | 3.8 | 7.7 |
| Guinea | — | 6.6 | 6.6 |
| Guyana | — | 17.3 | 17.3 |
| India | — | 425.2 | 425.2 |
| Indonesia | 60.4 | — | 60.4 |

|  | IBRD | IDA | Total |
|---|---|---|---|
| Indonesia | 65.0 | — | 65.0 |
| Indonesia | 99.0 | — | 99.0 |
| Malawi | — | 22.5 | 22.5 |
| Mali | — | 13.4 | 13.4 |
| Morocco | 54.0 | — | 54.0 |
| Panama | 35.0 | — | 35.0 |
| Paraguay | 24.5 | — | 24.5 |
| Senegal | — | 26.5 | 26.5 |
| Senegal | — | 12.6 | 12.6 |
| Sri Lanka | — | 64.1 | 64.1 |
| Thailand | 81.9 | — | 81.9 |
| Thailand | 31.6 | — | 31.6 |
| Trinidad and Tobago | 51.0 | — | 51.0 |
| Tunisia | 60.0 | — | 60.0 |
| Yemen | — | 24.3 | 24.3 |
| Total | 920.8 | 784.9 | 1,705.7 |

**Electric power and other energy**

|  | IBRD | IDA | Total |
|---|---|---|---|
| Albania | — | 29.5 | 29.5 |
| Bolivia | — | 5.1 | 5.1 |
| Cambodia | — | 40.0 | 40.0 |
| China | 400.0 | — | 400.0 |
| China | 440.0 | — | 440.0 |
| Colombia | 249.3 | — | 249.3 |
| El Salvador | 65.0 | — | 65.0 |
| India | 350.0 | — | 350.0 |
| Indonesia | 373.0 | — | 373.0 |
| Jamaica | 21.0 | — | 21.0 |
| Kyrgyz Republic | — | 20.0 | 20.0 |
| Lithuania | 5.9 | — | 5.9 |
| Madagascar | — | 46.0 | 46.0 |
| Mali | — | 27.3 | 27.3 |
| Pakistan | 350.0 | — | 350.0 |
| Philippines | 250.0 | — | 250.0 |
| Poland | 160.0 | — | 160.0 |
| Romania | 110.0 | — | 110.0 |
| Uruguay | 125.0 | — | 125.0 |
| Vietnam | — | 180.0 | 180.0 |
| Total | 2,899.2 | 347.9 | 3,247.1 |

**Environment**

|  | IBRD | IDA | Total |
|---|---|---|---|
| Algeria | 78.0 | — | 78.0 |
| Brazil | 50.0 | — | 50.0 |
| China | 125.0 | 25.0 | 150.0 |
| Ecuador | 15.0 | — | 15.0 |
| El Salvador | 50.0 | — | 50.0 |
| Lithuania | 6.2 | — | 6.2 |
| Slovenia | 23.9 | — | 23.9 |
| Uganda | — | 11.8 | 11.8 |
| Total | 348.1 | 36.8 | 384.9 |

**Finance**

|  | IBRD | IDA | Total |
|---|---|---|---|
| Bolivia | — | 9.0 | 9.0 |
| Croatia | 9.5 | — | 9.5 |

PROJECTS APPROVED FOR IBRD AND IDA          APPENDIX 14
ASSISTANCE IN FISCAL YEAR 1996,
BY SECTOR[a]  *(continued)*
*(amounts in millions of US dollars)*

| | IBRD | IDA | Total |
|---|---|---|---|
| Ghana | — | 23.9 | 23.9 |
| Guyana | — | 2.9 | 2.9 [b] |
| India | 200.0 | 5.0 | 205.0 |
| Jordan | 80.0 | — | 80.0 |
| Jordan | 40.0 | — | 40.0 |
| Kazakstan | 180.0 | — | 180.0 |
| Kyrgyz Republic | — | 45.0 | 45.0 |
| Kyrgyz Republic | — | 3.4 | 3.4 |
| Macedonia, Former Yugoslav Republic of | 12.0 | — | 12.0 |
| Morocco | 250.0 | — | 250.0 |
| Russia | 300.0 | — | 300.0 |
| Russia | 89.0 | — | 89.0 |
| Tanzania | — | 10.9 | 10.9 |
| Tunisia | 38.7 | — | 38.7 |
| Uganda | — | 12.3 | 12.3 |
| Vietnam | — | 49.0 | 49.0 |
| Zambia | — | 12.1 | 12.1 [b] |
| Total | 1,199.2 | 173.5 | 1,372.7 |
| | | | |
| **Industry** | | | |
| Bangladesh | — | 3.4 | 3.4 [b] |
| Bolivia | — | 8.0 | 8.0 [b] |
| Cape Verde | — | 11.4 | 11.4 |
| China | 170.0 | — | 170.0 |
| Indonesia | 47.0 | — | 47.0 |
| Total | 217.0 | 22.8 | 239.8 |
| | | | |
| **Mining and other extractive** | | | |
| Argentina | 30.0 | — | 30.0 |
| Bolivia | — | 11.0 | 11.0 |
| India | — | 63.0 | 63.0 |
| Mongolia | — | 35.0 | 35.0 |
| Russia | 500.0 | — | 500.0 |
| Russia | 25.0 | — | 25.0 |
| Ukraine | 15.8 | — | 15.8 |
| Total | 570.8 | 109.0 | 679.8 |
| | | | |
| **Multisector** | | | |
| Algeria | 300.0 | — | 300.0 |
| Argentina | 38.5 | — | 38.5 |
| Armenia | — | 60.0 | 60.0 |
| Azerbaijan | — | 65.0 | 65.0 |
| Cambodia | — | 40.0 | 40.0 |
| Chad | — | 30.0 | 30.0 |
| Chad | — | 9.5 | 9.5 |
| El Salvador | 16.0 | — | 16.0 |
| Georgia | — | 60.0 | 60.0 |
| Ghana | — | 4.8 | 4.8 [b] |
| Honduras | — | 26.4 | 26.4 [b] |
| Kenya | — | 90.0 | 90.0 |
| Kenya | — | 36.8 | 36.8 [b] |
| Lao People's Democratic Republic | — | 40.0 | 40.0 |
| Malawi | — | 102.0 | 102.0 |

| | IBRD | IDA | Total |
|---|---|---|---|
| Malawi | — | 4.4 | 4.4 [b] |
| Mali | — | 60.0 | 60.0 |
| Mauritania | — | 20.0 | 20.0 |
| Panama | 30.0 | — | 30.0 |
| Papua New Guinea | 50.0 | — | 50.0 |
| Romania | 280.0 | — | 280.0 |
| Russia | 24.0 | — | 24.0 |
| Sierra Leone | — | 0.3 | 0.3 [b] |
| Togo | — | 50.0 | 50.0 |
| Yemen | — | 80.0 | 80.0 |
| Total | 738.5 | 779.2 | 1,517.7 |

**Oil, gas, and coal**

| | IBRD | IDA | Total |
|---|---|---|---|
| Bolivia | — | 10.6 | 10.6 |
| Egypt | 20.0 | 15.0 | 35.0 |
| Moldova | 10.0 | — | 10.0 |
| Total | 30.0 | 25.6 | 55.6 |

**Population, health, and nutrition**

| | IBRD | IDA | Total |
|---|---|---|---|
| Argentina | 101.4 | — | 101.4 |
| Argentina | 350.0 | — | 350.0 |
| Argentina | 25.0 | — | 25.0 |
| Bosnia and Herzegovina | — | 5.0 | 5.0 |
| Brazil | 300.0 | — | 300.0 |
| Bulgaria | 26.0 | — | 26.0 |
| China | — | 100.0 | 100.0 |
| Côte d'Ivoire | — | 40.0 | 40.0 |
| Egypt | — | 17.2 | 17.2 |
| Georgia | — | 14.0 | 14.0 |
| India | — | 350.0 | 350.0 |
| Indonesia | 24.8 | — | 24.8 |
| Indonesia | 20.0 | — | 20.0 |
| Kyrgyz Republic | — | 18.5 | 18.5 |
| Macedonia, Former Yugoslav Republic of | — | 16.9 | 16.9 |
| Mexico | 310.0 | — | 310.0 |
| Morocco | 68.0 | — | 68.0 |
| Mozambique | — | 98.7 | 98.7 |
| Pakistan | — | 26.7 | 26.7 |
| Russia | 270.0 | — | 270.0 |
| Sierra Leone | — | 20.0 | 20.0 |
| Vietnam | — | 101.2 | 101.2 |
| Vietnam | — | 50.0 | 50.0 |
| Total | 1,495.2 | 858.2 | 2,353.4 |

**Public-sector management**

| | IBRD | IDA | Total |
|---|---|---|---|
| Albania | — | 4.0 | 4.0 |
| Argentina | 16.0 | — | 16.0 |
| Argentina | 500.0 | — | 500.0 |
| Armenia | — | 3.8 | 3.8 |
| Azerbaijan | — | 18.0 | 18.0 |
| Bolivia | — | 50.0 | 50.0 |
| Cameroon | — | 150.0 | 150.0 |
| Cameroon | — | 12.6 | 12.6 |

BY SECTOR *(continued)*
*(amounts in millions of US dollars)*

| | IBRD | IDA | Total |
|---|---|---|---|
| Cameroon | — | 30.3 | 30.3 [b] |
| Congo | — | 9.0 | 9.0 |
| Côte d'Ivoire | — | 180.0 | 180.0 |
| Croatia | 5.0 | — | 5.0 |
| Georgia | — | 4.8 | 4.8 |
| Ghana | — | 26.5 | 26.5 |
| Guinea | — | 12.2 | 12.2 |
| Honduras | — | 55.0 | 55.0 |
| Honduras | — | 9.6 | 9.6 |
| Lebanon | 20.0 | — | 20.0 |
| Mauritania | — | 0.8 | 0.8 [b] |
| Mexico | 30.0 | — | 30.0 |
| Moldova | 35.0 | — | 35.0 |
| Nicaragua | — | 5.8 | 5.8 [b] |
| Russia | 58.0 | — | 58.0 |
| Sri Lanka | — | 77.0 | 77.0 |
| Sri Lanka | — | 15.0 | 15.0 |
| Tajikistan | — | 5.0 | 5.0 |
| Turkey | 62.0 | — | 62.0 |
| Ukraine | 310.0 | — | 310.0 |
| Zambia | — | 140.0 | 140.0 |
| Zambia | — | 23.0 | 23.0 |
| Zimbabwe | — | 70.0 | 70.0 |
| Total | 1,036.0 | 902.4 | 1,938.4 |
| **Social sector** | | | |
| Algeria | 50.0 | — | 50.0 |
| Angola | — | 24.0 | 24.0 |
| Argentina | 152.0 | — | 152.0 |
| Armenia | — | 12.0 | 12.0 |
| China | 10.0 | 20.0 | 30.0 |
| Egypt | — | 120.0 | 120.0 |
| Eritrea | — | 17.5 | 17.5 |
| Ethiopia | — | 120.0 | 120.0 |
| Haiti | — | 50.0 | 50.0 |
| Honduras | — | 30.0 | 30.0 |
| Madagascar | — | 40.0 | 40.0 |
| Malawi | — | 56.0 | 56.0 |
| Mongolia | — | 10.0 | 10.0 |
| Morocco | 28.0 | — | 28.0 |
| Nicaragua | — | 30.0 | 30.0 |
| Yemen | — | 25.0 | 25.0 |
| Total | 240.0 | 554.5 | 794.5 |
| **Telecommunications/Informatics** | | | |
| Pakistan | 35.0 | — | 35.0 |
| Total | 35.0 | 0.0 | 35.0 |
| **Transportation** | | | |
| Albania | — | 25.0 | 25.0 |
| Armenia | — | 16.0 | 16.0 |
| Brazil | 350.0 | — | 350.0 |
| Bulgaria | 95.0 | — | 95.0 |
| Cameroon | — | 60.7 | 60.7 |

| | IBRD | IDA | Total |
|---|---|---|---|
| China | 260.0 | — | 260.0 |
| China | 210.0 | — | 210.0 |
| China | 210.0 | — | 210.0 |
| Colombia | 65.0 | — | 65.0 |
| Côte d'Ivoire | — | 20.0 | 20.0 |
| Georgia | — | 12.0 | 12.0 |
| Ghana | — | 100.0 | 100.0 |
| Indonesia | 86.9 | — | 86.9 |
| Kenya | — | 115.0 | 115.0 |
| Kenya | — | 50.0 | 50.0 |
| Lesotho | — | 40.0 | 40.0 |
| Nicaragua | — | 25.0 | 25.0 |
| Peru | 90.0 | — | 90.0 |
| Romania | 120.0 | — | 120.0 |
| Russia | 350.0 | — | 350.0 |
| Sierra Leone | — | 35.0 | 35.0 |
| Thailand | 150.0 | — | 150.0 |
| Turkey | 250.0 | — | 250.0 |
| Yemen | — | 37.0 | 37.0 |
| Total | 2,236.9 | 535.7 | 2,772.6 |

### Urban development

| | IBRD | IDA | Total |
|---|---|---|---|
| China | 125.0 | 25.0 | 150.0 |
| China | 250.0 | — | 250.0 |
| Colombia | 20.0 | — | 20.0 |
| Ghana | — | 71.0 | 71.0 |
| Indonesia | 142.7 | — | 142.7 |
| Latvia | 27.3 | — | 27.3 |
| Lebanon | 50.0 | — | 50.0 |
| Mauritania | — | 14.0 | 14.0 |
| Pakistan | — | 21.5 | 21.5 |
| Tanzania | — | 105.0 | 105.0 |
| Ukraine | 17.0 | — | 17.0 |
| Total | 632.0 | 236.5 | 868.5 |

### Water supply and sanitation

| | IBRD | IDA | Total |
|---|---|---|---|
| Bolivia | — | 20.0 | 20.0 |
| Colombia | 145.0 | — | 145.0 |
| Ethiopia | — | 35.7 | 35.7 |
| India | 167.0 | 25.0 | 192.0 |
| India | 59.6 | — | 59.6 |
| Morocco | 40.0 | — | 40.0 |
| Philippines | 57.0 | — | 57.0 |
| Poland | 21.5 | — | 21.5 |
| Russia | 200.0 | — | 200.0 |
| Venezuela | 39.0 | — | 39.0 |
| Total | 729.1 | 80.7 | 809.8 |
| Grand total | 14,488.1 [c] | 6,864.1 | 21,352.2 [c] |

— Zero.

a. Many projects include activity in more than one sector or subsector.

b. Supplementary financing to a previous loan but not counted as a separate operation.

c. Does not include the refinanced/rescheduled overdue charges of $167.8 million for Bosnia and Herzegovina.

## COMMUNIQUÉ

*The 51st Meeting of the Development Committee was held in Washington, D.C. on October 9, 1995, under the chairmanship of Mohamed Kabbaj, Minister of Finance and Foreign Investment of Morocco. Michel Camdessus, Managing Director of the International Monetary Fund and N'Goran Niamien (Côte d'Ivoire), Chairman of the Group of 24, also took part in the meeting. Observers from a number of international and regional organizations also attended.*

1. Ministers welcomed World Bank President James D. Wolfensohn to his first meeting of the committee. The committee was pleased that, for the first time, the United Nations Secretary General, Mr. Boutros Boutros-Ghali, addressed the committee.

2. *Support for poverty reduction.* Ministers reviewed the implications of the United Nations' Social Summit Declaration. They focused particularly on how World Bank and IMF efforts to reduce poverty could be strengthened through enhanced policy dialogue with governments, based in part on results of poverty assessments. Ministers agreed that multilateral development institutions should accelerate their investments in social sectors and poverty reduction programs. The committee encouraged the Bank to strengthen its efforts to promote broad-based, labor-intensive growth through increasing the access of the poor to land, credit, and basic infrastructure.

3. Ministers agreed that efforts to improve the composition and efficiency of public expenditures were needed. The committee urged the Bank and Fund to work closely with member governments to help them improve their public finances, especially by increasing attention to funding social and economic development programs and reducing nonproductive spending (including excessive military expenditures) within a framework of sustainable economic growth.

4. In this context, Ministers agreed that donors' support should be consistent with governments' public expenditure programs. The committee urged donor governments to continue to strengthen assistance for countries demonstrating strong commitment to social sector investments and other high priority poverty reduction programs. The committee also urged them to take steps to reduce administrative burdens on aid recipients.

5. *International Development Association (IDA).* Ministers recognized the importance of supporting the implementation of effective development policies and programs with adequate resource flows, especially of concessional funds, if poverty is to be reduced. The committee recognized that funding reductions facing IDA present a very serious risk to poverty reduction and economic growth in the world's poorest countries. Ministers agreed on the importance of a significant replenishment of IDA.

6. The Committee expressed great concern that potential reductions in contributions to IDA were likely to jeopardize its future and stressed the great importance donors attach to equitable burden sharing. The comittee urged all donors that have not done so to honor their commitments and continue the strong support that has marked IDA's thirty-five-year life.

7. Ministers agreed that every effort should be made to meet the essential financing requirements of poor countries as reflected in IDA's lending plans and to protect IDA's multilateral character.

8. *Multilateral debt.* Ministers agreed that current instruments should be sufficient to bring debt and debt service for the majority of heavily indebted poor countries (HIPCs) down to manageable levels. For a small group of countries, however, this may still leave an unsustainable debt situation, a problem for which appropriate approaches need to be further explored. Ministers requested the Bank and Fund to continue their work on this issue, including detailed country-specific analysis of debt sustainability, and after presenting their findings and recommendations to the Executive Boards, to report with proposals to the committee at its next meeting.

9. *Executive secretary.* The Committee selected Alexander Shakow as Executive Secretary.

## COMMUNIQUÉ

*The 52nd Meeting of the Development Committee was held in Washington, D.C. on April 23, 1996 under the chairmanship of Mohamed Kabbaj, Minister of Finance and Foreign Investment of Morocco. James D. Wolfensohn, President of the World Bank, Michel Camdessus, Managing Director of the International Monetary Fund, Qazi*

*Alimullah, Deputy Chairman of the Planning Commission of Pakistan for Finance and Economic Affairs and Chairman of the Group of 24, and Abdlatif Y. Al-Hamad, Director General of the Arab Fund for Economic and Social Development and Chairman of the Task Force on MDBs, addressed the plenary session. Observers from a number of international and regional organizations also attended.*

1. *International Development Association (IDA).* Ministers expressed appreciation to all donors that contributed to the three-year funding arrangement (a one-year interim trust fund, followed by a two-year replenishment of IDA's general resources) agreed upon in March 1996, and extended special recognition to those donors contributing to the FY97 Interim Trust Fund. Ministers noted that the funding pledged by donors, together with other resources expected to be available to IDA, will allow IDA to lend up to US$22 billion over three years, commencing in July 1996. Although this represents a significant achievement, reached under difficult circumstances, it leaves IDA with seriously constrained financial capacity to respond to countries' improved policy performance. Ministers praised those countries that have become new IDA donors and encouraged others to take similar action. They also thanked those that have made supplementary or increased contributions to IDA.

2. Ministers emphasized that the IDA-11 agreement reflects a strong consensus on IDA's importance to the support of effective development policies and programs in the poorest countries, with its core objective of poverty reduction supported by economic growth and environmental sustainability. Ministers urged IDA to raise its effectiveness and development impact.

3. Ministers reiterated the importance of maintaining IDA's capacity to transfer resources to countries with sound policy performance. They stressed the importance of fair burden sharing among IDA donors and called upon donors to honor their commitments on a timely basis to ensure successful implementation of IDA-11.

4. Noting with great concern the difficulties encountered in the replenishment of IDA-11, Ministers agreed that the prospects for IDA funding be a key issue for discussion by the committee in a year's time.

5. Ministers urged that rapid progress also be made in ensuring the continued financing of the IMF's Enhanced Structural Adjustment Facility (ESAF), a vital complement to IDA, for the multilateral effort to be fully effective.

6. *Resolving debt problems of the heavily indebted poor countries (HIPCs).* Ministers welcomed "A Framework for Action" presented by Bank and Fund management. The committee noted the progress achieved since its last meeting and expressed appreciation for the joint efforts of the Bank and the Fund.

7. Ministers agreed with the analysis of Fund and Bank staff that there were a number of HIPCs for whom the burden of debt, including multilateral debt, was likely to remain above sustainable levels over the medium term, even with strong policies and full use of existing debt-relief mechanisms.

8. Ministers agreed that for these countries further action is needed to address their debt problems, building on actions already being taken by official bilateral and commercial creditors. This would involve the use of both existing mechanisms and new arrangements, including contributions by the IFIs from their own resources, contributions by bilateral donors, and appropriate action by the Paris Club and other creditors.

9. Ministers agreed that the principal goal of the proposed framework should be to ensure for these countries that adjustment and reform efforts are not put at risk by continued high debt and debt-service burdens. They endorsed the following six principles to guide further action: (i) the objective should be to target overall debt sustainability on a case-by-case basis, thus providing an exit strategy from the rescheduling process; (ii) action will be envisaged only when the debtor has shown, through a track record, ability to put to good use whatever exceptional support is provided; (iii) new measures will build as much as possible on existing mechanisms; (iv) additional action will be coordinated among all creditors involved, with broad and equitable participation; (v) actions by the multilateral creditors will preserve their financial integrity and preferred creditor status; (vi) new external finance for the countries concerned will be on appropriately concessional terms.

10. While recognizing that many important aspects of the proposed framework of action need to be developed and refined further, Minis-

ters agreed that it provided an appropriate basis for further work. They requested that the Bank and Fund—in close consultation with concerned bilateral creditors, donors, debtors, the Paris Club, and other multilateral institutions—move swiftly to produce a program of action. Ministers urged that a decision be reached on this program and its financing as soon as possible, aiming to do so by the next IMF-World Bank annual meetings.

11. *Report of the Task Force on Multilateral Development Banks.* The committee welcomed this balanced and objective report. Ministers appreciated that it presented for the first time an overall assessment of the multilateral development banks.

12. Ministers believe the report provides an excellent analysis of the importance of multilateralism and the role of MDBs in a rapidly changing world. The committee appreciated the report's careful assessment of the performance of these five quite different institutions, with particular reference to its support for poverty reduction and sustainable development, investment in infrastructure, promotion of the private sector, operational orientation toward results on the ground, and to increasing cooperation among the MDBs.

13. The committee generally agreed with the report's conclusions and recommendations, recognizing that not all apply equally to each institution. Bearing in mind the value of diversity among the MDBs, Ministers urged the MDBs to act upon relevant recommendations as a matter of priority to strengthen further their policies and practices. Ministers invited the presidents of the MDBs to advise the committee, in about two years' time, on progress achieved in implementing the task force's major recommendations.

14. The committee expressed its great appreciation and gratitude to Abdlatif Al-Hamad for his chairmanship of the task force, as well as to the task force members and the Secretariat for their dedicated and productive work over the past fifteen months. The committee requested that the report be published and widely distributed.

# Index